Praise for

"Scripture is generally unambiguous and easy to understand. It is *perspicuous*. Yet the apostle Peter acknowledged that Scripture contains 'some things hard to be understood' (2 Peter 3:16). One of those difficult topics is the Sabbath. Colossians 2:16 and Romans 14:5, 6 suggest that confusion on this subject was a problem even in the earliest church. Over the years, much of what has been written about the Sabbath from both the church and the cults has only contributed to the confusion. That's why I am grateful for the clarity and biblical insight Dale Ratzlaff brings to the issue. *Sabbath in Christ* is a real treasure—a simple, straightforward, understandable digest of the best insights on a very difficult issue."—**Phil Johnson, Executive Director, Grace to You**

"Interpretation of Scripture correctly hinges on a proper understanding of the covenants, and a crucial decision of whether to let the old or new covenant define the other theologically. I greatly appreciate the assistance Dale Ratzlaff has given though *Sabbath in Christ* for all who are seeking a clearer understanding of the gospel of grace in Christ Jesus." — **Clay Peck, Senior Pastor, Grace Place, Berthoud, Colorado**

"You are certainly incisive when you point out that the various covenant sings have value only when they are celebrated in relationship to the covenant for which they have been designated as signs. Nothing is more important to an understanding of the Sabbath and other old covenant worship practices than your statement that we have been 'released from the law as a guide for Christian service' and that 'legal rules' have been replaced by spiritual and moral principles in Christ"—**Joseph Tkach, Pastor General, Worldwide Church of God**

"At last…an easily readable work that untangles every link of the formidable claims of sabbatarianism. Ratzlaff has done this by laying the plain Scriptures before our eyes and with great force of sweet persuasion causing us to see Jesus our Priceless Treasure."—**Geoffrey Drew, Grace Community Church, Sun Valley, California**

Sabbath in Christ

About the author

Dale Ratzlaff was a fourth generation Seventh-day Adventist (SDA) and was educated in SDA schools from first grade through seminary. He pastored in the Adventist church for 13 years, seven of these years as a Bible teacher at Monterey Bay Academy, La Selva Beach, California. In the 1980s, while nearing the end of his doctoral program at Andrews University, Dale Ratzlaff did an in-depth study of the SDA doctrine of the Investigative Judgment and Cleansing of the Heavenly Sanctuary, which Adventists teach started in 1844. He became convinced that this doctrine could not be supported by Scripture, was contrary to clear biblical teaching, and undermined the new covenant gospel of grace. As he could no longer teach this doctrine in clear conscience, Dale Ratzlaff and his wife, Carolyn, left the SDA denomination.

About two years after leaving the SDA church. Dale Ratzlaff lead a group of Christians in a seven-month inductive Bible study of the Sabbath. He continued studying the topic of the gospel, the covenants and the Sabbath and published *Sabbath in Crisis* in 1990. This book went through four printings and the present volume is a revised and enlarged study now entitled, *Sabbath in Christ*.

Dale Ratzlaff has authored two other books dealing with Seventh-day Adventist issues. He is president of Life Assurance Ministries, Inc. and editor of the by-monthly journal, *Proclamation*, which is targeted to former and inquiring Seventh-day Adventists, as well as other sabbatarian groups.

The Ratzlaffs live in Peoria, Arizona have two married sons, Bruce and Mike, and four grandchildren.

SABBATH IN CHRIST

Dale Ratzlaff

Life Assurance Ministries
PO Box 11587
Glendale, Arizona 85318

Copyright © 2003 by Dale Ratzlaff

Printed in the Unites States of America

All Scripture quotations—except where otherwise noted—are from the *New American Standard Bible,* © 1960, 1962, 1963, 1968, 1971, 1972, 1975, 1979, 1996 by The Lockman Foundation. Used by permission.

Cover design by Richard Tinker

Illustrated by Don Muth

Life Assurance Ministries Publications
P.O. Box 11587
Glendale, AZ 85318
623-572-9549
Email address: dale@ratzlaf.com
Internet web site: http://www.ratzlaf.com

Library of Congress Control Number: 2003091351

ISBN 0-9627546-1-7

DEDICATION

To my wife, Carolyn,

who is my best friend and has been a supportive life partner on our theological journey. I owe her a huge debt of gratitude for her numerous helpful suggestions and for the countless hours she spent in reading the many versions of this manuscript.

Foreword

"Sabbath in Christ" declares its main goal in the title, and then offers a well defended and much needed paradigm shift to the Christian community. Traditionally, Christian debate over the Sabbath has focused on Saturday versus Sunday. Through careful Biblical scholarship, *Sabbath in Christ* demonstrates how the heart of the 'Sabbath-for-Christians' issue (like all true Christian issues) is Christocentric, not a debate about days.

Dale Ratzlaff builds a strong case that arguing for one holy day or the other misses the New Testament's main point about the Sabbath: all old covenant holy days, including the seventh-day Sabbath, predicted and find their fulfillment in Jesus Christ. They were the shadows pointing to His substance (Colossians 2:17). In other words, Scripture offers only two real options for seeking *"God's rest"*:

A. The old covenant way of seeking rest in **a day**—whether it be Saturday or Sunday.

B. The new covenant way of entering God's rest through **the Person** of God's own Son, Jesus Christ, and His finished work of salvation: "Come unto Me, all you who are weary and heavily burdened, and *I will give you rest*" (Matthew 11:28).

This clarification, if true, is needed by *both* that great body of evangelical Christians who accept the absolute authority of Scripture; and by Seventh-day Adventists and other "Sabbath-keeping" groups who believe their seventh-day Sabbath doctrine sets them apart as God's true commandment-keeping people.

I'm honored to write this foreword for my friend, Dale Ratzlaff, and like him, I can speak to both the above groups with some authority. I wore the yoke of Adventism as a pastor, administrator, doctoral student at an SDA seminary and associate professor of theology at an SDA college. Over several decades I served on key church committees and wrote significant portions of the SDA secondary religion textbooks. Adventism is a denomination filled with so many wonderful and highly dedicated people.

But I came to realize that, in practice, the true integrating center of Seventh-day Adventist theology is not Jesus Christ, but the Sabbath. It defines their identity and ecclesiology. Contrary to Romans 11:5, SDA's are taught they are God's true remnant church *because* they keep the seventh-day Sabbath. It defines their soteriology and their eschatology: for Adventists, the Sabbath is the great issue that ultimately decides who wears the mark of the Beast and receives God's wrath (*because* of Sunday-worship); and those who are sealed by God for salvation (*because* of Sabbath-keeping).

In Adventism, anyone may openly question Christ's sinless nature or even the sufficiency of His atonement and still be accepted. But to deny the seventh-day Sabbath as a moral test is grounds for immediate disfellowship. My Adventist friends need to test this focus biblically, with honest hearts, and I know of no other book that could help them do that better than this volume.

Like Dale, the clarity of the Gospel led me to separate from Adventism and move into the larger Christian community as the senior pastor of a large, thriving evangelical church, relishing the profound truth of Romans 7:4–6. Yet on this side, I still find many Christians who fail to grasp and celebrate how Jesus Christ both completely fulfilled and simultaneously deepened the old covenant law given to Moses. They need greater clarity concerning the glory of John 1:17: *"The Law was given through Moses; but grace and truth came through Jesus Christ."*

This book is a treasure for any Christian who can still relate to the confusion of Peter, James and John on the Mount of Transfiguration (Matthcw 17:1–8), when faced with the glorified Christ *and* with Moses [the Law] *and* with Elijah [the prophets]. This volume will help you preserve all God's truth and yet, at the center, truly see *"**no one, except Jesus Himself alone**"* (17:8, NASB).

Dale is an expert guide through the covenantal tapestry in all of Scripture as God brings about eternal redemption and true rest in Jesus Christ for all humanity. Dale's analysis (in chapters 9–12) of why Jesus intentionally instigated so many Sabbath controversies, especially those recorded in John 5 and 9, is alone worth the price of the book—even just his exegesis of John 5:18. Powerful!

This is the second edition of *"Sabbath in Christ."* The first edition, titled *Sabbath in Crisis*, was honored with a forward by the eminent New Testament theologian, D. A. Carson, who said "the merits of this book are three, and they are considerable." He then cited Dale's very accessible writing style, especially his chapter summaries; Dale's own pilgrimage from Adventism into a deeper New Testament faith, and Dale's careful adherence to time-honored biblical hermeneutics. I echo Dr. Carson's sentiments that this volume, especially in its revised edition, could become the benchmark study of the Sabbath in Scripture.

Here is the bottom line. Dale calls us to realize that Jesus alone is the fullness of Prophet, Priest and King, Sacrifice and High Priest, Righteousness and Wisdom, Perfection, Covenant, Temple, Most Holy Place and Law. Jesus alone is our true Atonement, no longer a day. He alone is our true Passover, no longer a day. He is our true Provider of Pentecostal blessing, no longer a day; *and Jesus alone is our true Sabbath-rest*—it is no longer a day! We are complete *in Him* (Colossians 2:10). It is my prayer

Sabbath in Christ will help thousands to *"make every effort to enter that rest"* (Hebrews 4:6–11), so heaven's courts may indeed resound with joy.

Richard Fredericks, Ph.D.
Senior Pastor
Damascus Road Community Church
February 19, 2003

Contents

	Preface	11
1.	Sabbath Questions	13
2.	The Seventh Day in Genesis	21
3.	The Abrahamic Covenant	29
4.	The Old Covenant	41
5.	Shadows of Christ	67
6.	The New Covenant	89
7.	Jesus and Ritual Law	103
8.	Jesus and Old Covenant Moral Laws	113
9.	Jubilee Sabbath	119
10.	Lord of the Sabbath	133
11.	Sabbath Conflicts	147
12.	The Paradox of Sabbath Law	163
13.	Sabbath in Acts	177
14.	Sabbath in the Epistles	185
15.	New Covenant Documents and Signs	217
16.	A Better Covenant	229
17.	A Better Law	237
18.	Jesus, the Law's Fulfillment	265
19.	The Rest That Remains	279
20.	Righteousness Beyond the Law	293
21.	Life in the Spirit	301
22.	The First Day of the Week	315
23.	Sabbath Fulfillment in Christ	331
24.	Sabbath Arguments	351
25.	The Sabbath and Seventh-day Adventists	371
26.	Assembling and Resting	397
27.	The Testing Truth	409
	Selected Bibliography	421
	Scriptural Index	427
	Other LAM Publications	439

Abbreviations Used

Old Testament

Genesis	Gen.	
Exodus	Ex.	
Leviticus	Lev.	
Numbers	Num.	
Deuteronomy	Deut.	
Joshua	Josh.	
Judges	Jud.	
1 Samuel	1 Sam.	
2 Samuel	2 Sam.	
1 Kings	1 Ki	
2 Kings	2 Ki	
1 Chronicles	1 Chron.	
2 Chronicles	2 Chron.	
Nehemiah	Neh.	
Esther	Esth.	
Psalms	Ps.	
Isaiah	Isa.	
Jeremiah	Jer.	
Ezekiel	Ez.	
Daniel	Dan.	
Hosea	Hos.	
Joel	Joe.	
Amos	Amo.	
Micah	Mich.	
Malachi	Mal.	
1 Maccabees	1 Mac.	
2 Maccabees	2 Mac.	

New Testament

Matthew	Mt.
Mark	Mk.
Luke	Lk.
John	Jn.
Romans	Rom.
1 Corinthians	1 Cor.
2 Corinthians	2 Cor.
Galatians	Gal.
Ephesians	Eph.
Philippians	Phil.
Colossians	Col.
1 Thessalonians	1 Thess.
1 Timothy	1 Tim.
2 Timothy	2 Tim.
Titus	Tit.
Philemon	Phile.
Hebrews	Heb.
James	Jas.
1 Peter	1 Pet.
2 Peter	1 Pet.
1 John	1 Jn.
2 John	2 Jn.
Revelation	Rev.

PREFACE

I was leading a weekly Bible study, and questions were being raised regarding the Sabbath. At the time we were in an ideal position to do a truly inductive study of this subject. Most of us were former Seventh-day Adventists, and we were meeting for services on Sabbath (Saturday). It had been about two years since we had left the Seventh-day Adventist (SDA) church so we were far enough away from Adventism to not be bound by its theological paradigm, yet we felt no desire to change our day of worship. This proved to be the most rewarding Bible study most of us had ever done in that it was truly a "discovery" study. We were not seeking to prove anything.

We prayerfully studied the topic of the Sabbath every week for a period of about seven months. While the bulk of our research was done in Scripture itself, we also studied *From Sabbath to Sunday* and *Divine Rest for Human Restlessness,* both by Samuele Bacchiocchi, who is considered the leading SDA authority on this topic, *The Forgotten Day,* by SDA Desmond Ford, several articles by Robert Brinsmead, and *From Sabbath to Lord's Day,* edited by D. A. Carson. These as well as several other works on the Sabbath topic, including a set of taped lectures by Nordon Winger, made up the resources for this original study. I freely acknowledge that many of the insights presented in this book are gleaned from the above writers and lecturers.

I continued to study the subjects of the Sabbath, covenants and the gospel and published *Sabbath in Crisis* in 1990. It was revised at the second printing in 1995. Now after many thousands of readers have responded to *Sabbath in Crisis,* and the fourth printing is sold out, I have done a major revision and expansion of the original work. Some chapters have been extensively revised, others left almost unchanged and five new chapters have been added.

Dr. Richard Fredericks, former SDA pastor and scholar, and now Senior Pastor of the growing Damascus Road Community Church gave a series of messages on the topic of the Sabbath entitled, "Sabbath in Christ." I listened to this series on tape[1] and both Dr. Fredericks and I feel that this title not only reflects his study but also the theses of my book and he has graciously let me use this title.

I have chosen to write out most of the Bible references used. However, when this would be too cumbersome, I have summarized the key concepts and listed the Scripture reference for further study. At times I have emphasized a particular word or phrase by putting it in *italics*. Words added within a quotation will always be enclosed in brackets. All Bible references are taken from *The New American Standard Bible*[2] unless otherwise noted.

At the end of most chapters I have summarized what I consider to be the pertinent scriptural facts delineated within that chapter.

It is my earnest prayer that as you read this book you will be drawn into closer fellowship with the risen Lord, have a deeper understanding of the gospel of Christ and experience His true rest and real redemption; that you will accept Christ as your Covenant Keeper and the center of your joyous worship.

Dale Ratzlaff, M.Div.
Peoria, Arizona
March, 2003

---

[1] Available from Damascus Road Community Church, Damascus, MD at 301-253-5276 or www.damascus.com.
[2] Some are from the updated edition and others from the earlier edition.

CHAPTER ONE

SABBATH QUESTIONS

Time and again throughout the history of the Christian church, controversy has arisen over the importance of the Sabbath. Belief concerning the Sabbath varies considerably. There are almost as many interpretations of the Sabbath as there are shades of gray.

Although it is a great oversimplification, Sabbath belief can be divided into three main categories. First, there are those who believe Sunday is the Sabbath of the New Testament. They often refer to it as the Lord's Day and see it as a special day set aside for religious service. Those in this group feel free to use "Remember the sabbath day, to keep it holy" (Ex. 20:8), in admonishing Christians to observe the Sabbath, or the Lord's Day. Opinion regarding appropriate Sabbath behavior varies widely within this group. Some will not engage in regular employment on Sunday and try to keep at least some of the biblical rules for Sabbath observance.[1] We will refer to this group as

---

[1] "The Sabbath [in reference to Sunday] is to be sanctified by a holy resting all that day, even from such worldly employments and recreations as are lawful on other days; and spending the whole time in the public and private exercises of God's worship, except so much as is to be taken up in the works of necessity and mercy." Answer 60, of the *Westminster Shorter Catechism* as quoted in D.A Carson, *From Sabbath to Lord's Day*, (Zondervan, Grand Rapids, MI, 1982), pp. 326, 338.

holding the Transfer/Modification motif—*Transfer,* in that the Seventh-day Sabbath has been transferred to Sunday; *Modification,* in that the rules for Sabbath keeping have been modified.

The second motif of Sabbath understanding we will call Reformation/Continuation—*Reformation,* in the sense of needing to restore the Seventh-day Sabbath of the Fourth Commandment; *Continuation,* in that the Seventh-day Sabbath is to continue into the new covenant, and even to the world made new. In this group are those who believe Saturday is the true, biblical Sabbath and who continue to worship on the seventh day. There is also a wide variety of understanding within this group. Some hold the seventh day as the preferred day of worship but see no reason to try to persuade other Christian groups to observe the seventh day.[2] On the other end of the spectrum are those who worship on the seventh day and teach the seventh-day Sabbath will be God's final test of loyalty for *all* Christians living in the last days before the second coming of Christ.[3] They believe those who worship on Sunday will, in the final days, receive the mark of the beast[4] and the resulting wrath of God described in these words,

---

[2] From my personal conversations with Seventh-day Church of God pastors.

[3] This is the historic teaching of Seventh-day Adventist church.

[4] "The sign, or seal, of God is revealed in the observance of the seventh-day Sabbath, the Lord's memorial of creation. 'The Lord spake unto Moses, saying, Speak thou also unto the children of Israel, saying, Verily My Sabbaths ye shall keep: for it is a sign between Me and you throughout your generations; that ye may know that I am the Lord that doth sanctify you.' Exodus 31:12, 13. Here the Sabbath is clearly designated as a sign between God and His people. The mark of the beast is the opposite—the observance of the first day of the week. This mark distinguishes those who acknowledge the supremacy of the papal authority from those who acknowledge the authority of God." Ellen G. White, *Testimonies to the Church*, Vol. 8, p. 117. Author's note: Ellen G. White is considered by Seventh-day Adventists to have manifested the true gift of prophecy. She is seen as a "messenger of God" and

If any one worships the beast and his image, and receives a mark on his forehead or upon his hand, he also will drink of the wine of the wrath of God, which is mixed in full strength in the cup of His anger; and he will be tormented with fire and brimstone in the presence of the holy angels and in the presence of the Lamb (Rev. 14:9, 10).

A third motif of Sabbath understanding we will call Fulfillment/Transformation—*Fulfillment,* in that the Seventh-day Sabbath rest of the Old Testament has met its fulfillment in Christ; *Transformation,* in that the weekly Sabbath rest of the Fourth Commandment has been *transformed* into the rest of grace offered in the new covenant gospel of Christ. This motif we will refer to as "Sabbath in Christ." Those who hold this third view are Christians who believe the Sabbath as a special *day* no longer exists. They believe it is important to have a time of Christian worship but the day on which it takes place is unimportant. Usually, however, these people worship on Sunday and may also call it the Lord's Day, but do not hold it necessarily as a sacred day to be reverenced as do Sabbath keepers. They see the old covenant Sabbath, as all the other old covenant ceremonies, as a shadow of Christ who brings true rest for the soul.

We can immediately see the need for an accurate, biblical understanding of this subject. If Sabbath observance is going to be the final test in the last days before the coming of Christ, then we ought to make sure we carefully observe the Sabbath. Certainly none of us wants to experience the wrath of God. If we are going to observe the Sabbath then we ought to find out *for sure* upon which day it is to be kept. However, if the *day* of Sabbath observance—or the observance itself—is unimportant, then we ought to have sound, biblical evidence to support our

---

"...her writings are a continuing and authoritative source of truth...." The Fundamental Beliefs of Seventh-day Adventists, No. 17, "The Gift of Prophecy".

position. Then, if there is evidence for this view, we need to focus our attention on the gospel of Christ.

Why not do a thorough study of the Sabbath?

It is never wrong to study the foundation of our faith. Faith must be based upon a foundation of evidence; otherwise faith is folly. If the foundation is trustworthy, a thorough examination of it will only increase our faith. However, if, after a thorough examination of the biblical evidence, it is found that the timbers of our faith foundation are resting on nothing but damp earth and sand, then something ought to be done about it quickly, before the floods of the last days destroy our spiritual home.

Why not keep the fourth commandment?

While we would not insist that the mainstream of Christianity is always right, nevertheless the fact that so many sincere Christians throughout history have not observed the seventh-day Sabbath ought to cause us to examine their biblical reasons for not doing so. On the other hand, most Christians accept, believe in, and teach that the Ten Commandments are binding upon the Christian, yet they do not observe the fourth. Why?

Is the Sabbath moral or ceremonial?

The reformation/continuation school of thought argues that the Sabbath is a moral law and therefore it should be given the same weight as all moral laws. They point out that the Sabbath commandment is in the heart of the Ten Commandments and deserves equal, if not paramount, importance. Those who hold the "Sabbath in Christ" view believe that the Sabbath is a ritual law pointing forward to Christ. If this view is correct then why does the Sabbath find itself in the very heart of the Ten Commandments associated with many moral laws?

How did Jesus relate to the Mosaic Laws?

Did Jesus keep the letter of the biblical law? Did He always keep the Sabbath? If not, why? And if not, how can He be our Savior if He did not perfectly keep the law? If He did perfectly keep the Sabbath, then is Sabbath observance part of the righteousness that is imputed to the Christian who believes in Christ? If so, then should Sabbath observance be part of the sanctified life of the Christian? Was there a difference in the way Jesus related to the moral laws of the Mosaic code from the way He treated the ritual laws? If there is a difference then what light will this shed on our study of the Sabbath?

How should one observe the Sabbath?

If we are going to observe the Sabbath, whether it be on the seventh day or on the first day, *how* is it to be kept? Are we to observe the Sabbath according to Old Testament guidelines? If so, most of us would be under condemnation—and some would say justly so. If Sabbath observance is derived from the New Testament, there are few, if any, regulations to govern Sabbath behavior. Are we safe to take Jesus as our guide and example in Sabbath keeping while emulation of other acts of Jesus are condemned by the New Testament? For example, Jesus was born "under law" (Gal. 4:4). He was circumcised as prescribed by the law (Lk. 2:21), yet Paul states, "if you receive circumcision Christ will be of no benefit to you" (Gal. 5:2). As a Jew, Jesus participated in many of the other religious convocations and celebrations of the old covenant. What guidelines do we use if we make the example of Jesus normative for Christian life?

Does Sabbath observance bring Christian unity?

Some Sabbath keepers believe the Sabbath is *the* uniting force among God's true people. However, with such a wide variety of belief and practice relative to the Sabbath, *how* is this unity achieved? How the Sabbath is observed varies widely even among those of the same denomination. Does the history of the Christian church, or Sabbath-keeping denominational history for that matter, demonstrate the uniting influence of the Sabbath?

Does the Sabbath promote gospel clarity?

Some Christians believe Sabbath keepers allow the importance of the Sabbath to overshadow the gospel of Christ. On the other hand, some Sabbath keepers have charged non-Sabbath keepers with neglecting an important part of Christian duty designed to strengthen real godliness and they see the Sabbath as a vehicle for a better understanding of the gospel. Which is true?

It was seeking definitive answers to these and other questions that formed the basis of the Sabbath study out of which this book was born.

The Approach

How is a study of the Sabbath to be approached? Most of us come to this study with at least some previous understanding and prejudice. To do a thorough, objective study requires a great deal of discipline, commitment and, yes, even risk.

A highly developed and well-organized belief system can often be the most dangerous blinder to truth. We need only to look at history to see this demonstrated time and again. Jesus told His disciples about His imminent death, but they were unable to comprehend what He said because it did not fit within their theological, or should I say, political, framework.

Copernicus taught that the sun, not the earth, was at the center of the solar system. But this concept was not readily accepted because it did not fit within the approved teachings of the day.

Galileo met with the same resistance to his discovery of truth. He could demonstrate his findings by observable evidence. But when he did this, it often only infuriated those who watched. For a person of that day to accept the teachings of Copernicus or Galileo meant that his whole belief system came tumbling down. Many of the religious leaders felt that it was emotionally easier to hang on to the accepted teachings of the time, even if these teachings did have some problems, than to acknowledge new factual evidence which threatened their world view.

For us to entertain the idea that our own belief system may be wrong brings considerable insecurity. People have gone to great lengths to defend the indefensible in order to safely preserve what they considered to be "truth."

Those seeking truth must have a certain reverence for the evidence. The Bereans were said to be

> ...more noble-minded...for they received the word with great eagerness, examining the Scriptures daily, to see whether these things were so (Acts 17:11).

One who is honestly studying a doctrine must give serious consideration to the evidence that does not fit his belief system. He must be willing, if necessary, to humbly take apart his system of theology and put it back together again to fit the biblical evidence. This is not an easy task. It does, however, bring a great amount of confidence and peace when it is accomplished.

Genuine truth has nothing to fear from searching investigation. Therefore, as we begin this study, let us have a certain reverence for the evidence, let us seriously consider any evidence which does not fit our understanding of "truth," and let us humbly press on in our study eagerly awaiting the opportunity to understand what the Bible teaches about the Sabbath and what it means to the Christian.

It
was
very
good

CHAPTER TWO

THE SEVENTH DAY IN GENESIS

> Thus the heavens and the earth were completed, and all their hosts. And by the seventh day God completed His work which He had done; and He rested on the seventh day from all His work which He had done. Then God blessed the seventh day and sanctified it, because in it He rested from all His work which God had created and made (Gen. 2:1–3).

In harmony with what was presented in the previous chapter, our goal here at the beginning of our study is simply to find as many pertinent facts as possible: the obvious ones, and also those which may be less obvious. Then from these facts we will draw possible interpretations, but make few conclusions.

A study of these verses leads us to the following scriptural facts: The "work" of creation was completed by the end of the sixth day. God "rested" or "ceased" on the seventh day. God "blessed" the seventh day. God "sanctified" the seventh day. God sanctified the seventh day because He ceased from the work of creation.

A less obvious fact emerges as we look at the creation account in the first chapter of Genesis. Notice a recurring pattern. After God created day and night on the first day Scripture reads, "And there was evening and there was morning, one day" (Gen. 1:5). After God separated the waters to make the firmament we read, "And there was evening and there was morning, a second day" (Gen. 1:8).

This pattern continues throughout the first six days of creation. (See Gen. 1:13, 19, 23, 31.) However, when we look at the end of the seventh day we find no such formula. We would expect to read, "And there was evening and there was morning a seventh day," but it is missing.

An examination of the literary pattern of the creation record shows that this account was very carefully constructed. Note in the chart below that the first three days of creation correspond to the last three days of creation. With such precise and well-thought-out construction, could it be that the omission of "and there was evening and there was morning, a seventh day" was not accidental but by design?

Literary pattern of the creation record

Light	**Sun, moon and stars**
Evening and morning	Evening and morning
God saw it was good	God saw it was good
one day	a fourth day
Water and firmament	**Fish and birds**
Evening and morning	Evening and morning
God saw it was good	God saw it was good
a second day	a fifth day
Dry land	**Animals and man**
Evening and morning	Evening and morning
God saw it was good	God saw all that
a third day	He had made, it was very good
	a sixth day

Thus the heavens and the earth were completed

God rested (ceased) on the seventh day
God blessed the seventh day
God sanctified the seventh day
No "evening and morning a seventh day"

There is no mention of the word "Sabbath" in the Genesis account. However, the verb form for "rested" or "ceased" is used. Nothing is said about *man* resting; in fact, man is not even mentioned in connection with this seventh-day-creation rest.

What constituted God's "rest"?

With these scriptural facts well in mind, let us seek to discover what characterized God's "rest." Was He physically tired or mentally "worn out" at the end of Creation week? Exodus 31:17 reads, "on the seventh day He ceased *from labor* and was refreshed." "From labor" is not in the Hebrew but was added by the translator. So all we really have is that "He ceased and was refreshed." The Psalmist wrote, "He who keeps Israel will neither slumber nor sleep" (Ps. 121:4), indicating that God does not get physically tired and need rest as we do at the end of a day of work. Rather God's seventh-day-creation rest more likely relates to His *enjoyment* of His *finished* creation. He stepped back to view the world in its primeval beauty, which He characterized as "very good."

What could be more refreshing and restful than for God to be in fellowship with His "very good" creation? What beautiful visions come to mind when we contemplate what it must have been like before weed, decay, or death manifested their ugliness! Blue skies, clear waters, white sands, colorful flowers, and stately trees formed the background as the birds and animals played without fear when God walked through the garden delighted with His work.

One characteristic of that perfect world was that God had *freely* provided everything needed for the happiness of Adam and Eve. There was nothing for Adam and Eve to do but to enjoy God's gracious provision and fellowship with their Creator.

From the Genesis account we cannot determine how long it was before Adam and Eve sinned. One thing, however, we can be sure of: it was after the close of the first seventh day. That day stands out in Scripture as the *one* day when everything was in right relationship to God. The world sparkled with the freshness of a tropical morning. Adam and Eve held open fellowship with their Maker. Sin and its resulting curse were still unknown.

A rest designed to never end

We now come to an important question. Did God intend for this enjoyment of a finished creation to end at the close of the literal seventh day? According to the Genesis record "the heavens and the earth were completed" on the sixth day (Gen. 2:1). God's work of creation was completed. Adam and Eve had not yet sinned, so the open fellowship and communion which characterized that first seventh day rest continued. Therefore we may conclude that the *conditions* and *characteristics* of that first seventh day were designed by God to *continue* and would have continued had it not been for the sin of Adam and Eve. It was not God's design or intent that the open, face-to-face communion with man come to an end. It was not His design that the ground be cursed. No, it was the entrance of sin which interrupted Eden's perfection. "But your iniquities have made a separation between you and your God" (Isa. 59:2). By creating Adam and Eve with the power of choice, God allowed for the possibility of sin, but it was certainly not His will that sin should exist.

Could this be the reason why the Genesis record omits "and there was evening and there was morning, a seventh day"? This does not deny that the first seventh day had an evening and a morning, nor does it deny there was another day that followed the first seventh day. However, the *essence* of creation's seventh-day or the *conditions* that existed on that seventh day were intended to *remain*.

A sanctified day

What does the Genesis account mean when it says God "sanctified" the seventh day? The basic meaning of sanctify is to set apart as sacred. In this respect, then, God was setting apart the seventh day from the first six days for a special purpose. "God blessed the seventh day and sanctified it, *because* in it *He* rested..." (Gen. 2:3). This day was set apart from the first six days because it was the first day after creation was completed. It was, so to speak, a time to celebrate and enjoy the work of His hands. It was a time for fellowship and communion between the Creator and created life. Truly, the conditions of that day were sanctified and blessed.

Here we are told that God's rest is holy, set apart for some purpose. However, we must be careful not to read into this creation rest more than what is stated. The concept of rest is a theme which will be developed throughout Scripture. We will see that this "creation rest" will soon be lost, then it will be symbolized and then it will be restored.

The end of Eden's Rest.

While the Genesis account mentions nothing about people resting. Many have assumed, and probably correctly so, that Adam and Eve entered into "God's rest" on that first seventh day. For them this "rest" would not be a cessation from work as we know it for two reasons: First, the seventh day of creation was Adam and Eve's first full day of life! Second, work was part of the curse of sin. True, later they were instructed to cultivate and keep the garden (Gen. 2:15) but before the curse this should not be considered servile work. What we think of as work did not enter until after sin entered. Work was part of the curse of sin.

> To the woman He said, "I will greatly multiply your pain in childbirth, in pain you will bring forth children; yet your desire will be for your husband, and he will rule over you." Then to Adam He said,... "Cursed is the ground because of you; in toil you will eat of it all the days of your life. Both thorns and thistles it shall grow for you; and you will eat the plants of the field." (Gen. 3:16–18).

Sin brought creation's "rest" to an end. Women must now "labor" in childbirth. Men must "toil...all the days of their lives." Not only did Adam and Eve start working with the entrance of sin, in a sense it can be said that God too started work.

The beginning of a new work

The Genesis account does not mention an end to God's seventh-day rest. Rather it is presented as an ongoing state by the *omission* of the formula "and there was evening and morning, a seventh day." Nevertheless, it does mention a new work which God started immediately after Adam and Eve sinned. We read that "the Lord God *made* garments of skin for Adam and his wife, and clothed them" (Gen. 3:21). This event was the beginning of a work which would continue throughout the centuries until its significance would become fully revealed in the death and resurrection of Christ. The death of that first lamb, while not mentioned as such in the Genesis account, was the acorn of the great truth which, through the following centuries, would grow into the great, spreading oak of righteousness by faith. It pointed forward to Christ's substitutionary life and death for lost mankind. Naked Adam and Eve were clothed with robes made from the skin of the slain lamb—a substitute Who gave His life. Millennia later Paul would put this same truth in these words:

> He made Him who knew no sin to be sin on our behalf, that we might become the righteousness of God in Him (2 Cor. 5:21).
> All of you who were baptized into Christ have clothed yourselves with Christ (Gal. 3:27).

Jesus would say,

> Do not work for the food which perishes, but for the food which endures to eternal life, which the Son of Man shall give to you, for on Him the Father, even God, has set His seal. They said therefore to Him, "What shall we do, that we may *work* the *works* of God?" Jesus answered and said to them, "This is the

work of God, that you *believe in Him* whom He has sent" (Jn. 6:27–29).

The work of redemption was the work which God started[1] when man sinned and was driven from Eden's rest. This work would continue until man was once again restored to God's true rest.

Chapter Summary

1. Creation was completed in six days.
2. God rested on the seventh day.
3. God blessed the seventh day.
4. God sanctified the seventh day.
5. The reason God sanctified the seventh day was because He rested on it.
6. The seventh-day account does *not* have the formula "and there was evening and there was morning, a seventh day" as do the first six days of creation.
7. The creation record is carefully constructed.
8. There is no mention of the word "Sabbath" in the book of Genesis but its verb form is there.
9. There is no command for mankind to rest in the Genesis account.
10. Nothing is expressly mentioned regarding man in the seventh-day-creation rest.
11. The seventh-day "rest" of God was most likely characterized by His delight in His new creation and in open fellowship with Adam and Eve in the sin-free, perfect environment of Eden.
12. The conditions which characterized the "rest" of God would probably have continued had it not been for man's sin.
13. The fact that the Genesis account is so carefully constructed indicates that the omission of "and there was

---

[1] This does not deny that redemption had its roots before the foundation of the world. But the implementation of redemption started after man sinned.

evening and there was morning, a seventh day" was intentional.
15. When man sinned, the "rest" he experienced in Eden came to an end.
   a. Women would now have pain in the labor of childbirth.
   b. Men would toil all the days of their lives.
16. God began to implement the work of redemption which had been in place from before the foundation of world.

CHAPTER THREE

THE ABRAHAMIC COVENANT

There are only two covenants presented in the Bible that bear directly on one's salvation. They are the covenant with Abraham, also called the everlasting covenant, and the covenant with Israel at Sinai. True, God made a covenant with Noah and every living thing and also with David, but these covenants do not bear directly on our study of the Sabbath.

The covenant God made with Abraham is of great interest to our study for here are the roots of what will be called the new or everlasting covenant. On numerous occasions Jesus referred to Abraham and said that Abraham saw His day.[1] Abraham is the proto-type for the righteousness presented in the new covenant.[2] Therefore, we should expect to find many seeds of truth here that will later grow into a more developed theology of salvation.

God initiates the relationship

God found Abraham[3] in Ur and said to him,

---

[1] Jn. 8:56.
[2] Rom. 4:9–25; Gal. 3:14–18; Heb. 6:13–20.
[3] Abraham's name was really "Abram" before his name was changed by God as recorded in Gen. 17:5. I have used Abraham throughout to avoid confusion as does the New Testament.

Go forth from your country, and from your relatives and from your father's house to the land which I will show you; And I will make you a great nation, and I will bless you, and make your name great; and so you shall be a blessing; and I will bless those who bless you, and the one who curses you I will curse. And in you all the families of the earth will be blessed (Gen. 12:2, 3).

Here we see several things of importance: First, Abraham was asked to go into a country he had never seen. To obey God at this juncture was an expression of complete faith and trust.

Second, Abraham was given a three-fold personal promise that God would make him a great nation, would bless him and make his name great with the result that Abraham would be a blessing.

Third, God would bless those who blessed Abraham and curse those who cursed him.

Fourth,—and here is a key truth—"in you all the families of the earth will be blessed."

Abraham obeyed these commands. When he reached Canaan, he was soon confronted with a famine in the land so he went down to Egypt for survival. While in Egypt, God used Pharaoh to teach Abraham a needed lesson on integrity and then sent him back to Canaan with additional possessions given to him by Pharaoh.

Abraham then marshaled the men of his household and rescued Lot from the warring kings of the area and received the blessing of the King of Salem.

Doubtless Abraham was fearful that these warring kings would come against him.

After these things the word of the LORD came to Abram in a vision, saying, Do not fear, Abram, I am a shield to you; Your reward shall be very great (Gen. 15:1).

What a blessing this must have been to Abraham. God was his shield to protect him from the warring kings of the area. God again spoke of Abraham's reward being very great. Perhaps thinking of the great multitude of descendents God has promised, Abraham reflected on the fact that he had no heir. Therefore, Abraham suggested to God that because he was childless, Eliezer, his servant, should be considered his heir. However, God would not entertain this idea.

> This man will not be your heir; but one who will come forth from your body, he shall be your heir. And he took him outside and said, "Now look toward the heavens, and count the stars, if you are able to count them." And He said to him, "So shall your descendants be." Then he believed in the LORD and He reckoned it to him as righteousness (Gen. 15:4–6).

Here is an important point that was taught over and over again in God's dealing with Abraham. God is looking for complete faith (trust and belief) and when Abraham expressed this belief, God counted that belief as righteousness. Abraham would face other "faith-tests" as God sought to strengthen their relationship.

The burning oven and flaming torch

After this incident, God asked Abraham to prepare an offering of a three year old heifer, a three year old goat, a three year old ram, a turtledove and a young pigeon. He cut the larger animals in half and laid them opposite each other. Immediately the birds of prey came and tried to steal the fresh meat. The day wore on as Abraham was busy driving the pesky vultures away.

Then as the sun was going down, a deep sleep came upon Abraham, and a terrifying darkness fell upon him. God then spoke to him giving him a prophecy of things to come.

> It came about when the sun had set, that it was very dark, and behold, there appeared a smoking oven and a flaming torch which passed between these pieces. On that day the LORD made a covenant with Abram, saying, "To your descendants I have given this land, from the river of Egypt as far as the great river, the river Euphrates" (Gen. 15:17, 18).

What did the "smoking oven (or furnace)" and "flaming torch" represent? There is some evidence to believe that the "smoking oven" represents God the Father[4] and the "flaming torch" represents God the Son.[5] This would mean that both the Father and the Son were present confirming the covenant with Abraham.

During this confirmation event, *Abraham did nothing*. In fact, the way the story reads, it appears that Abraham was asleep. The active partners were God the Father and God the Son represented by the smoking furnace and burning torch. It should also be noted that there is no mention of blood in this confirmation event. When we get to the New Testament these facts will become important.

Helping God

Knowing that Eliezer could not be counted as an heir and Sarah's[6] childbearing years had come to an end,[7] Abraham listened to Sarah's attempt to "work things out" and took Hagar as a wife and to this relationship was born Ishmael. However, this attempt to assist God only brought sorrow, frustration and bitterness to the situation. God's purpose, however, was not to be thwarted by Abraham's taking things into his own hands.

> Now when Abram was ninety-nine years old, the LORD appeared to Abram and said to him, "I am God Almighty; walk before Me, and be blameless. And I will establish My covenant between Me and you, and I will multiply you exceedingly…As for Me, behold, My covenant is with you, and you shall be the father of a multitude of nations. No longer shall your name be

---

[4] Ex. 19:18; 20:18.

[5] Isa. 62:1; Many New Testament verses describe Christ as the "Light". See Sam Pestes, *The Stone Cutter's Bride,* for more support for this view. Cassette tapes and CDs of this study are available from Life Assurance Ministries Publications, Glendale, AZ, or may be obtained directly from Sam Pestes at s.pestes@shaw.ca.

[6] I have used "Sarah" even though her name at the time was "Sarai" to avoid confusion.

[7] Sarah was about seventy-five years old at this time.

The Abrahamic Covenant

> called Abram, but your name shall be Abraham; for I will make you the father of a multitude of nations. And I will make you exceedingly fruitful, and I will make nations of you, and kings shall come forth from you. And I will establish My covenant between Me and you and your descendants after you throughout their generations for an everlasting covenant, to be God to you and to your descendants after you. And I will give to you and to your descendants after you, the land of your sojournings, all the land of Canaan, for an everlasting possession; and I will be their God (Gen. 17:1–8).

Here we see that God made several covenant promises to Abraham: (1) His descendants would be multiplied exceedingly. (2) He would be a father of many nations. (3) Kings would come from Abraham. (4) God would give Abraham and his descendants the land of Canaan for an everlasting possession. This covenant is also called "an everlasting covenant".

Abraham was commanded to: (1) walk before God with integrity, (2) change his name from Abram to Abraham—a symbol of Abraham's belief in God's covenant promise that he would be father of a multitude. The only real requirement on the part of Abraham was to *believe God*.

The sign of God's covenant with Abraham was circumcision. But note well that this sign was given *after* God had previously counted Abraham righteous based solely on his faith.

> God said further to Abraham, "Now as for you, you shall keep My covenant, you and your descendants after you throughout their generations. This is My covenant, which you shall keep, between Me and you and your descendants after you: every male among you shall be circumcised. And you shall be circumcised in the flesh of your foreskin; and it shall be the *sign of the covenant* between Me and you (Gen. 17:9–11).

Giving up on personal ability to perform

Following this we have one of the most insightful episodes recorded about the life of Abraham;

> Then God said to Abraham, "As for Sarai your wife, you shall not call her name Sarai, but Sarah shall be her name. "I will bless her, and indeed I will give you a son by her. Then I will bless her, and she shall be a mother of nations; kings of peoples will come from her." Then Abraham fell on his face and laughed, and said in his heart, "Will a child be born to a man one hundred years old? And will Sarah, who is ninety years old, bear a child?" And Abraham said to God, "Oh that Ishmael might live before You!" (Gen. 17:15–18).

This section of Scripture has been variously interpreted and we will come back to it in later chapters for further development. However, at this point, may I suggest that Abraham expressed *no faith* that he and Sarah could have a son. The fact that he said, "Oh, that Ishmael might live before You!" indicates that he was still hoping that this contrived arrangement might fulfill God's promise. When Abraham fell on his face and laughed, could it be that his laugh was focused on the ridiculous impossibility of his and Sarah's ability to fulfill God's promise?

Sarah's faith was no better. While listening behind the tent door,

> Sarah laughed to herself, saying, "After I have become old, shall I have pleasure, my lord being old also?" (Gen. 18:12).

To this God said, "Is anything to difficult for the LORD?" and promised that Sarah would have a child at this time next year. When confronted with her laugh of *unbelief*, she denied that she had laughed, but God said, "No, but you did laugh."

If we are to take this whole incident as it reads, we must, it seems to me, recognize that both Abraham and Sarah had *absolutely no faith* that *they* could have a child. Underline this point in your thinking for it is vitally important for later understandings.

The Abrahamic Covenant

Regardless of Abraham's and Sarah's lack of faith in their ability to produce a child, God's promise was fulfilled and then there was true "laughter" in their home.[8]

God will provide for Himself the lamb

God was not through testing Abraham's faith. When he was about one hundred and fifteen years old the supreme test came when he was commanded to offer up Isaac as a burnt offering. Genesis 22 is one of the most gospel-centered "predictive events"[9] of the Old Testament. Here we see Abraham offering up his son, his only son, whom he loved. The mountain upon which Abraham was to do this was not just any mountain, but "*the* mountain I will show you". This was Mt. Moriah, where the temple was later built. Christians know it as Mt. Calvary. Climbing the mountain, the "beloved son", perfectly obedient to his father's will carried the "wood" needed for the sacrifice. Abraham, out of inspired faith said, "God will provide for Himself the lamb for a burnt offering." Isaac was "obedient to the point of death"—there is no mention of the young man trying to overpower his aged father. The aged Abraham now does not try to circumvent the clear command of God with human devisings. At last he has unwavering faith in God's promise and command. So great was Abraham's faith that he considered the Lord could raise Isaac from the dead so that God's promise would reach fulfillment.[10]

Yes, and God did provide the offering. With joy Abraham took the ram and offered it up in the place of his son. More than that, Abraham called the name of that place,

---

[8] Isaac means "laughter".

[9] I do not subscribe to the allegorical method of interpretation unless there is a "green light" to do so in the Scripture itself. This "green light" is found in Hebrews 11:19 where the writer calls Isaac a "type". In context the "type" represents Christ. To this consider the words of Jesus that "Abraham rejoiced to see My day." Jn. 8:56.

[10] Heb. 11:17–19.

"The LORD Will Provide." In the time of Moses, there was a saying, "In the mount of the LORD, it will be provided". Now, some four thousands years after Abraham, we sing, "Jehovah-Jirah, my Provider!" No wonder Jesus could say of Abraham that "he rejoiced to see my day, and he saw it and was glad."[11]

> Then the angel of the LORD called to Abraham a second time from heaven, and said, "By Myself I have sworn, declares the LORD, because you have done this thing and have not withheld your son, your only son, indeed I will greatly bless you, and I will greatly multiply your seed as the stars of the heavens and as the sand which is on the seashore; and your seed shall possess the gate of their enemies. "In your seed all the nations of the earth shall be blessed, because you have obeyed My voice" (Gen. 22:15–18).

Abraham's obedience

What was the nature of Abraham's obedience? Abraham obeyed and left Ur to follow God's directions to an unknown country. He walked throughout the land as God asked him to do.[12] Abraham obeyed the sign of the covenant and circumcised the males in his household. In his life we see a *decrease* of faith in his own abilities to fulfill God's promise and an *increase* of faith in trusting not only God's promise, but God's ability to fulfill His own promise. He did not pass all the tests of integrity[13] or faith[14] but he learned to be obedient to the *specific commands* of God as he received them. He learned it was better to wait on God's timing than to try to "work things out" on his own. In a word, Abraham believed God and that belief was counted as righteousness.

Some have quoted Genesis 26:5 as evidence that Abraham kept the Sabbath.

---

[11] Jn. 8:56.
[12] Gen. 13:17.
[13] Gen. 12:13.
[14] Gen. 17:17:17, 18.

> I will multiply your descendants as the stars of heaven, and will give your descendants all these lands; and by your descendants all the nations of the earth shall be blessed; because Abraham obeyed Me and kept My charge, My commandments, My statutes and My laws (Gen. 26:4, 5).

This interpretation, however, cannot stand the biblical test. Sometimes what is not mentioned is as important as what is mentioned. In the story of Abraham, or all of Genesis for that matter, the word "law" or "Sabbath" does not appear even once. The plural form, "laws", appears but once and that occurrence is in the text above. Neither "Sabbath" nor "Sabbaths" is mentioned in Genesis. Further, if one looks at the context of Genesis 26:5 it will be seen that it is almost identical to Genesis 22:16.

> Then the angel of the LORD called to Abraham a second time from heaven, and said, "By Myself I have sworn, declares the LORD, because you have done this thing and have not withheld your son, your only son, indeed I will greatly bless you, and I will greatly multiply your seed as the stars of the heavens and as the sand which is on the seashore; and your seed shall possess the gate of their enemies. In your seed all the nations of the earth shall be blessed, because you have obeyed My voice" (Gen. 22:15–18).

It is "because you have done this thing"—the offering of Isaac, not the keeping of a Sabbath—that caused God to swear by an oath the promised blessing.

It is clear that Abraham's obedience was an obedience of faith to the *specific commands* of God given to him and not to any Ten Commandment law. There are numerous New Testament texts which show that Abraham's promises and blessings were *not* based on law or law keeping but only on faith. Therefore to argue that Genesis 26:4, 5 implies that Abraham kept the Sabbath is in direct contradiction to the clear statements of Scripture. Consider the following:

> For the promise to Abraham or to his descendants that he would be heir of the world was not through the Law, but through the righteousness of faith (Rom. 4:13).

For this reason it is by faith, in order that it may be in accordance with grace, so that the promise will be guaranteed to all the descendants, not only to those who are of the Law, but also to those who are of the faith of Abraham, who is the father of us all (Rom. 4:16).

For if the inheritance is based on law, it is no longer based on a promise; but God has granted it to Abraham by means of a promise (Gal. 3:18).

We must conclude, then, that the nature of Abraham's obedience centered on the specific commands and promises that God gave to him. Further, his obedience is not seen as following a given set of rules, rather it is an obedience of faith—trusting God.

Chapter Summary

1. God initiated the relationship with Abraham.
2. God's covenant blessings were not based on anything that Abraham had previously done.
3. In the Abrahamic Covenant God's blessings included:
   a. A promise to multiply Abraham's descendants.
   b. Make him a father of many nations.
   c. Have kings of people come from him.
   d. Give to Abraham and his descendants the land of Canaan as an everlasting possession.
   e. A promise that all the families of the earth would be blessed in Abraham's descendants.
   f. God would be Abraham's shield and very great reward.
4. The Abrahamic Covenant is also called the Everlasting Covenant.
5. The sign of the Abrahamic Covenant was circumcision.
6. The sign of circumcision was given *after* Abraham had been declared righteous based solely on his faith.
7. Abraham did not actively participate in the confirmation of the covenant.

The Abrahamic Covenant

8. There is some evidence to believe that the smoking oven and flaming torch represented God the Father and God the Son who were present at the confirmation of the covenant with Abraham.
9. While Abraham expressed faith in God's promise, he and Sarah had no faith that *they* could fulfill God's promise.
10. When Abraham and Sarah attempted to "help God" fulfill His own promise it caused untold harm to themselves and others.
11. God's tests to Abraham were always "faith tests".
12. Abraham's obedience centered in his faith obedience to the specific commands that God gave him.
13. There is not the slightest hint that Abraham kept the Sabbath.

So He declared to you His **Covenant** which He commanded you to perform, that is, **the Ten Commandments**

CHAPTER FOUR

THE OLD COVENANT

The Concept of Covenant

An understanding of the concept of covenant is fundamental to a right interpretation of the whole Bible and it is absolutely imperative to a correct understanding of the Sabbath and the Sinaitic Covenant. It has been shown that the covenants God made with His people, especially the Sinaitic Covenant, closely follow the structure of the ancient Near East treaty covenant documents.[1] A covenant is simply an agreement or promise between two parties. One party is the suzerain, or ruling party. The other is the vassal, or ruled party. The suzerain—God in the case with Israel—was the one who dictated the terms of the covenant. Usually these terms were written out in duplicate so each party to the covenant had an identical copy[2] much the way a bank contract is made today. The covenant documents contained the promise made by the suzerain to the ruled party and the requirements, or obligations, of the ruled party to the suzerain. The covenant documents contained an outline of what would happen if the ruled party did not abide by the covenant obligations: blessings if they kept the

---

[1] Meredith G. Kline, *Treaty of the Great King*, (Wm. B. Eerdmans Publishing Company, Grand Rapids, MI, 1963), pp. 13, 14.
[2] *Ibid.,* p. 19.

covenant and cursings if they did not. Each covenant had a sign which was *arbitrarily* assigned by the suzerain and placed in the very *center* of the covenant document[3] and was *unique to that covenant agreement*. The ruled party was to keep or display the sign of the covenant as a symbol of their obedience to the covenant stipulations. Failure to do so would be considered by the suzerain a sign of rebellion and called for drastic consequences.

We see, then, that there are five main parts of each covenant: (1) the promise from the suzerain to the ruled party, (2) the requirements of the ruled party to the suzerain and (3) the sign of the covenant. (4) A list of the blessings that would occur if they were obedient to the covenant and (5) a list of the cursings that would come upon them for disobedience to the covenant stipulations. All of these were detailed in two *identical* covenant documents; one for the suzerain and one for the ruled party. In the ancient Near Eastern treaties,

> ...enshrinement of the treaty before the gods was expressive of their role as witnesses and avengers of the oath.[4]

Introduction to the Old Covenant

Before we consider the place that the Sabbath holds in the old covenant it is important that we first see the overall, larger view of this covenant. We want to get a concept of the size and form of the forest before we examine the trees. The old covenant has three aspects: (1) the exodus from Egypt, (2) the giving of the covenant at Sinai, and (3) the settlement in the land of Canaan.

The Old Testament is divided into law, history, psalms and prophets, and each relates to the covenant. Genesis gives the history of the covenant people and the covenant-keeping God. Exodus, Leviticus, Numbers and Deuteronomy

---
[3] *Ibid.*, p. 18.
[4] *Ibid.*, p. 19.

are the books of the covenant, or the books of the law.[5] The history of the Israelites is a history of the covenant people. The kings of Israel were evaluated with respect to the covenant. The Lord said to King Solomon,

> Because you have done this, and you have not kept My covenant and My statutes, which I have commanded you, I will surely tear the kingdom from you, and will give it to your servant (1 Ki. 11:11).

The overriding theme of the prophets is to call Israel and Judah, God's Old Testament covenant people, back to covenant loyalty. The prophets point out that the underlying reason for Israel's problems is that they have broken the covenant.

> "The house of Israel and the house of Judah have broken My covenant which I made with their fathers." Therefore thus says the Lord, "Behold I am bringing disaster on them" (Jer. 11:10, 11).

The exodus, the giving of the law at Sinai, and the settlement in the land of Canaan are inseparably linked in that they are all events connected with the giving of the covenant.

The exodus from Egypt must be seen as a covenant of redemption.

> Now it came about in the course of those many days that the king of Egypt died. And the sons of Israel sighed because of the bondage, and they cried out; and their cry for help because of their bondage rose up to God. So God heard their groaning; and God remembered His covenant with Abraham, Isaac, and Jacob …"So I have come down to deliver them from the power of the Egyptians" (Ex. 2:23, 24; 3:8).

As the great, redemptive activity of the old covenant, the exodus becomes the foundation for many of Israel's laws. The prologue to the Ten Commandments is,

---

[5] Genesis is also considered part of the law.

> I am the LORD your God, who brought you out of the land of Egypt, out of the house of slavery (Ex. 20:2).
>
> If your kinsman, a Hebrew man or woman, is sold to you, then he shall serve you six years, but in the seventh year you shall set him free. And when you set him free, you shall not send him away empty-handed. You shall furnish him liberally from your flock and from your threshing floor and from your wine vat; you shall give to him as the LORD your God has blessed you. And you shall remember that you were a slave in the land of Egypt, and the LORD your God redeemed you; therefore I command you this today (Deut. 15:12–15).
>
> When your sons ask you in time to come, saying, "What do the testimonies and the statutes and the judgments mean which the LORD commanded you?" then you shall say to your son, "We were slaves to Pharaoh in Egypt; and the LORD brought us from Egypt with a mighty hand" (Deut. 6:20, 21).

To rightly understand the old covenant laws, we must see them pictured in the frame of the old covenant redemption—the exodus from Egypt.

The redemptive event of the exodus not only serves as the foundation for Israel's law, it supplies the motivation for obedience. Time and again we find God instructing Israel to rehearse His "mighty deeds" so that they will "not forget" His covenant acts and will remember to keep the covenant laws, and thus receive the covenant blessings. When faced with the apparently overwhelming task of driving out the inhabitants of the land in order to fulfill God's covenant promise they were told:

> If you should say in your heart, "These nations are greater than I; how can I dispossess them?" you shall not be afraid of them; you shall well remember what the LORD your God did to Pharaoh and to all Egypt: the great trials which your eyes saw and the signs and the wonders and the mighty hand and the outstretched arm by which the LORD your God brought you out. So shall the LORD your God do to all the peoples of whom you are afraid (Deut. 7:17–19).

The Psalms record the worship of the covenant people. The mighty acts of God manifested in their redemption from Egyptian slavery is one of the major recurring themes of Israel's worship.

> Praise the LORD! Oh give thanks to the LORD, for He is good; for His lovingkindness is everlasting. Who can speak of the mighty deeds of the LORD, or can show forth all His praise?... Nevertheless He saved them for the sake of His name, that He might make His power known. Thus He rebuked the Red Sea and it dried up; and He led them through the deeps, as through the wilderness (Ps. 106:1, 2, 8, 9).

After the waters of the Red Sea covered the Egyptian armies and Israel experienced the promised covenant redemption, they broke out in joyous, worshipful celebration to the Almighty God who had delivered them from the Egyptian army.

> I will sing to the LORD, for He is highly exalted; the horse and its rider He has hurled into the sea. The LORD is my strength and song, and He has become my salvation; He is my God, and I will praise Him; my father's God and I will extol Him (Ex. 15:1, 2).

In addition to the exodus from Egypt, another major theme of Israel's worship was creation. Their God, YHWH, not only had redeemed them from Egyptian bondage, but He was the Creator of the heavens and the earth.

> O come, let us sing for joy to the LORD; let us shout joyfully to the rock of our salvation. Let us come before His presence with thanksgiving; let us shout joyfully to Him with psalms. For the LORD is a great God, and a great King above all gods, in whose hand are the depths of the earth; the peaks of the mountains are His also. The sea is His, for it was He who made it; and His hands formed the dry land (Ps. 95:1–5).

Thus we find these two dominant themes in Israel's worship: Giving adoration to the God who created the world and who redeemed them from Egypt.

The old covenant must be seen as interaction between two parties: God and Israel. While much space is devoted to Israel and her shortcomings, there is also ample coverage of God and His faithfulness. The book of Genesis outlines the history of the covenant people and the covenant-keeping God. The genealogies trace this history back to the "day" when God and man were in perfect fellowship—that "day" of "rest" when all was "very good." We see, then, that Old Testament history is indeed covenant history. It is a history of the God of creation patiently acting and interacting with man. He made a covenant with Noah and all the earth. Later He singled out Abraham as a covenant partner. Then He entered into covenant agreement with Isaac, Jacob and the "sons of Israel."

The Sinaitic Covenant

Covenant documents

The Ten Commandments: the basic covenant

What comprises the Sinaitic Covenant? The answer to this question is extremely important to our study of the Sabbath. The words "testament" and "covenant" are nearly identical in meaning—a very important fact to remember. Read carefully the following verses.

> And when He had finished speaking with him upon Mount Sinai, He gave Moses the two *tablets of the testimony,* the tablets of stone, written by the finger of God (Ex. 31:18).
>
> So he [Moses] was there with the LORD forty days and forty nights; he did not eat bread or drink water. And he wrote on *the tablets the words of the covenant, the Ten Commandments* (Ex. 34:28).
>
> So He declared to you *His covenant* which He commanded you to perform, that is, *the Ten Commandments;* and He wrote them on *two tablets of stone* (Deut. 4:13).
>
> When I went up to the mountain to receive the *tablets of stone, the tablets of the covenant* which the LORD had made with you ...(Deut. 9:9).
>
> And it came about at the end of forty days and nights that the LORD gave me the *two tablets of stone, the tablets of the covenant* (Deut. 9:11).

The Old Covenant

> So I turned and came down from the mountain while the mountain was burning with fire, and the *two tablets of the covenant* were in my two hands (Deut. 9:15).
>
> There was nothing in the ark except the two tablets of stone which Moses put there at Horeb, where the LORD made a covenant with the sons of Israel, when they came out of the land of Egypt…And there I have set the place for the ark in which is the covenant of the LORD, which He made with our fathers when He brought them out of Egypt (1 Ki. 8:9, 21).

These verses state unequivocally that the covenant between God and Israel which was made at Sinai was the Ten Commandments. This truth is underlined by the fact that the Ten Commandments were kept in the "ark of the covenant." "Then he [Moses] took the testimony and put it in the ark" (Ex. 40:20).

> Then I turned and came down from the mountain, and put the *tablets in the ark* which I had made; and there they are, as the LORD commanded me…At that time the LORD set apart the tribe of Levi to carry the ark *of the covenant* of the LORD (Deut. 10:5, 8).

The ark of the covenant was called the ark of the covenant because it was the box or container which held the covenant (Ten Commandments). It was a common practice in the ancient Near East for treaty documents to be placed in the sanctuary of the vassal (ruled party) and a duplicate copy to be placed in the sanctuary of the suzerain (ruling party).

> Similar instructions were given Moses at Sinai concerning the two tables. They were to be deposited in the ark, which in turn was to be placed in the tabernacle (Ex. 16:21; 40:20; Deut. 10:2). Because Yahweh was at once Israel's covenant Suzerain and God of Israel and Israel's oath, there was but one sanctuary for the depositing of both treaty duplicates.[6]

Considering the above, nothing could be stated more straightforwardly or more clearly and nothing is more important to a biblical understanding of the Sabbath than the

---

[6] *Ibid*, p. 19.

fact that the Ten Commandments are the *"words of the covenant."*

The "other laws": the expanded covenant

The Sinaitic Covenant, however, comprised more than just the Ten Commandments. In Exodus 21:1–23:33 God gives Moses applications and interpretations of the Ten Commandments. This same truth can be demonstrated in the book of Deuteronomy, which means "second law." A quick scanning through this book will show that most of it is quotation. Moses is repeating to the children of Israel the covenant of the Lord.

> These are the words of the covenant which the LORD commanded Moses to make with the sons of Israel in the Land of Moab, besides the covenant which He made with them at Horeb [Sinai] (Deut. 29:1).

In other words, the laws and judgments of the book of Deuteronomy become part of the covenant for two reasons. First, they repeat the Ten Commandments, the covenant itself, and second, they are a further *interpretation* of that covenant as Moses renewed the covenant with the Israelites as they were about to enter the promised land.

The "other laws" in the expanded version of the covenant interpret the Ten Commandments. Following are just a few examples to show the relationship between the Ten Commandments, the Sinaitic Covenant itself, and the expanded version of that covenant. The reader is encouraged to look up these verses, read them in their context and note how they interpret, explain, and apply the Ten Commandments.

1. No other gods:
   Sacrifice to another god (Ex. 22:20)
   Not worship any other (Ex. 34:14)
   I am the Lord your God (Lev. 20:24)
   Fear the Lord your God (Deut. 10:12)
2. Not worship idols:
   Not make idols (Lev. 26:1)

The Old Covenant

      Never forgiven for (Deut. 29:17–21)
      Makes God angry (Deut. 32:21)
      Do not turn to (Lev. 19:4)
3. Not profane God's name:
      Visit iniquity to four generations (Ex. 34:7)
      Not profane My holy name (Lev. 22:32)
      Put to death for profaning (Lev. 24:16)
      Put to death for cursing God (Lev. 24:10–13)
4. Remember the Sabbath:
      Perpetual covenant (Ex. 31:13)
      Put to death for violation (Ex. 31:14)
      Violator to be "cut off" (Ex. 31:14)
      Not kindle a fire on (Ex. 35:3)
      Keep evening to evening (Lev. 23:32)
5. Honor father and mother:
      Death penalty for cursing parents (Ex. 21:17)
      Death penalty for hitting father (Ex. 21:15)
      Reverence father and mother (Lev. 19:3)
      Rebellious to parents (Deut. 21:18–21)
6. Not kill:
      Killed in a quarrel and fistfight (Ex. 21:18)
      Killed by beating with a rod (Ex. 21:20)
      Killed by ox, first offense (Ex. 21:28)
      Killed by ox, several offenses (Ex. 21:29)
7. Not commit adultery:
      With another man's wife (Lev. 20:10)
      With father's wife (Lev. 20:11)
      With daughter-in-law (Lev. 20:12)
      A number of situations (Lev. 18:16–30)
8. Not steal:
      Steals an ox (Ex. 22:1)
      Thief caught while breaking in (Ex. 22:2–4)
      Animal grazing in neighbor's field (Ex. 22:5)
      Thief not caught until later (Ex. 22:8)
9. Not bear false witness:
      Lied and sworn falsely (Lev. 6:3–8)
      Swears thoughtlessly (Lev. 5:4)
      Not give false report (Ex. 23:1)
      Punishment for a false witness (Deut. 19:18–21)

10. Not covet:
    Not covet gold on destroyed idols (Deut. 7:25)
    Not covet the land (Ex. 34:24)

The expanded version of the covenant was placed in a receptacle on the side of the ark of the covenant showing its relationship to the Ten Commandments which were placed inside the ark of the covenant.

> Take this book of the law and place it beside the ark of the covenant of the LORD your God, that it may remain there as a witness against you (Deut. 31:26).

The covenant reduced to a sign

There is yet a third dimension to the Sinaitic Covenant. In Exodus 31:12–17 we see that the Sabbath is called a covenant.

> So the sons of Israel shall observe the sabbath, to celebrate the sabbath throughout their generations *as a perpetual covenant*. It is a *sign* between Me and the sons of Israel forever; for in six days the LORD made heaven and earth, but on the seventh day He ceased from labor, and was refreshed (Ex. 31:16, 17).

Here the Sabbath is called a "perpetual covenant." It was a "sign" between God and Israel. In the Hebrew Bible if one counts the words of the Ten Commandments he will find the central phrase is "remember the sabbath day to keep it holy." As the sign of the covenant was placed in the very center of the ancient Near East treaty documents, so the Sabbath, as the sign of the Sinaitic Covenant, rightfully finds its place in the *very center* of the Ten Commandments.

Therefore, we may look at the covenant documents in three ways: (1) the Ten Commandments are the basic Sinaitic Covenant, the very *words of the covenant,* (2) the "other laws" or the "book of the law" is the *covenant expanded and interpreted* and (3) the Sabbath is the *covenant reduced to a sign.*

The Old Covenant: One Law

There are some who teach that the Ten Commandments are the Moral Law and the Book of the Law that was placed by the side of the ark is the Ceremonial Law. However, this is unbiblical and simplistic. The Book of the Law should be understood to be Genesis to Deuteronomy and it contained the Ten Commandments as in Exodus 20 and Deuteronomy 5, as well as all the other regulations and laws. We must see the law of the old covenant as one law.[7] While there are moral, ceremonial and societal aspects of the law, they comprise but one law. Often these aspects of the law are intermingled. There is no sharply defined separation between them.

So far we have seen that the Ten Commandments are the "words of the covenant" God made with Israel at Sinai. We have also seen that the expanded version of the covenant— the interpretation of the Ten Commandments to their specific life situations—is also called "the words of the covenant" (Deut. 29:1, 9) or "the book of the covenant" (Ex. 24:7). The Ten Commandments were placed inside the Ark of the Covenant, and "the book of the covenant" was placed at the side of the Ark of the Covenant and these comprised the law of the old covenant or simply "the law".

God's covenant promise to Israel

God's covenant promise to Israel was broad. By the time Israel had arrived at Sinai, God had already delivered them from Egyptian bondage, opened up the Red Sea, provided water for them in the desert and given them manna from heaven. He would yet bring them into the Promised Land, protect them from their enemies, upon the offering of sacrifices he would forgive their sins. Therefore, God's

---

[7] See H.M. Riggle, *The Sabbath and the Lord's Day* (Faith Publishing House, Guthrie, OK, 1922) Now published by Life Assurance Ministries Publications Glendale, AZ), pp. 46–60 for much supporting documentation.

claim upon Israel was both past and future and rooted in His gracious redemption. In Exodus 19, Moses communicates to the people this message from God.

> You yourselves have seen what I did to the Egyptians, and how I bore you on eagles' wings, and brought you to Myself. Now then, if you will indeed obey My voice and keep My covenant, then you shall be My own possession among all the peoples, for all the earth is Mine (Ex. 19:4–5).[8]

Israel's covenant promise to God

Moses then takes the covenant offered by God to the Israelites and records their response.

> So Moses came and called the elders of the people, and set before them all these words which the LORD had commanded him. And all the people answered together and said, "All that the LORD has spoken we will do!" And Moses brought back the words of the people to the LORD (Ex. 19:7–8).

> Moses came and recounted to the people all the words of the LORD and all the ordinances; and all the people answered with one voice, and said, "All the words which the LORD has spoken we will do!" And Moses wrote down all the words of the LORD (Ex. 24:3).

> Then he [Moses] took the Book of the Covenant and read it in the hearing of the people; and they said, "All that the LORD has spoken we will do, and we will be obedient" (Ex. 24:7).

Stipulations of the covenant

The covenant requirements that Israel promised to keep are too numerous to mention. They included the Ten Commandments, the "other laws" recorded in Exodus through Deuteronomy and the covenant signs in all totaling 613 commandments.[9]

---

[8] See also the many other promises mentioned in Exodus and Deuteronomy.

[9] See Rabbi Joseph Telushkin, *Biblical Literacy* [William Morrow and Company, Inc.] 1948, for a detailed description of each of the 613 commandments, their biblical foundation and Jewish interpretation.

The Sinaitic Covenant vs. the Abrahamic Covenant

From the biblical text itself, it is evident that the stipulations of the Sinaitic Covenant were not included in the covenants God made with Abraham. A quotation from Deuteronomy confirms this point. Some have tried to read back into Abrahamic Covenant the requirements of the Sinaitic Covenant. Note how clear Scripture is on this point:

> The LORD our God made a covenant with us at Horeb [another name for Sinai]. The LORD did *not* make this covenant with our fathers, but with us, with *all of those of us alive here today* (Deut. 5:3).

Some who reviewed this manuscript argued that the "our fathers" in this text refers back to the generation who died in the wilderness and not to Abraham, whom they claim, was a Sabbath keeper. However, this cannot be the case because the above reference clearly states that the "LORD our God made a covenant with *us* at Horeb. The "us" includes not only Moses but all the children of Israel. The "our fathers" must refer to Abraham, Isaac and Jacob who were not included in the Sinaitic Covenant. "Our fathers" is a term often used by Moses to refer to Abraham, Isaac and Jacob.[10]

Moses then lists the Ten Commandments (Deut. 5:1–21) and the other laws in the "book of the covenant" that were not given to Abraham or to "the fathers" as part of the covenant stipulations God made with them. However, the Israelites were the descendants of Abraham, and therefore came under the covenant of circumcision. In Lev. 12:1–3 God repeated the commandment of circumcision, indicating its continuing importance for the men of Israel.

The Israelites living after the Sinaitic Covenant were under both covenants.

---

[10] See Ex. 3:15; 4:5; Deut 1:8; 6:10; 9:5; 30:20.

Remember His covenant forever, the word which He commanded to a thousand generations, the covenant which He made with Abraham, and His oath to Isaac. He also confirmed it to Jacob for a statute, to Israel as an everlasting covenant (1 Chron. 16:15–17; cf. Ps. 105).

Covenant signs

The Sinaitic Covenant had one unique sign, yet because the Israelites were part of the Abrahamic Covenant, for all practical purposes, the old covenant could be considered to have two signs. The unique sign of the Sinaitic Covenant was the Sabbath and then there was the sign of circumcision—from the Abrahamic Covenant. Only those households where the males were circumcised were included in the covenant community of Israel. Notice the parallel in language between these two covenant signs: Circumcision "C" and Sabbath "S" as recorded in Genesis 17: 9–14 and Exodus 31:12–18; 20:12:

C. "You shall keep My covenant" 17:9
S. "You shall surely observe My sabbath" 31:13

C. "Me and you and your descendants" 17:9
S. "Me and the sons of Israel" 31:17

C. "And you shall be circumcised" 17:11
S. "You are to observe the sabbath" 31:14

C. "Throughout your generations" 17:12
S. "Throughout your generations" 31:13

C. "The sign…between Me and you" 17:11
S. "A sign between Me and you" 31:13

C. "An everlasting covenant" 17:13
S. "A perpetual covenant" 31:16

C. "Uncircumcised…cut off" 17:14
S. "Whoever does any work…cut off" 31:14

C. Servant to be circumcised 17:12
S. Servant to keep Sabbath 20:10

C. Sign of circumcision given at time of giving of the covenant 17:1–9
S. Sign of Sabbath given at time of giving of the covenant 31:18
C. Circumcision mentioned 6 times
S. Sabbath mentioned 6 times

The similarities in wording, style and time of giving, are too striking to be accidental. And the similarity is even more apparent in the original language. For example, "everlasting" (Gen. 17:13) and "perpetual" (Ex. 31:16) are translations from the same Hebrew word, *olam*. It is important that we understand the relationship between circumcision and Sabbath and see the role they play in the Sinaitic Covenant. Circumcision was the entrance sign into the covenant God made with Abraham and his descendants. It was the initiatory or entrance sign of the covenant by which one became a member of the covenant community. The Passover feast was a celebration for the covenant community only. In the following reference circumcision served as the entrance sign into the covenant community and thus gave one the right to participate in the Passover (or covenant) celebration.

> And the LORD said to Moses and Aaron, "This is the ordinance of the Passover: no foreigner is to eat of it; but every man's slave purchased with money, *after you have circumcised him,* then he may eat of it…if a stranger sojourns with you, and celebrates the Passover to the LORD, let all his males be circumcised, and then let him come to celebrate it; and he shall be like a native of the land. But *no uncircumcised* person may eat of it" (Ex. 12:43, 44, 48).

The Sabbath, in a similar way, was the continuing sign the covenant people—now under the Sinaitic covenant—were to "remember." It was a ceremony observed weekly as a renewing of the covenant. As in the case with circumcision, if a foreigner desired to join in covenant fellowship he was to observe the Sabbath.

> The seventh day is the sabbath of the LORD your God; in it you shall not do any work, you...or *the sojourner* who stays with you (Ex. 20:10).

Notice how in the time of Isaiah the Sabbath was related to the covenant and how foreigners who joined themselves to Israel were expected to observe the Sabbath of the covenant.

> Let not the foreigner who has joined himself to the LORD say, "The LORD will surely separate me from his people." Neither let the eunuch say, "Behold, I am a dry tree." For thus says the LORD, "To the eunuchs who *keep My sabbaths,* and choose what pleases Me, and *hold fast My covenant,* to them I will give in My house and within My walls a memorial, and a name better than that of sons and daughters; I will give them an everlasting name which will not be cut off. Also the *foreigners who join themselves to the LORD,* to minister to Him, and to love the name of the LORD, to be His servants, *every one who keeps from profaning the sabbath, and holds fast My covenant"* (Isa. 56:3–6).

Circumcision was given to the descendants of Abraham as the one-time entrance sign into the covenant community. The Sabbath was given as a repeatable sign of the Sinaitic Covenant Israel was to "remember."

Covenant partners

In many of the above quotations the covenant partners were clearly stated, nevertheless it is important that we thoroughly understand who they were. Scripture makes it very clear that the Sinaitic Covenant was made with the nation of Israel *only.*

The prologue to the Ten Commandments clearly identifies the covenant partners.

> Then God spoke all these words, saying, "I am the LORD your God, who brought you out of the land of Egypt, out of the house of slavery" (Ex. 20:1, 2).

Who were the people who were brought out of the land of Egypt? The people of Israel.

In connection with the covenant of Sabbath (which stood for the whole of the Ten Commandments) we read,

> Speak to the sons of Israel, saying, "You shall surely observe My sabbaths; for it is a *sign between Me and you throughout your generations"* (Ex. 31:13).
>
> So the sons of Israel shall observe the sabbath, to celebrate the sabbath throughout their generations as a perpetual covenant. It is a sign between Me and the sons of Israel forever (Ex. 31:16, 17).
>
> Then Moses summoned all Israel, and said to them, "Hear, O Israel, the statutes and the ordinances which I am speaking today in your hearing…The LORD our God made a covenant with us at Horeb [Sinai]. The LORD did not make this covenant with our fathers, but with us, with all those of us alive here today" (Deut. 5:1–3).

The Sinaitic Covenant partners were God and the sons of Israel only. Others could join the covenant community, but only if the males were circumcised and all kept the Sabbath.

Old Covenant righteousness

The old covenant was given in a grace/redemption setting. God had just delivered Israel from hundreds of years of Egyptian slavery. We will also see in the next chapter that grace was abundantly prefigured through the sacrificial system. However, the righteousness of the Sinaitic Covenant is markedly different from that of the Abrahamic Covenant. Abraham was accounted righteous solely on the basis of his faith.[11] The righteousness of the old covenant, however, was based on personal obedience to the law.

> So the LORD commanded us to observe all these statutes, to fear the LORD our God for our good always and for our survival, as it is today. It will be righteousness for us if we are careful to observe all this commandment before the LORD our God, just as He commanded us (Deut. 6:24, 25).

---

[11] Gen. 15:6.

At the giving of the covenant at Sinai, the sons of Israel felt that they could keep God's law of commandments.

> All the people answered together and said, "All that the LORD has spoken we will do!" And Moses brought back the words of the people to the LORD (Ex. 19:8).[12]

Abraham had learned the lesson of faith that Israel never did. He finally came to the point where he no longer trusted in his ability to perform but trusted God to fulfill His own promises. The sons of Israel, however, felt they could go it on their own. Perhaps this is why God gave them the 613 detailed commandments to teach them the hard lesson that they could not be good enough without His grace and power.

Duration of the covenant

How long was the Sinaitic Covenant to last? All Old Testament scriptural references dealing expressly with the giving of the covenant indicate that it was to last forever. The following references are only samplings; others could be listed. Notice how many aspects of the covenant are said to be perpetual or everlasting. I encourage the reader to look in a Bible concordance and note how many of the entries under perpetual, everlasting, forever, and permanent have to do with some aspect of the Sinaitic Covenant.

> It [describing the service of the *lamps* in the tent of meeting] shall be a *perpetual* statute throughout their generations for the sons of Israel (Ex. 27:21).
>
> Thus shall My covenant [circumcision] be in your flesh for an *everlasting* covenant (Gen. 17:13).
>
> And you shall gird them with sashes, Aaron and his sons, and bind caps on them, and they shall have the priesthood by a *perpetual statute* (Ex. 29:9).
>
> There shall be *perpetual incense* before the LORD *throughout your generations* (Ex. 30:8).

---

[12] See also Ex. 24:3; 24:7; Lev. 18:5; Gal. 3:12.

The Old Covenant

> It is a *perpetual statute throughout your generations* in all your dwellings: you shall not eat any fat or any blood (Lev. 3:17).
>
> Do not drink wine or strong drink, neither you nor your sons with you, when you come into the tent of meeting, so that you may not die—it is a *perpetual statute throughout your generations* (Lev. 10:9).

The seasonal yearly feasts are said to be perpetual statutes (Lev. 23:14, 21, 41).

> But *pasture fields* of their [the Levites'] cities shall not be sold, for that is their *perpetual possession* (Lev. 25:34).
>
> All the *offerings of the holy gifts,* which the sons of Israel offer to the LORD, I have given to you and your sons and your daughters with you, as a *perpetual allotment.* It is an *everlasting covenant* of salt before the LORD to you and your descendants with you (Num. 18:19).

With rare exception everything connected with the covenant God made with Israel was said to be permanent, perpetual, everlasting, forever, or "throughout your generations." It was not until Israel had broken the covenant and the nation was headed into captivity that we get mention of a new covenant (Jer. 31:31).

Purpose of the covenant

The covenant served as the basis of the relationship that existed between God and Israel. There were blessings and cursings associated with the covenant: blessings if Israel was obedient and kept the covenant, and cursings if Israel disobeyed and forsook the covenant. The covenant agreement also included provision for forgiveness if Israel sinned but later repented and returned to God.

One purpose the covenant held was to be a witness or testimony between God and Israel. When Israel disobeyed, they had no excuse when the cursing came upon them, for the "testimony" was there. In fact, the very presence of Israel in captivity was a witness of God's faithfulness as a covenant partner.

Indeed all Israel has transgressed Thy law and turned aside, not obeying Thy voice; so the curse has been poured out on us, along with the oath which is written in the law of Moses the servant of God, for we have sinned against Him. Thus He has confirmed *His words* which He had spoken against us and against our rulers who ruled us, to bring on us great calamity (Dan. 9:11, 12).

The covenant was said to be written on two tablets of stone (Ex. 34:1). Artists often picture these tablets as written only on one side. But Scripture states they were written on both sides.

Then Moses turned and went down from the mountain with the two tablets of the testimony in his hand, tablets which were written on both sides; they were written on one side and the other (Ex. 32:15).

The tablets of the covenant served a purpose much like a present-day contract. Today when we purchase a car or a home with a bank loan we get one copy of the contract (covenant) and the bank keeps a second, identical copy of the contract. In like manner some feel these two tables of the covenant were identical.[13] One copy was for the vassal (Israel) and the other was for the Suzerain (God).[14] The expanded version of the covenant, called "the book of the law," was placed at the side of the ark and later copied so Israel could have free access to the stipulations of the covenant.

Violations of the covenant

It is important to recognize that a serious violation of *any* of the covenant stipulations could "break" the covenant. This could be a violation of the basic covenant, the Ten Commandments; a violation of the "book of the covenant" or a violation of the Sabbath, the covenant sign.

---

[13] Kline, *Treaty of the Great King,* p. 19.
[14] Ibid., p. 59.

The Old Covenant

In such cases the people were to be "cut off" from the covenant community.

> But if you do not obey Me and do not carry out all these commandments, if, instead, you reject My statutes, and if your soul abhors My ordinances so as not to carry out all My commandments, and so break My covenant…(Lev. 26:14, 15).

We see this concept illustrated when Moses was on his way to Egypt: "It came about at the lodging-place on the way that the LORD met him and sought to put him to death." At this point Zipporah, the wife of Moses, circumcised their sons "So He [the LORD] let him alone" (Ex. 4:24, 25). This incident shows how important it was for member of the covenant community to comply with the sign of the covenant if he expected God's covenant blessings. In this case even Moses was considered a violator of the covenant and would have been killed or "cut off" from the covenant community had he not complied with the sign of the covenant—a sobering thought indeed!

God allowed for a difference in punishment between intentional and unintentional sin.

> Also if one person sins unintentionally, then he shall offer a one year old female goat for a sin offering…The person who does anything defiantly, whether he is native or an alien, that one is blaspheming the LORD; and that person shall be cut off from among his people (Num. 15:27, 30).

In this same context a man was found gathering sticks on the Sabbath day. He was put in custody and

> Then the LORD said to Moses, "The man shall surely be put to death; all the congregation shall stone him with stones outside the camp." So all the congregation brought him outside the camp, and stoned him to death with stones, just as the LORD had commanded Moses (Num. 15:35, 36).

We see here that a violation of the Sabbath, the sign of the Sinaitic Covenant, was considered to be open rebellion against the covenant. Note the many ways for which one could be "cut off" from the covenant people:

The offense:	Scripture:
Not circumcised	Gen. 17:14
Breaking the Sabbath	Ex. 31:14
Eating anything leavened	Ex. 12:15
Misuse of anointing oil	Ex. 30:33
Misuse of incense	Ex. 30:38
Eating sacrifice while unclean	Lev. 7:20
Misuse of sacrifice	Lev. 7:21
Eating fat of sacrifice	Lev. 7:25
Eating blood	Lev. 7:27
Killing sacrifice wrongly	Lev. 17:1–4
Incest	Lev. 18:6–18, 29
Intercourse during menstruation	Lev. 18:19, 29
Homosexual activity	Lev. 18:22, 29
Intercourse with animals	Lev. 18:23, 29
Eating a sacrifice wrongly	Lev. 19:1–8
Offering children to Molech	Lev. 20:3
Contact with spiritists	Lev. 20:6
Not humbling oneself	Lev. 23:29
Neglecting the Passover	Num. 9:13

Covenant characteristics

Those who start to read the Bible through usually do well until they come to the latter part of Exodus. From there through Deuteronomy it is usually rough going because they get bogged down in all the *laws*. These books contain literally hundreds of laws because the Sinaitic Covenant is a *law covenant*. While God's grace was represented in His gracious provision of forgiveness on condition of repentance and the offering of certain sacrifices, the emphasis, nonetheless, is on law. It is characteristically a *law covenant*.

Not only is this covenant primarily law, but it is law in *great detail*. This covenant law does not simply ask people to bring an offering to the LORD, but it spells out exactly what kind of an offering to bring.

The Old Covenant

> You shall also offer one male goat for a sin offering and two male lambs one year old for a sacrifice of peace offerings (Lev. 23:19).

This law does not simply say to bring a cereal offering, but it tells how much cereal to bring and how to mix it.

> Its grain offering shall then be two-tenths of an ephah of fine flour mixed with oil (Lev. 23:13).

This law does not simply say bring oil but it instructs the people to bring "clear oil from beaten olives" (Lev. 24:2).

This law does not simply say to bring cakes of bread to the LORD but:

> You shall take fine flour and bake twelve cakes with it; two-tenths of an ephah shall be in each cake. And you shall set them in two rows, six to a row, on the pure gold table before the LORD (Lev. 24:5, 6).

This great detail of law is characteristic of the Sinaitic Covenant. I am reminded of times when I was teaching high school students, especially the freshmen. I was forced to go into great detail in making my assignments. Anything that could be misunderstood often was. I could not just say, "Answer these questions," but would have to instruct them to, "Write answers to questions 1–10, page 56, and be ready to turn them in at the beginning of class on Tuesday, September 25. Please use 8 1/2 x 11 lined paper and write clearly. Place your name in the upper left-hand corner and the date in the upper right-hand corner." From the great amount of detail and minute instructions included in the old covenant it appears that God was treating the Israelites as children. Israel had just spent several hundred years in slavery to Egypt, and God met them where they were.

Another characteristic of the Sinaitic Covenant is that it is a mediated covenant.[15] Moses, and later Joshua and other leaders, served as a mediator between God and the sons of

---

[15] See D. A. Carson, *Showing the Spirit*, (Baker Book House, 1987), p. 151 ff.

Israel. What the people knew about God they received through a mediator (Ex. 24:1–7). Only the prophets and certain other leaders of the people were filled with the Holy Spirit and had a personal knowledge of God. At times this mediatorial role was even intercessory. When the Israelites were bitten with snakes, Moses interceded with God and God gave him directions for making the brazen serpent. If the snake-bitten Israelite simply looked at the uplifted serpent he lived (Num. 21:4–9). On one occasion when the people grumbled against Moses and Aaron,

> The LORD spoke to Moses, saying, "Get away from among this congregation, that I may consume them instantly." Then they fell on their faces...Then Aaron took it [the censer of incense] as Moses had spoken, and ran into the midst of the assembly, for behold, the plague had begun among the people. So he put on the incense and made atonement for the people. And he took his stand between the dead and the living, so that the plague was checked (Num. 16:44–48).

Chapter Summary

1. The biblical covenants in general, and the Sinaitic Covenant in particular, closely follow the form of other ancient, Near East treaties.
   a. There is a covenant promise of the suzerain to the vassal.
   b. There is a covenant promise of the ruled party to suzerain.
   c. The document which contains the covenant agreement has the sign of that covenant in the very center of the document.
   d. Two identical copies of the covenant documents are made.
   e. The documents are placed in the house of the vassal's god who is called to witness the oath of the covenant.
2. The stipulations of the Sinaitic Covenant were not a part of the covenant God made with Abraham.

The Old Covenant

3. The elements of the Sinaitic Covenant are three:
   a. The Ten Commandments are the words of the Sinaitic Covenant.
   b. The "other laws" found in Exodus through Deuteronomy are the expanded version of the Sinaitic Covenant and are usually called "the book of the covenant," or "the book of the law."
   c. The Sabbath was the sign of the Sinaitic Covenant and, as such, was placed in the very center of the Ten Commandments.
4. The "book of the law" interpreted and applied the "tables of the law" to specific situations in the life of Israel.
5. The wording of the covenant of circumcision is nearly identical with the wording of the covenant of Sabbath. What is said of one is said of the other.
6. The covenant partners were God and the nation of Israel only. No other people were included within this covenant.
7. Old covenant righteousness was based upon personal obedience to the law.
8. The provisions of the Sinaitic Covenant were open to others, but *only* if they became circumcised, kept the Sabbath and were willing to abide by all the covenant stipulations.
9. The duration of the Sinaitic Covenant was said to be forever, eternal, perpetual, or "throughout your generations."
10. The purpose of the covenant was to provide the basis of fellowship between God and Israel and to serve as a witness in case of covenant violations.
11. Violations of the covenant included violations of the Ten Commandments, the other laws in the "book of the covenant," or the signs of the covenant: circumcision and Sabbath.
12. Provision was made for the difference between intentional and unintentional sin.

a. An Israelite was put to death or cut off from the covenant community for intentional sin.
   b. An Israelite who committed unintentional sin was provided atonement conditional on the fulfillment of certain sacrifices.
13. The Sinaitic Covenant is characteristically a law covenant.
14. The Sinaitic Covenant is minutely detailed as if it were written for children.
15. The Sinaitic Covenant is a mediated covenant with Moses, or at times Aaron, standing between God and the sons of Israel.

CHAPTER
Five

SHADOWS OF CHRIST

The purpose of this chapter is to get an overview of the religious services connected with the Sinaitic Covenant, to discover how and why the Sabbath was observed in the Old Testament and to observe relationships between the Sabbath and other old covenant ceremonies. It will not serve our purpose to articulate the details of the old covenant sacrificial services or rituals. However, their significance as a means of displaying God's grace should not be diminished. It is, nonetheless, beyond the scope of this study to do so. This chapter will, of necessity, cover a vast amount of material. Passages closely related to our topic have been included. In places you may want to scan some of the miscellaneous detail. If you do, please note that which is in italics as this will prove important to our study. Some of the evidence in this chapter will not have immediate application but will prove to be of enormous value for later understanding.

Covenant convocations

In this section we will look at an array of religious services prescribed within the Sinaitic Covenant linked to a specific time for their performance.

Leviticus 23 lists most of the appointed times or holy convocations for the covenant people.

> The LORD spoke again to Moses, saying, "Speak to the sons of Israel, and say to them, 'The LORD's appointed times which

you shall proclaim as holy convocations—My appointed times are these'" (Lev. 23:1, 2).

The Seventh-day Sabbath

For six days work may be done; but on the seventh day there is a sabbath of complete rest, a holy convocation. You shall not do any work; it is a sabbath to the LORD in all your dwellings (Lev. 23:3). So the sons of Israel shall observe the sabbath, to celebrate the sabbath throughout their generations as a perpetual covenant (Ex. 31:16).

The Passover

In the first month, on the fourteenth day of the month...is the LORD's Passover (Lev. 23:5). Now this day will be a memorial to you, and you shall celebrate it as a feast to the LORD; throughout your generations you are to celebrate it as a permanent ordinance (Ex. 12:14).

The Feast of Unleavened Bread

Then on the fifteenth day of the same month there is a Feast of Unleavened Bread to the LORD; for seven days...on the first day you shall have a holy convocation; you shall *not do any laborious work*...on the seventh day is a holy convocation; you shall *not do any laborious work* (Lev. 23:6–8). You also shall observe the Feast of Unleavened Bread...*you shall observe this day throughout your generations as a permanent ordinance* (Ex. 12:17).

First Fruits

You shall bring in the sheaf of the first fruits of your harvest...on the day after the sabbath the priest shall wave it...*it is to be a perpetual statute throughout your generations* (Lev. 23:10–14).

Pentecost

You shall count fifty days to the day after the seventh sabbath; then you shall present a new grain offering to the LORD...*you shall do no laborious work*. It is to be *a perpetual statute* in all your dwelling places *throughout your generations* (Lev. 23:15–21).

Blowing of Trumpets

In the seventh month on the first of the month, you shall have a rest, a reminder by blowing of trumpets, a holy convocation. You *shall not do any laborious work* (Lev. 23:23–25).

Day of Atonement

On exactly the tenth day of the seventh month is the day of atonement…It is to be *a sabbath of complete rest to you* (Lev. 23:27–32). And this shall be *a permanent statute* for you: in the seventh month, on the tenth day of the month, you shall humble your souls, and *not do any work,* whether the native, or the alien who sojourns among you…*It is to be a sabbath of solemn rest for you…it is a permanent statute* (Lev. 16:29, 31).

Feast of Booths

On the fifteenth of the seventh month is the Feast of Booths for seven days to the LORD. On the first day is a holy convocation; *you shall do no laborious work of any kind…*On the eighth day you shall have a holy convocation…*You shall do no laborious work…*So Moses declared to the sons of Israel the appointed times of the LORD (Lev. 23:33–44).

New Moons

Then at the beginning of each of your months you shall present a burnt offering to the LORD (Num. 28:11). To offer burnt offerings morning and evening, *on sabbaths and on new moons* and on the appointed feasts of the LORD our God, *this being required forever in Israel* (2 Chron. 2:4).

Sabbatical Years

Speak to the sons of Israel, and say to them, "When you come into the land which I shall give you, then *the land shall have a sabbath to the LORD…*Six years you shall sow your field, and six years you shall prune your vineyard and gather in its crops, but *during the seventh yea*r *the land shall have a sabbath rest, a sabbath to the LORD;* you shall *not sow* your field *nor prune* your vineyard. Your harvest aftergrowth you shall *not reap,* and your grapes of trimmed vines you shall *not gather; the land shall have a sabbatical year.* And all of you shall have the *sabbath products* of the land for food: yourself, and your male and female slaves, and your hired man and your foreign resident, those who live as aliens with you. Even your cattle and the animals that are in your land shall have all its crops to eat" (Lev. 25:2–7).

Jubilee

You are to count off *seven sabbaths of years* for yourself, seven times seven years, so that you have the time of the *seven sabbaths of years,* namely, *forty-nine years*. You shall then sound a ram's horn abroad on the tenth day of the seventh month; *on the day of atonement* you shall sound a horn all through your land. You shall thus consecrate the fiftieth year and *proclaim a release through the land to all its inhabitants. It shall be a jubilee for you and each of you shall return to his family.* You shall have the fiftieth year as a *jubilee:* you shall not sow, nor reap its aftergrowth, nor gather in from its untrimmed vines. For it is a jubilee; it shall be holy to you. *You shall eat its crops out of the field...*But if you say, "What are we going to eat on the seventh year if we do not sow or gather in our crops?" then I will so order My blessing for you in the sixth year that it will bring forth the crop for *three years* (Lev. 25:8–12, 20, 21).

In the preceding references we see a developing sabbatical cycle: the weekly Sabbath, the seven annual, or seasonal sabbaths, every seven years a sabbatical year, every seven sabbatical years a Jubilee.

In each of these "sabbaths" we find that work is prohibited. They are all called "holy" or are said to be a "sabbath to the Lord." These are said to be perpetual and were to be practiced "throughout your generations". Animals as well as the land itself are included in the "rest." There is an underlying sense of freedom in the sabbath concept. Everyone is free from the responsibility of work; the Israelites, the slaves, the foreigners, the animals and even the land itself. There seems to be a rising crescendo in the sabbatical cycle which reaches its peak in the Jubilee. On that fiftieth year there was a whole year of Sabbaths, a special sabbatical year! The Jubilee was ushered in on the Day of Atonement by the blowing of a ram's horn. The Jubilee was a time of release to the members of the covenant community, a time to return to the family property, a time to cancel all debts, a time to wipe the

Shadows of Christ

record clean and begin anew. It was designed to be a joyous time of celebration and fellowship!

As joyful as the Jubilee sounds, there is no record it was ever observed. It seems to have been something that was written about but never experienced. Perhaps the people were too selfish to proclaim freedom to all the inhabitants of the land. Perhaps they were too fearful of monetary loss should they not sow or reap. Whatever the reason, the celebration of the Jubilee seems to have remained for the "days to come" when God would give them *three years* worth of blessings!

Sabbath Observance

When it comes to Sabbath observance the Old Testament is very specific. It should be noted that the following Sabbath laws usually apply to *all* the Sabbaths, not just the weekly Sabbath. I have included all the Old Testament rules for Sabbath observance. It should be noted that some of these are not from the books of the law and serve as a biblical interpretation of the original Sabbath commands.

Things not to do on the Sabbath:

Do not go out of your place

Then the LORD said to Moses...Remain every man in his place; let no man go out of his place on the seventh day (Ex. 16:29).

Do not bake or boil

This is what the LORD meant: Tomorrow is a sabbath observance, a holy sabbath to the LORD. Bake what you will bake and boil what you will boil, and all that is left over put aside to be kept until morning (Ex. 16:23).

Do not do any work

But the seventh day is a sabbath unto the LORD your God; in it *you shall not do any work,* you or your son or your daughter, your male servant or your female servant or your cattle or your sojourner who stays with you (Ex. 20:10).

The prohibition of working is set forth in very clear terms.

> You shall work six days, but on the seventh day you shall rest, even during plowing time and harvest you shall rest (Ex. 34:21).

Do not build a fire

> These things are the things that the LORD has commanded you to do...You shall not kindle a fire in any of your dwellings on the sabbath day (Ex. 35:1, 3).

Do not carry a load

> But if you do not listen to Me to keep the sabbath day holy by not carrying a load and coming in through the gates of Jerusalem on the sabbath day, then I shall kindle a fire in the gates, and it will devour the palaces of Jerusalem and not be quenched (Jer. 17:27; cf. Neh. 1:15).

Do not buy or sell

> As for the peoples of the land who bring wares or any grain on the sabbath day to sell, we will not buy from them on the sabbath or a holy day (Neh. 10:31; cf. Amos 8:5 ff.).

Do not do your own pleasure

> If because of the sabbath, you turn your foot *from doing your own pleasure* on My holy day, and call the sabbath a delight, the holy of the LORD honorable, and shall honor it, *desisting from your own ways, from seeking your own pleasure, and speaking your own word*... (Isa. 58:13, 14).

Things to do on the Sabbath:

Keep it holy

> Remember the sabbath day, to keep it holy (Ex. 20:8).

Rest

> For six days work may be done, but on the seventh day there is a sabbath of complete rest (Ex. 31:15).

Shadows of Christ

Observe or celebrate

So the sons of Israel shall *observe* the sabbath, to *celebrate* the sabbath throughout their generations as a perpetual covenant (Ex. 31:16).

Delight in the Lord

Then you will take delight in the Lord (Isa. 58:14).

Convocate

For six days work may be done, but on the seventh day there is a sabbath of complete rest, a holy *convocation*. You shall not do any work; it is a sabbath to the LORD in all your dwellings (Lev 23:3).

The instructions regarding a holy convocation, or sacred assembly, are the same for seventh-day Sabbath and all the seasonal feasts.[1]

Time of Sabbath observance:

"From evening until evening you shall keep your sabbaths" (Lev. 23:32).

It should be noted that this instruction is given in connection with the Day of Atonement but was interpreted by the Jews to apply to all sabbaths.

Penalties for violation of Sabbath law:

Put to death

Therefore you are to observe the sabbath, for it is holy to you. Every one who profanes it shall surely be *put to death*... Whoever does any work on the sabbath day shall surely be *put to death* (Ex. 31:14,15). For six days work may be done, but on the seventh day you shall have a holy day, a sabbath of complete rest to the LORD; whoever does *any work on it shall be put to death* (Ex. 35:2).

---

[1] See Lev. 23:7, 21, 24, 27, 35; 28:18, 28:25; Num. 29:1, 7, 12.

Cut off from Israel

> Whoever does any work on it, that person shall be *cut off* from among his people (Ex. 31:14).

Reflections of Eden

As we look at what the covenant people were either told to do, or told not to do, on the Sabbath, and then reflect back upon the first seventh-day rest at the end of creation week, there seems to be a definite connection. It appears that the Sabbath laws given to the Israelites were designed to cause them to behave very much as Adam and Eve behaved in Eden. While this fact is not clearly brought out in the scriptural record, it is strongly implied in the wording of the fourth commandment.

> For in six days the LORD made the heavens and the earth, the sea and all that is in them, and rested on the seventh day; therefore the LORD blessed the sabbath day and made it holy (Ex. 20:11).

Nearly all the prohibitions given in connection with these Sabbaths would have been completely meaningless to Adam and Eve on that first seventh day *before sin entered*. On the other hand, what Israel was commanded to do on the Sabbath would have been done naturally by Adam and Eve; therefore, no command would have been needed. Consider the following reasoning:

Prohibitions:

Do not go out of your dwelling place

> Adam and Eve did not leave the garden until after sin entered.

Do not bake or boil

> We have no record of Adam and Eve using fire in their Eden home. Some assume they ate their food fresh from the garden.

Shadows of Christ

Do not do any work

Adam and Eve did not "work" until after they sinned and were driven from the garden (Gen. 3:17–19). The Genesis account does mention that they were to "cultivate and keep" the garden. But whatever is intended here certainly was not work *as we know it*. Their garden was not filled with pesky weeds nor did they have to water it continually!

Do not carry a load

There was no need for Adam and Eve to carry a load or burden. What would they have carried? They did not have to store their crops for winter. They surely did not have irrigation pipes or shovels etc., for a "mist used to rise from the earth and water the whole surface of the ground" (Gen. 2:6).

Do not build a fire

Before sin entered, clothes were not even needed, therefore we can assume that the weather was not cold and a fire was not needed.

Do not buy or sell

Whom would they have purchased from and to whom would they have sold? They were told to eat "freely…"

Do not do your own pleasure

With the brevity of the written record in Genesis it is difficult to prove how this would or would not have applied to our first parents. Before sin entered into the lives of Adam and Eve we might assume it would have only been natural for God to be first in their thinking.

Admonitions:

Keep the Sabbath holy

Holiness is a term used for something that is set apart for God or is connected to Him in some way. This would automatically have been carried out in Eden as perfect Adam and Eve were in perfect fellowship with their Creator.

Rest

If we understand the "rest" of the seventh-day-creation record to be fellowship with God, this admonition would have been unneeded as it was the activity most cherished in the garden. God had provided everything man needed for health and happiness.

Observe, do, or celebrate

There would have been no need to tell our first parents to do these things, because the very doing of these things was that of which their life consisted.

Convocate

Adam and Eve were in perfect fellowship on Eden's seventh day.

Delight yourself in the Lord

It must have been Adam and Eve's highest delight to fellowship with their Maker in that perfect Eden home.

In connection with the greatest of the Sabbaths of the covenant people, the Jubilee, Israel was told "it shall be holy to you, you shall eat its crops out of the field" (Lev. 25:12). The Creator's words to Adam and Eve were "From any tree of the garden you may eat freely" except from the tree in the middle of the garden (Gen. 2:16, 17). The behavior of Adam and Eve on that first seventh day must have been very much like the directions given to Israel for the observance of Jubilee.

The Sabbaths of the old covenant appear to be "mini rest stops." They were like a "pretend game" where Israel behaved like Adam and Eve on that first seventh day, the big difference being that Adam and Eve were in open fellowship with the Creator, a fellowship which was not hindered by sin. The Israelites, on the other hand, did not even desire to be in God's presence.

And all the people perceived the thunder and the lightning flashes and the sound of the trumpet and the mountain smoking; and when the people saw it, they trembled and stood at a distance. Then they said to Moses, "Speak to us yourself and we will listen; but let not God speak to us, lest we die" (Ex. 20:18, 19).

Shadows of hope

Within the Sabbath concept there were shadows of hope, hints of better things to come. The Sabbaths pointed the Israelites *back* to the perfect fellowship of the seventh-day-creation "rest," (Ex. 20:11) before sin with its resulting curse of labor and work occurred. The Sabbaths were a reminder that they were now free from Egyptian slavery where there was no *physical* rest. (Deut. 5:15), the Sabbaths also directed their tired souls *forward* to the time when the fellowship of that seventh day would be restored and they would find true, spiritual rest for their *souls* and true redemption from *sin*. The Sabbaths gave them reason to look *forward* with hope to that time when freedom would be proclaimed to the captives, when that year of release[2] from all debt would arrive. They eagerly waited for the time they could return to the land of the fathers, when they could again eat freely the natural produce of the land, when they could cease from their heavy burdens and enter into the "rest" of the Jubilee. Each of the Sabbaths pointed them *forward* with hope to the next sabbatical event. The seventh-day Sabbath was a weekly reminder of the *coming*

---

[2] The word used here later became a word used for forgiveness in the New Testament via the Septuagint.

seasonal sabbaths. The seasonal sabbaths were a reminder of the *coming* sabbatical year. The sabbatical year was a reminder of the *coming* Jubilee. This kept hope alive.

Sabbath Relationships

While some of the following may appear to be somewhat repetitious, this information is very important to a thorough understanding of the Sabbath and will be needed for later interpretations.

In the following references be aware of the close association between the seventh-day Sabbath and the other religious duties connected with the Sinaitic Covenant, such as the morning and evening burnt offerings. Note especially the close connection between the seventh-day Sabbaths, the new moons, and the seven yearly sabbaths or "fixed festivals." Recognize that when these convocations of the old covenant are listed as a group they usually appear in either ascending or descending order.

Sabbaths (days)
new moons (months)
fixed festivals (seasons)
or
fixed festivals (seasons)
new moons (months)
Sabbaths (days)

This is brought out here as it will be of importance for later interpretations.

...offer all *burnt offerings* to the LORD, on the *sabbaths,* the *new moons* and the *fixed festivals* in the number set by the ordinance concerning them, continually before the LORD (1 Chron. 23:31).

Behold, I am about to build a house for the name of the LORD my God, dedicating it to Him, to burn fragrant incense before Him, and to set out the showbread continually, and to offer *burnt offerings* morning and evening, on *sabbaths* and on *new moons,* and on the *appointed feasts* of the LORD our God, this being required forever in Israel (2 Chron. 2:4).

Then Solomon offered *burnt offerings* to the LORD on the altar of the LORD which he had built before the porch; and did so according to the daily rule, offering them up according to the commandment of Moses, for the *sabbaths,* the *new moons,* and the three *annual feasts*—the feast of unleavened bread, the feast of weeks, and the feast of tabernacles (2 Chron. 8:12, 13).

He also appointed the king's portion of his goods for the burnt offerings, namely, of the morning and evening *burnt offerings,* and the burnt offerings for the *sabbaths* and for the *new moons* and for the *fixed festivals,* as it is written in the law of the LORD (2 Chron. 31:3).

And it shall be the prince's part to provide the *burnt offerings,* the *grain offering* and the *drink offerings,* at *the feasts,* on the *new moons,* and on the *sabbaths,* as all the appointed feasts of the house of Israel (Ez. 45:17).

The following references show a close relationship between the Sabbath and the new moon celebrations. Observe that they have nearly identical offerings prescribed for them.

The gate of the inner court shall be shut the six working days; but it shall be opened on the *sabbath day,* and opened on the *day of the new moon...*The people of the land shall also worship at the doorway of that gate before the LORD on the *sabbaths* and on the *new moons...*And the burnt offering which the prince shall offer to the LORD on the *sabbath day* shall be *six lambs* without blemish and a *ram* without blemish...the *grain offering...*a *hin of oil...*And on the day of the *new moon* he shall offer...*six lambs* and a *ram,* which shall be without blemish...*grain offering...*a *hin of oil...*(Ez. 46:1–7).

I will also put an end to all her gaiety, her feasts, her new moons, her sabbaths, and all her festal assemblies (Hos. 2:11).

Why will you go to him today? It is neither *new moon* nor *sabbath* (2 Ki. 4:23).

...for the continual burnt offering, the *sabbaths,* the *new moon,* for the appointed times...(Neh. 10:33).

Bring your worthless offerings no longer, their incense is an abomination to Me. *New moon* and *sabbath,* the calling of assemblies—I cannot endure iniquity and the solemn assembly. I hate your new moon festivals and your appointed feasts...(Isa. 1:13, 14).

"And it shall be from *new moon* to *new moon* and from *sabbath* to *sabbath,* all mankind will come to bow down before Me," says the Lord (Isa. 66:23).

In the foregoing references we see a very close connection between the seventh-day Sabbath and the yearly feasts or "appointed times of the Lord." Notice that <u>when the word "Sabbath" is used in connection with the other "times of the Lord," it *always* refers to the seventh-day Sabbath.</u>

Covenant Relationships

In the last section, "Sabbath Relationships," we saw how the Sabbath is closely related to all the other covenant *convocations*. This section will show how the Sabbath is tied to the *whole* Sinaitic Covenant.

The Sabbath is related to the Ten Commandments in that it is one of the Ten Commandments; it finds itself at the very center of the Ten Commandments and it is the sign of the covenant (Ex. 20:8–11; 31:13–18). Thus, the Sabbath of Sinai is inseparably linked to the Sinaitic Covenant.

The Ten Commandments are related to the ark of the covenant. The ark was the special wooden box in which the covenant was placed (Ex. 25:16). Thus, the Sabbath is related to the ark of the covenant.

The ark of the covenant was placed in the most holy place of the "tabernacle of the testimony" (Ex. 38:21; Num. 1:50, 53). The ark, the Ten Commandments, and the Sabbath are all related to the tabernacle of the testimony. So we see that the Sabbath is related to the tabernacle of the testimony.

The tabernacle of the testimony was the center for the worship of the covenant people. They were directed to take their offerings there. The priests were directed to offer special offerings there on the Sabbath. The weekly Sabbath is related to *all* the other religious services and holy convocations of the covenant people as they worshiped around the tabernacle of the covenant according to covenant stipulations (2 Chron. 2:4).

The religious celebration of the covenant had a strong, underlying sabbatical cycle. There were Sabbaths every seven days (Lev. 23:1–3). There were seven seasonal sabbaths—each of which was observed as a seventh-day Sabbath (Lev. 23). Every seven years there was a sabbatical year when the land was to have "a sabbath to the Lord" (Lev. 25:1–7). The high point of the sabbatical cycle was the Jubilee. It was a special sabbatical year, a whole year of sabbaths with additional blessings including the proclamation of freedom to the captives (Lev. 25:8–17). All of these observances had their foundation in the covenant of which the Sabbath was the sign. Thus, the Sabbath was closely connected to *all* covenant celebrations.

As the Sinaitic Covenant partners were God and Israel and the Sabbath was a sign between God and the sons of Israel forever (Ex. 31:17), the Sabbath is therefore inseparably linked to the "sons of Israel forever."

To become a member of the covenant community the males of every household had to be circumcised (Gen. 17:9–14; Lev. 12:3) and all had to observe the Sabbath (Ex. 31:13–17; Isa. 56:1–8). A foreigner was forbidden to partake in the covenant celebrations unless he was circumcised (Ex. 12:48). If you take away circumcision, then you take away the covenant people. If you take away covenant people, then you must take away the Sabbath of Sinai, for it is the sign between God and the covenant people. Therefore, the Sabbath and circumcision were closely linked as signs of the covenant.

The covenant blessings and promises were specifically related to the "covenant people" living in the "promised land" (Gen. 13:15; Deut. 4:40). The borders of this land were clearly spelled out in the book of the covenant (Ex. 23:31; Deut. 1:6, 7; Deut. 3). The land which was to enjoy its sabbaths was the "promised land." Thus the promised land and the Sabbath were closely linked (Lev. 25:1–4; 26:34, 35). Nothing could be more clearly stated. Everything in the covenant was related to everything else in the covenant, and the seventh-day Sabbath is in the very heart of these complex relationships. A correct understanding of the seventh-day Sabbath requires that we see it *in relationship* to the totality of old covenant life and experience. It is closely connected to the covenant, the covenant people, the tabernacle of the covenant, the services of the covenant, the laws of the covenant, the promises of the covenant, the blessings of the covenant, the cursings of the covenant and the land of the covenant. The Sabbath "is a sign between Me and the sons of Israel for ever" (Ex. 31:17).

Sabbath Observers

Who were commanded to observe the Sabbath?

But the seventh day is a sabbath of the LORD your God; in it *you* shall not do any work, you or *your son* or *your daughter, your male servant* or *your female servant* or *your cattle* or *your sojourner* who stays with you (Ex. 20:10).

But during the seventh year the land shall have a sabbath rest, a sabbath to the Lord; you shall not sow your field nor prune your vineyard (Lev. 25:4).

Six days you are to do your work, but on the seventh day you shall cease from labor; in order that your *ox* and your *donkey* may rest, and the *son of your female slave,* as well as *your stranger,* may refresh themselves (Ex. 23:12).

The children of Israel, their cattle, their land and their sojourners were all required to keep the Sabbath. It was the sign of the covenant between the Lord and the "sons of Israel".

Purposes of the Sabbath

A reminder of the seventh-day-creation rest

> Remember the sabbath day, to keep it holy...For in six days the Lord made the heavens and the earth, the sea and all that is in them, and rested on the seventh day; therefore the Lord blessed the sabbath day and made it holy (Ex. 20:8, 11).

A reminder of redemption from Egyptian slavery

> Observe the sabbath day to keep it holy...And you shall remember that you were a slave in the land of Egypt, and the LORD your God brought you out of there by a mighty hand and by an outstretched arm; therefore the LORD your God commanded you to observe the sabbath day (Deut. 5:12, 15).

Here the purpose of the Sabbath is said to be a sign of Israel's redemption from Egyptian slavery. In this version of the fourth commandment no mention is made of the seventh-day-creation rest. This purpose is closely related to the Sabbath as a sign of the covenant, for the redemption from Egypt was covenant redemption.

> God remembered His covenant...So I have come down to deliver them from the power of the Egyptians (Ex. 2:24; 3:8).

Physical rest

The root meaning of Sabbath is *rest,* and a primary purpose of the Sabbath was to provide physical rest. The first occurrence in Scripture of the word "Sabbath" occurs in connection with the giving of the manna. "So the people *rested* on the seventh day" (Ex. 16:23, 30). In the fourth commandment we read:

> You shall not do any work...for in six days the LORD made the heavens and the earth, the sea and all that is in them, and *rested* on the seventh day (Ex. 20:10, 11).

In the section which explicitly states that the seventh-day Sabbath is the sign of the covenant between the Lord "and the sons of Israel" it says, "on the seventh day there is a sabbath of *complete rest"* (Ex. 31:15, 17).

Exodus 23:12 specifies who and what were to be included in the Sabbath rest.

> Six days you are to do your work, but on the seventh day you shall cease from labor; *in order* that your *ox* and your *donkey* may *rest,* and the *son of your female slave,* as well as your *stranger,* may *refresh themselves.*

Here it is expressly stated that the purpose of the Sabbath is to provide rest for the work animals and slaves. The Sabbath rest also includes the land of Israel. "During the seventh year the *land* shall have a sabbath *rest"* (Lev. 25:4). The same concept applies to the Jubilee (Lev. 25:11).

A test of covenant loyalty

A careful examination of the first Sabbath incident reveals a third purpose of the Sabbath.

> Then the Lord said to Moses, "Behold, I will rain bread from heaven for you; and the people shall go out and gather a day's portion every day that I may *test* them, whether or not they will walk in My instruction. And it will come about on the sixth day, when they prepare what they bring in, it will be twice as much as they gather daily" (Ex. 16:4, 5).

Here, the Sabbath functions *as a test of loyalty* for the covenant people. This is in harmony with the concept later in the book of Exodus, which shows the Sabbath to be a sign of the covenant. So in the first occurrence of the Sabbath its purpose is stated as a "test" of Israel's loyalty. Later in this same account we read:

> And it came about on the seventh day that some of the people went out to gather, but they found none. Then the LORD said to Moses, "How long do you refuse to keep My commandments, and My instructions?" (Ex. 16:27, 28).

Sign of the covenant

> So the sons of Israel shall observe the sabbath, to celebrate the sabbath throughout their generations as a *perpetual covenant.* It is a *sign* between *Me* and the *sons of Israel forever* (Ex. 31:16, 17).

Sign of sanctification

In Exodus 31:13 we read:

> But as for you, speak to the sons of Israel, saying, "You shall surely observe My sabbaths; for this is a sign between Me and you throughout your generations, that you may know that I am the LORD who *sanctifies* you."

Here the Sabbath is said to be a sign of sanctification. Some read back into this text a present-day theological definition of sanctification and interpret this text to say that the observance of the Sabbath is a sign that God makes a person holy. God does make us holy, but we should interpret this passage using the basic meaning of sanctify, which is "to set apart." In other words, the Sabbath is a sign that Israel was *set apart* or elected by God. For all practical purposes, this is just another way of saying that the Sabbath is a sign of the covenant. Israel was chosen or set apart by God.

There seems to be one underlying element in all of the purposes of the Sabbath which are all related to the Sinaitic Covenant in some way.

Chapter Summary

1. The "Lord's appointed times" were:
    a. Seventh-day Sabbath
    b. Passover
    c. Feast of Unleavened Bread
    d. Feast of First Fruits
    e. Pentecost
    f. Blowing of Trumpets
    g. Day of Atonement
    h. Feast of Booths
    i. New moon celebrations
2. The seven yearly appointed times of the Lord were all kept like the seventh-day Sabbath with similar offerings and no laborious work was to be done.

3. *All* of the Sabbaths of Israel were said to be perpetual, everlasting, or "throughout your generations."
4. Additional religious services closely connected with the Sabbath were:
   a. Morning and evening burnt offerings
   b. New moon festivals
5. When the "Lord's appointed times" are listed they usually are listed in either ascending or descending order (days, months, seasons or seasons, months, days).
6. When the word "Sabbath" is listed with the yearly "sabbaths" or "appointed times of the Lord," it *always* refers to the weekly Sabbath.
7. The sabbatical cycle consisted of:
   a. Weekly, seventh-day Sabbaths
   b. Seven seasonal sabbaths
   c. Sabbatical years (every seventh year)
   d. Jubilee (after the seventh sabbatical year)
8. The prohibitions for observing the Sabbaths were:
   a. Not going out of one's place
   b. Not baking or boiling
   c. Not doing any work
   d. Not building a fire
   e. Not buying or selling
   f. Not carrying a load or burden
   g. Not doing own pleasure
9. The commands for Sabbaths were:
   a. Keep it holy
   b. Rest completely
   c. Observe, do, or celebrate
   d. Convocate
   d. Delight in the Lord
10. Penalties for the violation of Sabbath law were:
    a. Put to death
    b. Cut off from the covenant people
11. Sabbaths were to be observed from evening until evening.

12. The seventh-day Sabbath is in the very center of, and is linked to, all old covenant relationships.
    a. It is closely linked with the Sinaitic Covenant.
    b. It is closely linked to the Ark of the Covenant.
    c. It is closely linked to the tabernacle of the covenant.
    d. It is closely linked to all covenant convocations.
    e. It is closely linked to the sons of Israel.
    f. It is closely linked to circumcision.
    g. It is closely linked to the Promised Land.
    h. It is closely linked with the blessings and curses of the covenant.
13. Sabbath observers were to be:
    a. You (implies both the Israelite husband and wife),
    b. Your son
    c. Your daughter
    d. Your male servant
    e. Your female servant
    f. The son of your female slave
    g. The sojourner (stranger) who stays with you
    h. Your cattle
    i. Your ox
    j. Your donkey
    k. Your land
14. Purposes for the Sabbath included:
    a. A reminder of the seventh-day-creation rest
    b. A sign of redemption from Egypt (covenant)
    c. The physical rest of the Israelites, their slaves, and their sojourners
    d. The physical rest of the Israelites' animals
    e. A test to see if Israel would obey the Lord's commandments and laws
    f. A sign of the covenant between the Lord and the "sons of Israel"
    g. A sign of being sanctified or set apart
15. There is a relationship between the Sabbath laws and the seventh-day-creation rest.

16. The Sabbath concept seems to be a reminder of Eden before sin entered.
17. Most, if not all, of the Sabbath prohibitions would have been meaningless to Adam and Eve before sin entered.
18. Most, if not all, of the Sabbath commands would have been done naturally by Adam and Eve and thus would have been unneeded before sin.
19. Israel's observance of the various Sabbath laws of the Sinaitic Covenant seems to be an acting out in a sinful world of what Adam and Eve did in a sinless world.
20. While the Sabbath laws of the Sinaitic Covenant pointed back to the seventh-day rest in Eden and Israel's redemption from Egyptian slavery, there was also an element of hope for the future, especially in looking forward to the rest of the Jubilee.

CHAPTER SIX

THE NEW COVENANT

This chapter will give a sweeping overview of the new covenant, determine how the New Testament defines the old covenant, and seek to find the proper relationship that exists between these two covenants. Several chapters later we will come back to this topic for further development.

The three main aspects of the old covenant were (1) the redemptive deliverance of Israel from Egypt, (2) the giving of the covenant at Sinai, and (3) the settlement of Israel in the land of Canaan. What are the main features of the new covenant?

When we come to the New Testament the dominant feature is the life, death and resurrection of Christ. Here we have a new saving activity and a new redemption that is greater than that experienced by Israel in the exodus. As the saving activity of the exodus served as the foundation for Israel's law, service and worship, so for God's new covenant people the saving activity of Christ serves as the foundation for their law, the motivation for their service and the theme of their worship. To the degree that the new saving activity is better than the old, to that same degree the new law is better than the old, the new motivation for service is better than the old motivation, and the new theme of worship is better than the old.

Christ, the basis of New Testament law

The redemption of Christ serves as the moral basis for New Testament law. While morality is clearly taught in the Old Testament, the New Testament writers seldom refer to Old Testament law as the *reason* for moral living, and when the law of the old covenant is mentioned in the epistles it is usually by way of illustration, rather than by way of command. In old covenant life, morality was seen as an *obligation to numerous specific laws*. In the new covenant, morality springs from *a response to the living Christ*. In 1 Corinthians 6 Paul admonishes Christians to stay away from prostitution and immorality. His reason for pure living is not based upon the laws of Sinai but upon the believer's relationship with Christ.

> Do you not know that your bodies are members of Christ? Shall I then take away the members of Christ and make them members of a harlot? May it never be! Or do you not know that your body is a temple of the Holy Spirit who is in you, whom you have from God, and that you are not your own? For you have been bought with a price: *therefore* glorify God in your body (1 Cor. 6:15, 19, 20).

Paul could have referred to the old covenant laws that prohibited impure living, such as "You shall not commit adultery," and to portions of the Sinaitic Covenant which interpreted this law to apply to situations similar to the problems Paul was dealing with in Corinth. There was plenty of material in the old covenant he could have used but he chose rather to use a better moral foundation: union with Christ.

In Philippians 2:1–4, Paul is seeking to guide the Christian believers to care for each other, to do nothing from selfishness or conceit. In the old covenant we find the reason to treat one another with loving care to be something like this:

> He executes justice for the orphan and the widow, and shows His love for the alien by giving him food and clothing. So show

your love for the alien, for you were aliens in the land of Egypt (Deut. 10:18, 19).

In the new covenant the focus of morality is no longer Sinai or the exodus from Egypt. The new covenant has a better focus.

> Have this attitude in yourselves which was also in Christ Jesus, who, although He existed in the form of God, did not regard equality with God a thing to be grasped, but emptied Himself, taking the form of a bondservant, and being made in the likeness of men. And being found in appearance as a man, He humbled Himself by becoming obedient to the point of death, even death on a cross (Phil. 2:5–8).

We will come back to the topic of new covenant law for further development in Chapters 15 and 16, nevertheless in this introductory chapter it is important to understand that new covenant law has its moral foundation in the spotless righteousness of Christ.

Christ, the motivation for holy living

Under the new covenant the motivation for Christian living is centered in our love for Christ.

> For the love of Christ controls us (2 Cor. 5:14). I am under compulsion; for woe is me if I do not preach the gospel (1 Cor. 9:16). If you love me, you will keep my commandments (Jn. 14:15).

In his great masterpiece on salvation, the book of Romans, Paul first builds a solid foundation for man's acceptance by God based upon *faith* in the perfect, finished work of Christ. Then, and only then, does he admonish in holy living. His motivation for Christian living is based upon the work of Christ, not the laws of Sinai.

> Knowing that Christ, having been raised from the dead, is never to die again; death no longer is master over Him. For the death He died, He died to sin, once for all; but the life that He lives He lives to God. Even so consider yourselves to be dead to sin, but alive to God in Christ Jesus. *Therefore,* do not let sin reign in your mortal body that you should obey its lusts…But

thanks be to God that though you were slaves of sin, you became *obedient from the heart* to that form of teaching to which you were committed, and *having been freed from sin,* you became slaves of righteousness (Rom. 6:9–12, 18).

Justification by faith in Christ is a better motivation than deliverance from Egypt.

Overthrowing the strongholds of Satan

As Old Testament history records the covenant people overthrowing the Canaanites and settling themselves in the land of Canaan, so New Testament history documents the acts of the apostles and the early Christians taking the "land" of the Gentile nations. In the old covenant God manifested His mighty works in overthrowing the walls of Jericho and driving out the inhabitants of the land of Canaan. In the new covenant we see Christians filled with the power of the Holy Spirit overthrowing the strongholds of Satan, casting out demons, healing the sick, raising the dead and setting the captives free.

Christ, the theme of new covenant worship

> Through Him then let us continually offer up a sacrifice of praise to God, that is, the fruit of lips that give thanks to His name. And do not neglect doing good and sharing; for with such sacrifices God is pleased (Heb. 13:15, 16).

When we come to understand that the One who died on the cross for our sins is KING OF KINGS AND LORD OF LORDS (Rev. 19:16), then we will join the millions who with a loud voice proclaim,

> "Worthy is the Lamb that was slain to receive power and riches and wisdom and might and honor and glory and blessing." And every created thing which is in heaven and on the earth and under the earth and on the sea, and all things in them, I heard saying, "To Him who sits on the throne, and to the Lamb, be blessing and honor and glory and dominion forever and ever" (Rev. 5:12–14).

When we understand and experience the new covenant gospel, when we realize that we who are sinners can stand without fault before the throne of God; when we experience the indwelling Christ, then we, too, will fall down and worship.

Christ, a better revelation

Just as the old, slow, cumbersome, hand-operated calculator has been antiquated by the new, fast, compact, electronic computer, so the old covenant has been antiquated by the new. It was the best for its time, but now, new, *better* things have come.

> God, after He spoke long ago to the fathers in the prophets in many portions and in many ways, in these last days has spoken to us in His Son...and He is the radiance of His glory and the exact representation of His nature (Heb. 1:1–3).
>
> But if the ministry of death, in letters engraved on stones, came with glory so that the sons of Israel could not look intently at the face of Moses because of the glory of his face, fading as it was, how shall the ministry of the Spirit fail to be *even more* with glory? For if the ministry of condemnation has glory, *much more* does the ministry of righteousness *abound in glory*. For indeed what had glory, in this case has no glory on account of the glory that surpasses it. For if that which fades away was with glory, *much more* that which *remains is in glory* (2 Cor. 3:7–11).

The flickering candle of truth which lighted the shadowy pathways of Old Testament history must give way to the unveiled glory of the *Risen Son!*

New Testament definitions of old covenant

Before we seek to discover what the New Testament teaches regarding the relationship that should exist between the old and new covenants, we must first determine what the New Testament defines as the old covenant. It is clear and definitive.

In our study of the old covenant we found that the Ten Commandments were the covenant. They were called the "tablets of the testimony" (Ex. 31:18), the "words of the covenant, the Ten Commandments" (Ex. 34:28), "the testimony" (Ex. 40:20), "the covenant of the Lord" (1 Ki. 8:8, 9, 21).

We also found that the other laws in the books of Exodus through Deuteronomy were called the "book of the covenant" (Ex. 24:7) or "the book of the law" (Deut. 31:26). We saw that these laws served as an interpretation or expansion of the Ten Commandments. Does the New Testament agree with our findings?

> Now even the *first covenant* had regulations of divine worship and the earthly sanctuary. [The writer of Hebrews is now going to list things which were included in the "first covenant."] For there was a tabernacle prepared, the outer one, in which were the lampstand and the table and the sacred bread; this is called the holy place. And behind the second veil, there was a tabernacle which is called the Holy of Holies, having a golden altar of incense and the *ark of the covenant* covered on all sides with gold, in which was a golden jar holding the manna, and Aaron's rod which budded, and *the tables of the covenant* (Heb. 9:1–4).

The writer of Hebrews defines the "first covenant" as the Sinaitic Covenant and specifically mentions "the tables of the covenant" (the Ten Commandments).

In the following reference both aspects of the old covenant are mentioned.

> You are our letter, written in our hearts, known and read by all men; being manifested that you are a letter of Christ, cared for by us, *written not with ink,* but with the Spirit of the living God, not on *tablets of stone,* but on tablets of human hearts. And such confidence we have through Christ toward God. Not that we are adequate in ourselves to consider anything as coming from ourselves, but our adequacy is from God, who also made us adequate as servants of a *new covenant,* not of the letter, but of the Spirit; for the letter kills, but the Spirit gives life. But if the ministry of death, in letters *engraved on stones,* came with glory...(2 Cor. 3:2–7).

In these verses Paul is contrasting the new covenant with the old and in so doing defines the old covenant exactly as we found in our study of the Old Testament. The old covenant was not only on "tablets of stone" but "written with ink"—a reference to the "book of the covenant." Both are included in Paul's definition of old covenant.

In the book of Galatians Paul specifically mentions that the old covenant comes from Mt. Sinai.

> This contains an allegory; for these women are two covenants, one proceeding from Mount Sinai bearing children who are to be slaves (Gal. 4:24).

We see, then, that the New Testament confirms our conclusions regarding old covenant documents. The Sinaitic Covenant is called the "old" or the "first" covenant in the New Testament. The New Testament speaks of the "old" or "first" covenant as being "engraved on stone," and calls it the "tablets of the covenant"; both are clear references to the Ten Commandments. The New Testament also includes "the book of the covenant" which was "written with ink," in its definition of the old, or first, covenant.

Old and new covenant relationships

Now that we have confirmed what the New Testament means when it refers to the old, or first, covenant, we must next address the proper relationship that should exist between these two covenants. Their relationship is very important and often highly controversial. From New Testament times to the present day this subject has been vigorously debated. There were Judaizing Christians whom Paul confronted who said that unless a person kept all the laws of the old covenant, one could not be saved. Then, on the other extreme, there have been those like Marcion, a second-century Christian philosopher in Asia Minor, who felt the Christian church should not even include the Old Testament in its accepted canon of Scripture.

Some take a simplistic approach to the relationship that should exist between the new and old covenants: "I believe in the whole Bible. It doesn't really matter whether God says it in the New Testament or in the Old Testament; if He says it, it's good enough for me." In practice, however, even those who feel this way *must* pick and choose among the old covenant laws. What Christian today is willing to stone a person to death for a violation of Sabbath law? What married Christian man is willing to take his brother's wife and raise up children for a deceased brother while still married to his wife? Who is going to insist that Christians wear tassels on the four corners of their garments?[1] Yet all of these are old covenant laws (Ex. 31:14; Deut. 25:5–10; 22:12).

In practical Christian experience, we usually try to find a church where we feel "comfortable." We like the way the pastor "explains the Bible," or "teaches truth." When this takes place, consciously or unconsciously, we are often led to accept the "system of truth" that is taught. The church will, by applying its theological framework, choose to accept, and perhaps even enforce, certain of the Old Testament laws, while choosing to ignore certain others. Thus the church system, whatever that system is, becomes the grid by which to filter out the Old Testament laws which "still apply," while letting others fall into the hopper labeled, "not for today." The problem here is that the "system of truth" is often taken for granted. The point I am making is that we, ourselves, ought to be conscious of what we are doing and seriously evaluate whether certain old covenant laws should be enforced and others discarded. We need to have clear, scriptural principles to guide us in our application of old covenant laws. Too often those who enforce old covenant laws do so on the basis of the old covenant statements themselves without letting the new

---

[1] Certain "Christian" groups are now insisting that this should be done!

covenant interpret, modify, or transform these laws with reference to Jesus Christ, the new covenant center.

Let us now carefully examine the New Testament evidence which compares and contrasts the old covenant with the new. In doing so our purpose is to discover principles of interpretation which will help us correctly understand which covenant is to have precedence and why.

> God, after He spoke long ago to the fathers in the prophets in many portions and in may ways, in these last days has spoken to us in His Son, whom He appointed heir of all things, through whom also He made the world. And He is *the radiance of His glory and the exact representation of His nature,* and upholds all things by the word of His power (Heb. 1:1–3).

The Old Covenant:	**The New Covenant:**
God spoke	God has spoken with finality
to the fathers	to us
long ago	in these last days
in the prophets	in His Son
in many portions,	Who is the radiance of His glory
and in many ways.	the exact representation of His nature.

In the old covenant God did speak. He spoke to the fathers: Abraham, Isaac, Jacob, Moses, and others. His revelation to them was fragmentary: a few direct statements and a few other revelations in summary and shadowy form. For example, the statement, "In you all the families of the earth shall be blessed" (Gen. 12:3), was not fully understood by the fathers. It would take hundreds, yes, thousands, of years before the meaning of that succinct statement would be fully understood.

The prophets often were at a loss to know the full intent of their own visions. For example, in the following quotation we see the prophet Daniel wondering what his vision meant.

> Then I, Daniel, was exhausted and sick for days. Then I got up again and carried on the king's business; but I was astounded

at the vision, and there was none to explain it...Go your way, Daniel, for these words are concealed and sealed up until the end time (Dan. 8:27;12:9).

The high point of God's revelation in the old covenant was the giving of the Ten Commandments on Mt. Sinai. Yet even this fades into nothingness when compared with the revelation of the life of Jesus, who could say, "He who has seen Me has seen the Father" (Jn. 14:9).

The old covenant was given "to the fathers" "long ago," for the time then present. The new is given "to us" "in these last days." The old revelation of truth was incomplete, fragmentary: "God spoke." In the new revelation God speaks with finality: "God has spoken." Jesus is God's final word. Why? Because "He is the radiance of His glory and the exact representation of His [God's] nature."

The Hebrew Christians, to whom the book of Hebrews was written, had been driven from their synagogues and the pageantry of the temple service. They were being persecuted; some had given up their lands and houses. Living the humble Christian life, meeting in homes for Christian services did not compare outwardly to the safe, comfortable "good old days" when they were still practicing Judaism. Some were tempted to go back to the easy life of Judaism. So the writer shows these suffering Christians that the reality of their new life in Christ far supersedes that possible within the framework of the old covenant. The book of Hebrews was written to help Jewish Christians move away from the old covenant as a source of truth and as a guideline for worship. It does this by showing how much *better* the new covenant is over the old. A quick survey of this book shows the relationship between these two covenants.

Jesus: The better new covenant

- Is a better revelation of truth (Heb. 1:1–3)
- Is better than the angels (Heb. 1:3–14)
- Is worthy of more glory than Moses (Heb. 3:13)
- Gives a better hope (Heb. 6:9–11)
- Has a better guarantee in Christ (Heb. 7:22)
- Has a more excellent ministry (Heb. 8:6)
- Has a better mediator in Christ (Heb. 8:6)
- Is enacted on better promises (Heb. 8:6)
- Cleansed with better sacrifices (Heb. 9:23)
- Promises a better country (Heb. 11:16)
- Promises a better resurrection (Heb. 11:35)
- Gives us something better (Heb. 11:40)
- Has a better mediator (Heb. 8:6; 12:24)
- Speaks with better blood (Heb. 12:24)

We must remember that the writer of Hebrews was writing to a people who loved the old covenant services. While his writing is to the point and at times very strong, he nevertheless couched his words so he would not offend his intended readers. Therefore, he chooses to use the often-repeated word "better" to describe the difference between the two covenants. However, when we turn to comparisons of the two covenants in documents which were written to Gentile audiences we find stronger language used.

> Who also made us adequate as servants of a new covenant, not of the letter, but of the Spirit; for the letter kills, but the Spirit gives life. But if the ministry of death, in letters engraved on stones, came with glory, so that the sons of Israel could not look intently at the face of Moses because of the glory of his face, fading as it was, how shall the ministry of the Spirit fail to be even more with glory? For if the ministry of condemnation has glory, much more does the ministry of righteousness abound in glory. For indeed what had glory, in this case has no glory on account of the glory that surpasses it. For if that which fades

away was with glory, much more that which remains is in glory (2 Cor. 3:6–11).

2 Corinthians 3:3–18

Old Covenant:	New Covenant:
written with ink	written with the Spirit
on tablets of stone	on tablets of human hearts
inadequate (implied)	adequate servants
of the letter	of the Spirit
letter kills	Spirit gives life
ministry of death	ministry of the Spirit
came with glory	abounds in glory
ministry of condemnation	ministry of righteousness
glory fades	glory surpasses it
now has no glory	remains in glory
veil remains unlifted	veil removed in Christ
veil lies over their heart	veil taken away
bondage (implied)	liberty
unable to change heart (implied)	being transformed

In the next few verses, Paul comes to more practical matters. What about reading the old covenant?

> But their minds were hardened; for until this very day at the reading of the old covenant the same veil remains unlifted, because it is removed in Christ. But to this day whenever Moses is read, a veil lies over their heart. But whenever a man turns to the Lord, that veil is taken away. Now the Lord is the Spirit; and where the Spirit of the Lord is, there is liberty. But we all, with unveiled face beholding as in a mirror the glory of the Lord, are being transformed into the same image from glory to glory, just as from the Lord, the Spirit (2 Cor. 3:12–18).

What is Paul saying here? First, the people with the veil over their faces (in his case the Jews) are those who accept the old covenant as it reads or read it through old covenant eyes. Paul is saying that to understand the old covenant correctly we must see it from the new covenant perspective. This is a very important principle of interpretation. *The new*

The New Covenant

covenant, which is a better and more nearly complete revelation of truth, must be allowed to interpret, modify or transform all old covenant statements in a Christ-centered way.

Second, if we continue to read the old covenant from any other perspective it will be as though we are looking through a veil and we could come to the wrong conclusions. This means that *we should not accept any old covenant laws or practices on the basis of the old covenant statements themselves. Rather, we must examine every old covenant law and statement from the new covenant perspective: Jesus Christ.*

Applying this principle to the topic of the Sabbath means that as Christians we are *not* to go *directly* to old covenant laws and statements regarding Sabbath rest. Rather, we are to discover what the new covenant teaches about God's rest and allow it to modify or transform all old covenant Sabbath law from a Christ-centered perspective.

Before we leave the discussion of Paul's comparison of the two covenants, I would like to point out his frequent mention of the Holy Spirit in connection with the new covenant. We will deal more fully with this concept a few chapters later, but for now keep your eyes and hearts open for insights regarding the work of the Holy Spirit in the new covenant. The Holy Spirit is vitally important to a correct understanding and application of new covenant law!

We will next examine the way Jesus related to the ritual and moral laws of the old covenant to find a pattern which will help us better understand the Sabbath encounters of Jesus recorded in the Gospels.

Chapter Summary

1. The new covenant centers around the life, death and resurrection of Christ.
2. The redemption from sin brought by the life, death and resurrection of Jesus serves as the moral founda-

tion for new covenant law, the motivation for Christian living and the theme of Christian worship.
3. The new covenant calls the Sinaitic Covenant the "old covenant" or the "first covenant."
4. The new covenant defines the old covenant as both the Ten Commandments and the other laws which made up the old covenant.
5. The new covenant is much better than the old in every way.
6. The new covenant has greater authority than the old covenant.
7. Unless the old covenant is interpreted by the new and read in a Christ-centered way, the reader will not understand it correctly.

CHAPTER SEVEN

JESUS AND RITUAL LAW

One of the most important tasks we face in our study of the Sabbath is to determine if the Sabbath is a moral or ceremonial law. Is the Sabbath a moral requirement that all peoples are to observe, or is the Sabbath a Jewish institution that pointed forward in some way to the gospel of Christ? Before we get to the four chapters dedicated to Jesus and the Sabbath we want to discover how Jesus related to the other laws of the Old Testament. In this chapter we want to discover how Jesus dealt with the ritual or ceremonial laws of the old covenant. In the next chapter we will examine how Jesus treated the moral laws of the old covenant. In so doing we will find a pattern in His treatment of these laws and this pattern, in turn, will give us insight into the many Sabbath incidents in the life of Jesus that will help us reach definitive answers in our Sabbath study.

As the gospel record advances from the beginning of Christ's ministry to the end we will see a development in the way Jesus dealt with ritual or ceremonial law. At first there are inferences that he was not too concerned with ritual law, then we will find additional evidence supporting this conclusion and then finally clear, scriptural proof. We start with the Gospel of Mark.

> And a leper came to Jesus, beseeching Him and falling on his knees before Him, and saying, "If You are willing, You can

make me clean." Moved with compassion, Jesus stretched out His hand and touched him, and said to him, "I am willing; be cleansed." Immediately the leprosy left him and he was cleansed. And He sternly warned him and immediately sent him away, and He said to him, "See that you say nothing to anyone; but go, show yourself to the priest and offer for your cleansing what Moses commanded, as a testimony to them" (Mk. 1:40–44).

If Jesus could heal by a word of command[1] why did He *choose* to heal this unclean leper with a *touch*? Why did Jesus sternly warn this man to say nothing to anyone about this healing? The answer was obvious to the original readers of Mark's gospel who knew the law and its interpretation. By touching this leper, Jesus made Himself unclean. While there is no specific biblical law stating that someone touching a leper becomes ritually unclean, it is nevertheless, clearly assumed in the passage below.

As for the leper who has the infection, his clothes shall be torn, and the hair of his head shall be uncovered, and he shall cover his mustache and cry, "Unclean! Unclean!" He shall remain unclean all the days during which he has the infection; he is unclean. He shall live alone; his dwelling shall be outside the camp (Lev. 13:45, 46).

This explains Mark 1:45.

But he went out and began to proclaim it freely and to spread the news around, to such an extent that Jesus could no longer publicly enter a city, but stayed out in unpopulated areas; and they were coming to Him from everywhere.

Could it be that the reason Jesus was forced to stay out in unpopulated areas was that He was considered unclean because of His contact with the leper?

One could argue that Jesus, in His purity and sinlessness, could not become unclean. Yet we are not dealing with intrinsic moral laws here, rather, ritual law. In any event it appears that Jesus was at least near a violation of ritual custom if not law.

---

[1] See Mark 1:25.

Jesus and Ritual Law

For the next example of Christ's relationship to ritual law let us examine the episode of the healing of Jairus' daughter in Mark 5:21–43. Jesus is approached by a synagogue official who implored Christ to come and heal his daughter who was "at the point of death." As Jesus and the crowd that followed Him were on their way, a ritually unclean woman touched His garment. This was against custom and was understood to make Jesus ritually unclean.[2] At this point some people from the synagogue official's home arrived and announced that the girl was dead to which Jesus responded, "Do not be afraid any longer, only believe."

When they arrived at the home of Jairus, Jesus said, "Why make a commotion and weep? The child has not died, but is asleep." and they began laughing at him. Then Jesus taking only his three closest disciples and the child's mother and father went into the room where the girl was.

> Taking the child by the hand, He said to her, "Talitha kum!" (which translated means, "Little girl, I say to you, get up!"). Immediately the girl got up and *began* to walk, for she was twelve years old. And immediately they were completely astounded. And He gave them strict orders that no one should know about this…(Mk. 5:41–43).

Again, we note that Jesus took the girl by the hand and the Gospel writer under the guidance of the Holy Spirit chose to record this fact. We see nearly the same instruction given to the parents as to the leper in the previous incident we considered, "And He gave them *strict orders* that no one should know about this." In this incident, we now have moved from inference to fact. Note the following:

> The one who touches the corpse of any person shall be unclean for seven days. That one shall purify himself from uncleanness with the water on the third day and on the seventh day, *and then* he will be clean; but if he does not purify himself on the third day and on the seventh day, he will not be clean. Anyone who

---

[2] See Lev. 15:19–25.

touches a corpse, the body of a man who has died, and does not purify himself, defiles the tabernacle of the LORD; and that person shall be cut off from Israel. Because the water for impurity was not sprinkled on him, he shall be unclean; his uncleanness is still on him. (Num. 19:11–13).

According to this biblical law Jesus made himself unclean by touching the dead girl. Further, according to this law, "He defiled the tabernacle of the LORD" and should have been "cut off from Israel."

> What so links these two episodes that they are intertwined? That in both the recipient of the miracle was a female seems in itself insignificant. More importantly, in both Jesus becomes ritually unclean: in one when the woman touches him; in the other when he touches the girl. But the fact of Jesus' uncleanliness is not mentioned, and there I believe lies the point of intertwining the episodes. Mark is making a strong statement about Jesus' indifference. To Jesus, the uncleanliness has no importance. Jesus is paying no attention to the scriptural provisions.[3]

Some will argue that the girl was not really dead because Jesus said, "She is not dead, but sleeping." However, this is the same term Jesus used when he described Lazarus who clearly was dead.[4] In Luke's account we read, "he took her by the hand and called, saying, 'Child arise!' and *her spirit returned...*" indicating the girl had come back to life.

In Mark 7:14–23 Jesus moves from *doing* things that were contrary to ritual law to *teaching* things contradictory to biblical ritual law.

> After He called the crowd to Him again, He *began* saying to them, "Listen to Me, all of you, and understand: there is nothing outside the man which can defile him if it goes into him; but the things which proceed out of the man are what defile the man. ["If anyone has ears to hear, let him hear."] When he had left the crowd *and* entered the house, His disciples questioned Him

---

[3] Alan Watson, *Jesus and the Law,* (University of Georgia Press, Athens GA, 1996), p. 54.
[4] John 11:11.

> about the parable. And He said to them, "Are you so lacking in understanding also? Do you not understand that whatever goes into the man from outside cannot defile him, because it does not go into his heart, but into his stomach, and is eliminated?" (*Thus He* declared all foods clean.) And He was saying, "That which proceeds out of the man, that is what defiles the man. "For from within, out of the heart of men, proceed the evil thoughts, fornications, thefts, murders, adulteries, deeds of coveting *and* wickedness, *as well as* deceit, sensuality, envy, slander, pride *and* foolishness. "All these evil things proceed from within and defile the man" (Mk. 7:14–23).

The statement, "Thus he declared all foods clean" is in the best manuscripts and therefore, should not be treated as some late scribal insertion but the insertion of the writer, Mark.[5] This teaching is in *direct contradiction* to the food laws in Leviticus 11 and Deuteronomy 14 but in harmony with new covenant understanding.[6]

The next incident in the life of Jesus we will examine relates to the half-shekel tax required of everyone in the old covenant.

> The LORD also spoke to Moses, saying, "When you take a census of the sons of Israel to number them, then each one of them shall give a ransom for himself to the LORD, when you number them, so that there will be no plague among them when you number them. "This is what everyone who is numbered shall give: half a shekel according to the shekel of the sanctuary (the shekel is twenty gerahs), half a shekel as a contribution to the LORD. "Everyone who is numbered, from twenty years old and over, shall give the contribution to the LORD. The rich shall not pay more and the poor shall not pay less than the half shekel, when you give the contribution to the LORD to make atonement for yourselves." (Ex. 30:11–15).

This law is a law given directly by the Lord to Moses. It is not some rabbinical interpretation, but a requirement of the old covenant law. It applies to everyone who is

---

[5] Even if this were a scribal addition, it shows how the teaching of Jesus was understood by the early church.
[6] See Acts 10, 11; Rom. 14:14.

numbered in Israel. It is very insightful to see how Jesus related to this old covenant law.

The motive behind the questioners is unclear. However, the very fact that they asked if Jesus paid this tax indicates that they had reason to question Jesus' careful adherence to old covenant law. Perhaps they had seen or heard of other instances where Jesus took exception to the law, at least as they understood it.

> When they came to Capernaum, those who collected the two-drachma tax came to Peter and said, "Does your teacher not pay the two-drachma tax?" He said, "Yes." And when he came into the house, Jesus spoke to him first, saying, "What do you think, Simon? From whom do the kings of the earth collect customs or poll-tax, from their sons or from strangers?" When Peter said, "From strangers," Jesus said to him, "Then the sons are exempt. "However, so that we do not offend them, go to the sea and throw in a hook, and take the first fish that comes up; and when you open its mouth, you will find a shekel. Take that and give it to them for you and Me" (Mt. 17:24-27).

Here Jesus declares that He and His disciples are actually exempt from this tax because they are "sons". That this is the same half-shekel tax referred to in Exodus 30 seems certain.[7] Clearly, Jesus did not consider paying this ritual tax[8] to be necessary except not to do so would offend them. In other words, Jesus paid little attention to the intrinsic value of obedience to this old covenant requirement.

While there are many more examples we could cite,[9] we can now make two general conclusions.

---

[7] See R.C.H. Lenski, *Commentary on the New Testament, Matthew*, (Hendrickson Publishers, 1998), pp. 672, 673; Hendriksen, *New Testament Commentary, The Gospel of Matthew*, (Baker Book House, Grand Rapids, MI, 1973), pp. 677–680. Carson, *Gospel of Matthew, The Expositor's Bible Commentary*, (Zondervan, Grand Rapids, MI, 1984), Vol. 8, pp. 393–395.

[8] I see this as a ritual law as it related to "making atonement" (Ex. 30:15).

[9] See Alan Watson, *Jesus and the Law*, for many more examples.

First, Jesus *always* let the moral and ethical considerations of a given situation dictate his actions[10] whether or not his actions were in violation of rabbinical or even biblical ritual law.

Second, at times it seems that Jesus *purposely* went out of His way to violate ritual law. He would often heal by a word of command when a touch would have been appropriate. Yet when a touch would make Him ritually unclean, He often chose to heal in that manner.

Why did Jesus violate biblical ritual laws?

Jesus was without sin

Some of the ritual laws dealt with cleansing from sin and Scripture is clear that Jesus was without sin.[11] This would excuse Jesus from having to offer the various sin offerings.

Ritual laws were Jewish, Jesus was universal

A number of ritual laws dealt with "clean and unclean". Some of these laws may have had something to do with health and hygiene but were given religious significance. We have shown that one could break the covenant in numerous ways, including violating ritual law.[12] As we saw in our study of the old covenant, this covenant was made between God and Israel *only*. It was the adherence to ritual practices that gave the Jews a unique national identity. The new covenant gospel of Christ, by contrast, was to go to all nations, peoples and tongues. Christ must do two difficult things: First, He must fulfill the many prophecies of the old covenant that pointed forward to Him. Second, He had to give instruction that would be applicable to all people. Therefore, we see him purposely—but not sinfully—

---

[10] I recognize that Jesus never did anything without the Father's approval. See John 8:28.
[11] Heb. 4:15; 2 Cor. 5:21.
[12] See page 60–62.

moving away from "Israel only" laws to universal principles in His teachings and practice. To bring about this change He purposely put little value on the old covenant ritual laws.

Old covenant ritual law pointed forward to Christ

Many, if not most, of the ritual laws of the old covenant in some way pointed forward to Christ. The New Testament is replete with testimony that the life, death and resurrection of Christ and the forgiveness thereby offered are all foreshadowed in the old covenant. Now that Christ had come, these laws lost much of their useful function. When a person reaches his destination he folds up the map and puts it away. The map served a good and useful purpose but is now no longer needed, except to review the road traveled.

As one reads through the Gospels and carefully examines the controversies Jesus had with the Pharisees who were strict adherents to the law, it becomes evident that the very laws that the Pharisees were so meticulously keeping became the things that kept them from accepting Christ as the Messiah. What follows is a vitally important point to understand with reference to old covenant ritual law: <u>Once Christ had come, the observance of old covenant ritual laws which had performed an important function by pointing Israel forward to Christ now actually *became a hindrance* to His acceptance.</u> The very people who were most intent on carefully following old covenant law were the same people who rejected Him.

> From the days of John the Baptist until now the kingdom of heaven suffers violence, and violent men take it by force. For all the prophets and the Law prophesied until John (Mt. 11:12, 13).

This verse[13] indicates that there was a change in the *function* of the law and the prophets with the coming of John the Baptist. Greek scholar, R.C.H. Lenski, gives the meaning of this verse to be the kingdom "'is brought

---

[13] See also Lk. 16:16.

Jesus and Ritual Law

forward powerfully' by John and by Jesus."[14] *The Message* paraphrase is:

> For a long time now people have tried to force themselves into God's kingdom. But if you read the books of the Prophets and God's Law closely, you will see them culminate in John...[15]

We will see that behind nearly every controversy between Jesus and the Jewish leaders, Jesus is trying desperately to move the people *away from* the old covenant laws *to* Himself. In so doing, Jesus was not violating the *intent* of old covenant law even when He was violating the letter of the biblical ritual laws. This is true because the *main function* of old covenant law, prophecy and history was to point to Christ.[16]

Summary

1. Jesus always let the moral and ethical considerations of a given situation dictate his actions whether or not they were in violation of old covenant ritual law.
2. At times Jesus went out of His way to heal in such a manner that his actions would be considered a violation of old covenant ritual law.
3. At times Jesus' teaching was diametrically contrary to old covenant ritual law.
4. Jesus gave little weight to old covenant ritual law for several reasons:
   a. Many of these laws dealt with sin and He was sinless.
   b. Old covenant ritual laws were for Israel only, Jesus' teachings were universal.

---

[14] Lenski, *Matthew*, p. 437
[15] Eugene H. Peterson, *The Message,* (Navpress, Colorado Springs, CO., 1994), p. 30.
[16] The book of Hebrews is replete with illustrations. See the many "fulfills" in Matthew; see Jn. 5:39 and the many "untils" in John and Galatians 3.

c. Old covenant ritual laws were designed to point forward to the Messiah. Now that the Messiah had come these laws were of little value and actually were a hindrance to many who could not move from the legalism of law into the kingdom of Grace. Many were unable to leave the familiar symbolic shadow and walk in the reality of the light of the Savior's presence. The dry and brittle old covenant wine skin could not hold the fresh squeezings of new covenant gospel wine.

CHAPTER EIGHT

JESUS AND OLD COVENANT MORAL LAWS

In this chapter we will see a marked difference in the way Jesus treated the moral laws of the old covenant in contrast to the way He regarded the ritual laws. Perhaps the best illustrations of this are found in the Sermon on the Mount in Matthew 5.

> You have heard that the ancients were told, "YOU SHALL NOT COMMIT MURDER" and "Whoever commits murder shall be liable to the court." But I say to you that everyone who is angry with his brother shall be guilty before the court; and whoever says to his brother, "You good-for-nothing," shall be guilty before the supreme court; and whoever says, "You fool," shall be guilty *enough to go* into the fiery hell (Mt. 5:21, 22).

Here Jesus refers to the sixth commandment with its rabbinical interpretation. Note how Jesus starts with the old covenant moral law, which in itself, is actually quite narrow in scope dealing only with murder. He then *contrasts* His teaching which greatly expands the reach of this moral law by showing that the evil passions of anger and angry, insulting talk are sins that when committed bring guilt worthy of fiery hell. In other words, Jesus takes this moral *law* of the old covenant and expands it from the *act* of murder to the *principle* of angry emotions and insulting talk. This is no small change! In doing this Jesus raises the moral bar high above the old covenant law.

In Matthew 5:27, 28 Jesus does the same thing with the seventh commandment.

> You have heard that it was said, "YOU SHALL NOT COMMIT ADULTERY"; but I say to you that everyone who looks at a woman with lust for her has already committed adultery with her in his heart.

Again, Jesus quotes an old covenant moral law and then *contrasts* His Teaching which *modifies* and *expands* the old covenant *act* of adultery to include even the *principle* of a lustful look or thought.

Of special interest is Matthew 5:33–37 where Jesus refers to the law of vows found in Numbers 30:1–15 and Deuteronomy 23:21–23. I list this in the "moral law" section because making a vow (promise) to God is certainly a moral act and should be seen as an expansion of "You shall not bear false witness against your neighbor" which, by itself, is very narrow in scope.

> Again, you have heard that the ancients were told, "YOU SHALL NOT MAKE FALSE VOWS, BUT SHALL FULFILL YOUR VOWS TO THE LORD." But I say to you, make no oath at all, either by heaven, for it is the throne of God, or by the earth, for it is the footstool of His feet, or by Jerusalem, for it is THE CITY OF THE GREAT KING. Nor shall you make an oath by your head, for you cannot make one hair white or black. But let your statement be, "Yes, yes" *or* "No, no"; anything beyond these is of evil (Mt. 5:33–37).

Granted, the Jews of Jesus' day were abusing vows, however, a careful reading of the above statement compared with the old covenant law indicates that Jesus is condemning something permitted, even approved, in old covenant law.

> When you make a vow to the LORD your God, you shall not delay to pay it, for it would be sin in you, and the LORD your God will surely require it of you. However, if you refrain from vowing, it would not be sin in you. You shall be careful to perform what goes out from your lips, just as you have voluntarily vowed to the LORD your God, what you have promised (Deut. 23:21–23).

Jesus and Old Covenant Moral laws

There is no hint in the law that making an oath is bad or even undesirable. Note the following record of Jephthah.

> Now the Spirit of the LORD came upon Jephthah, so that he passed through Gilead and Manasseh; then he passed through Mizpah of Gilead, and from Mizpah of Gilead he went on to the sons of Ammon. Jephthah made a vow to the LORD and said, "If You will indeed give the sons of Ammon into my hand, then it shall be that whatever comes out of the doors of my house to meet me when I return in peace from the sons of Ammon, it shall be the LORD'S, and I will offer it up as a burnt offering (Jug. 11:29–31).

Jephthah was horrified to see his daughter come out the door to welcome him. He sent her away to weep for two months and then we read,

> At the end of two months she returned to her father, who did to her according to the vow which he had made…(Jug. 11:39).

Hebrews 11:32 lists Jephthah in the faith hall of fame.

Therefore, oath making in and of itself was approved in the law.[1] Jesus, however, *contrasts* His *better teaching* on oaths. This better teaching corrected the abuse some of the Jews of Christ's day were making relative to oath taking. It also simplified the *principle* of oaths to simply telling the truth.

In Matt. 5:43–48 Jesus said,

> You have heard that it was said, "YOU SHALL LOVE YOUR NEIGHBOR and hate your enemy." But I say to you, love your enemies and pray for those who persecute you, so that you may be sons of your Father who is in heaven; for He causes His sun to rise on *the* evil and *the* good, and sends rain on *the* righteous and *the* unrighteous. For if you love those who love you, what reward do you have? Do not even the tax collectors do the same? If you greet only your brothers, what more are you doing *than others?* Do not even the Gentiles do the same? Therefore you are to be perfect, as your heavenly Father is perfect.

---

[1] See also Deut. 6:13; 10:20 where there is a command to "swear by the His name."

While Scripture does not say, "hate your enemy," we should not be too quick to condemn the Jewish leaders for teaching this for it could be implied from other portions of the law. There are many statements in the law that show a distinction in the moral and ethical nature of how an Israelite was to treat a fellow Israelite compared to how he was to treat a foreigner. For example,

> You shall not charge interest to your countrymen: interest on money, food, *or* anything that may be loaned at interest. You may charge interest to a foreigner, but to your countrymen you shall not charge interest...(Deut. 23:19, 20).

Jesus *contrasts* His law of love with that of the old covenant. The old covenant law taught that one should love his Jewish neighbor. However Jesus modified and expanded this law beyond geographical and ethnic boundaries to include even foreign enemies who persecute us!

In doing this, Jesus is moving away from the old covenant which had an Israel/Palestine center, to the coming new covenant which had application to all nationalities, worldwide. While the new covenant did not come into full force until the death and resurrection of Christ, Christ's teaching anticipated this change.

While there are many other examples that could be given,[2] we can now make a generalized summary of Christ's attitude toward the moral laws in the Mosaic Code.

Summary of Christ and Old Covenant Moral Law

1. Jesus felt free to *modify* and *expand* the moral laws of the old covenant.
2. The moral and ethical dimensions of Christ's law are so far above the old covenant moral laws that Jesus could *contrast* His moral teaching with old covenant moral law.

---

[2] See Alan Watson, *Jesus and the Law,* for a number of other examples.

Jesus and Old Covenant Moral laws

3. Jesus *modified* and *expanded* the moral laws of the old covenant changing them from legal rules to moral and ethical principles.
4. Jesus modified and expanded the *scope* of the moral laws of the old covenant moving them *beyond* laws for Israel alone to ethical and moral principles for every nation tongue and people.[3]

---

[3] See Matt. 28:18–20.

Today this Scripture has been fulfilled in your hearing

CHAPTER NINE

JUBILEE SABBATH

As we study the life of Jesus in the four Gospels we should keep several concepts well in mind.

Transition between the covenants

The Gospels record the historical time period between the old and new covenants. Sometime between the baptism of Jesus by John the Baptist[1] and the outpouring of the Holy Spirit on the day of Pentecost[2] the transition from the old covenant to the new covenant was fully made.

Transition: a process with a point in time

The transition from the old covenant to the new covenant is made in stages. Certain aspects of the new covenant seem to come into play before others. We should expect this, as the giving of the old covenant to the sons of Israel was done in increments starting at the exodus from Egypt and continuing to just before they entered into the

---

[1] "From the days of John the Baptist until now the kingdom of heaven suffers violence, and violent men take it by force. For all the prophets and the Law prophesied until John." Mt. 11:12, 13; "The Law and the Prophets *were proclaimed* until John; since that time the gospel of the kingdom of God has been preached, and everyone is forcing his way into it." Lk. 16:16.

[2] Acts 2.

land of Canaan.[3] Within that forty-year period, however, the giving of the Ten Commandments on Mt. Sinai and the events connected with it are usually seen to be the starting point of the old covenant. In the same way we will find the new covenant comes in stages over a three-and-a-half-year period with the resurrection of Christ as the key point of the transition.

The example of Jesus is limited

We should not be surprised to find Jesus observing and even teaching about old covenant convocations. We know that He was "born under law" (Gal. 4:4). We know that he was circumcised according to the direction of the law (Lk. 2:21). He observed the Passover on more than one occasion (Lk. 2:41, 42; Jn. 2:13; Jn. 5:1; Lk. 22:11), as well as other old covenant convocations (Jn. 7:2, 10; 10:22). He wore tassels on the bottom of His garment as prescribed in old covenant law (Num. 15:38 cf. Mt. 9:20). Even Jesus' teaching includes demands that the people hallow the temple (Mk. 11:15–18) and present old covenant sacrifices (Mt. 5:23, 24). We cannot use Christ's example in Sabbath observance to enforce present-day Sabbath keeping unless we are also willing to use His example to enforce circumcision, the Passover, temple worship, the wearing of tassels on the bottom of garments and the other old covenant practices.

Examine how Jesus related to Sabbath law.

We have seen that Jesus always let the moral and ethical considerations of a given situation dictate his actions regardless of the constraints of ritual law. We have also seen that when Jesus was teaching on the moral laws of the old covenant he always modified and expanded the moral laws

---

[3] For example, the laws regarding the Passover were given as Israel was leaving Egypt. Later, in the wilderness of Sin, Israel was given the Sabbath. At Sinai more laws were given. Then just before the entered the land of Canaan more were given.

to a much higher moral plain and broader scope. By carefully examining Jesus' teaching and behavior relative to the Sabbath we should be able to tell if He considered the Sabbath to be a moral or ritual law.

The Gospels are history and theology

Fourth, while the Gospels are historical accounts of the life of Jesus, they are more than history. They are theological works as well. Under the guidance of the Holy Spirit the Gospel writers selected and recorded certain events from the life of Jesus for theological reasons. While they all did this, John is the most forthright in stating this fact.

> Many other signs therefore Jesus also performed in the presence of the disciples, which are not written in this book; but these have been written that you may believe that Jesus is the Christ, the Son of God; and that by believing you may have life in His name (Jn. 20:30, 31).
>
> And there are also many other things which Jesus did, which if they were written in detail, I suppose that even the world itself would not contain the books which were written (Jn. 21:25).

Therefore, we ought to look for the theological reasons for the inclusion of certain incidents and historical details in the life of Jesus. Also, we should thoughtfully observe the exact wording and what may appear as miscellaneous factual detail. Sometimes in these facts we may find hints of truth which the casual reader would miss. As the Gospels were written many years after the resurrection, the writers may have chosen to include certain Sabbath incidents which would, by their inclusion, speak to the theological needs of that time.

Method of study

In this study of the life and ministry of Jesus as it relates to the Sabbath we will seek to discover what He *taught* regarding the Sabbath, and what Jesus *did* on Sabbath days. We will examine both the immediate and wider context.

Jubilee Fulfilled

(Lk. 4:16–30; Mk. 6:1–6; Mt. 13:53–58)

This chapter starts out, "And Jesus, full of the Holy Spirit, returned from the Jordan and was led about by the Spirit in the wilderness" (Lk. 4:1). While in the wilderness Jesus was tested by the devil for forty days. After successfully withstanding Satan's temptations,

> Jesus returned to Galilee in the power of the Spirit...And He came to Nazareth, where He had been brought up; and as was His custom, He entered the synagogue on the Sabbath, and stood up to read. And the book of the prophet Isaiah was handed to Him. And He opened the book, and found the place where it was written, "The Spirit of the Lord is upon Me, because He anointed Me to preach the gospel to the poor, He has sent Me to proclaim release to the captives, and recovery of sight to the blind, to set free those who are downtrodden, to proclaim the favorable year of the Lord." And He closed the book, and give it back to the attendant, and sat down; and the eyes of all in the synagogue were fixed upon Him. And He began to say to them, "Today this Scripture has been fulfilled in your hearing" (Lk. 4:14,16–21).

Picture yourself in the synagogue at Nazareth as Jesus reads this portion of Old Testament Scripture, which all recognize as a prophecy of the Messiah proclaiming the Jubilee, the favorable year of the Lord. Watch as Jesus takes His seat, which was the approved place for a teacher to give further comments on the reading. Then listen to Jesus say, *"Today* this Scripture has been fulfilled in your hearing!"

The first sermon of Jesus consisted of three points: (1) He was the Messiah, (2) the Jubilee had come, and (3) His mission was one of liberation, of setting the captives free! Let us consider each point.

Jesus, the promised Messiah

We immediately note that Jesus quotes Isaiah 61:1, a Messianic prophecy couched in Jubilee language and a phrase from Isaiah 42:7, "To open blind eyes, to bring out prisoners from the dungeon, and those who dwell in darkness from the prison." The context of this second passage must not escape our attention. This is a prophecy of the coming Messiah, set forth in the terms of "My Servant" with overtones of the Jubilee.

> Behold, My Servant, whom I uphold; My chosen one in whom My soul delights. I have put *My Spirit* upon him; He will bring *justice* to the *nations*...I am the Lord, I have called you [the Messiah] in righteousness, I will also hold you by the hand and watch over you, and *I will appoint you as a covenant to the people,* as a light to the *nations.* To open blind eyes, *to bring out* prisoners from the dungeon, and those who dwell in darkness from the prison...Behold, the *former things* have come to pass, now I declare *new things.* Sing to the Lord a *new song* (Isa. 42:1, 6, 7, 9, 10).

Here we see several things of major importance to our study that relate to this "Servant," the Messiah.

Descriptions of the nature and work of the Messiah:

1. He is God's Chosen (elect) One (v. 1)
2. He has the Spirit of God upon Him (v. 1)
3. His ministry brings justice to the nations (plural) (v. 1)
4. He is a covenant to the people (v. 6)
5. His work is to free those living in bondage (v. 7)
6. He declares "new things" (v. 9)

This ministry cannot fit within the framework of the old covenant. The Messiah is now *the elect One.* Through the long centuries from the day when God told Abraham, "in you all the families of the earth shall be blessed," God had slowly been narrowing His elect. "For through Isaac your descendants shall be named" (Gen. 21:12). It is narrowed further as Esau is rejected and the covenant is through Jacob (Gen. 27, 28). Years later the covenant promise of rulership is narrowed to the house of David (2 Chron. 13:5). Then it is limited even further to One who was to be born in Bethlehem (Mich. 5:2). The prophecy quoted above says that God would have an elect "One." We can sense the excitement of the disciples as they announced, "We have found the Messiah!" (Jn. 1:41). Jesus was that One. Then, as this One perfectly fulfills God's will and makes reconciliation for the sins of the world, from this Elect One *flows out* a joyful proclamation of blessing and forgiveness to *all nations*.

The ministry of the Messiah was to be a Spirit-filled ministry. Thus we read of Jesus, "And Jesus, full of the Holy Spirit, returned from the Jordan...And Jesus returned to Galilee in the power of the Spirit" (Lk. 4:1, 14).

No longer is the covenant limited to the "sons of Israel throughout their generations," but Jesus is to bring justice to the *nations*.

But He said to them, "I must preach the kingdom of God to the *other cities* also, for I was sent for this purpose" (Lk. 4:43).

> For forgiveness of sins should be proclaimed in His name to all the *nations* (Lk. 24:47).

No longer is the covenant the words engraved on two tablets of stone; *Jesus is the covenant*. He, Himself, is "a covenant to the people" (Isa. 42:6).

The ministry of this Servant is a liberating ministry. We see Jesus releasing the demonized (Lk. 4:31–36), rebuking fever (Lk. 4:38, 39), healing various diseases (Lk. 4:40) and preaching the gospel to the oppressed poor (Lk. 7:22).

The coming of the Messiah is a new revelation.

> And amazement came upon them all, and they began discussing with one another, and saying, "What is the message? For with authority and power He commands the unclean spirits, and they come out" (Lk. 4:36).

The passage in Luke 4:16–30 and the Old Testament scriptures quoted by Jesus in these verses openly teach that Jesus is the promised Messiah.

Jesus, the fulfillment of Jubilee

The context of Isaiah 42 fits perfectly within the prophecy of Isaiah 61:1, 2. Both have strong overtones of Jubilee. As we review the queen of the Sabbaths, the Jubilee, we find the following facts:

The Jubilee (Lev. 25:8–17)

1. Started on the Day of Atonement (v. 9).
2. Was ushered in with the blowing of a ram's horn (v. 9).
3. Was a proclamation of release to all inhabitants of the land (v. 10).
4. Made provision for each to return to his own family and property (v. 10).
5. Allowed for no sowing or reaping (v. 11).
6. Instructed the people to eat the crops directly out of the field (v. 12).
7. Brought justice to all (vv. 14–17).

The "year of release" points to forgiveness of sin

The heart of the Jubilee was the proclamation of *release* to all the inhabitants of the land. The word "release" as used in Luke 4:18 is the same word that the Septuagint Greek translation of the Old Testament used in translating the Jubilee Scripture in Lev. 25:10. However, the New Testament expands the meaning of this word to include not only release, but also *forgiveness of sin*.[4] In fact, it becomes one of the key words used in the New Testament for forgiveness.

As we look at the ministry of Jesus, we immediately see Him proclaiming both release and forgiveness. "Woman, you are *freed* from your sickness…Should not this woman have been *released* from this bond on the Sabbath day?"

---

[4] Gerhard Kittel, *Theological Dictionary of the New Testament,* (Wm. B. Eerdmans Publishing Co., Grand Rapids, MI., 1963), Vol. I, p. 510.

(Lk. 13:10–17). "My son, your *sins are forgiven*" (Mk. 2:5). Scripture stated that at the coming of the Jubilee each person was to return to his own family and the land of his fathers. Therefore, it is no accident that Luke records the coming of Jesus to Nazareth in these words: "And He came to Nazareth, *where He had been brought up*" (Lk. 4:16). There, in His hometown, with His family present, Jesus announced that Jubilee had arrived.

While the Day of Atonement is not mentioned by name in the New Testament, the book of Hebrews shows how this old covenant sabbath pointed forward to the atonement brought by Christ's death on the cross. In the old covenant the Day of Atonement had to be repeated every year. By contrast Jesus,

> ...having offered one sacrifice for sins for all time, sat down at the right hand of God...For by *one offering* He has perfected for all time those who are sanctified (Heb. 10:1–4, 12, 14).

Jesus not only fulfilled the Day of Atonement, but the atonement He brought far superseded the old covenant concept of atonement. The Day of Atonement served as a pointer to direct the people to the death of Christ. But when that "one offering" was sacrificed, the function of the yearly Day of Atonement ceased to exist in the presence of the true atonement for sin: Jesus Christ.

The Jubilee was ushered in by the blowing of a ram's horn. It was a way of *proclaiming the good news* of freedom, rest, and release to the captives. With the coming of Jesus, the fulfillment of the Jubilee, we see a proclamation of even better news than the old covenant Jubilee.

> I bring you good news of a great joy which shall be for all the people; for today in the city of David there has been born for you a Savior, who is Christ the Lord (Lk. 2:10, 11).
> And Jesus returned in the power of the Spirit; and news about Him spread through all the surrounding district (Lk. 4:14).

Later, after the death and resurrection of Jesus, Luke records:

> And He [Jesus] said to them, "Thus it is written, that the Christ should suffer and rise again from the dead the third day; and that repentance for forgiveness of sins should be *proclaimed* in His name to all the nations" (Lk. 24:46, 47).

The proclamation of the Jubilee pointed forward to the proclamation of the gospel. During the Jubilee there was to be no sowing or reaping; people were to eat the crops out of the field. Correspondingly we read of Jesus:

> And at that time Jesus went on the Sabbath through the grainfields, and His disciples became hungry and began to pick the heads of grain and eat (Mt. 12:1).

Jesus ushered in and fulfilled the Jubilee. The Jubilee was a shadow of a greater rest, a greater release, a greater redemption and a greater proclamation. The Gospels teach that Jesus "fulfilled" that to which the Jubilee pointed. As the Messiah, He proclaimed the favorable year of the Lord—the Kingdom rule of Christ.

The Jubilee ministry of Jesus

Cast out an unclean demon	Lk. 4:31–36
Rebuked a fever and it left	Lk. 4:38, 39
Healed those with various diseases	Lk. 4:40
Cast out many demons	Lk. 4:41
Preached the kingdom of God	Lk. 4:43, 44
Forgave sin	Lk. 5:20
Opened the eyes of the blind	Lk. 7:21
Released a woman bound by Satan	Lk. 13:10–17

Not only did Jesus announce that Jubilee had arrived, but His ministry testified to that truth.

Sabbath Behavior of Jesus

In the foregoing section we studied the Sabbath teaching of Jesus. In this short section we will see what we can learn from His Sabbath behavior.

> And He came to Nazareth, where He had been brought up; and as was His custom, He entered the synagogue on the Sabbath, and stood up to read (Lk. 4:16).

As a good Jew, it was the habit, or custom, of Jesus to attend Sabbath services in the synagogue. This is reinforced several times in this chapter.

> And He came down to Capernaum, a city of Galilee. And He was teaching them on Sabbath days (Lk. 4:31).

We should also note that we have no record of Jesus ever attending a Sabbath service when He was not the teacher. One could argue that Jesus' Sabbath attendance at the synagogue was primarily to gain a hearing. We will later see that this was also Paul's reason for synagogue attendance.

Summary of Luke 4:16-30

1. The Spirit of the Lord was upon Jesus.
2. Jesus was anointed (as Messiah) by the Spirit to:
   a. Preach the gospel to the poor
   b. Proclaim release (and forgiveness) to the captives
   c. Proclaim recovery of sight to the blind
   d. Proclaim freedom to the downtrodden
   e. Proclaim the favorable year of the Lord (Jubilee)
3. The ministry as set forth in the whole of Luke 4 was a ministry of liberation which included:
   a. Freeing the demonized
   b. Rebuking fever
   c. Healing the sick
   d. Proclaiming the kingdom of God
4. In this passage nothing is *taught* regarding the Sabbath.

5. Jesus declared that:
   a. He was God's chosen (elect) One
   b. He had the Spirit of God upon Him
   c. His ministry was to bring justice to the nations
   d. He was a covenant to the people
   e. His work was to free those living in bondage
   f. His coming was a new revelation
6. Sabbath behavior of Jesus:
   a. It was the custom of Jesus to attend the synagogue services on the Sabbath.
   b. On this occasion Jesus participated in the synagogue service by reading and commenting upon the Scripture read.
   c. There is no record of Jesus attending synagogue Sabbath services when He was not the speaker.

Jubilee Experienced

(Luke 13:10–17)

Luke is the only Gospel writer to record this Sabbath healing. Since this incident falls within the scope of Jesus' Jubilee ministry I have included it with this chapter.

> And He was teaching in one of the synagogues on the Sabbath, and behold, there was a woman who for eighteen years had had a sickness caused by a spirit; and she was bent double, and could not straighten up at all. And when Jesus saw her, He called her over and said to her, "Woman, you are freed from your sickness." And He laid His hands upon her; and immediately she was made erect again, and began glorifying God. And the synagogue official, indignant because Jesus had healed on the Sabbath, began saying to the multitude in response, "There are six days in which work should be done; therefore come during them and get healed, and not on the Sabbath day." But the Lord answered him and said, "You hypocrites, does not each of you on the Sabbath untie his ox or his donkey from the stall, and lead him away to water him? And this woman, a daughter of Abraham as she is, whom Satan has bound for eighteen long years, should she not have been

released from this bond on the Sabbath day?" And as He said this, all His opponents were being humiliated; and the entire multitude was rejoicing over all the glorious things being done by Him (Lk. 13:10-17).

It appears that Jesus considered the Sabbath not only as an appropriate day upon which to heal, but a most desirable day for this activity. He took the initiative to call this bent-over woman to Himself as soon as He saw her. It should be recognized that her illness was not life threatening, because she had already been in this condition for eighteen years. Jesus obviously could have waited until the Sabbath was over to minister to her, but *He chose to heal her in the synagogue in the presence of the multitude with Jewish leaders closely observing His actions.*

Luke states that her condition was "caused by a spirit" (Lk. 13:11). In harmony with this, Jesus said that Satan had bound her for the duration of her illness. The fact that Jesus calls her "a daughter of Abraham" indicates that she was a believing Israelite, a member of the covenant community.

The actions of Jesus must be seen as spiritual warfare. Satan had made inroads upon God's true child. He had "bound" this daughter of Abraham for eighteen long years. In the presence of Jesus, however, Satan's kingdom is driven back, the woman is "released" from her bondage, and this captive is set free. This is Jubilee ministry; it is a demonstration of the kingdom rule of God. How fitting that Jesus should overthrow the power of Satan on the Sabbath, a day which was a reminder of the deliverance from Egyptian bondage (Deut. 5:15) and restore this woman to the "rest" which existed before Satan had overcome Eve, the first daughter of God.

Isaiah prophesied that when the Messiah would come, a new song of praise would be sung (Isa. 42:10). As soon as this woman was made erect by the touch of Jesus she "began glorifying God" (Lk. 13:13). This praise was not something required by the law. It was the natural response of the woman's heart which overflowed in gratitude to God

Jubilee Sabbath

for her "release" from the power of Satan. This woman, who had been bound as a captive of Satan, was called by Jesus into personal fellowship, delivered from the power of her oppressor and healed from her physical condition. She *experienced* the true rest of the Jubilee Sabbath! She now had a new motive for service. She was experiencing new covenant life.

The Jewish leaders, on the other hand, were enslaved under the letter of the old covenant Sabbath law and could not experience the release of the new covenant nor could they rejoice with the woman in her healing.

Jesus defended His Sabbath conduct of releasing this woman by referring to the Sabbath behavior of the Jewish leaders who would untie their ox or donkey on the Sabbath and lead it to water. In doing so the opponents of Jesus were humiliated and the multitude rejoiced over what Jesus was doing.

Summary of Luke 13:10–17

1. The woman healed was not in a life-threatening condition.
2. Jesus, upon seeing this woman, immediately called her to Himself.
3. This woman's physical condition was caused by a spirit.
4. Jesus spoke freedom to this woman and then, after laying His hands upon her, released her from the power of Satan.
5. After being healed this woman immediately began praising God.
6. The synagogue official considered the actions of Jesus as a violation of Sabbath law.
7. Jesus defended His Sabbath conduct on the basis of the Sabbath behavior of the Jewish leaders. If Sabbath law allowed the Jewish leaders to untie and water their animals on the Sabbath, in the same way

Sabbath law must allow for a true child of God to be "released" from the power of Satan on the Sabbath.
8. The underlying theme of this Sabbath healing is one of release from the power of Satan and freedom in the presence of Christ—themes found in the Jubilee and the Sabbath.
9. It appears that Jesus considered this Jubilee-type ministry to be especially appropriate on the seventh-day Sabbath.
10. While seeking to enforce the letter of Sabbath law, the Jewish leaders completely missed the experience to which these laws pointed: freedom from the power of Satan and fellowship with God.

CHAPTER TEN

LORD OF THE SABBATH

In this chapter we will examine two occurrences in the ministry of Jesus where He clearly exerts His authority over old covenant Sabbath law.

Authority over the Demonized
(Mark 1:21–34; Luke 4:31–44)

These passages describe three Sabbath events: (1) a Sabbath morning synagogue encounter with a demonized man, (2) the Sabbath afternoon healing of Simon's mother-in-law, and (3) the "after sundown" ministry to the multitudes.

> And they [Jesus and some of His disciples] went into Capernaum; and immediately on the Sabbath He entered the synagogue and began to teach. And they were amazed at His teaching; for He was teaching them as one having authority, and not as the scribes. And just then there was in their synagogue a man with an unclean spirit; and he cried out, saying, "What do we have to do with You, Jesus of Nazareth? Have you come to destroy us? I know who You are—the Holy One of God!" And Jesus rebuked him, saying, "Be quiet, and come out of him!" And throwing him into convulsions, the unclean spirit cried out with a loud voice, and came out of him. And they were all amazed, so that they debated among themselves, saying, "What is this? A new teaching with authority! He commands even the unclean spirits, and they obey Him." And immediately the news

about Him went out everywhere into all the surrounding district of Galilee (Mk. 1:21–28).

While this portion of Scripture speaks of Jesus' teaching method, nothing is said about the content of His teaching. The people were amazed at His teaching authority—"He was teaching them as one having authority" (v. 22)—and His authority over the forces of evil—"He commands even the unclean spirits, and they obey Him" (v. 27). However we have no record of what He taught; only what He did.

Note that the unclean spirit recognized Jesus. The spirit knew Jesus was from Nazareth and that He was "The Holy One of God." It can be inferred that the unclean spirit knew what the outcome was to be. "Have you come to destroy us?" Jesus' answer in essence was, "Yes!" Jesus demonstrated the "gospel of the kingdom"—the rule and reign of God over the forces of evil.

One of the purposes of the Sabbath, perhaps the main purpose,[1] was that it was a sign of redemption—deliverance from bondage. The Jubilee was to be a day of freeing the captives. How appropriate that Jesus takes these sabbatical concepts and on the Sabbath frees the captive of Satan, delivering this person from the bondage of enemy enslavement.

After the synagogue meeting Jesus and the disciples go to the home of Simon and Andrew.

> And immediately after they had come out of the synagogue, they came into the house of Simon and Andrew, with James and John. Now Simon's mother-in-law was lying sick with a fever; and immediately they spoke to Him about her. And He came to her and raised her up, taking her by the hand, and the fever left her, and she began to wait on them (Mk. 1:29–31).

---

[1] See "The Roman Catholic Church and the Decalogue", *Proclamation*, (Life Assurance Ministries, Inc. Glendale, AZ, 2001), Vol. 2, Nos. 5&6. where Dr. Streifling gives evidence that the Ten Commandments as listed in Deuteronomy is the original version.

Again, nothing is expressly taught about the Sabbath in this incident but much can be learned from observing Christ's activities. The disciples, who had recently been called by Jesus, seemed to understand that His ministry was a healing ministry, for they immediately told Him about the sickness of Peter's mother-in-law, indicating they expected Jesus to heal her. By healing her during the hours of the Sabbath Jesus made it clear He considered healing an acceptable, or even desirable, Sabbath activity even though this was not the accepted custom of the Jewish leaders. In Luke's account Jesus "rebukes" the fever (Lk. 4:39) as if He were speaking to an intelligent entity. It can be inferred that the fever was probably caused by some malevolent spirit which Jesus rebuked.

> This time in the cure there does seem to be in some sense a breach of the Sabbath prohibition [as understood by the Rabbis] on working. Touching by itself was not work, but touching to effect a cure may have been regarded as a breach of the law as E.P. Sanders claims.[2]

After this spirit left Peter's mother-in-law she immediately began to serve them. Word of this healing must have spread immediately to the surrounding communities because a few hours later,

> When evening had come, after the sun had set, they began bringing to Him all who were ill and those who were demon possessed. And the whole city had gathered at the door. And He healed many who were ill with various diseases, and cast out many demons; and He was not permitting the demons to speak, because they knew who He was (Mk. 1:32–34).

Scripture does not say why the people waited until after the Sabbath to bring their sick to Jesus. The fact that Jesus felt free to heal Simon's mother-in-law on the Sabbath indicates that it was not so much His desire that the people wait until after sundown to come for healing as it was their own ideas regarding Sabbath observance.

---

[2] Alan Watson, *Jesus and the Law,* p. 14.

Jesus was continually performing a liberating, freeing ministry, healing those sick with various diseases and casting out demons. Both Mark and Luke indicate Jesus continued this type of ministry on other Sabbaths.

> And He went into their synagogues throughout all Galilee, preaching and casting out the demons (Mk. 1:39).
> And He was teaching them on Sabbath days (Lk. 4:31).

Note how Jesus describes His liberating and healing activities in Luke 4:43, 44.

> But He said to them, "I must preach the kingdom of God to the other cities also, for I was sent for this purpose." And He kept on preaching in the synagogues of Judea.

Jesus defines the "kingdom of God" as His liberating, jubilee ministry of healing the sick and casting out demons, a ministry that demonstrated His authority or kingdom rule over the forces of evil.

Summary of Mark 1:21–34 and Luke 4:31–44

In summary, nothing in this incident is expressly taught regarding the Sabbath. However, from the *activity* of Jesus we learn the following:

1. Jesus' Sabbath teaching was with such authority it amazed His hearers.
2. Jesus commanded an unclean spirit to come out of a demonized person on the Sabbath. It obeyed.
3. Jesus felt free to heal (by taking Simon's mother-in-law's hand and rebuking the fever) on the Sabbath.
4. This method of healing on the Sabbath was probably considered a violation of Sabbath law by the Jewish leaders.
5. Simon's mother-in-law, who had just been healed, waited on them while it was Sabbath.
6. Just after sundown, which marked the end of the Sabbath, Jesus healed many people with various diseases and cast out many demons.

7. Jesus continued His liberating ministry on other Sabbath days in the synagogues of Galilee and Judea.
8. Jesus called His ministry of healing and of casting out demons "preaching the kingdom of God."
9. Jesus seems to be fulfilling one of the purposes of the Sabbath—a sign of deliverance from bondage.

Authority over Sabbath Law

(Mk. 2:23–28; Mt. 12:1–8; Lk. 6:1–5)

This is a very important Sabbath encounter, recorded by all the Synoptic Gospels. Matthew adds some additional details not in Mark and also has some contextual material that must be studied in connection with it. The thrust of this incident bears directly on the topic of Sabbath behavior; therefore we must give our most careful attention to this passage. We will first examine the reference from Mark and then consider the additional material found in Matthew. Luke adds no additional insights.

The Mark account comes immediately after Jesus' discussion about putting new wine into old wineskins. Most interpret this section to refer to the *contrast* between Judaism and Christianity or the old and new covenants. In essence, Jesus was saying by this illustration that the fullness of the new covenant gospel could not be put into the rigid forms of Judaism. The gospel of Christ must be placed in a new "wineskin"—the church.

> And it came about that He was passing through the grainfields on the Sabbath, and His disciples began to make their way along while picking the heads of grain. And the Pharisees were saying to Him, "See here, why are they doing what is not lawful on the Sabbath?" And He said to them, "Have you never read what David did when he was in need and became hungry, he and his companions: How he entered into the house of God in the time of Abiathar the high priest, and ate the consecrated bread, which is not lawful for anyone to eat except the priests, and he gave it also to those who were with him?" And He was saying to them, "The Sabbath was made for man, and not man for the

Sabbath. Consequently, the Son of Man is Lord even of the Sabbath" (Mk. 2:23–28).

Matthew's account of this Sabbath occurrence follows *immediately after* Christ made this proclamation:

> Come unto Me, all who are weary and heavy laden, and I will give you *rest*. Take My yoke upon you, and learn from Me, for I am gentle and humble in heart; and you shall find *rest* for your souls. For My yoke is easy, and My load is light (Mt. 11:28–30).

In the Matthew account we also find that Christ's defense of His disciples' activities has two additional arguments not listed in Mark.

> Or have you not read in the Law, that on the Sabbath the priests in the temple *break* the Sabbath, and are innocent? But I say to you, that something greater than the temple is here. But if you had known what this means, "I desire compassion, and not sacrifice," you would not have condemned the innocent (Mt. 12:5–7).

First, let us look carefully at what the disciples were doing and why the Pharisees considered them to be breaking the Sabbath. It is very easy for us to denounce the Pharisees for their narrow interpretation of Sabbath law. Yet to rightly understand this incident and what Jesus was really teaching we must see it from their perspective. In this case the Pharisees understood the Sabbath law to require "complete rest" (Ex. 31:15) and refraining from all work (Ex. 20:10). The Pharisees recognized that these laws applied even to plowing and harvest time (Ex. 34:21). They were familiar with the instruction which said that on the Sabbath they were "to remain every man in his place" (Ex. 16:29). Further, they knew the Scripture which taught that food was to be gathered and prepared on the day before the Sabbath so no gathering or cooking would interfere with the rest of the Sabbath day (Ex. 16:23–26).

Looking through the eyes of the Pharisees we can see why they considered Christ's disciples to be breaking the

Lord of the Sabbath

Sabbath on at least three counts: (1) They were "harvesting and threshing" the grain in their hands, which was work and therefore a violation of the Sabbath. (2) They were not completely resting, which was required on the Sabbath. (3) They had failed to "remember the Sabbath" in that they apparently had not prepared their food the day before.

Whether or not the disciples actually broke the letter of the biblical Sabbath law is not the most important point. Rather, it is the way Jesus responded to the accusations as He took *authority over Sabbath law* and defended His disciples by giving four powerful arguments to show that His disciples did not come under condemnation for their questionable Sabbath activities. Consider each of the arguments Christ put forward to show why His disciples were free from condemnation.

Argument one is:

> Have you never read what David did when he was in need and became hungry, he and his companions: how he entered into the house of God in the time of Abiathar the high priest, and ate the consecrated bread, *which is not lawful* for anyone to eat except the priests, and he gave it also to those were with him? (Mk. 2:25, 26).

In 1 Samuel 21:1–6 we are told that David was fleeing from King Saul, who was seeking to kill him. He came to the priest and in answer to the priest's question as to why David was alone he answered,

> The king has commissioned me with a matter, and has said to me, "Let no one know anything about the matter on which I am sending you with which I have commissioned you and I have directed the young men to a certain place."

This was a lie. Nevertheless the priest believed it and gave David "consecrated bread" which he later shared with his men. It is important to note that David was not reprimanded by God for the violation of this ritual law regarding eating the sacred bread, as he was when he violated a moral law by taking another man's wife.[3]

There are two possible conclusions which may be drawn from this illustration, both of which are valid. First, human need takes precedence over ritual law. This is a pattern we discerned when we earlier studied Christ's relationship with ritual law and we will see this pattern played out over and over again in a later chapter. Second, David was exempted from the law because of who he was: the anointed of God, the coming King of Israel. It was all right for *his* men to eat this bread because they were *associated* with the coming King of Israel, who was above the letter of *ritual* law by virtue of his kingly office.

Correspondingly, Jesus was arguing that His disciples were innocent, not so much because they were hungry, but because they were involved with Him in His work, which took precedence over ritual, Sabbath law. Jesus was the anointed of God, the coming King of Israel; therefore, they were free from condemnation by virtue of their association with Christ. This offers a preview of the coming redemption of the new covenant gospel: you are complete in Him.

The second argument Christ placed before the Pharisees to justify His disciples' questionable Sabbath activity is this:

> Or have you not read in the Law, that on the Sabbath the priests in the temple *break* the Sabbath, and are innocent? (Mt. 12:5).

The priests are instructed in the law to do certain things on the Sabbath which would fall into the category of work and would normally be considered Sabbath breaking. These activities were probably the making and deploying of fresh showbread (Lev. 24:5-9) and the sacrificing of certain Sabbath offerings (Num. 28:9, 10). However, because these activities were commanded in the old covenant law, the priests were innocent. Most pastors can relate to this argu-

---

[3] 2 Sam. 11, 12.

ment. The day of worship is often, if not always, the hardest and most tiring day of their week.

Now notice how Christ applies this argument to the situation at hand. "But I say to you, that something greater than the temple is here" (Mt. 12:6). Jesus used this phrase several other times in this chapter and it becomes evident what He means.

> The men of Nineveh shall stand up with this generation at the judgment, and shall condemn it because they repented at the preaching of Jonah; and behold, *something greater* than Jonah is here (Mt. 12:41).
>
> The Queen of the South shall stand up with this generation at the judgment, and shall condemn it; because she came from the ends of the earth to hear the wisdom of Solomon; and behold, *something greater* than Solomon is here (Mt. 12:42).

That "something greater" is Jesus Himself and the kingdom He brings. It was God's presence which made the tabernacle service important enough to allow the priests to violate the letter of *ritual* Sabbath law and yet be innocent. The presence of Jesus tabernacling (Jn. 1:14) in the temple of His body (Mt. 26:61) took precedence over ritual Sabbath law. Therefore, just as the priests could violate the *letter* of Sabbath law to fulfill the more important services of the temple, so the disciples of Jesus could violate the letter of ritual Sabbath law because they were engaged in the more important service of One who is greater than the temple.

The third argument of Jesus is:

> But if you had known what this means, "I desire compassion, and not a sacrifice," you would not have condemned the innocent (Mt. 12:7).

This is a quotation from Hosea 6:6. It reads,

> For I delight in loyalty rather than sacrifice, and in the knowledge of God rather than burnt offerings.

This text cuts to the very heart and meaning of covenant law. It shows that God is more concerned with the attitude of the heart than He is with ritual, even ritual which pointed forward to Christ's death on the cross. In this argument, Jesus proves the disciples are innocent because of their heart loyalty and close association to Him, even though they may have broken the letter of Sabbath law.

Here again is the irony of the old covenant Sabbath laws as observed by the Pharisees. On one hand the Pharisees, who were keeping the very letter of the Sabbath laws, had no compassion or loyalty to the God of the covenant. On the other hand the disciples, who appear to have broken the letter of the old covenant Sabbath law, were loyally following their Lord!

The fourth argument of Jesus is:

> The Sabbath was made for man, and not man for the Sabbath. Consequently, the Son of Man is Lord even of the Sabbath (Mk. 2:27, 28).

The meaning of this verse has been vigorously debated. Some have argued it teaches that the Sabbath was instituted *at creation* for all mankind.[4] However, this interpretation runs completely contrary to the Jewish understanding that the Sabbath was given *only* to the nation of Israel.[5] While we agree that there was a seventh-day rest in Eden, we will find that it was not identical to the Sabbath of Sinai.

Here Jesus is saying that the Sabbath was made for the *benefit* of man and not man for the *benefit* of the Sabbath. Because of this, Jesus, as the Son of Man, controls the

---

[4] Desmond Ford, *The Forgotten Day*, (Desmond Ford Publications, Newcastle, CA 1981) p. 81.

[5] Harold H. P. Dressler, "The Sabbath in the Old Testament", in *From Sabbath to Lord's Day*, p. 34. C. Rowland, "A summary of Sabbath Observance in Judaism at the Beginning of the Christian Era", in *From Sabbath to Lord's Day*, p. 46. Max M. B. Turner, "The Sabbath, Sunday and the Law in Luke/Acts", in *From Sabbath to Lord's Day*, p. 128.

Sabbath and is not to be controlled by it.[6] The term, *the Son of Man,* which Jesus used in reference to Himself, comes from Daniel 7:13, where it is used in connection with the dawning of the eschatological (end time) reign of God. Thus, in defense of Jesus' disciples' questionable Sabbath activities, Jesus announces His own authority as the Son of Man who is bringing the eschatological reign of God.

The thrust of Jesus' argument is not in defining appropriate Sabbath behavior or a correct interpretation of old covenant Sabbath law; rather it is in <u>showing how old covenant law, including Sabbath law, points to *Him*</u>. In this respect it seems obvious that the Sabbath is a ritual law. Even Jewish scholars recognize that the Sabbath as a ritual and not moral law.[7] Thus, like the other ritual laws, the importance of the shadow falls away in the presence of the reality of the Messiah.

In summary, we see that Jesus is taking authority over Sabbath law. His *presence* allows greater freedom regarding Sabbath observance just as the priests were not bound by all the Sabbath laws in their temple services where God was present. His *office* as the Anointed, coming King of Israel, gave Him and those associated with Him freedom to infringe upon ritual Sabbath law. As the Son of Man, who has the *mission* of bringing in the eschatological reign of God, He is above the control of ritual Sabbath law.

We can safely conclude even more than this. When we consider that in both Mark and Luke this incident immediately follows the discussion about putting new wine in new wineskins we get overtones of coming changes. Remembering also that in Matthew this incident (Mt. 12:1, 2) is

---

[6] D. A. Carson, "Jesus and the Sabbath in the Four Gospels", in *From Sabbath to Lord's Day,* p 65.

[7] Although the Sabbath's importance is suggested by its being the only ritual law in the Ten Commandments, there is little specific Sabbath legislation in the Bible. Rabbi Joseph Telushkin, *Biblcal Literacy,* p. 429.

connected to the three verses of the preceding chapter (Mt. 11:28–30) by the use of the phrase "at this time" (Mt. 12:1), leads us to conclude that the Sabbath itself may be associated with the eschatological rest of God.

At the same time, there is evidence for the fact that the Sabbath itself is associated with the theme of restoration and the messianic age. Within such a framework the fact that Jesus is the Lord of the Sabbath becomes the more significant, for the very concept of Sabbath begins to undergo transformation. That Jesus Christ is Lord of the Sabbath is not only a messianic claim of grand proportions, but it raises the possibility of a future change or reinterpretation of the Sabbath, in precisely the same way that His professed superiority over the Temple raises certain possibilities about ritual law. No details of that nature are spelled out here, but the verse arouses expectations.[8]

The way this incident contextually unfolds leads us to conclude that Jesus is the reality prefigured in old covenant rituals. More than that, He is showing that a violation of ritual law which was designed to point to Him now has little significance.

Summary of the Sabbath in a Grainfield

1. The disciples may have violated the *letter* of old covenant law.
2. In proving His disciples "innocent," Jesus presented four powerful arguments, all of which show His authority over Sabbath law.
   a. David and his men violated the letter of the law by eating the consecrated bread. It is implied that David was innocent because of who he was: the anointed of God, the coming King of Israel. It is implied that his men were innocent because they were with David. Correspondingly, Jesus, by virtue of His kingly office, is above the letter of the law, and His disciples are innocent because

---

[8] *Ibid.*, p. 66.

they are with the Anointed of God, the coming King of Israel.

b. The priests are innocent of breaking the Sabbath because their Sabbath "work" was necessary to the temple service. But "Something" greater than the temple was there with the disciples in the grainfield that Sabbath day. That "Something" was none other than God, who was "tabernacling" in the flesh—the temple of His body. Correspondingly, the disciples are innocent because they are in the service of Jesus, Someone greater than the old temple.

c. God desired real, heartfelt compassion and loyalty over the ritual of sacrifice. Thus, the disciples were innocent of their violation of ritual law, because by following Jesus they demonstrated their heartfelt compassion and loyalty to Him, which took precedence over the letter of the law.

d. The Sabbath was made for man and not man for the Sabbath. Consequently the Son of Man is Lord (has authority) over the Sabbath.

3. The thrust of Jesus' argument is not so much in defining appropriate Sabbath conduct as in showing how old covenant law points to Him.
4. When taken as a whole and considering the context, Jesus' response to the Pharisees lays the groundwork for the possibility of future changes.
5. Jesus did not seem concerned with minor violations of Sabbath law. This indicates that Jesus understood the Sabbath law to be ritual and not moral.

He not only was breaking the Sabbath, but also was calling God His own Father

CHAPTER
ELEVEN

SABBATH CONFLICTS

A Sabbath in a Synagogue

(Lk. 6:6–11; Mt. 12:9–14; Mk. 3:1–6)

In all the synoptic gospels, this Sabbath episode follows the one we have just studied in the previous chapter. Each account varies somewhat from the others, but the thrust of the teaching is the same in all three. I will quote the account as found in Luke and then add the additional material found in Matthew and Mark.

> And it came about on another Sabbath, that He entered the synagogue and was teaching; and there was a man there whose right hand was withered. And the scribes and Pharisees were watching Him closely, to see if He healed on the Sabbath, in order that they might find reason to accuse Him. But He knew what they were thinking and He said to the man with the withered hand, "Arise and come forward!" And he arose and came forward. And Jesus said to them, "I ask you, is it lawful on the Sabbath to do good, or to do evil, to save a life, or to destroy it?" And after looking around at them all, He said to him, "Stretch out your hand!" And he did so; and his hand was completely restored. But they themselves were filled with rage, and discussed together what they might do to Jesus (Lk. 6:6–11).

Matthew states that the Pharisees were questioning Jesus instead of Jesus questioning them (Mt. 12:10). Luke records that Jesus, "knowing their thoughts," questioned the Pharisees. This is not a contradiction, as the Pharisees could have been questioning Jesus in their thoughts. Matthew also records the reasoning of Jesus.

> What man shall there be among you, who shall have one sheep, and if it falls into a pit on the Sabbath, will he not take hold of it, and lift it out? Of how much more value then is a man than a sheep! So then it is lawful to do good on the Sabbath (Mt. 12:11,12).

Mark's account adds more detail regarding Jesus' reaction to the people in the synagogue and the anger He felt toward their hardness of heart.

> And after looking around at them with anger, grieved at their hardness of heart, He said to the man, "Stretch out your hand" (Mk. 3:5).

This story deals specifically with Sabbath behavior. The Jewish rabbis had interpreted healing, caring for the sick, as work and therefore a violation of Sabbath law. However, they had modified this so that one could care for those who were in a life-threatening situation.[1] It is obvious that the man with a withered hand was *not* in a life-threatening condition. This incident appears to be a direct confrontation by Jesus upon the commonly accepted interpretation of Sabbath law.

Jesus showed His attitude by "looking around at them with anger, grieved at their hardness of heart." Then he demonstrated His authority to interpret the Sabbath law by openly calling the man to the front and healing him.

Jesus asks the question, "Is it lawful to do good on the Sabbath?" Then He follows up His own question with action and heals the man. The result of this open confrontation with the accepted interpretation of Sabbath law was that the Pharisees immediately counseled with the Herodians and set out to "destroy Him."

As we pointed out in the last chapter, when the disciples of Jesus were accused of Sabbath violation, Jesus carefully

---

[1] Rowland, "A summary of Sabbath Observance in Judaism at the Beginning of the Christian Era", in *From Sabbath to Lord's Day*, p. 46

laid out five reasons why He and His disciples did not come under the authority of Sabbath law. In this account He *demonstrated* His authority and lordship over the Sabbath laws (as they were currently interpreted) in an open, public confrontation with the leaders of Judaism.

Summary of a Sabbath in a synagogue

1. Jesus specifically stated that it was lawful to do good on the Sabbath.
2. Jesus openly and publicly confronted the Jewish leaders regarding the commonly accepted interpretation of Sabbath law.
3. Jesus healed a man whose condition was not life threatening on the Sabbath.
4. Jesus was openly angry and grieved at the hardness of the Pharisees' hearts.

A Sabbath Dinner with the Pharisees

(Luke 14:1–6)

And it came about that when He went into the house of one of the leaders of the Pharisees on the Sabbath to eat bread, they were watching Him closely. And there in front of Him was a certain man suffering with dropsy. And Jesus answered and spoke to the lawyers and Pharisees, saying, "Is it lawful to heal on the Sabbath, or not?" But they kept silent. And He took hold of him, and healed him, and sent him away. And He said to them, "Which one of you shall have a son [some manuscripts read donkey] or an ox fall into a well, and will not immediately pull him out on the Sabbath day?" And they could make no reply to this.

This episode is very much like the one we just studied with the exception that this one is *planned* by the Pharisees. One gets the idea that the Pharisees and lawyers invited Jesus to dinner for the one purpose of documenting evidence they could use against Him in regard to the violation of the Sabbath. It appears they "planted" this person with dropsy so that he was sitting right in front of Jesus.

Jesus accepted their challenge but first asked them if it was lawful to heal on the Sabbath. Like schemers running a sting operation, they kept silent. Jesus then healed the man and justified His actions by referring to their own Sabbath behavior in relationship to their animals, implying that a man is more valuable than an animal, and thus deserving of greater Sabbath privileges.

Summary of a Sabbath dinner with the Pharisees

1. It appears that this episode was set up by the Jewish leaders to entrap Jesus:
   a. The man with dropsy just happened to be there in front of Him.
   b. The Pharisees and lawyers did not answer Jesus' question, probably for fear that Jesus would disclose their true motives.
2. Jesus healed the man with dropsy on this Sabbath day.
3. Jesus justified His Sabbath behavior on the basis of how the Pharisees, and the others present, took care of their animals on the Sabbath.

A Sabbath at Bethesda

(John 5:1–18; 7:14–24)

The gospel of John was written later than the other gospels and was clearly written to express certain theological perspectives. John takes for granted that his readers have access to the other gospel accounts and is not concerned with merely giving his account of the events which are recorded in the other gospels unless these events fit his overall goals that the reader "may believe that Jesus is the

Sabbath Conflicts

Christ, the Son of God; and that believing you may have eternal life" (Jn. 20:31).

Not only this, but John includes events in the life of Jesus which the other gospel writers did not record, because *from John's perspective in time* these events contribute to the theological needs of his day. There is good evidence that John is distancing himself from the "Jewish" understanding of things. We see this in statements like "the *Jewish* day of preparation" (Jn. 19:42). If Sabbath observance were a Christian requirement, and if the Sabbath were celebrated according to biblical guidelines when this gospel was written, then we would expect John simply to write, "the day of preparation." The fact that he calls it *"the Jewish* day of preparation" was a clear message to his readers. Likewise, John calls the Passover "the feast *of the Jews"* (Jn. 6:4). This is evidence that the New Testament church was moving away from the Sabbath and other ritual laws *of the old covenant*. For this reason we believe John included certain Sabbath episodes which are not recorded by the other gospel writers.

This Sabbath incident is very involved and warrants our careful attention. We will divide the text, and our study of it, into three sections.

> After these things there was a feast of the Jews; and Jesus went up to Jerusalem. Now there is in Jerusalem by the sheep gate a pool, which is called in Hebrew Bethesda, having five porticoes. In these lay a multitude of those who were sick, blind, lame, withered...And a certain man was there, who had been thirty-eight years in his sickness. When Jesus saw him lying there, and knew that he had already been a long time in that condition, He said to him, "Do you wish to get well?" The sick man answered Him, "Sir, I have no man to put me into the pool when the water is stirred up, but while I am coming, another steps down before me." Jesus said to him, "Arise, take up your pallet, and walk" (Jn. 5:1–9).

We should note again this was not a life-threatening emergency. This man had already been there thirty-eight years and a few more days would probably have done him no harm. Jesus initiated the conversation and in His healing command ordered this man to arise, lift up his bed, and walk.

This healing took place on the Sabbath. The question has often been asked if Jesus commanded this man to break the Sabbath. Without question, Jesus asked him to openly break the Halakah, the rabbinical laws which were an interpretation of the biblical laws.[2] This man's "pallet" probably consisted of a pad to protect him from the hard stone floor and several blankets to keep him warm during the cold Jerusalem nights. In other words, his "pallet" probably consisted of what would normally be the covers on a bed. Having personally backpacked several hundred miles with modern, lightweight equipment, it is my conclusion that this man's "pallet" would have constituted a "load," which was forbidden to be carried on the Sabbath (Jer. 17:27).

It should also be noted that there was no good reason why this man had to carry his "pallet" that day. Jesus could have healed him on the Sabbath and then asked him to go back after sundown, or on the next day, and carry away his bed. One gets the idea that Jesus *purposefully* chose to heal this man on the Sabbath and *deliberately* asked him to do something which would be considered a violation of Sabbath law.

If we take the position that Jesus did command this man to break the Sabbath, it raises theological questions which must be answered. The only suitable answer is that Christ considered the Sabbath to be a ritual law that pointed forward to the rest He would bring and now it had little, if any, value. If we hold the Sabbath to be a moral law, then we are faced with either trying to make this act fit within biblical Sabbath law or charging Christ with sin. What we

---

[2] D. A. Carson, "Jesus and the Sabbath in the Four Gospels", in *From Sabbath to Lord's Day,* p. 81.

can say for certain, however, is that the people of Christ's day understood the actions of this man as breaking the Sabbath law *as they perceived it.*

> And immediately the man became well, and took up his pallet and began to walk. Now it was the Sabbath on that day. Therefore the Jews were saying to him who was cured, "It is the Sabbath, and it is not permissible for you to carry your pallet." But he answered them, "He who made me well was the one who said to me, 'Take up your pallet and walk.'" They asked him, "Who is the man who said to you, 'Take up your pallet, and walk.'" But he who was healed did not know who it was; for Jesus had slipped away while there was a crowd in that place. Afterward Jesus found him in the temple, and said to him, "Behold, you have become well; do not sin any more, so that nothing worse may befall you." The man went away, and told the Jews that it was Jesus who had made him well. And for this reason the Jews were persecuting Jesus because He was doing these things on the Sabbath. But He answered them, "My Father is working until now, and I Myself am working." For this cause therefore the Jews were seeking all the more to kill Him because He not only was breaking the Sabbath, but also was calling God His own Father, making Himself equal with God (Jn. 5:9–18).

Looking at these verses in Greek adds additional insight. In verse 18 we read, "because He not only *was breaking* the Sabbath..." "Was breaking" is in the continuous tense in Greek, implying that Jesus was repeatedly involved in such activity.[3] The Greek verb here is *eluen,* which comes from the root *luo,* and has the idea of "destroy." This same verb is used by John in the following verses: *"Destroy* this temple, and in three days I will raise it up" (Jn. 2:19). "The Son of God appeared for this purpose, that He might *destroy* the works of the devil" (1 Jn. 3:8). Kittel's *Theological Dictionary of the New Testament* gives the following possible meanings to this verb *as used in the context of John 5:18:* "to break up," "to destroy," "to

---

[3] Leon Morris, *The New International Commentary of the New Testament, The Gospel of John,* (Wm. B. Eerdmans Publishing Co, Grand Rapids, MI, 1971), p. 307.

dismiss," "to set aside," "to invalidate."[4] Therefore, a correct alternate translation would be "because He was not only *destroying* the Sabbath..."

This passage says that the Jews were persecuting Jesus because He was destroying, or invalidating, the Sabbath. We should not be too hasty to denounce the Jews. Old covenant Sabbath law clearly required that a person who openly broke the Sabbath was to be put to death (Ex. 31:14,15; 35:2). The Pharisees had the old covenant record of the man who was caught gathering sticks on the Sabbath and was stoned to death at the express command of God for this violation (Num. 15:32–36). They also had the later scriptural interpretations of Sabbath law to prohibit carrying a load on the Sabbath (Jer. 17:27). One could excuse the man carrying sticks before he could excuse a man carrying his bedroll except for the fact that he did it at the express command of Jesus. It is assumed that the man gathering sticks was doing so to meet some kind of human need, perhaps for warmth or to cook food, while there was no good reason mentioned why the man in this incident had to carry his bed away *that day*. Therefore, when limiting oneself to the Old Testament Sabbath laws the Jewish leaders seemed to be doing the very thing the law required: setting about to put to death one whom they understood to have openly and purposefully set aside Sabbath law.

Next we should note Christ's defense of His Sabbath activities. "But He answered them, My Father is *working* until now, and I Myself am *working*." It is very important to note that Jesus did not try to prove that His healing activities or His command to "Arise, take up your pallet, and walk" were within the scope of Sabbath law. Rather He boldly states that His Father and He are *working*—something clearly forbidden in Sabbath law. Jesus then moved the discussion *away from* the violation of Sabbath

---

[4] Kittel, *Theological Dictionary of the New Testament*, (Wm. B. Eerdmans Publishing Co., Grand Rapids, MI, 1967), Vol. IV, p. 336.

law *to* His close association with His Father. The Jewish rabbis had correctly concluded that the rest which God entered on the seventh day after creation did not apply to God's work of upholding the universe.[5] We remember from our study of Genesis that God began the "work" of redemption immediately after the fall of Adam and Eve. It was this "work" that Jesus was continually doing which caused the Jewish leaders to persecute Him. As upholding creation is above the rest of Sabbath law, so is Christ's work of redemption. This work far supersedes the Sabbath laws of the Pharisees and even the letter of the Old Testament Sabbath laws. It is the goal of redemption to restore the conditions which existed on that first seventh day when God rested.

Look carefully at the whole of verse 18. These are the words of the Gospel writer, John.

> For this cause the Jews were seeking all the more to kill Him, because He not only *was breaking* [or destroying] *the Sabbath,* but also was calling God His own Father, *making Himself equal with God* (Jn. 5:18).

Were these accusations correct? Throughout the gospel of John the divinity of Jesus is portrayed as a major theme. "The Word was God...The Word became flesh" (Jn. 1:1–3, 14). "Before Abraham was, I AM" (Jn. 8:58), etc. The clear wording and the literary structure force us to conclude that *both* of these statements (that Jesus was breaking or destroying the Sabbath and calling God His own Father) were true, and because they were true, they were the reasons the Jews sought all the more to kill Jesus.

In the next few verses Jesus gives thirteen reasons which prove two things. First, they show the close association between Himself and His Father, confirming the fact that Jesus is indeed equal with the Father. Second, they show

---

[5] D. A. Carson, *Commentary on John,* (Wm. B. Eerdmans Publishing Co., Grand Rapids, MI, 1991), p. 247.

why He, like His Father, must continue to *work,* even if His work was a violation of Sabbath law.

- He does only what the Father does (Jn. 5:19).
- The Son gives (eternal) life to whom He wishes (Jn. 5:21).
- The Father has given all judgment to the Son (Jn. 5:22).
- All are to honor the Son just as they honor the Father (Jn. 5:23).
- The one who believes (in Jesus) is not judged (Jn. 5:24).
- The Son of God will raise the dead (Jn. 5:25).
- The Son has life in Himself (Jn. 5:26).
- As the Son of Man, Jesus has the authority to execute judgment (Jn. 5:27).
- Jesus' judgment is just (Jn. 5:30).
- Jesus' authority is backed by two witnesses (to make it legal according to Jewish law), the Father and John the Baptist (Jn. 5:31–33).
- The purpose of Jesus' taking all authority is for the Jews' salvation (Jn. 5:34).
- If they reject the witness of John, which the Jewish leaders did, then the two legal witnesses are the Father and the very works of Jesus (Jn. 5:35–37).
- The Scriptures also testify of Jesus (Jn. 5:39).

At this point Jesus, as the Son of Man who has authority to sit in judgment, takes the judgment seat and confronts the Pharisees by saying,

> Do not think that I will accuse you before the Father; the one who accuses you is Moses, in whom you have set your hope. For if you believed Moses, you would believe Me; for *he wrote of Me.* But if you do not believe his writing, how will you believe My words? (Jn. 5:45–47).

These last few verses give additional insight regarding the Sabbath. First, they corroborate what we have concluded before: Jesus, by virtue of His divinity, is above the letter of ritual Sabbath law. Secondly, Jesus, *in the context of this Sabbath incident,* says that Moses wrote of Him. Could it be that Jesus was saying that the Sabbath, as set forth in the old covenant, was an institution which was to point forward to the coming of Jesus and His work? Could it be that the Sabbath, which was a memorial of a finished creation also pointed forward to a finished redemption? Could it be that the redemption from Egyptian bondage also foreshadowed the true redemption in Christ? Could it be that the Sabbath which pointed back to the open fellowship Adam had with God before sin entered, also pointed forward to the open fellowship a justified believer can have with God? Could it be that the laws of the Sabbath, over which the Pharisees were stumbling, were the very laws which should have directed them to the only One who could bring in the true rest of God? Could it be that the true Sabbath is in Christ!?

Two chapters later, in John 7, Jesus refers back to this Sabbath incident. Notice His comments.

> Jesus answered and said to them, "I did one deed [Greek is 'work'], and you all marvel. On this account Moses has given you circumcision (not because it is from Moses, but from the fathers), and on the Sabbath you circumcise a man. If a man receives circumcision on the Sabbath that the Law of Moses may not be broken, are you angry with Me because I made an entire man well on the Sabbath? Do not judge according to appearance, but judge with righteous judgment" (Jn. 7:21–24).

Jesus is defending His previous act of healing the man at the pool of Bethesda. It is of interest to note that He does not focus on the man's carrying his bedroll, but on the healing. Notice His two arguments. First, He shows that in Jewish law circumcision took precedence over the Sabbath. From our previous study of the old covenant we saw why this was so. The Sabbath was a sign between God and the "sons of Israel" (Ex. 31:17). However, to become a "son of Israel" a male had to be circumcised. It was then and then only that the Sabbath law applied. Jesus' first argument draws a parallel between the Jewish practice of circumcising on the eighth day, even if it fell on the Sabbath, and His "work" of making an entire man well on the Sabbath.

The first argument is based upon old covenant law. The second argument is based upon a different reference point. The Jews saw, and judged, the actions of Jesus from the reference point of the old covenant law. They were judging "according to appearance." Jesus, on the other hand, has a different reference point: "judge with righteous judgment." What is "righteous judgment"? He told them in the last part of Chapter 5:

> For not even the Father judges any one, but He has given all judgment to the *Son* (Jn. 5:22). He gave *Him* [the Son] authority to execute judgment, because He is the Son of Man (Jn. 5:27). *My judgment* is just; because I do not seek My own will but the will of Him who sent Me (Jn. 5:30).

Here, Jesus asserts His deity by showing that He will be the one who sits as Judge in the final judgment. And because of this, His conduct is above question.

It appears Jesus openly and willfully commanded this man to do something which the Jewish leaders would consider to be a violation of biblical Sabbath law as Jesus continued His "work" of redemption. *Jesus did this in order that He might show them who He really was and thus move their reference point of life and judgment from the old covenant laws to Himself.* He was seeking to help them make a transition from the old covenant (Sinai laws) to the new covenant (His words). Jesus was showing the Jewish leaders that He, as the Son of Man, was now the true reference point for all life and judgment. Further, these Jewish leaders stood condemned by the very Sabbath laws which they were using to condemn Jesus, because a primary purpose of ritual Sabbath law was to point them to the coming Messiah. The "work" of the Messiah was to bring redemption by deliverance from the bondage of sin and to restore Eden's rest of intimate fellowship with God. Jesus was seeking to move the Jewish leaders away from old covenant ritual Sabbath law which pointed forward to Him. This would happen only as the people acknowledged His authority as greater than the authority of the old covenant.

Jesus took great personal risk by commanding this man to take up his bed and walk on the Sabbath. His Sabbath activities were the foundation of a major part of the hatred that developed between Jesus and the Jewish leaders which ultimately led to His crucifixion. Jesus knowingly and purposefully took this risk to bring redemption and the true "rest" of God where man once again would be at peace with his Creator.

It seems clear from the wording of this incident that we must understand Sabbath law as ritual law and not moral law. To conclude otherwise one must do a number of questionable hermeneutical gymnastics.

Summary of a Sabbath at Bethesda

1. The man Jesus healed was not in a life-threatening situation.
2. Jesus purposely commanded this man to carry his pallet which the Jews understood to be a violation of Old Testament Sabbath law.
3. The story gives no reasons why this man had to carry his pallet on the Sabbath.
4. When accused of Sabbath breaking, Jesus' answer was, "My Father is working until now, and I Myself am working."
5. The Greek verb used in Jn. 5:18 indicates that Jesus was *continually* involved in activities which the Jews considered to be breaking, destroying or invalidating the Sabbath.
6. John reflects the Pharisees' charge against Jesus by saying that Jesus was breaking or destroying the

Sabbath and making Himself equal with God, both of which were true.
7. Because of Jesus' Sabbath breaking and His claim to equality with God, the Jewish leaders sought all the more to kill Him.
8. Rather than explaining how this healing incident fit within Sabbath law, Jesus established His own authority by showing the close association between Himself and the Father and why He must continue to work.
   a. He did only what the Father was continually doing.
   b. He gives eternal life to whom He wishes.
   c. The Father had given all judgment to the Son.
   d. All should honor the Son just as they honor the Father.
   e. The one who believes in Jesus is not judged.
   f. The Son of God will raise the dead.
   g. The Son has life in Himself.
   h. As the Son of Man He has authority to execute judgment.
   i. His judgment is just.
   j. His authority is legal because it is backed by two witnesses: John the Baptist and His Father.
   k. The purpose of Jesus' taking authority is for their salvation.
   l. If they didn't accept John's witness, then He had two more: His own works and the Scriptures.
   m. The Scriptures testify of Jesus.
9. Jesus took His prerogative as the Son of Man, who is to execute judgment, by telling His accusers Moses would accuse them, for Moses wrote of Him. It can be assumed, by considering the context of this Sabbath incident, that Jesus is referring to the Sabbath as the means by which Moses spoke of Jesus.

Sabbath Conflicts

10. It seems evident that Jesus considered the Sabbath a ritual, or ceremonial law that pointed forward to Him and thus it had fulfilled its purpose.
11. When considering this incident as a whole, it appears that Jesus was purposefully seeking to move the Jewish leaders' reference point of life and judgment from the old covenant laws to Himself.
12. Jesus took great personal risk in this attempt to show Himself as the reference point of life and judgment in the new covenant.
13. This incident is strong evidence that Jesus considered the Sabbath as a ritual law pointing forward to the redemption which He would bring.

You are His disciple, but we are disciples of Moses

CHAPTER TWELVE

THE PARADOX OF SABBATH LAW

John 9

This story, like those in John 5 and 7, is a very important one and deserves our most careful attention. Again, we must not lose sight of any of the details in this chapter for they will give us insight into the deeper meaning intended by the author. This is a long chapter in John's gospel and we cannot overlook any part of it. We will study it in sections, then at the conclusion try to pull all the ideas together.

> And as He [Jesus] passed by, He saw a man blind from birth. And His disciples asked Him, saying "Rabbi, who sinned, this man, or his parents, that he should be born blind?" Jesus answered, "It was neither that this man sinned, nor his parents; but it was in order that the *works* of God might be displayed in him. We must *work* the *works* of Him who sent Me, as long as it is day; night is coming, when no man can *work*. While I am in the world, I am the light of the world" (Jn. 9:1–5).

This chapter starts with a man who was born blind. The reason for this blindness is that "the *works* of God might be displayed in him" (Jn. 9:3). It is important to note the frequent use of the word "work" in the beginning of this Sabbath incident. It is to alert us to the underlying theme of what follows. Jesus will again be accused of Sabbath breaking because of His *work* in healing this man. This, perhaps more than any other *work* of Jesus, will demonstrate the true nature of the redemption and "rest" of the new covenant.

We will soon see that Jesus and the Jewish leaders were thinking and conversing from two different reference points. It is almost as if they were "talking past" each other. Jesus understood what was going on, but the Jewish leaders seemed to have clouded reasoning and completely misunderstood Jesus. The reason for this misunderstanding is clear. They were still looking through the clouded veil of the old covenant law.[1] It is equally true that Jesus continued to speak from His reference point: Himself, the new covenant center.

For Jesus the word "work" refers to doing the works of God—kingdom work, Jubilee ministry: healing the sick, casting out demons, releasing the captives, binding up the brokenhearted, opening the eyes of the blind, preaching the gospel to the poor, proclaiming the favorable year of the Lord. This work was designed to bring redemption from the bondage of sin and restore the rest of Eden's seventh day—the true "rest" of God. The Jewish leaders, on the other hand, understood "work" to be that which was forbidden by a literal, perhaps rigid, interpretation of old covenant Sabbath law.

We note that Jesus seemed to express a certain sense of urgency. "We *must* work the works of Him who sent Me, as long as it is day; night is coming, when no man can work." Jesus included His disciples as fellow participants in this urgent work, "*We* must work..." They, too, were to be engaged in the kingdom, Jubilee "work" of proclaiming the "rest" of God.

Jesus declared Himself to be the "light of the world." We will see that those who do not believe in Him remain in the "blindness" of sin.

---

[1] 2 Cor. 3:14–18

The Paradox of Sabbath Law

> When He had said this, He spat on the ground, and made clay of the spittle, and applied the clay to his eyes, and said to him, "Go, wash in the pool of Siloam" (which is translated, Sent). And so he went away and washed, and came back seeing (Jn. 9:6, 7).

As was noted in the previous chapter, it appears that Jesus again intentionally healed this man in such a way that His actions would be seen to be an open violation of Sabbath law. To us, making a little clay seems trivial and certainly not work. However, to the Jewish leaders, who operated from a literal interpretation of the old covenant, "making" clay was working and the law said, "you shall not do any work" (Ex. 20:10). They felt this action was not in accord with the admonition of the law to have a "sabbath of complete rest" (Ex. 31:15). Further, they felt that Jesus' instruction to send this man across town was not adhering to the command which said, "Remain every man in his place" (Ex. 16:29). Nor was "washing" in the pool of Siloam, which was big enough to swim in, an appropriate Sabbath activity. Washing was to be taken care of on the day of preparation.

As is often encountered in the writings of John, small, apparently insignificant details provide additional evidence to support John's underlying purpose in writing this gospel: that the reader would come to "believe that Jesus is the Christ, the Son of God; and that by believing, you may have life in His name" (Jn. 20:31). In the passage at hand we have such details. Not only does John record that Jesus sent this blind man to the pool of Siloam, but he includes the translation of the meaning of the name, Siloam, as "sent." This little clue is to remind us of other passages in John's gospel. "My food is to do the will of Him who *sent* Me, and to accomplish His work" (Jn. 4:34). "And the Father who *sent* Me, He has borne witness of Me" (Jn. 5:37). John is seeking to lead his readers to a true understanding of who Jesus is.

> And so he went away and washed, and came back seeing (Jn. 9:7).

Nothing could be more direct and to the point or less flamboyant. At the same time we see the possible connections to the "washing" of baptism and the "seeing" of saving faith.

> The neighbors therefore, and those who previously saw him as a beggar, were saying, "Is not this the one who used to sit and beg?" Others were saying, "This is he," still others were saying, "No, but he is like him." He kept saying, "I am the one." Therefore they were saying to him, "How then were your eyes opened?" He answered, "The man who is called Jesus made clay, and anointed my eyes, and said to me, 'Go to Siloam, and wash'; so I went and washed, and I received sight." And they said to him, "Where is He?" He said, "I do not know" (Jn. 9:8–12).

At first this short passage appears to have little to do with our study of the Sabbath, yet in reality it encompasses the very essence of new covenant Sabbath understanding. It is full of subtle insights regarding the gospel. First, notice the saving action of Jesus. This beggar did not ask to be healed! The entire action proceeded from Jesus. Second, note the kind of people Jesus chooses to save: blind beggars, people who have a strong sense of personal need. Third, note the simplicity of salvation: "I washed, and I received sight." Fourth, note the transformation that takes place: his friends could hardly recognize him! Fifth, note the drawing power of the gospel: "Where is He?"

We begin to see that in each Sabbath exposure there is a progressive movement *away from* the details of the old covenant laws *toward* the one, central theme of the new: Jesus Christ and the redemption and "rest" He brings.

> They brought to the Pharisees him who was formerly blind. Now it was a Sabbath on the day when Jesus made the clay, and opened his eyes. Again therefore the Pharisees also were asking him how he received his sight. And he said to them, "He applied clay to my eyes, and I washed, and I see." Therefore some of the Pharisees were saying, "This man is not from God, because he does not keep the Sabbath." But others were saying, "How can a

The Paradox of Sabbath Law

man who is a sinner perform such signs?" And there was a division among them (Jn. 9: 13–16).

It appears from this passage that Jesus was making some headway in moving the reference point of judgment held by the Jewish leaders. In previous instances involving Sabbath breaking the Jewish leaders presented a united front against Jesus. Now, only "some of the Pharisees" stumbled over the old covenant Sabbath law and said, "This man is not from God, because he does not keep the Sabbath" (v. 16). Now, some are apparently willing to look at Him from the "Jubilee ministry" perspective of the new covenant. They evaluate the ministry of Jesus saying, "How can a man who is a sinner perform such signs?" So "there was a division among them."

> They said therefore to the blind man again, "What do you say about Him, since He opened your eyes?" And he said, "He is a prophet." The Jews therefore did not believe it of him, that he had been blind, and had received sight, until they called the parents of the very one who had received his sight, and questioned them, saying, "Is this your son, who you say was born blind? Then how does he see?" His parents answered them, and said, "We know that this is our son, and that he was born blind but how he now sees, we do not know; or who opened his eyes, we do not know. Ask him; he is of age, he shall speak for himself." His parents said this because they were afraid of the Jews; for the Jews had *already agreed,* that if any one should confess Him to be Christ he should be put out of the synagogue. For this reason his parents said, "He is of age; ask him" (Jn. 9:17–23).

This is a very enlightening, and tragic, portion of Scripture. Through the healing of this man born blind, Jesus desperately sought to bring sufficient evidence for an intelligent, saving faith to the leaders of the people He came to save. He knew that the new wine of the gospel would not fit within the rigid framework of Judaism. Jesus, through this healing incident, tried to reach their hearts with the truth of who He was. This truth, and this truth alone, could save them. The tragedy of their situation was that they were so deeply entrenched within their own belief system most of them could not even entertain the idea they could possibly be wrong. "The Jews had already agreed that if any one should confess Him to be Christ, he should be put out of the synagogue." This prejudice, or prejudgment, blinded their minds. It appears from time to time, however, there were some of the Jewish rulers who, at least for a period of time, seemed almost persuaded to believe in Jesus as the Messiah. What kept the majority back? Several times in this book I have referred to the fact that our own belief system is often our greatest hindrance to the openness essential to the discovery of new truth. The Jews had their system, which in itself was a major factor in their inability to believe. Yet there was more to their system than just what they considered to be "truth." It provided them with a complete lifestyle, a social community, power, wealth, and influence. To break out of the system was costly in many ways. Thus the books of Hebrews and First Peter were written to encourage Jewish Christians who had paid the price and had broken out of the Jewish system. These people had lost their wealth, their lands, their friends, and their influence. They had nothing left but Jesus—Jesus only! Yet, as Paul so beautifully says,

> I count all things to be loss in view of the surpassing value of knowing Christ Jesus my Lord, for whom I have suffered the loss of all things, and count them but rubbish in order that I may gain Christ and may be found in Him (Phil. 3:8, 9).

Throughout history Christians who have stood for truth, regardless of the consequences, and paid the price for so doing, know that to be found "in Christ" is of greater value even if it means the loss of all other things. Jesus is sufficient.

> Now a second time they called the man who had been blind, and said to him, "Give glory to God; we know that this man is a sinner." He therefore answered, "Whether He is a sinner, I do not know; one thing I do know, that, whereas I was blind, now I see." They said therefore to him, "What did He do to you? How did He open your eyes?" He answered them, "I told you already,

The Paradox of Sabbath Law

and you did not listen; why do you want to hear it again? You do not want to become His disciples too, do you?" (Jn. 9:24–27).

One gets the idea that the Pharisees were struggling in the valley of decision. The evidence before their eyes must have been like sharp needles pricking their consciences. It appears they recognized the far-reaching consequences of the decision which confronted them and they made every effort to find sufficient reason to escape making a decision. They wanted more time. Then, as this formerly blind beggar suggested the idea that perhaps they too were considering becoming disciples of Jesus, they revolted and their decision was made.

And they reviled him, and said, "You are His disciple, but we are disciples of Moses" (Jn. 9:28).

This is a key verse in this chapter and a very important one in our study of the Sabbath. *Here is the confrontation between the old covenant and the new covenant.* This is Moses (Sinai) pitted against Christ. One *cannot* go both directions; either he is a *disciple of Jesus,* or a *disciple of Moses.*[2] In the next few verses we can sense the deep spiritual insight of this formerly blind beggar, and the appalling spiritual blindness of the Pharisees still under the veil of the Torah, who had been confronted with the truth of Jesus and who He was, but had opted to remain disciples of Moses.

The Pharisees answered this new disciple of Jesus with,

"We know that God has spoken to Moses; but as for this man, we do not know where He is from." The man answered and said to them, "Well, here is an amazing thing, that you do not know where He is from and yet He opened my eyes" (Jn. 9:29, 30).

To fully understand what is taking place here we must look at a passage in John 7 which immediately follows the discussion of the Sabbath incident regarding the healing of the man at the pool of Bethesda.

---

[2] Moses stands for the whole law.

> Therefore some of the people of Jerusalem were saying, "Is this not the man whom they are seeking to kill? And look, He is speaking publicly, and they are saying nothing to Him. The rulers do not really know that this is the Christ, do they? However we know where this man is from; but whenever the Christ may come, no one knows where He is from" (Jn. 7:25-27).

This new disciple of Jesus picks up the foolishness of the people's reasoning. In one incident the Jewish leaders reject Jesus because they know He is from Galilee and state that when the Messiah comes they will not know where He is from. The next moment they reject Jesus as the Christ because they do not know where he is from! Yet He is opening the eyes of the blind; doing the very things Messiah was to do!

This "seeing" disciple of Jesus continues to witness to the learned, but "blind," Pharisees, bringing insight after insight which must have hit their spiritual pride like burning arrows.

> We know that God does not hear sinners; but if any one is God-fearing, and does His will, He hears him. Since the beginning of time it has never been heard that any one opened the eyes of a person born blind. If this man were not from God, He could do nothing (Jn. 9:31-33).

This was a powerful argument which could not be answered. The credentials of Jesus were founded in His kingdom work, His Jubilee ministry. The Pharisees had no answer, and, utterly humiliated by the logic and spiritual insight of this new disciple of Jesus, they answer, "You were born entirely in sins, and are you teaching us?" And they put him out (Jn. 9:32-34).

The Pharisees did to this new disciple of Christ what religious (in contrast to truly Christian) leaders have done throughout the centuries to those who have taken a stand for truth. They "put him out." His parents had avoided speaking in favor of Jesus so they would not be disfellowshipped,

The Paradox of Sabbath Law

> For the Jews had *already agreed,* that if any one should confess Him to be Christ, he should be put out of the synagogue (Jn. 9:22).

Consider carefully the Sabbath theology taught, the depth of meaning uncovered, the love expressed, and the needs met in the next few verses. These verses are the high point of our study on Jesus and the Sabbath. They lead us to the true redemption and "rest"—yes, here we come to Sabbath in Christ.

> Jesus heard that they had put him out; and finding him, He said, "Do you believe in the Son of Man?" He answered and said, "And who is He, Lord, that I may believe in Him?" Jesus said to him, "You have both seen Him, and He is the one who is talking with you." And he said, "Lord, I believe." And he worshipped Him (Jn. 9:35–38).

Jesus not only knew that His new disciple had been disfellowshipped, but He cared. He still knows and cares. Jesus set out to find this man so young in his newfound faith. I am reminded of the parable of the lost sheep in Luke 15. The Good Shepherd searched for the lost sheep *until* He found him. He still does. Jesus gave this young-in-faith disciple an opportunity to receive a further revelation of truth. The new disciple's understanding of Christ at this point was very limited. He understood Christ to be "a prophet" (Jn. 9:17). Yet, with his limited knowledge of Jesus, his uneducated background, this previously blind beggar who had no ax of self-interest to grind, openly confessed himself on the side of Jesus. His only motive was that of gratitude. As he began to move out in his limited knowledge and experience, Jesus met him and said, "Do you believe in the Son of Man?" Today that same Son of Man still gives opportunity for greater revelations of truth to those who walk in the full knowledge of what they have already received, no matter how limited that truth is. Jesus did not condemn or make fun of this young disciple's lack of insight. By asking this man if he believed, it appears Jesus expected His new disciple to recognize Him as the

Son of Man, but the man answered, "Who is He, Lord, that I may believe?" I thank God that He still treats with kindness and patience those of us who seem to be so dull of hearing and so slow to receive spiritual insight. Jesus gave His new disciple a revelation of truth which met his greatest need: *He revealed Himself.* Today the greatest longing in the heart of God is still to make Himself known to us. It is only His presence which will bring redemption and spiritual rest and meet the real need of our heart. John records the simplicity, and workability, of the new covenant gospel. "Lord, I believe." The new covenant gospel is still simple and it still works. Do you believe? If you do, then the last insight of this passage will be your highest priority, your greatest joy: "and he worshipped Him."

Consider the paradoxical nature of this incident. The Pharisees, who were known to be meticulous observers of old covenant Sabbath laws, *by their meticulous observance of these laws,* rejected the Messiah, to whom these laws pointed. As disciples of Moses, their point of reference and judgment was like a yoke around their neck which bound them. In striving hard to obtain, they failed. The blind beggar, on the other hand, did not strive. Rather his healing, his insight, his acceptance, his restored relationship to God and intimate, face-to-face fellowship with Jesus were the result of nothing but God's sovereign grace! *Here, in stark contrast, are the principles of the two covenants operating side by side. If one is to be a disciple of Jesus, he cannot, at the same time, be a disciple of Moses.*

> But to this day whenever Moses is read, a veil lies over their heart; but whenever a man turns to the Lord, the veil is taken away (2 Cor. 3:15,16).

Here, too, is a great paradox. As mentioned before, the Pharisees were strict Sabbath keepers. They followed the old covenant Sabbath laws to the letter. Yet in following these laws they completely missed the redemption and true "rest" to which the Sabbath laws pointed. On the other hand, this "sin blinded"[3] beggar, redeemed from the curse of sin and saved by faith, entered *without works* into the true "rest" of God.

Whether one draws the purpose of the Sabbath from the commandments as listed in Exodus (rest) or Deuteronomy (redemption), there is no question that Jesus fulfilled that purpose.

With these insights let us come back to the passage in John. This previously blind beggar has become a "new creation."

> If any man is in Christ, he is a new creation; the old things passed away; behold, new things have come (2 Cor. 5:17).

This child of God is now a new man: healed, washed, found, accepted, and worshipping in intimate, face-to-face fellowship with none other than the Creator Himself. Here is true redemption; here is the true "rest of God" to which the old covenant Sabbath laws pointed. No work was done by this man! All was of grace. This blind man was found, healed, washed, and accepted, by the "work" of Jesus on that Sabbath day. This redeemed man entered into the "rest" which "remains" for the one who believes! Jesus' "work" on that Sabbath brought redemption and Eden's "rest" to this man.

> And Jesus said, "For judgment I came into this world, that those who do not see may see; and that those who see may become blind." Those of the Pharisees who were with Him heard these things, and said to Him, "We are not blind too, are we?" Jesus said to them, "If you were blind, you would have no sin; but now you say, 'We see,' your sin remains" (Jn. 9:39–41).

These are sad, tragic words of Jesus. Yet they serve as a solemn warning to those who are deeply entrenched within their belief system and believe they have the truth and are the true people of God. They are fearful words for those

---

[3] It was commonly believed that this deformity was caused by sin. See John 9:1, 2

who are still bound to Sinai for their reference point of life and judgment.

Chapter Summary

1. The "work" of Jesus was kingdom work—Jubilee ministry.
2. The disciples of Jesus were included in this urgent "work."
3. It appears that Jesus again, openly and intentionally, healed in such a way that caused the Jewish leaders to believe He had violated old covenant Sabbath law.
4. The Pharisees, when confronted with the truth of Jesus, rejected Him *because* they were blinded by their reference point of judgment: Sinaitic laws.
5. This chapter points out in stark contrast the two systems: Christ (the new covenant) and Moses (the old covenant).
6. This incident is paradoxical in nature.
    a. The Pharisees cast this man out of their fellowship.
    b. Jesus took this man into fellowship with Himself.
    c. The Pharisees meticulously observed the Sabbath laws but totally missed the redemption and real rest to which these laws pointed.
    d. The blind beggar, who did not work but was saved by grace, was redeemed from sin and entered into the true "rest of God": intimate, face-to-face fellowship with the Creator.
    e. The learned Pharisees, who almost knew the Old Testament law by heart, seemed to be steeped in spiritual blindness because the veil of Sinai was still over their eyes.
    f. The previously blind beggar, who knew little, if any, of the law, and was considered to be totally born in sin, showed deep spiritual insight.

The Paradox of Sabbath Law

    g. The "work" of Jesus was to bring redemption and establish His "rest."
    h. According to the Jews, Jesus broke the Sinaitic Sabbath, but in doing so He brought redemption and true "rest."
7. Jesus pronounced a solemn warning upon those who say "they see" (know the truth) yet in reality they are "blind" and "remain" in sin.
8. The underlying dynamic of Jesus was to move the reference point of the Pharisees from Sinai to Himself.
9. The way Jesus related to the Sabbath indicates that He considered the Sabbath to be a ritual or ceremonial law that pointed forward to the rest and redemption He would bring.

On the Sabbath day they went into the synagogue

CHAPTER THIRTEEN

SABBATH IN ACTS

This chapter will examine all the Sabbath incidents in the book of Acts to discover what, if anything, is *taught* regarding the Sabbath and what can be learned by the Sabbath *behavior* of the early believers. It is important to look carefully at each Sabbath episode.

Acts 13:13–52

> But going on from Perga, they arrived at Pisidian Antioch, and on the Sabbath day they went into the synagogue and sat down. And after the reading of the Law and the Prophets the synagogue officials sent to them, saying, "Brethren, if you have any word of exhortation for the people, say it." And Paul stood up, and motioning with his hand, he said…(Acts 13:14–16).

At this point Paul begins a sermon which continues through verse 41. It becomes immediately evident that Paul's subject matter is not the Sabbath, but the good news of Christ. Paul does, however, make an incidental reference to the Sabbath.

> For those who live in Jerusalem, and their rulers, recognizing neither Him nor the utterances of the prophets which are read every *Sabbath,* fulfilled these by condemning Him (Acts 13:27).

At the conclusion of Paul's exhortation Luke records,

And as Paul and Barnabas were going out, the people kept begging that these things might be spoken to them the next *Sabbath*. Now when the meeting of the synagogue had broken up, many of the Jews and the God-fearing proselytes followed Paul and Barnabas, who, speaking to them, were urging them to continue in the grace of God. And the next *Sabbath* nearly the whole city assembled to hear the word of God. But when the Jews saw the crowds, they were filled with jealousy, and began contradicting the things spoken by Paul, and were blaspheming. And Paul and Barnabas spoke out boldly and said, "It was necessary that the word of God should be spoken to you first; since you repudiate it, and judge yourselves unworthy of eternal life, behold, we are turning to the Gentiles" (Acts 13:42–46).

At this word the Gentiles rejoiced (Acts 13:48), and the gospel spread through the whole region (Acts 13:49). The Jews then instigated a persecution against Paul and Barnabas, and drove them out of their district (Acts 13:50).

This event was early in Paul's ministry. These Sabbath meetings were held in a Jewish synagogue, for the benefit of a Jewish congregation; they were not meetings of Christian believers.

Summary of Acts 13:13–52

1. Nothing is taught regarding the seventh-day Sabbath.
2. These two Sabbath meetings were held in a Jewish synagogue.
3. Paul and Barnabas went to this synagogue to preach the gospel of Christ because they felt the Jews should hear it first.
4. The only mention of the Sabbath in Paul's sermon is in connection with the Jews at Jerusalem who rejected the very Christ whom they read about in the Prophets each Sabbath.

Acts 16:11–40

Paul and his companions came to Philippi, where they stayed for some days.

Sabbath in Acts

> And on the *Sabbath* day we went outside the gate to a river side, where we were supposing that there was a place of prayer; and we sat down and began speaking to the women who had assembled. And a certain woman named Lydia, from the city of Thyatira, a seller of purple fabrics, a worshipper of God, was listening; and the Lord opened her heart to respond to the things spoken by Paul. And when she and her household had been baptized, she urged us, saying, "If you have judged me to be faithful to the Lord, come into my house and stay" (Acts 16:12–15).

Following this the narrative tells of Paul casting out a spirit of divination from a certain slave girl. The masters of this girl, having now lost their source of monetary profit, complained to the authorities regarding Paul and his companions. This in turn led to their beating, arrest and incarceration. While in jail, there was an earthquake which resulted in the jailer's conversion. After the jailer and his house were baptized, Paul was freed, spoke briefly with the new converts in the home of Lydia, and then left town.

Summary of Acts 16:11–40

1. Nothing is taught regarding the Sabbath.
2. On the Sabbath day Paul and his companions sought out a gathering of Jewish proselytes (God worshippers) who met for prayer by a river side. (Apparently there was no synagogue in Philippi at that time.)
3. Paul's message was the gospel of Christ.
4. Paul preached the gospel to the jailer and baptized his whole household.

Acts 17:1–9

> Now when they had traveled through Amphipolis and Apollonia, they came to Thessalonica, where there was a *synagogue of the Jews*. And according to Paul's custom, he went to them, and for *three Sabbaths reasoned with them* from the Scriptures, explaining and giving evidence that the Christ had to suffer and rise again from the dead, and saying, "This Jesus whom I am proclaiming to you is the Christ" (Acts. 17:1–3).

A few of the Jews, a "great multitude of the God-fearing Greeks and a number of the leading women" accepted the gospel. The Jews created such a disturbance that Paul and his companions had to leave town.

Summary of Acts 17:1–9

1. Nothing is taught regarding the Sabbath.
2. The message of Paul was the gospel of Jesus.
3. It was Paul's custom to go to the Jewish synagogue on the Sabbath and from the Scriptures seek to persuade those present that Jesus was the Christ.
4. Paul "reasoned" with the Jews here for three Sabbaths.

Acts 18:1–11

In this section we find Paul coming to the city of Corinth.

> And he was reasoning in the synagogue every Sabbath and trying to persuade Jews and Greeks (Acts 18:4).

Soon, however, the Jews began to resist his efforts.

> And when they resisted and blasphemed, he shook out his garments and said to them, "Your blood be upon your own heads, I am clean; from now on I shall go to the Gentiles." And he departed from there and went to the house of a certain man named Titus Justus, a worshipper of God, whose house was next to the synagogue. And Crispus, the leader of the synagogue, believed in the Lord with all his household, and many of the Corinthians when they heard were believing and being baptized (Acts 18:6–8).

God gave Paul a vision encouraging him to keep on speaking about Christ, so Paul

> ...settled there a year and six months, teaching the word of God among them (Acts 18:11).

Some have used this passage to prove Paul "kept" seventy-eight Sabbaths while in Corinth. To do this they read verse 4, which says that Paul was in the synagogue "every" Sabbath. Then they read verse 11, which states Paul stayed in Corinth a year and six months. Every Sabbath for a year and six months equals seventy-eight Sabbaths that Paul kept.

However, a careful study of this passage makes it clear that this argument and resulting conclusion are in error. First, "every Sabbath", cannot refer to the whole time Paul was in Corinth since verse 7 shows that Paul was forced to leave the synagogue and go to a house next door. So he reasoned with the Jews *in their synagogue* only three weeks. He did stay there a year and six months, but these facts alone neither support nor deny his Sabbath keeping.

In Acts 19 we have a similar account of Paul's ministry both in and out of the synagogue.

> And he entered the synagogue and continued speaking out boldly for three months, reasoning and persuading them about the kingdom of God. But when some were becoming hardened and disobedient, speaking evil of the Way before the multitude, he withdrew from them and took away the disciples, reasoning *daily* in the school of Tyrannus (Acts 19:8, 9).

When Paul was forced to leave the Jewish synagogue, where it is assumed he met on Sabbath, he then had *daily* meetings in the School of Tyrannus.

Summary of Acts 18:1–11

1. Nothing is taught regarding the Sabbath.
2. Paul's message was to convince those present that Jesus was the Christ.
3. We know that Paul was "reasoning in the synagogue every Sabbath," but the fact that he was forced to leave the synagogue, apparently quite early in his stay in Corinth, shows that this "synagogue" practice did not necessarily continue for the full year and a half.

Incidental References to the Sabbath in Acts

Acts 1:12

> Then they [the disciples] returned to Jerusalem from the mount called Olivet, which is near Jerusalem, a Sabbath day's journey away.

Here, Luke, the writer of Acts, is describing how far the mount of Olives is from Jerusalem by the use of the term "a Sabbath day's journey."

Acts 15:21

This verse mentions the Sabbath in connection with the Jerusalem Council. The context of this verse is the final decision of the Council, which stated that the Gentiles did not have to keep the law of Moses, rather they were only required to

> ...abstain from things contaminated by idols and from fornication and from what is strangled and from blood (Acts 15:20).

Then follows this verse,

> For Moses from ancient generations has in every city those who preach him, since he is read in the synagogues every Sabbath (Acts 15:21).

It is clear these Sabbath meetings where Moses was read were *Jewish* meetings. Note that (1) they are places which have been established "from ancient generations," (2) they are synagogues," (3) they are "in every city." These characteristics would not fit the early Christian assemblies, many of which met in homes (cf. Rom. 16:5, 1 Cor. 16:19, Col. 4:15, Phile. 1:2). Of greater interest to our study is the fact that it is in these *Jewish synagogues* where Moses is read every Sabbath.

Chapter Summary

1. In all the Sabbath meetings recorded in the Book of Acts, *not once* is the Sabbath the point of discussion. Nothing is taught regarding the Sabbath.
2. In *every* Sabbath incident recorded in the Book of Acts Paul is seeking to persuade the Jews, and others, that Jesus is the Christ. The subject of the teaching is *always* the gospel.
3. *Every* Sabbath incident recorded in the Book of Acts is in connection with a Jewish meeting. All but one are in a Jewish synagogue, the one exception being the meeting by a river side in Philippi where there was no synagogue. Here again, it was a meeting place for "God-worshippers"—a name used to describe converts to Judaism.
4. When going to a new city it was Paul's custom, or method of approach, to first go to the Jewish synagogue and "reason with them from the Scriptures." He would do this every Sabbath until the Jews threw him out, usually only two or three weeks, then he would direct his ministry to the Gentiles.
5. It is in the Jewish synagogues where Moses is read every Sabbath.

Things which are a mere shadow

CHAPTER FOURTEEN

SABBATH IN THE EPISTLES

In the last chapter we studied about Paul and his companions as they went to Jewish synagogues to preach Christ. We found that in every instance their Sabbath activities were in connection with Jewish services. In contrast, this chapter deals with letters written to Christian churches. We will now study three key verses that relate to the Sabbath (Colossians 2:16, 17; Galatians 4:10, 11; Romans 14:5, 6), examine Paul's method of evangelism, and then consider "the missing controversy."

Colossians 2:16, 17

> Therefore let no one act as your judge in regard to food or drink or in respect to a festival or a new moon or a *Sabbath day*—things which are a mere shadow of what is to come; but the substance belongs to Christ.

Unlike the references to the Sabbath in the book of Acts, this passage is a direct teaching on the subject of the Sabbath. In this verse Paul includes the Sabbath with other old covenant ritual convocations such as new moon celebrations and festivals. This verse has been vigorously debated and the debate often centers on three key areas. (1) What does Paul mean by "Sabbath day"? Is he referring to the weekly Sabbath, the seven seasonal sabbaths such as the Passover, etc., or is he addressing the problem of Sabbath perversion? (2) What are the "elementary principles" Paul mentions in Colossians 2:8, 20? Is he referring to a rudiment of some syncretistic heresy that the Colossians had fallen into or is he referring to old covenant convocations or perhaps both? (3) How are we to understand "Let no man judge you" (Col. 2:16)? Were certain members of the Colossian church keeping certain celebrations while *others* judged them? Or were the ones *practicing* the celebrations judging the ones who did not?

Let us first study the context, then we will define "elementary principles" and "Sabbath day(s)" and then draw some conclusions regarding the ones who were judging and how all of this relates to our study of the Sabbath.

Local context

A quick scan of Colossians 2:8–23 will help us in our interpretation.

> See to it that no one take you captive through philosophy and empty deception, according to the tradition of men, according to *the elementary principles of the world,* rather than according to Christ. For in Him all the fullness of Deity dwells in bodily form, and *in Him you have been made complete,* and He is the head over all rule and authority; and in Him you were also circumcised with a circumcision made without hands, in the removal of the body of the flesh *by the circumcision of Christ; having been buried with Him in baptism,* in which you were also raised up with Him through faith in the working of God, who raised Him from the dead. And when you were dead in your transgressions and the uncircumcision of your flesh, He made you alive together with Him, having forgiven us all our transgressions, *having canceled out the certificate of debt consisting of decrees against us and which was hostile to us; and He has taken it out of the way, having nailed it to the cross.* When He had disarmed the rulers and authorities, He made a public display of them, having triumphed over them through Him. *Therefore let no one act as your judge in regard to food or drink or in respect to a festival or a new moon or a Sabbath day—things which are a mere shadow of what is to come; but the substance belongs to Christ.* Let no one keep defrauding you of your prize by delighting in self-abasement and the worship of the angels, taking his stand on visions he has seen, inflated without cause by his fleshly mind, and not holding fast the

> Head, from whom the entire body, being supplied and held together by the joints and ligaments, grows with a growth which is from God.
>
> If you have *died with Christ to the elementary principles of the world,* why, as if you were living in the world, do you submit yourself to decrees, such as, "Do not handle, do not taste, do not touch!" (which all refer to things destined to perish with the using)—in accordance with the commandments and teachings of men? These are matters which have, to be sure, the appearance of wisdom in self-made religion and self-abasement and severe treatment of the body, but are of no value against fleshly indulgence.

In Colossians 2 Paul is writing about the completeness of Christ and His sacrifice. In verse 8 Paul begins by warning his readers against several things which can take them away from this completeness and thus make them captive to discouragement and loss.

"Elementary principles of the world"

> See to it that no one take you captive through philosophy and empty deception, according to the tradition of men, according to the *elementary principles of the world,* rather than according to Christ (Col. 2:8).

What does Paul mean by the "elementary principles of the world"? Notice how he uses this term (identical in Greek) elsewhere.

> Now I say, as long as the heir is a child, he does not differ at all from a slave although he is owner of everything, but he is under guardians and managers until the date set by the father. So also we, while we were children, *were held in bondage under the elementary things of the world.* But when the fullness of time came, God sent forth His Son, born of a woman, born under the Law, in order that He might redeem those who *were under the Law,* that we might receive the adoption as sons (Gal. 4:1–5).

In the above passage Paul says that before the coming of Christ the Jews were "held in bondage under the elementary things of the world." He explains what he means by this term when he says that God sent forth His Son to redeem "those who were under the Law." Here he defines the "elementary things of the world" as the old covenant law.

In Hebrews 5 this term is also used. Here again "the elementary principles" are "the oracles of God"—*the old covenant writings.* In explaining how Christ is a better High Priest than the priests of the old covenant the writer says:

> For though by this time you ought to be teachers, you have need again for someone to teach you *the elementary principles of the oracles of God,* and you have come to need milk and not solid food (Heb. 5:12).

In Colossians 2:20,21 Paul speaks about *dying* to the elementary principles of the world.

> If you *have died with Christ to the elementary principles of the world,* why, as if you were living in the world, do you submit yourself to decrees such as, "Do not handle, do not taste, do not touch!"

In Romans 7 Paul writes,

> Therefore, my brethren, you also were made to *die to the Law* through the body of Christ, that you might be joined to another, to Him who was raised from the dead, that we might bear fruit for God (Rom. 7:4).

In Colossians Paul speaks of *dying* with Christ to the *elementary principles* of the world; in Romans He speaks of *dying* to the *law* through Christ. Again Paul uses "elementary principles" in connection with the old covenant law.

Since Paul uses the term "elementary principles" to apply to old covenant law on several other occasions, we can and should use this meaning in Colossians unless the context forbids it. The Colossian heresy doubtless included more than this, but old covenant teachings certainly formed a significant part of it.

You are complete in Christ

> For in Him all the fullness of Deity dwells in bodily form, and *in Him you have been made complete,* and He is the head over all rule and authority (Col. 2:9, 10).

This is Paul's central argument. He courageously defends the position that Jesus *alone* is the testing truth for salvation. He is forthright in stating that the believer in Christ is *complete*. This is the truth he is defending against those who are saying, "Yes, Paul, Jesus is the truth, *but* 'It is necessary to circumcise them, and to direct them to observe the Law of Moses'!" (Acts 15:5) Remember, that the reason circumcision is often mentioned is that it served as the entrance sign into the old covenant community. It stood for *all* old covenant law.

Circumcision ⟶ *baptism*

> And *in Him you were also circumcised* with a circumcision made without hands, in the removal of the body of the flesh *by the circumcision of Christ; having been buried with Him in baptism,* in which you were also raised up with Him through faith in the working of God, who raised Him from the dead. And when you were dead in your transgressions and the uncircumcision of you flesh, He made you alive together with Him, having forgiven us all our transgressions (Col. 2:11–13).

In these passages Paul takes the old covenant sign of circumcision and shows how Christ *symbolically fulfilled* this concept and then links *circumcision with baptism*. This is no accident! As circumcision was the *entrance sign* into the old covenant community for the sons of Israel, so baptism is the *entrance sign* into the new covenant community.

Circumcision not only served as the entrance sign to the old covenant, Paul shows how it *also pointed forward to Christ,* yet it does *not* continue as a sign in the new covenant. Rather, in the new covenant, circumcision is *transformed* into baptism which *replaces* circumcision as the entrance sign of the covenant. This shows that when ritual law meets its fulfillment it no longer serves a useful purpose.

Decree nailed to the cross

> Having canceled out the certificate of debt consisting of decrees against us and which was hostile to us; and He has taken it out of the way, having *nailed it to the cross*. When He had disarmed the rulers and authorities, He made a public display of them, having triumphed over them through Him (Col. 2:14, 15).

What was the "certificate of debt" or the "decrees" which were nailed to the cross? In context, Paul has been speaking about the old covenant. Was the old covenant "against us"? We should remember from our study of the old covenant that one of its functions was to act as a "testimony" against Israel if they sinned.

> Take this book of the law and place it beside the ark of the covenant of the Lord your God, that it may remain there as a witness *against* you (Deut. 31:26).

The cursings associated with the broken law *and* the ability of the law to condemn were both taken away when Christ was nailed to the cross.

> There is therefore now no condemnation for those who are in Christ Jesus (Rom. 8:1).

Other hang-ups

According to Paul *one way* the Christians at Colossae could lose the precious freedom of being complete in Christ was to place themselves back under old covenant law. In Colossians 2:18–23 he speaks of *other ways* they could do the same thing. Here he mentions such things as worship of angels, self-made religion, self-abasement, severe treatment of the body, etc., all of no value. Paul may have reference here to certain strict sects of Judaism, such as the Essenes, who practiced extreme self-discipline, or perhaps to certain pre-gnostic influences that were invading the Colossian church.

Sabbath in the Epistles

Sabbath days

The word for Sabbath in Colossians 2:16 is plural in Greek and could be translated "Sabbath days." However, the fact that it is plural does *not* mean it cannot have a singular meaning. For example, in *all* the following passages the word "Sabbath" is plural in Greek but the context requires a singular meaning.

> "Jesus went on the Sabbath through the grainfields" (Mt. 12:1), "Is it lawful on the Sabbath to do good?" (Lk. 6:9), "On the Sabbath day we went outside the gate to a river side" (Acts 16:13).

In these verses it is clear that the Greek word for "Sabbath days" *must* be translated with a singular meaning. One cannot, therefore, say that because in Colossians 2:16, 17 the word for Sabbath is plural in Greek it must therefore not refer to the seventh-day Sabbath. In many other New Testament references the plural Greek word for Sabbath is translated as the seventh-day Sabbath.

Weekly or seasonal Sabbaths?

Is the Sabbath day mentioned in verse 16 the seventh-day Sabbath or does it refer to the yearly, seasonal Sabbaths?

> Therefore, let no one act as your judge in regard to food or drink or in respect to a festival or a new moon or a Sabbath day (Col. 2:16).

From the local context it is evident that the items in Colossians 2:16 are derived from the old covenant, but we cannot, from the local context, make a definitive conclusion whether or not the Sabbath is the weekly Sabbath or the yearly seasonal feasts such as Passover, the Day of Atonement, etc. However, the Old Testament usages of the terms listed in Colossians 2:16 (food, drink, festival, new moon, and Sabbath) make it clear beyond question that the weekly Sabbath is here in view.

Old Testament context

In the chapter, Shadows of Hope, We discovered that when these ritual laws of the old covenant were mentioned together, *never* are the seasonal feasts called "sabbaths" leaving the word "Sabbath" for the seventh-day Sabbath to avoid confusion. We also saw that when the old covenant convocations such as Sabbaths, new moons, festivals (yearly feasts), etc., were mentioned, they were listed in either ascending or descending order.

> days
> months
> seasons
> or
> seasons
> months
> days

The following references are *all* the verses from the Old Testament which use the term Sabbath and two or more of the *key terms* mentioned in Colossians 2:16. In each verse you can readily see "Sabbath" refers to the *weekly* Sabbath, *not* the seasonal, yearly sabbath festivals.

Several of the following passages employ a typical Hebrew literary device known as parallelism. Note how the new moon is *equated* with the *weekly Sabbath*.

> Why will you go to him today? It is neither *new moon* nor *sabbath."* (2 Ki. 4:23).
>
> Thus says the LORD God, "The gate on the inner court facing east shall be shut the six working days; but it shall be opened on the *sabbath day,* and opened on the day of the *new moon*...The people of the land shall also worship the doorway of that gate before the LORD on the *sabbaths* and on the *new moons.* And burnt offerings which the prince shall offer to the LORD on the *sabbath day* shall be six lambs...the grain offering with the lambs...a hin of oil...and on the day of the *new moon*...six lambs, a grain offering...a hin of oil..." (Ez. 46:1, 3–7).

> When will the *new moon* be over so that we may buy grain, and the *sabbath,* that we may open the wheat market? (Amos 8:5).
>
> "And it shall be from *new moon* to *new moon* and from *sabbath* to *sabbath,* all mankind will come to bow down before Me," says the Lord (Isa. 66:23).

In the following quotations carefully note that the seven yearly sabbaths are *never* called "sabbaths" but are always known by other terms such as "annual feasts," "fixed festivals," etc.

> ...and to offer all burnt offerings to the LORD, on the *sabbaths,* the *new moons* and the *fixed festivals* in the number set by the ordinance concerning them, continually before the LORD (1 Chron. 23:31).
>
> ...to burn fragrant incense before Him, and to set out the showbread continually, and to offer burnt offerings morning and evening, on *sabbaths* and on *new moons* and on the *appointed feasts* of the LORD our God, this being required forever in Israel (2 Chron. 2:4).
>
> Then Solomon offered burnt offerings to the LORD according to the daily rule, offering them up by the commandment of Moses, for the *sabbaths,* the *new moons,* and the three *annual feasts*—the *feast of unleavened bread,* the *feast of weeks,* and the *feast of tabernacles* (2 Chron. 8:12, 13).
>
> He also appointed the king's portion of his goods for the burnt offerings, namely, for the morning and evening burnt offerings, and the burnt offerings for the *sabbaths* and for the *new moons* and for the *fixed festivals,* as it is written in the law of the LORD (2 Chron 31:3).
>
> ...for the continual burnt offering, the *sabbaths,* the *new moon,* for the *appointed times*...(Neh. 10:33).
>
> Bring your worthless offerings no longer, their incense is an abomination to Me. *New moon* and *sabbath,* the calling of assemblies—I cannot endure iniquity and the solemn assembly. I hate your *new moon festivals* and your *appointed feasts,* they have become a burden to Me (Isa. 1:13, 14).

Note the close parallel between the following two references and that of Colossians 2:16.

> I will also put an end to all her gaiety, her *feasts,* her *new moons,* her *sabbaths* (Hos. 2:11).

> And it shall be the prince's part to provide the burnt offerings, the grain offerings [*food*], and the drink offerings [*drink*], at the feasts [*festival*], on the *new moons,* and on the *sabbaths,* at all the appointed feasts of the house of Israel (Ez. 45:17).

Samuele Bacchiocchi's attempt to make "Sabbaths" refer to "week-days" is a desperate and futile attempt to avoid the clear implications of this Scripture.[1]

> It is significant that in 59 of 60 occurrences in the NT, Adventists affirm that the [words "Sabbath"] refer to the weekly Sabbath, but in the 60th occurrence they maintain it does not, although all grammatical authors contradict this.[2]

Conclusions

The evidence is weighted *overwhelmingly* in favor of interpreting "Sabbath day" in Colossians 2:16 as the *weekly seventh-day Sabbath* for the following reasons:

First, in the immediate context of Colossians (2:11–13), Paul shows that Jesus symbolically fulfilled the one other sign of the old covenant, circumcision. Elsewhere (Gal. 5:1–6) Paul clearly states that this sign of the old covenant no longer applies to Christians, and he asserts that those who do practice it for *religious* reasons have fallen from grace! Logic would lead us to believe that if *one* of the signs of the old covenant was symbolically fulfilled by Christ and no longer applies, it is very likely the *other* sign of the old covenant (the seventh-day Sabbath) was also symbolically fulfilled by Christ and would no longer apply as a required practice. We will deal more fully with the

---

[1] "The fact that the Galatian list begins with "days" (*hemeras*, plural), suggests the possibility that the "sabbaths" in Colossians may also refer to week-days in general rather than to the seventh-day Sabbath in particular." Samuele Bacchiocchi, *The Sabbath in the New Testament,* (Biblical Perspectives, Berrien Springs, MI, 1990), p. 117.
[2] Walter Martin, *The Kingdom of the Cults,* (Bethany House, Bloomington, MN, 1997), pp. 465–467.

symbolic fulfillment of the Sabbath and the continuing sign of the new covenant in later chapters.

Second, in the Old Testament references which list the terms used in Colossians 2:16, "Sabbath(s)" *always* refers to the weekly Sabbath.

Third, when these terms are listed they are listed in either *ascending* or *descending order*. Thus, in Colossians 2:16 we find "festival (season), new moon (month), sabbath (day)." Since Paul is making use of an established sequence of terms from the Old Testament, one would expect the meaning to be the same.

Fourth, in the Old Testament references which list the terms found in Colossians 2:16, the yearly sabbaths (Passover, Tabernacles, Day of Atonement, etc.) are *never* called "sabbaths" but *always* called "fixed festivals," "appointed feasts," "annual feasts," etc. While some of the yearly "appointed feasts" are *elsewhere* said to be "a sabbath of rest" (Lev. 23), they are *not* called by the term "sabbaths," probably to avoid confusion with the weekly Sabbath. For this reason the term "festival" in Colossians 2:16 *must* refer to the annual "sabbaths," leaving the word "Sabbath day" for the weekly Sabbath.

Fifth, in the old covenant listing of the appointed times of the Lord, the seventh-day Sabbath is *closely associated* with new moons and the other items mentioned in Colossians 2:16 such as "food" and "drink."

Sixth, to hold that "Sabbath(s)" in Colossians 2:16 must refer to yearly Sabbaths is contrary to the weight of evidence. It is also contrary to the immediate context where Paul is writing about the other sign of the old covenant: circumcision.

Seventh, it makes Paul's writing redundant. One must interpret "festivals" as the yearly sabbaths, and then turn around and *also* interpret "Sabbath day" as the yearly sabbaths.

Eighth, it destroys the natural order which is so apparent in the other biblical listings of these terms. It is contrary to the unity of the old covenant, where everything in the old covenant is related to everything else within the old covenant.

We must conclude, then, that the Sabbath mentioned in Colossians 2:16 is indeed the seventh-day Sabbath.

Let no one judge you...

To which group in Colossae did Paul write, "Let no one judge you"? From the context of Colossians it is my conclusion that the ones doing the judging were the very ones who were practicing the old covenant convocations and certain aberrations of Christianity. Therefore Paul says to those who were being urged to practice these things,

> ...let no one act as your judge in regard to food or drink or in respect to a festival or a new moon or a Sabbath day—things which are a mere shadow of what is to come; but the substance belongs to Christ. Let no one keep defrauding you of your prize by delighting in self-abasement...(Col. 2:16–18).

Some have argued that the "Sabbaths" in Colossians 2:16 were perversions of the weekly Sabbath[3] or were part of a syncretistic heresy.[4] However, the evidence is weighted

---

[3] "But what is clear is the fact that the Sabbath observance in the apostle's mind is that connected with the perversion, not the fulfillment of the fourth commandment." Desmond Ford, *The Forgotten Day*, p. 105.

[4] "Christians presumably were led to believe that by submitting to these ascetic practices, they were not surrendering their faith in Christ, but rather they were receiving added protections and were assured of full access to the divine fullness. This bare outline suffices to show that the Sabbath is mentioned not in the context of a direct discussion on the nature of the law, but rather in the context of syncretistic beliefs and practices advocated by the Colossian "philosophers."...Paul's warning against the "regulations" of the false teachers, can hardly be interpreted as a condemnation of the Mosaic laws regarding food and festivals, since what the Apostle condemns is not the teachings of Moses but their perverted use by the Colossian false teachers. A *precept* is not nullified by the condemnation of its *perversion*." Samuele Bacchiocchi, *The Sabbath in the New Testament*, p. 110.

heavily against these arguments for several reasons. First, if the problem in Colossae was a perversion of the weekly Sabbath and Paul was seeking to correct this perversion he certainly missed his opportunity, for he never mentions anything about Sabbath reformation either here or in any of his epistles to young Christian churches. Second, Paul states in the local context (Col. 2:17) that these old covenant convocations (festivals, new moons, and Sabbaths) were a *shadow* of things to come. It is clear he has reference to these convocations as pointing forward to Christ. If Paul were directing his comments to a *perversion* or to some *syncretistic heresy* he could not at the same time call it a shadow of Christ.

Implications

If we accept that the seventh-day Sabbath *is* intended by Paul in Colossians 2:16, then what is he saying and how does this affect those who continue to observe the seventh-day Sabbath as a necessary Christian duty?

First, Paul's comments regarding the other convocations of the old covenant, such as new moon celebrations and the annual feasts, also apply to the seventh-day Sabbath. He, like the old covenant writers, considered *all* these convocations as *inseparable*. They were all ritual laws pointing forward to Christ. This is especially true since in verse 17 he says that these are a mere shadow and he makes no distinction between the first two terms and the third. The Greek, referring back to the three terms, literally reads, "which things are a shadow", linking them inseparably together.

Second, he tells the Christians they should allow no one to judge them regarding the Sabbath. The context makes it clear that Paul is against those who are trying to force the Colossians to keep the Sabbath and other old covenant convocations. They are to allow no one to make them feel guilty for *not* observing these.

Third, the observance of the Sabbath and other ceremonies in old covenant times was meant to point forward to Christ. They were a *mere shadow* of what was to come. As a shadow they lose their significance in the presence of the reality to which they pointed. We saw this principle worked out with Jesus and the Pharisees. The ritual laws of Sabbath were designed to point forward to Christ who brings true rest and redemption. Yet when these ritual laws were understood by the Pharisees to be required moral laws, they actually kept the Jewish leaders from accepting their Messiah!

Fourth—and here is the heart of Paul's argument in Colossians 2—*any* practice which seeks to add to the completeness the believer already has in Christ only undermines that relationship and the believer's assurance. "...Things which are a mere shadow of what is to come; but the substance belongs to Christ" (Col. 2:17). The Greek literally reads, "but the body is of the Christ." Christ, and Christ alone, is the "body" in which dwells *our complete righteousness*. Anytime the Christian seeks to add to that "body of righteousness," he is saying that Christ's righteousness is insufficient and he undermines his own standing with God. The good news of the gospel is that we are complete *in Him!*

Galatians 4:9–11

> But now that you have come to know God, or rather to be known by God, how is it that you turn back again to the *weak* and *worthless elemental things,* to which you desire to be *enslaved* all over again? You observe *days* and *months* and *seasons* and *years*. I fear for you, that perhaps I have labored over you in vain.

To understand these verses correctly we must again see them in their context. The central issue in the book of Galatians is the old covenant law and its relationship to righteousness for the Christian. There were some in the

Galatian church who were teaching that Christians must observe the old covenant law.

> Tell me, you who want to be under law, do you listen to the law (Gal. 4:21)?

Paul's answer to these false teachers is very clear. We will discuss more fully Paul's argument in relationship to the law in subsequent chapters; nevertheless for now note his clear, powerful statements regarding old covenant law.

> Therefore the Law has become our tutor to lead us to Christ, that we may be justified by faith. But now that faith has come, we are no longer under a tutor (Gal. 3:24, 25).

Paul likens the law to a tutor and then in the next verse says we are no longer under a tutor. Christians are no longer under old covenant law. Nothing could be stated more clearly.

With this context clearly in mind, look again at our passage.

Days, months, seasons, and years

> But now that you have come to know God, or rather to be known by God, how is it that you turn back again to the *weak* and *worthless elemental things,* to which you desire to be *enslaved* all over again? You observe *days* and *months* and *seasons* and *years.* I fear for you, that perhaps I have *labored over you in vain* (Gal. 4:9–11).

Notice that Paul again uses the term "elemental things." This is a term he uses elsewhere to refer to old covenant law. What were the *days, months, seasons and years?* The central issue in the church of Galatia was the law and its relationship to righteousness for the Christian. Paul's opponents were seeking to persuade the Galatians to observe the law. This is what Paul is fighting. He shows that the observance of the law as a requirement puts one under a curse for *any* failure to keep it perfectly. In the context of what was taking place in Galatia and with what we have learned from our study of Colossians 2:16, it should be clear that some of the Galatians had been persuaded by the Judaizers to observe the convocations of the old covenant. These days, months, seasons and years can be nothing other than Sabbaths (days), the new moon celebrations (months), the annual feasts (seasons) and sabbatical years (years). Notice these are listed in ascending order as they often are in the Old Testament record.

There are some who attempt to say that the problem with the Galatian teachers was not that they were teaching against the rituals of the old covenant law, rather they were "motivated by superstitious beliefs in astral influences"[5] and were teaching "the perverted use of cultic observations".[6] This, I believe is without foundation. If one reads through the whole book of Galatians at one time, it becomes patently evident that Paul is, indeed, dealing with Judaizers who were promoting the rituals of old covenant law. Paul does, however, equate the false gospel of the Judaizers with witchcraft and in that sense, even paganism.

> You foolish Galatians, who has bewitched you, before whose eyes Jesus Christ was publicly portrayed *as* crucified (Gal. 3:1)?

The reason for this is that the false gospel of Christ *plus* works of the law denies the very heart of the Gospel and places Christianity on the same level as Christless Judaism, even paganism. Because Christ and the Father are One, when the Jews rejected Christ, they in essence, rejected the Father as well.

> ... he who rejects Me rejects the One who sent Me (Lk. 10:16).

Conclusion

We have a clear reference to the seventh-day Sabbath in this passage for the following four reasons. (1) The context of the book of Galatians, including chapter 4, is dealing with those "who want to be under law." (2) Paul's use of

---

[5] Bacchiocchi, *The Sabbath in the New Testament,* p. 122.
[6] *Ibid.*, p. 123.

"elemental things" usually, if not always, refers to that which is contained in the old covenant. (3) The Galatians were observing days, months, seasons, and years, thus placing themselves back under old covenant law. (4) These convocations are listed in ascending order.

Implications

If we accept that the seventh-day Sabbath is here in view, what are the implications? There are many of deep significance. For the Christian, the Sabbath is "weak and worthless" (v. 9). This fits in perfectly with the other ritual laws of the old covenant which were a shadow of Christ. For the Christian the Sabbath is enslaving (v. 9). Some Sabbath-keepers would disagree strongly with this. However, those who have tried to observe the Sabbath *according to biblical guidelines* know that it is nearly impossible to keep the Sabbath. For the Christian, the observance of the Sabbath may undermine his standing in Christ. "I fear for you, that perhaps I have labored over you in vain" (v. 11). For the Christian the Sabbath should be treated just like the new moons, the annual feasts, and the sabbatical years of Judaism—not required or expected practice for new covenant Christians.

We have studied Colossians 2 and Galatians 4; we now turn our attention to Romans 14.

Romans 14:5, 6

> One man regards one day above another, another regards every day like. Let each man be fully convinced in his own mind. He who observes the day, observes it to the Lord, and he who eats, does so for the Lord, for he gives thanks to God; and he who eats not, for the Lord he does not eat, and gives thanks to God.

Are the "days" mentioned here Sabbath days? They probably are but the evidence is not as strong as it is for the passage in Galatians 4:10 and Colossians 2:16.

A different method for a different church

The context of this passage is *apparently* quite different from that in both Galatians and Colossians. However, it may not be as different as it first appears. Rather, what is different may be the way Paul is dealing with the situation. Galatia and Colossae were both largely Gentile churches. It is apparent, however, that some of these believers in Galatia and Colossae had strong Jewish-centered backgrounds. Many of them probably were "God-worshippers" before they became Christians. We noticed in our study of Acts that Paul's evangelistic method was first to go to the synagogue and preach until he was thrown out, then he witnessed to the Gentiles in the area. Because Paul followed this method it appears that many of the early Gentile converts to Christianity had strong old covenant backgrounds because they were often regular attendees at the Jewish synagogues before their conversion. This explains why, in writing to the Gentile churches, this old covenant background is so apparent.

When we come to the church at Rome, however, we have a different situation. In New Testament times more Jews lived in Rome than in Jerusalem. Thus, when Paul wrote to the church at Rome, he was writing to a church which, although it had many Gentile converts, had many members who were from the Hebrew race and were converts from Judaism.

Because of this Paul deals with nearly the same subject matter in the book of Romans—old covenant law—but uses a different method. His treatment of the old covenant law is much softer in Romans than in his letters to Gentile churches because many of his readers in Rome were Jewish nationals.

Diversity in the New Testament church

It appears that the New Testament church was not as uniform in its practices and beliefs as some would like to

Sabbath in the Epistles

think. From Acts and the Epistles of Paul we can subdivide the New Testament church into five groups.

First, there were Jewish Christians who kept the old covenant laws *and* insisted that the Gentile Christians do the same.

> Certain ones of the sect of the Pharisees who had *believed,* stood up, saying, "It is *necessary* to circumcise them, and to direct them to observe the Law of Moses" (Acts 15:5).

Second, there were those who felt the Jewish Christians had to keep the old covenant laws, but the Gentile converts did not.

> You see, brother, how many thousands there are among the *Jews* of those who have *believed,* and they are all zealous for the Law; and they have been told about you, that you are teaching all the *Jews* who are among the Gentiles to forsake Moses, telling them not to circumcise their children nor to walk according to the customs...But concerning the *Gentiles who have believed,* we wrote, having decided [at the Jerusalem Council] that they should abstain from meat sacrificed to idols and from blood and from what is strangled and from fornication (Acts 21:20,21,25).

Third, there were Gentile Christians who were seeking to keep the old covenant law. Paul wrote to these people in Colossae and Galatia.

> Tell me, *you who want to be under law,* do you not listen to the law (Gal. 4:21)?

Fourth, there were Gentiles who did not keep the old covenant law.

> For it seemed good to the Holy Spirit and to us to lay upon you no greater burden than these essentials: that you abstain from things sacrificed to idols and from blood and from things strangled and from fornication; if you keep yourselves free from such things, you will do well. Farewell (Acts 15:28,29).

Fifth, Paul, himself, represents those who were free from old covenant law keeping, yet he had no problem observing the law when in the company of those who kept it *if* it would give him an opportunity to proclaim the gospel to these people.

> And to the Jews I became as a Jew, that I might win Jews; to those who are under the Law, as under the Law, though not being myself under the Law, that I might win those who are under the Law; to those who are without law, as without law, though not being without the law of God but under the law of Christ, that I might win those who are without law (1 Cor. 9:20, 21).

All five of these groups can be found within the New Testament Christian church. They were all considered as "believers" but that does not mean they all had the right theology. Paul was in sharp disagreement with two groups, the first and third, but was much softer in his disagreement with the second group (Christians converted from Judaism) although his disagreement with them is decided and very clear.

The church at Rome

The church at Rome, as stated before, was a mixed group made up of many Jewish Christians as well as Gentile Christians. Doubtless there were many disputes between these two groups. We can understand Paul's treatment of law and observances in the book of Romans only with an understanding of this background.

Let us now come back to the passage in Romans 14. Paul is writing to this mixed church in Rome telling them to quit judging one another. In this chapter he mentioned several points of argument: There were those who ate "all things" and others who ate "vegetables only" (v. 2). There were those who regarded some things as "unclean" and others who did not (vv. 14, 20). There were those who drank wine and others who did not (v. 21). There were those who regarded and observed one day above another, and others who regarded every day alike (vv. 5,6).

It should be noted that Paul's position on several of these arguments is clear even if his approach is tactful and diplomatic. He is always on the side of Christian liberty and he is always against those who would force certain observances. It is the man who is "weak in faith" that eats vegetables only (v. 2). Paul says,

> I know and am convinced in the Lord Jesus that nothing is unclean of itself; but to him who thinks anything to be unclean, to him it is unclean...All things indeed are clean (Rom. 14:14, 20).

Notice that Paul traces the cessation of the clean/unclean issue to Jesus' teaching.

> After He called the crowd to Him again, He began saying to them, "Listen to Me, all of you, and understand: there is nothing outside the man which can defile him if it goes into him; but the things which proceed out of the man are what defile the man. ["If anyone has ears to hear, let him hear."] When he had left the crowd and entered the house, His disciples questioned Him about the parable. And He said to them, "Are you so lacking in understanding also? Do you not understand that whatever goes into the man from outside cannot defile him, because it does not go into his heart, but into his stomach, and is eliminated?" (Thus He declared all foods clean.) (Mk. 7:14–19).

The Jewish Christians, with their background in the old covenant, doubtless were the ones who considered some foods unclean (Lev. 11). Yet Paul clearly says "All things indeed are clean"[7] (Rom. 14:20), showing his disagreement with those who would enforce old covenant law on Christians.

The "days" mentioned in this chapter, that some "regard" and "observe" over other days, are most likely Sabbath days, although the evidence is not conclusive. If, indeed, this passage does refer to Sabbath days then Paul simply says "let each man be fully convinced in His own mind" (v. 5). This is a much softer, gentler answer than he gave to the Colossians and Galatians. And we can see why. There were many Jewish Christians in the Roman church to

---

[7] Paul is dealing with "clean" and "unclean" from a religious, ritual purity point of view.

which Paul was writing who still kept *many* of the old covenant regulations.

It is of utmost importance to note the difference between the situation mentioned in Rome and that of Galatia. In Galatia the false teachers were saying that one must observe the old covenant rituals for salvation, thus compromising the gospel.[8] In Rome, however, some of the believers were passing judgment on each other's "opinions" regarding a number of issues including the observance of "days". The problem in Rome, then, was not one of a compromise of the gospel; rather it was diversity of opinions that caused disunity within the church.

An additional insight that is worthy of our attention has been suggested by Douglas R. de Lacey. He shows that some of the early Greek manuscripts have the word "for" in verse 5. "*For* one man regards one day above another…" If one permits the "for" to have its full force

> We need only allow that the "days" issue had arisen earlier in the history of the Roman church, and had already been solved. And it is not improbable that in such a cosmopolitan milieu this should have been the case. Paul will then be saying to the church that *just as* they accept differing practices over "days" *so also* they should entertain differing practices over "meats." It is then easy to see why "days" form no further part of the discussion.[9]

This interpretation does not change the conclusion that for Paul the mixed body of Christians in Rome was free to decide for itself regarding the value of observing certain "days." It was not a matter of salvation for them, rather one of preference and in choosing their preferences they were not to judge another who had different "opinions" for the sake of Christian love and unity.

---

[8] Gal. 1:6–9.
[9] Douglas R. de Lacey, "The Sabbath/Sunday Question and the Law in the Pauline Corpus", in *From Sabbath to Lord's Day,* p. 182.

Conclusions

The "days" in Romans 14 probably refer to the Sabbath but we cannot be dogmatic in this conclusion.

Implications

If one concludes that Paul is here referring to Sabbath days, what are the implications? Again, there are several. Sabbath observance is a matter of personal conviction. Church unity is more important than arguments over the Sabbath. Paul did not believe Sabbath observance, or nonobservance, was important in itself. There is evidence that Jewish Christians in Rome were the ones who were observing the Sabbath, while the Gentile Christians there regarded "every day alike."

Paul's method of evangelism

> For though I am free from all men, I have made myself a slave to all, that I might win the more. And to the Jews I became as a Jew, that I might win those who are under the Law; to those who are without law, as without law, though not being without the law of God but under the law of Christ, that I might win those who are without law. To the weak I became weak, that I might win the weak; I have become all things to all men, that I may by all means save some. And I do all things for the sake of the gospel, that I may become a fellow-partaker of it (1 Cor. 9:19–23).

Paul's fundamental evangelistic method was to adapt his customs—even his religious practices—to those for whom he was working as long as this did not compromise the simplicity of the gospel of salvation in Christ alone plus nothing. This method, I believe, gives considerable insight as to why we find Paul doing certain things which would otherwise seem to contradict his own teaching.

Paul made some very straight and strong statements about Christians who received circumcision; however, he circumcised one of his Christian helpers.

> Behold I, Paul, say to you that if you receive circumcision, Christ will be of no benefit to you. And I testify again to every

man who receives circumcision, that he is under obligation to keep the whole Law. You have been severed from Christ, you who are seeking to be justified by law; you have fallen from grace (Gal. 5:2–4).

Paul is unyielding when it comes to compromising the gospel. He will not allow anything to be added to faith in Christ alone. Yet when the purity of gospel is not the issue, Paul was very flexible in allowing and even promoting following old covenant observance when to do so would further the spread of the gospel. Note the different approach Paul took in the reference below.

> Paul wanted this man [Timothy] to go with him; and he took him and circumcised him because of the Jews who were in those parts, for they all knew that his father was a Greek (Acts 16:3).

Paul was not teaching one thing and doing another; rather, he was following a basic principle: do all things for the sake of the gospel. In essence what Paul said to the Galatians was that if they were circumcised for religious reasons as a gospel requirement, it was an exercise in futility without giving the slightest advantage in regard to their relationship with Christ. Required circumcision *for Christians* implied that Christ's grace was insufficient for salvation. When Paul had Timothy circumcised it was *not* for religious reasons and it was not part of his gospel message, rather it was because of the *prejudice of the Jews* who were in those parts.

The same principles are at work on several other occasions in Paul's life. He told the Galatians not to observe days, months, seasons and years—the holy times of the old covenant—yet we see him "hurrying to be in Jerusalem, if possible, on the day of Pentecost" (Acts 20:16). On another occasion Paul "had his hair cut, for he was keeping a vow" (Acts 18:18). When returning to Jerusalem after his last missionary journey Paul and some of his friends

> ...went into the Jewish temple, giving notice of the completion of the days of purification, until sacrifice was offered for each one of them (Acts 21:23–26).

Doubtless, Paul underwent these purification rites so that he could enter the Jewish gatherings in the temple and there witness to the gospel of Christ. It seems that Paul bent over backward to please the Jewish Christians in Jerusalem, as well as in other parts of the world. Yet at the same time, he stood firmly on the premise that to observe the old covenant ceremonies as a salvation requirement was contrary to the Christian gospel.

Paul instructed his pastors in training to

> ...shun foolish controversies and genealogies and strife and *disputes about the Law;* for they are unprofitable and worthless (Tit. 3:9).

Paul's method of evangelism explains why he went to the synagogues on the Sabbath. He was not "keeping the Sabbath" for religious reasons, rather he says,

> ...to the Jews I became as a Jew, that I might win Jews; to those who are under the Law, as under the Law, though not being myself under the Law, that I might win those who are under the Law (1 Cor. 9:20).

Paul's method of evangelism and his instruction to the young Gentile churches seem at times to be contradictory. Yet upon careful study we see that he was guided in both by the new covenant law of love. He would allow nothing to separate the believer from the completeness he already had in Christ. Therefore we have his strong warnings against the continued practice of old covenant convocations. However, his genuine love for his Jewish kinsmen caused him to comply with old covenant practices when to do so would further the interests of the gospel. Here we see an illustration of how workable the new covenant really is. Rather than being governed by large numbers of specific rules, as in the old covenant, Paul was guided by the Holy

Spirit in applying the principle of love to God and love to man in different ways for different situations.

How does this relate to our study of the Sabbath? From these principles we must conclude that to observe the Sabbath for religious reasons as a *necessary* Christian duty, or as a *requirement of salvation,* seriously undermines one's standing in Christ. For Paul this would be another gospel of a different type, completely separate from the true gospel and should be vigorously confronted. At the same time one is free to observe the Sabbath with those who are prejudiced regarding the Sabbath if that observance furthers the spread of the gospel.

The missing controversy

There is yet another *strong evidence* that Paul in his ministry to the Gentile churches did not promote the keeping of the Sabbath. It is clear from the Gospels and Jewish history that the Jews of New Testament times had built up numerous rules to keep themselves from breaking the biblical Sabbath laws. Sabbath rules were legion and varied from one rabbi to the next. One was not to travel beyond 2000 cubits from his lodging. No sexual intercourse was permitted on the Sabbath. Better food was to be served on the Sabbath than on other days. No fasting was allowed on the Sabbath. One could not prepare, or eat anything prepared on the Sabbath. One could not carry an object from his home into a public area on the Sabbath. The Essenes even said that defecation was a work prohibited on the Sabbath. A tailor was not to carry a needle on the Sabbath. A householder was not to reach out of his house and place something in the hand of a poor person on the Sabbath.[10]

---

[10] C. Rowland, "A Summary of Sabbath Observance in Judaism at the Beginning of the Christian Era", in *From Sabbath to Lord's Day,* p. 45–51.

Sabbath in the Epistles

Sometimes we laugh at all the rules the Jews made regarding the Sabbath. However, having come from a background where we tried to keep the biblical laws for the Sabbath, I can recall countless hours discussing what was appropriate and what was not appropriate Sabbath keeping.

When I was a boy, my mother did not cook or wash the dishes on the Sabbath. However, for Sabbath dinner she did reheat the food she had prepared the day before. When we began to use frozen vegetables she found that it was no more "work" to take frozen peas and cook them than it was to reheat the ones which were cooked the day before plus they tasted much better and were probably better for us. I remember the discussion we had in making this transition. However, we never did face the fact that even making a fire on the Sabbath was wrong![11] If we did, would it have been wrong to build a fire in a wood stove? What if you kept coals overnight so you did not have to light a match, would that be building a fire? And what about a modern gas cooktop which lights with a turn of the knob. Is that building a fire?

When we took long trips we tried not to travel on the Sabbath. However, we often took short trips in the car on Sabbath afternoon to "enjoy nature." I remember on several occasions we compromised and decided to "enjoy nature" at the same time we "traveled." However, when we did this, we always would gas up on Friday night and drive until the gas tank was about empty. We would then find a place to observe the rest of the Sabbath. As soon as the sun was down, we would gas up and continue our trip.

When I was pastoring in the Seventh-day Adventist church I remember a lady who was baptized and joined our church. I studied with her the biblical principles of Sabbath keeping and encouraged her to follow them. Some time later she called me and said that her husband did not like

---

[11] You shall not kindle a fire in any of your dwellings on the sabbath day. Ex. 35:3.

her keeping the Sabbath because she was not making the beds on Sabbath morning. I assured her that making the beds was acceptable Sabbath keeping. I had, in our previous study, instructed her that she should not use the sacred hours of the Sabbath to do her house-work, such as washing clothes, etc. In interpreting my instruction, coupled with the biblical rules for Sabbath keeping, she felt that there was more "work" in making a bed than there was in washing clothes in an automatic washing machine. I was hard pressed to defend my definition of what was "work" and what was right and what was wrong to do on the Sabbath.

Samuele Bacchiocchi, Seventh-day Adventist theologian, in his book, *The Sabbath in the New Testament,* has some twenty-one pages devoted to modern Sabbath observance. In these pages he asks many questions about Sabbath keeping and then gives his interpretation. For example: (1) "...holding of weddings on the Sabbath should be discouraged."[12] (2) "As a general rule, however, it is advisable to avoid conducting funerals on the Sabbath, since they disrupt the spirit of rest, joy, and celebration of the Sabbath."[13] (3) "A distinction must be made between essential services rendered on the Sabbath in a Seventh-day Adventist institution and those rendered in a non-SDA institution." The reason for this, says Dr. Bacchiocchi, is that in a non-SDA institution, such as a fire station, the Sabbath keeper might be asked to do routine maintenance work which would not be accepted Sabbath observance.[14] (4) "Purchasing goods or services on the Sabbath, such as eating out in restaurants, will turn the mind of the believer away from the sacredness of the Sabbath to the secularism and materialism of the world."[15] (5) Dr. Bacchiocchi states

---

[12] Samuele Bacchiocchi, *The Sabbath in the New Testament,* p. 217.
[13] *Ibid.,* p. 218.
[14] *Ibid.,* p. 222.
[15] *Ibid.,* p. 225.

that "Historically, Seventh-day Adventists have endeavored to follow the principle of sunset reckoning [to mark the beginning and end of Sabbath] even in the Arctic regions by broadening the meaning of 'sunset' to include, for example, the end of twilight, the diminishing of light, the moment when the sun is closest to the horizon."[16] Having said this, however, he then argues for Sabbath to be reckoned in arctic regions using equatorial sunset time, 6 p.m. to 6 p.m.[17]

I include these few examples, from the Jews of Christ's day, from my own experience and the counsel of Dr. Bacchiocchi, not because they are unusual or wrong, for I believe this counsel is good and *necessary* for those who keep the Sabbath. The point I want to underline is that *when one really sets out to observe the Sabbath according to biblical guidelines there are hundreds of "gray areas" that must be addressed.* Anyone who has *seriously* tried to keep the Sabbath according to *biblical guidelines* knows this from experience.

We must thoughtfully consider the following facts. There is real need for the *interpretation* of the Sabbath laws for *anyone who is going to keep the Sabbath.* Just going to church on Saturday is not "keeping" the Sabbath. The New Testament milieu was one where there were differing interpretations regarding Sabbath observance among the various sects of Judaism. Jesus took issue with at least several of the Jewish interpretations of Sabbath keeping and from their perspective seemed to go out of His way to "break" the Sabbath. It is totally inconceivable that Paul, in forming, instructing and nurturing young Gentile churches over a period of many years, would have said nothing about appropriate Sabbath observance. That the Gentiles knew many of the Jewish customs is evident from the New

---

[16] *Ibid.,* p. 227.
[17] *Ibid.,* p. 228.

Testament.[18] If Sabbath observance was a part of the theology and practice of the Gentile Christians they would have needed instruction on *how* to observe the Sabbath. The believers in Corinth asked many questions about Christian conduct; why did they not include "How do we keep the Sabbath?" Coupled with the other evidence in this chapter, it is obvious that Sabbath keeping was not required, expected or even recommended in the Gentile Churches.

Chapter Summary

1. Unlike the book of Acts, the epistles contain explicit teaching regarding the Sabbath.
2. The evidence is heavily weighted in favor of understanding the "Sabbath day(s)" in Colossians 2:16 to be the seventh-day Sabbath.
3. There is strong evidence to believe that the "days" referred to in Galatians 4:10 refer to the seventh-day Sabbath.
4. There is evidence to believe that the "days" in Romans 14:5, 6 refer to the seventh-day Sabbath.
5. In *every instance* in the epistles where there is teaching about the Sabbath, that teaching suggests that the Sabbath either undermines the Christian's standing in Christ, or is nonessential.
6. The Sabbath is linked with other old covenant ritual laws and convocations.
7. The implications for the continued *required* observance of the Sabbath by Christians run from unimportant—probably for the believing Jew who wants to observe the Sabbath knowing that it is not part of Christian duty—to a dangerous undermining of one's standing in Christ for the believing Gentile.
8. The Sabbath is described by such terms as: "a mere shadow," "elemental things," "weak," and "worthless."

---

[18] See Jn. 4:8; Mk. 7:3; Acts 10:20; Acts 13:43; Acts 16:3; Acts 17:13; Acts 18:4; Acts 18:28; Acts 26:2; Gal. 2:13.

Sabbath in the Epistles

9. The Sabbath is said to be enslaving.
10. The required observance of the Sabbath, and related old covenant convocations, made Paul "fear" that he had labored in vain because they were following a different and false gospel.
11. The required observance of the Sabbath by Christians seriously undermines the finished work of Christ.
12. It was Paul's stated and practiced method of evangelism to adapt his practices in order to break down prejudice and by so doing win more people to Christ as long as these practices were seen to be optional and not a requirement of salvation.
13. The fact that the Epistles contain instruction on almost every conceivable topic relative to Christian conduct but are silent in regard to Sabbath observance indicates that Sabbath observance was not required, expected or even recommended to the Gentile churches.

Do this in remembrance of Me

CHAPTER FIFTEEN

NEW COVENANT DOCUMENTS AND SIGNS

It is now time to return to the new covenant and study it in greater depth. In Chapter 6 we had a brief overview of this subject and covered two aspects of the new covenant. First, we found the New Testament defines the Sinaitic Covenant just the way the Old Testament did as comprising both the Ten Commandments and the other laws which were an application and interpretation of the ten principles. The New Testament specifically mentions "the tables of the covenant" (Heb. 9:1–4), "Letters engraved on stones," as referring to the "first" or "old" covenant.

Second, we saw that the old covenant, while being a revelation of truth, was very incomplete and fragmentary. The new covenant revelation of Jesus, on the other hand, is a "better" revelation because, unlike the laws of the old covenant, Jesus is the radiance of God's glory and He is the exact representation of God's nature (Heb. 1:1,2). Thus we concluded that if the two covenants were to come into conflict, the new covenant would *always* take precedence over the old.

Jesus, the new covenant

Jesus is the new covenant. He is the Elect of God. As we read in Isaiah 42:6, a prophecy of the coming Messiah, *"I will appoint you* [The Messiah] *as a covenant to the people, as a light to the nations."* "I will keep You and *give You for a covenant of the people"* (Isa. 49:8). "For on Him [Jesus] the Father, even God, has set His seal" (Jn. 6:27).

> But now He has obtained a more excellent ministry, by as much as *He* is also the mediator of a *better covenant* which has been enacted on *better promises* (Heb. 8:6).

The old covenant partners were God and the "sons of Israel." The new covenant partners are the Father and Jesus. Jesus is the one who rendered perfect obedience to His Father's will. We enter into that covenant by faith in Him. Over and over again we hear Jesus saying,

> My food is to do the will of Him who sent Me, and to accomplish His work...I do not seek my own will, but the will of Him who sent Me...I have kept My Father's commandments (Jn. 4:34; 5:30; Jn. 15:10).

On that Friday afternoon when our Covenant Keeper was dying on the cross for our sins, His last words were, "It is finished" (Jn. 19:30). Just before these triumphant words we read, "Jesus, knowing that all things had already been accomplished..." (Jn. 19:28). He finished the work!

Jesus only

In the old order of things at the very center of the camp of Israel was the tabernacle of the covenant, and in the center of the Most Holy Place was the ark of the covenant and in the ark of the covenant was the covenant and above the mercy seat was the shekinah glory. At the death of Christ, however, the old order of things came to an end.

> And Jesus uttered a loud cry, and breathed His last. And the veil of the temple was torn in two from top to bottom (Mk. 15:37, 38).

In the new order of things we see Jesus only.

- Jesus is the way   Jn. 14:6
- Jesus is the truth   Jn. 14:6
- Jesus is the life   Jn. 14:6
- Jesus is the Good Shepherd   Jn. 10:11,14

New Covenant Documents and Signs

- Jesus is the light   Jn. 8:12
- Jesus is the door   Jn. 10:7
- Jesus is the first   Rev. 22:13
- Jesus is the last   Rev. 22:13
- Jesus is the I AM   Jn. 8:58
- Jesus is the unique Son   Jn. 3:16
- Jesus is the beloved Son   Jn. 3:17
- Jesus is the bread of life Jn. 6:48
- Jesus is the water of life Jn. 7:37, 38
- Jesus is the resurrection   Jn. 11:25
- Jesus is the judge   Jn. 5:27

Throughout the Gospels the constant endeavor is to move the focus of the people away from Sinai to Jesus. Why? Because God no longer dwells in the tent of the tabernacle of testimony (or the temple) but is now tabernacling in the person of His Son, Jesus, and through the Holy Spirit He indwells in the Christian.

The discerning reader of the New Testament will see a parallel between the life of Jesus, who is the new covenant, and certain things connected with the old covenant. In the parallel, however, there is also a contrast. Jesus is much, much better! Consider the following.

Israel, as a nation, was born at the exodus from Egypt. Thus, we read of the birth of Jesus,

> And he [Joseph] arose and took the Child and His mother by night, and departed for Egypt; and was there until the death of Herod; that what was spoken by the Lord through the prophet might be fulfilled, saying, "Out of Egypt did I call My Son" (Mt. 2:15).

In the old covenant God gave the Ten Commandments on Mt. Sinai. In the new covenant Jesus went to the "Mount" and gave His people His blessings (Mt. 5:1–12). In the old covenant six of the Ten Commandments dealt with man's relation to man. It is no accident that Jesus quotes six of the old covenant laws, some from the Ten

Commandments and some from the "book of the law" and then says, "But I say to you..." In so doing Jesus shows that He is the one who understands the true meaning of the old covenant law and has authority over the old covenant law.

> 1. You have heard that the ancients were told, "You shall not commit murder."...But I say to you that every one who is angry with his brother shall be guilty (Mt. 5:21, 22).
> 2. You have heard that it was said, "You shall not commit adultery"; But I say to you, that every one who looks on a woman to lust for her has committed adultery with her already in his heart (Mt. 5:27, 28).
> 3. And it was said, "Whoever divorces his wife..." But I say to you that every one who divorces his wife, except for the cause of unchastity, makes her commit adultery (Mt. 5:31, 32).
> 4. You have heard that the ancients were told, "You shall not make false vows..." But I say to you, make no oath at all (Mt. 5:33, 34).
> 5. You have heard it was said, "An eye for an eye and a tooth for a tooth." But I say to you, do not resist him who is evil (Mt. 5:38–42).
> 6. You have heard it was said, "You shall love your neighbor, and hate your enemy." But I say to you, love your enemies (Mt. 5:43–47).

What is Jesus doing here? He is showing that He, as the Messiah and Son of God, has authority over the law and can interpret (or even change) it at will. As we noted in the chapter, Jesus and Old Covenant Moral Law, when Jesus taught on a moral law from the old covenant, He felt free to *modify* and *expand* the moral laws of the old covenant. We found that the moral and ethical dimensions of Christ's law are so far above the old covenant moral laws that Jesus could *contrast* His moral teaching with old covenant moral law. Jesus also *modified* and *expanded* the moral laws of the old covenant changing them from legal rules to moral and ethical principles. Jesus modified and expanded the *scope* of the moral laws of the old covenant moving them *beyond* laws for Israel alone to ethical and moral principles for every nation tongue and people.

New Covenant Documents and Signs

What does the experience on the mount of transfiguration teach?

> And He was transfigured before them; and His garments became radiant and exceedingly white, as no launderer on earth can whiten them. And *Elijah* appeared to them along with *Moses;* and they were conversing with Jesus. And Peter answered and said to Jesus, "Rabbi, it is good for us to be here; and let us make three tabernacles [sacred tents], one for You, and one for Moses, and one for Elijah." For he did not know what to answer; for they became terrified. Then a cloud formed, overshadowing them, and a voice came out of the cloud, *"This is My beloved Son, listen to Him!"* And all at once they looked around and *saw no one with them any more, except Jesus only* (Mk. 9:3–8).

Peter volunteered to make *three* "sacred tents," one for Moses, one for Elijah and one for Jesus. By making this suggestion Peter was unconsciously making Jesus equal with the Law (Moses) and the Prophets (Elijah). But suddenly a cloud shuts out Moses and Elijah, the voice of God booms forth—He will have no one equal with His Son!—"This is My beloved Son, *listen to Him!"* Then they saw no one but *Jesus only!* While the event of the transfiguration may include other insights, the revelation of the superiority of Jesus over the law and prophets is certainly the central theme.

There are many illustrations that could be given to show that Jesus, and Jesus only, is the center of new covenant truth. He far supersedes the shadowy revelation which lighted the pathways of old covenant history. The underlying motif of all of the controversies Jesus had with the Jewish leaders had to do with who He was and the authority of His word and actions in relationship to the old covenant law and the accepted interpretation of those laws.

> "Unless you believe that I am He, you shall die in your sins" (Jn. 8:24).

New covenant law

Because Jesus is the Elect of God; because He is God's final revelation to man; because He is the exact representation of God's nature; because He is the Way, the Truth, and the Life; because He is the Light of the world; because He always did the Father's will; because He never did anything but what the Father was doing—because of these things He, Himself, becomes the basis for new covenant law. "If you abide in My word, then you are truly disciples of Mine" (Jn. 8:31). "If anyone keeps *My word* he shall never see death" (Jn. 8:51).

> I have come as the light into the world, that everyone who believes in Me may not remain in darkness...He who rejects Me, and does not receive My sayings, has one who judges him; the word I spoke is what will judge him at the last day. For I did not speak on My own initiative, but the Father Himself who sent Me has given Me commandment, and what to say, and what to speak. And I know that His commandment is eternal life; therefore the things I speak, I speak just as the Father has told Me (Jn. 12:46–50).

The words of the covenant

As we saw in our study of the old covenant, the Ten Commandments were the words of the covenant. There was also an expanded version of the covenant: the laws recorded in Exodus through Deuteronomy. We also saw that the covenant's ongoing sign was the Sabbath. What is the new covenant law or commandment?

> *A new commandment* I give to you, that *you love one another,* even as I have loved you, that you also love one another. By this all men will know that you are My disciples, if you have love for one another (Jn. 13:34, 35).

Part of this "new commandment" was not new. The old covenant had instructed them to love one another. The part that was new was "as I have loved you." And as we see the way that Jesus loved those dull, slow to learn, stumbling,

New Covenant Documents and Signs

sleeping, denying, and forsaking disciples, we indeed have a new commandment!

What made other nations know the Israelites were the chosen people? Not the way they loved, but what they ate and what they did not eat; where they worshipped, when they worshipped, the clothes they wore, etc. However, in the new covenant, Christ's true disciples will be known by the way they love!

This commandment to love is repeated a number of times in the New Testament, just as the Ten Commandments were repeated in the old.

> If you love Me, you will keep My commandments (Jn. 14:15). He who has My commandments, and keeps them, he it is who loves Me; and he who loves Me shall be loved by My Father, and I will love him, and will disclose Myself to him (Jn. 14:21). If you keep my commandments, you will abide in My love; just as I have kept My Father's commandments, and abide in His love...This is My commandment, that you love one another, just as I have loved you (Jn. 15:10–12).
>
> You are My friends, if you do what I command you (Jn. 15:14). This I command you, that you love one another (Jn. 15:17). And this is His commandment, that we believe in the name of His Son Jesus Christ, and love one another, just as He commanded us (1 Jn. 3:23). And this commandment we have from Him, that the one who loves God should love his brother also (1 Jn. 4:21).

The Book of the Covenant: the New Testament

As the old covenant had an expanded version of the Ten Commandments known as the book of the law, so the new covenant contains more than just the simple command to love one another as Christ loved us. We have the Gospels which demonstrate how Jesus loved us enough to give His very life so that we might be saved. We have in these records the additional words of Christ. Then, in the epistles we have interpretations of the love and work of Christ. Like the old covenant, some of the interpretations of the covenant are moral and eternal and some are specifically set forth for the culture in which the writers lived.

The epistles interpret and apply the meaning of Christ's life, death and resurrection, and this application is valid for all peoples and time. They also contain instructions which are clearly intended for a specific culture, time and place.[1]

So the core, or heart, of the new covenant is to love one another as Christ loved us. This is expanded and interpreted in the rest of the New Testament, and also becomes part of the new covenant.

New covenant signs

The sign of the Abrahamic Covenant was circumcision,[2] and the sign of the Sinaitic Covenant was the Sabbath.[3] As both covenants applied to the children of Israel circumcision served as the entrance sign for the old covenant and the sign Israel was to "remember" was the Sabbath. What are the signs of the new covenant?

The entrance sign of the new covenant is baptism. When Jesus came to John the Baptist, John said,

> I have need to be baptized by You, and do You come to me? But Jesus answering said to him, "permit it at this time; for in this way it is fitting for *us* to fulfill all righteousness" (Mt. 3:14, 15).

The "us" in the passage above is plural indicating that Jesus is being baptized, not only for his own compliance with the way of salvation, but also as an example for us. We see in this incident reflections of an Old Testament event. When Moses was on the way to Egypt to deliver Israel, he was met by the Lord, who "sought to put him to death" because his sons were uncircumcised. Quickly the rite of circumcision was performed and the Lord then permitted him to continue His mission of deliverance (Ex. 4:24–26). So in the new covenant when Jesus is on His way—starting His ministry—he accepts the sign of the new covenant, baptism, and then goes on to deliver "Israel."

---

[1] See 1 Cor. 11:6.
[2] Gen. 17:9–14.
[3] Ex. 31:13–17.

New Covenant Documents and Signs

In the great commission passage in Matthew 28:19, 20 we read:

> Go therefore and make disciples of all nations, baptizing them in the name of the Father and the Son and the Holy Spirit, teaching them to observe all that I commanded you; and lo, I am with you always, even to the end of the age.

The following diagram will help show how this passage is constructed in Greek.

Go therefore and make disciples of all nations:

1. Baptizing them in the name of the Father and the Son and the Holy Spirit,

2. Teaching them to observe all that I commanded you;

And lo,

I am with you always, even to the end of the age.

The way to make disciples was *first* to baptize them, *then* teach them to observe all that Jesus taught—how to love as He loved.

We find the same order in the old covenant. The people of Israel were first to be circumcised and then, as members of the covenant community, they were to receive ongoing instruction.

It is of interest to note that every time the New Testament uses the words "into Christ" it is in connection with baptism.

> Or do you not know that all of us who have been *baptized into Christ Jesus* have been baptized into His death? (Rom. 6:3).
>
> For all of you who were *baptized into Christ* have clothed yourselves with Christ (Gal. 3:27).

And in Him you were also circumcised with a circumcision made without hands...having been buried with Him in baptism (Col. 2:11, 12).

For by one Spirit we were all baptized into one body (1 Cor. 12:13).

Baptism fills the place in the new covenant that circumcision filled in the old. It is the entrance sign or ceremony into the covenant community.

Having shown this, we must also remember that baptism, *per se,* does not have effective force. We are not saved by baptism, rather we are saved by belief in Christ. Baptism is the outward sign that we have committed ourselves to Jesus Christ as our Savior and Lord.

What is the continuing, repeatable sign of the New Testament that we are to "remember"?

And while they were eating, Jesus took some bread, and after blessing, He broke it and gave it to the disciples, and said, "Take, eat; this is My body." And He took a cup and gave thanks, and gave it to them, saying, "Drink from it, all of you; for this is My blood *of the covenant,* which is to be shed on behalf of many for forgiveness of sins" (Mt. 26:26–28).

Do this *in remembrance of Me*...This cup which is poured out for you is the *new covenant* in My blood (Lk. 22:19, 20).

While there is yet much to discuss regarding the new covenant and its relation to the old which will shed light on our study of the Sabbath, nevertheless we are ready for the following comparisons:

The old covenant: **The new covenant:**

Covenant partners
God and Israel   The Father and Jesus

Words of the covenant
Ten Commandments   Love as Christ loved

Book of the covenant
Genesis to Deuteronomy   Gospels and Epistles

	Entrance sign	
Circumcision		Baptism
	Remembrance sign	
Sabbath		The Lord's Supper

Chapter Summary

1. The center of the new covenant is in the person of Jesus.
2. Because of who Jesus is (God tabernacling in the flesh), His revelation of truth greatly supersedes that given in the old covenant.
3. The Sermon on the Mount shows that Jesus' authority is greater than that of the old covenant.
4. The experience of the transfiguration teaches that God does not want His Son made an equality with the old covenant. We are to see "Jesus only."
5. The new covenant in summary form is: "And this is His commandment, that we believe in the name of His Son Jesus Christ, and love one another, just as He commanded us."
   a. Our duty to God is to believe in Jesus.
   b. Our duty to man is to love as God loved us.
6. The new covenant, in expanded form, is recorded in the gospels and epistles. These interpret and apply the basic message of belief in Christ and love for our fellow men.
7. The entrance sign in the new covenant is water baptism and the sealing of the Holy Spirit.
8. In the new covenant the Christian is to "remember" the continuing sign of the Lord's Supper.

God…in these last days has spoken to us in His Son

CHAPTER SIXTEEN

A BETTER COVENANT

In this section we come to the heart of the new covenant.

> But now He has obtained a more excellent ministry by as much as He is also the mediator of a *better covenant* which has been enacted on *better promises*. For if the first covenant had been faultless, there would have been no occasion sought for a second. For finding fault with them [the sons of Israel]...I will effect a *new covenant* with the house of Israel and with the house of Judah; *not like* the covenant which I made with their fathers (Heb. 8:6–10).

Now comes the essence of what the new covenant is to be:

First,

> I will put My laws into their minds. And I will write them upon their hearts (Heb. 8:10).

How is this done?

> Written not with ink, but with the Spirit of the living God, not on tablets of stone, but on tablets of human hearts (2 Cor. 3:3).

Second,

> And they shall not teach every one his fellow citizen... For all shall know Me, from the least to the greatest of them (Heb. 8:11).

Here, in stark contrast to the old covenant where only the key leaders such as Moses, Joshua, David, etc., were in touch with the Holy Spirit and had a personal relationship with God, under the new and better covenant everyone is to have a personal knowledge of God, and thus be taught personally by Him. In the old covenant the people said to Moses,

> ...speak to us yourself and we will listen, but let not God speak to us, lest we die (Ex. 20:19).

In the new, better covenant everyone is to know the Lord personally.

Third,

> For I will be merciful to their iniquities, and I will remember their sins no more (Heb. 8:12).

Here we have one foundational truth expressed in two ways: God is going to be merciful regarding our sins. While we certainly see God's mercy in the old covenant, we also see him dealing justly with sinners. Note the threatened results if Israel disobeyed. Witness also what happened to Israel when they did disobey.

> But it shall come about, if you will not obey the Lord your God, to observe to do all His commandments and His statutes which I charge you today, that all these curses shall come upon you and overtake you. Cursed shall you be in the city, and cursed shall you be in the country. Cursed shall be your basket and your kneading bowl. Cursed shall be the offspring of your body and the produce of your ground, the increase of your herd and the young of your flock. Cursed shall you be when you come in, and cursed shall you be when you go out. The Lord will send upon you curses, confusion, and rebuke, in all you undertake to do, until you are destroyed and until you perish quickly, on account of the evil of your deeds, because you have forsaken Me (Deut. 28:15–20).

The new covenant is much, much better than the old. While in the old covenant we see God's mercy time and again, nevertheless, complete forgiveness was only typified, as Christ had not yet died for the sins of the world. In the new covenant God deals with grace and mercy, and Christ, as our substitute and surety, fulfills the covenant

A Better Covenant

stipulations for us. This will be discussed further in a later chapter.

Another way of saying the same truth is that God will not remember our sins. In Scripture when we read of God "remembering" it is often associated with impending action. When God "remembered" Rachel she conceived and bore a son (Gen. 30:22). When God "remembered" His covenant He took action to deliver Israel (Ex. 2:24; 3:8). So when we read in the new and better covenant that God is not going to "remember" our sins, the underlying concept is that He is not going to take action regarding our sins! Why?

> He made Him who knew no sin to be sin on our behalf, that we might become the righteousness of God in Him (2 Cor. 5:21).

The following chart contrasts the old and new covenants on these three items:

Old covenant:	**New covenant:**
Laws written on stone	Laws written on heart
Only leaders knew God	All personally know God
Sinners punished	Christ suffered on our behalf

General principles

The new covenant has general principles rather than detailed laws. Hebrews 8:9 says the new covenant is *not* like the old. In the old we saw that everything was spelled out in minute detail as if it were given to children. However, the new covenant is set forth as given to "sons" who know what their Father is doing.

Springing from this intimate friendship where all know the Lord, we find a completely different style in the new covenant. In the old covenant the laws regarding the showbread were set forth as follows.

> You shall take fine flour and bake twelve cakes with it; two-tenths of an ephah shall be in each cake. And you shall set them in two rows, six to a row, on the pure gold table before the Lord (Lev. 24:5, 6).

When we come to the new covenant all we have is,

> ...as often as you eat this bread and drink this cup you show the Lord's death until He comes (1 Cor. 11:26).

There is no recipe telling us how to make communion bread, no instruction regarding what kind of plate to use. We are not even told how often to practice it. Rather, the new covenant deals with the heart and central issues in general principles giving us the freedom to be guided by the Holy Spirit to find an appropriate recipe, plate and time.

The following chart illustrates this principle:

OC = old covenant
NC = new covenant

OC   Showbread: detailed recipe, how to arrange it, what kind of plate to use, when to put it out, etc. (Lev. 24:5, 6).

NC   Communion bread: no recipe, no directions other than "When He had given thanks, He broke it and said, 'This is My body, which is for you; do this in remembrance of Me'!" (1 Cor. 11:24, 25).

OC   When to worship: Sabbaths, new moons, fixed festivals, etc., (Lev. 23).

NC   When to worship: not forsaking the assembling of yourselves together (Heb. 10:25). Continually offer up a sacrifice of praise (Heb. 13:15).

OC   Where to worship: tabernacle (temple in Jerusalem) (Jn. 4:20).

NC   Where to worship: Where two or three are gathered together (Mt. 18:20).

OC   How to worship: as prescribed by the law.
NC   How to worship: in Spirit and in truth (Jn. 4:24).

OC   What to bring: one male goat and two male lambs (Lev. 23:19).

NC   What to bring: present your bodies a living and holy sacrifice (Rom. 12:1).

This illustrates how the old covenant is characterized by great detail. In contrast the new covenant is presented in general principles.

A covenant of grace

While the old covenant made provision for forgiveness and grace was present, nevertheless its focus was law. In contrast, while the new covenant has law, its focus is on grace.

A personal covenant

In the old covenant only the key leaders were filled with the Holy Spirit and had a personal knowledge of God. However, in the new covenant all are to know God personally and be taught by Him.

A covenant for all nations

The old covenant was limited to the "sons of Israel" and those who would "join themselves to the Lord" by being circumcised, keeping the Sabbath and thus coming under the Torah. By contrast the new covenant is good news for all the nations. Whosoever will may come. All may join the new covenant community by believing in Jesus, demonstrating this belief by being baptized and observing the Lord's Supper.

The new covenant an extension of the Abrahamic or everlasting Covenant

Some have tried to make the new covenant a continuum of the old covenant with the only difference being that the law of the old covenant is now written on the heart and in the new covenant we trust Christ's righteousness rather than trying to establish our own. However, I do not believe this harmonizes with the whole of New Testament teaching. Rather, I believe the new covenant is a continuum of the everlasting covenant or the Abrahamic Covenant that has its foundation before the creation of the world. Notice the following similarities between the Abrahamic Covenant and the new covenant and the dissimilarities between the Abrahamic Covenant and the old covenant.

Abrahamic Covenant (AC)
New Covenant (NC)
Old Covenant (OC)

AC	All the families of the earth (Gen. 12:3).
NC	All nations (Mt. 28:19).
OC	Sons of Israel only (Ex. 20:22; 31:13; Deut. 5:1, 2).
AC	Not under the law (Gal. 3:17).
NC	Not under the Sinaitic Law (Rom. 7:6; 10:4; Gal. 3:25; 5:18).
OC	The old covenant is the law (Ex. 34:28; Deut. 4:13; Deut. 9:11, 15).
AC	Belief (faith) counted as righteousness (Gen. 15:6).
NC	Belief (faith) counted as righteousness (Rom. 3:28; Eph. 2:8, 9).
OC	Righteousness based upon personal obedience to law (Deut. 6:25; Rom. 10:5, Gal. 3:12).

Abraham was the father of two groups of people that have symbolic religious significance. Isaac represents those who have a personal relationship with God *by faith* and can be truly called "spiritual Israel" regardless of nationality.[1] Ishmael represents those who trust their good works or their physical connection to Abraham for righteousness.[2]

Those who can rightly be called "spiritual Israel" have gone through a personal experience where they have learned to distrust themselves and trust only in God. Jacob had his personal, life-changing experience at the brook Jabbok when his name was changed from Jacob to Israel.[3]

---

[1] See Gal. 3:26–29; Gal. 4:21–31.
[2] See Gal. 4:21–31; Rom. 9:6–8.
[3] See Gen. 32:24–30.

Those who continue to trust their Sinai-law keeping and/or their nationality for righteousness are, according to Paul, still in the slavery of bondage and are to be counted as spiritual descendants of Ishmael and are still under the old covenant.[4]

So we see that the new covenant is a continuum of the Abrahamic Covenant. However, it connects to Abraham *before* Abraham was circumcised so it could apply to all nations.[5]

The covenant that was ratified by the blood of Christ was, then, not the Sinaitic covenant, but the Abrahamic Covenant or the new covenant. Although it was presented before the old or first covenant, it was ratified after the Sinaitic Covenant and therefore is called "new". In the following chart note the superiority of the new covenant over the old.

OC   Based upon the promise of the Israelites (Ex. 19:8; 24:3).
NC   Based upon the promise of God's Son and the oath of God (Heb. 6:13–20, 8:6; Isa 42:6; Gen. 22:15–18).

OC   Ratified by the blood of animals (Ex. 24:3–8).
NC   Ratified by the blood of Christ (Heb. 9:14; 12:24).

OC   A human (Moses) mediator (Ex. 19, 24).
NC   Mediated by Jesus, God's Son (Heb. 12:24).

OC   A faulty covenant (Heb. 8:7, 8).
NC   A better covenant (Heb. 8:6).

OC   An obsolete covenant (Heb. 8:13).
NC   An everlasting or eternal covenant (Heb. 13:20).

---

[4] See Gal. 4:21–31.
[5] Rom. 4:9–11.

Chapter Summary

1. According to Hebrews 8 the three main aspects of the new covenant are:
   a. God's law is written on the heart by the Spirit.
   b. All will know God personally.
   c. God will not remember (take action regarding) our sins.
2. The general characteristics of the new covenant are:
   a. General principles rather than specific details.
   b. The emphasis is on grace (done) rather than on law (do).
   c. It is a personal covenant.
   d. It is a covenant for all nations.
3. The new covenant is an extension of the Abrahamic Covenant and has the following similarities:
   a. Has application to all nations.
   b. Righteousness is based solely upon faith.
   c. Not under the Sinaitic law.
   d. Based upon the promise and oath of God.
   e. Mediated by Jesus, God's Son.
   f. Is an everlasting or eternal covenant.
4. A true "Israelite" is one who has a personal relationship with God and distrusts himself and places all his trust in God regardless of his nationality.
5. Someone who trusts his nationality or law keeping for acceptance with God is considered to be a spiritual descendant of Ishmael and remains in the spiritual bondage of slavery.

CHAPTER SEVENTEEN

A BETTER LAW

Now we are ready for the heavyweight and often misunderstood truth of the New Testament: Christians are no longer under old covenant law. On one hand this truth is one of the most dangerous revelations within the new covenant in that it has been misunderstood, misapplied, and used as an excuse for sin. On the other hand, understood in its fullness, it is one of the most rewarding, refreshing and practical truths. Let us carefully examine Scripture on this topic. Let us not try to explain away anything to make it fit our theology, rather let us accept each statement for what it teaches and align our theology with Scripture.

It is important to recognize that not all passages of Scripture have equal teaching authority. There are passages in either highly symbolic or poetic language. These passages have little teaching authority. There are also passages which refer to a subject matter in passing, but the context deals with other subject matter. An illustration of this was seen in the chapter on the Sabbath in Acts. Nothing was *taught* regarding the Sabbath, but the Sabbath was mentioned in connection with Paul's evangelistic method of first preaching Christ to those attending the Jewish synagogue. This type of reference has some teaching authority. However, when a passage expressly teaches on a given subject *within the context of that subject,* the passage has the very highest teaching authority.

Hebrews

The book of Hebrews was written to Jewish believers who had been members of the old covenant community. The contextual teaching of this book deals with the very point of our study: how Christians are to relate to old covenant law. Therefore, we should accept the following statements as having the *highest teaching authority.* After the writer of Hebrews has shown the three fundamental aspects of the new covenant (Heb. 8:6–12) he adds,

> When He said, "A new covenant," He has made the *first obsolete.* But whatever is becoming obsolete and growing old is ready to disappear (Heb. 8:13).

A literal translation from the Greek would be, "In saying 'new' he has made old the first; but that which grows old and aged is near disappearing." With the coming of the new covenant the "first covenant" grows old and aged and is near disappearing. Both the Old Testament and The New Testament define the old covenant as the Ten Commandments *and* the other laws in the books of Moses. But can we be sure that is what the author here has in mind?

The very next verse makes it clear beyond doubt.

> Now even the first covenant had regulations of divine worship [Greek word is *service*] (Heb. 9:1).

It is unquestionably clear that the Sabbath was one of those regulations of divine worship or service (Lev. 23). Following this reference the author of Hebrews lists other aspects of the "first covenant," then in verse 4 he lists "the tables of the covenant." Let me clarify by reviewing what is said here. First, our author calls the Sinaitic Covenant the "first covenant" (called old in other places). Then he says it had regulations for divine worship. He goes on to list the things included in this "first covenant," including "the tables of the covenant"—a clear reference to the Ten Commandments. These are facts of Scripture in their contextual setting. Thus the "tables of the covenant," which include the Sabbath commandment, and the "laws for divine worship," which include the Sabbath, are old and ready to disappear.

In Hebrews 9:4–10 the author continues to describe aspects of old covenant worship and then in verse 10 states that these were "imposed *until* a time of reformation." What is that "time of reformation"? The next verse tells us, "But when Christ appeared..." (Heb. 9:11).

In the next chapter we read,

> ...He *takes away the first in order to establish the second.* By this will we have been sanctified through the offering of the body of Jesus Christ once for all (Heb. 10:9, 10).

From our previous study we remember that the Ten Commandments were the "words of the Sinaitic Covenant." Hebrews 8:8, quoting from Jeremiah 31:32, states that the new covenant is "not like" the one God made with Israel when they came out of Egypt. In other words, <u>the new covenant is not like the Ten Commandments</u>.

Galatians

The book of Galatians teaches the same thing. Remember that the book of Galatians was written to those who had been misled by the Judaizing teachers and who "wanted to be under law" (Gal. 4:21). The context deals expressly with our subject matter. Therefore, it, too, has the highest teaching authority. In Galatians 3:17 Paul states that the Law "came four hundred and thirty years" *after* the promise to Abraham. Thus, Paul agrees with the old covenant record that this covenant "was not made with the fathers" (Deut. 5:3). In answer to "Why the Law?" Paul says, "It was added because of transgressions...*until* the seed should come to whom the promise had been made" (Gal. 3:19). Verse 16 defines this "seed" as Christ.

Paul continues,

But before faith came, we were kept in custody under the law, being shut up to the faith which was later to be revealed. Therefore, the *Law has become our tutor to lead us to Christ,* that we may be justified by faith. But *now that faith is come, we are no longer under a tutor* (Gal. 3:22).

The following chart illustrates Paul's teaching:

Here, in contextual teaching, Paul calls the law our tutor and then says we are no longer under a tutor. In other words he is saying that *the old covenant law no longer has authority over the life of a Christian.* But can we be sure this is what Paul really means? Yes. Note carefully his powerful allegory.

Tell me, you who want to be under law, do you not listen to the law? For it is written that Abraham had two sons, one by the bondwoman and one by the free woman. But the son of the bondwoman was born according to the flesh, and the son by the free woman through the promise. This contains an allegory: for these women are *two covenants,* one proceeding from *Mount Sinai* bearing children who are to be slaves; she is Hagar. Now this Hagar is Mount Sinai in Arabia, and corresponds to the present Jerusalem, for she is in slavery with her children. But the Jerusalem above is free; she is our mother...And you brethren, like Isaac, are children of promise. But as at that time he who was born according to the flesh persecuted him who was born according to the Spirit, so it is now also. But what does the Scripture say? Cast out the bondwoman and her son, for the son of the bondwoman shall not be an heir with the son of the free woman. So then, brethren, *we are not children of a bondwoman,* but of the free woman (Gal. 4:21–31).

The following chart will help us understand this passage:

A Better Law

Old Covenant	New Covenant
Hagar = Bondwoman	**Sarah = Free woman**
Sinai-Jerusalem	The Jerusalem above
Son of the bondwoman	Son of the free woman
Born of flesh	Born of promise
In slavery	In freedom
Persecuting	Persecuted
(Like Ishmael)	Like Isaac
Born according to flesh	Born according to Spirit

Conclusions: (Gal. 4:30, 31)
1. "Cast out the bondwoman." = Cast out the old covenant.
2. Cast out "her son." = Cast out those who promote the old covenant.
3. "For the son of the bondwomen shall not be an heir with the son of the free woman." = The terms of covenants are mutually exclusive.
4. "We are not children of a bondwoman." = We are not under the old covenant.
5. We are children "of the free woman." = We are under the new covenant.

Here, in clear contextual teaching over several chapters, Paul states in three specific ways that Christians are not under the authority of the old covenant. (1) The Law was given 430 years *after* Abraham and was in effect *until* the coming of Christ. (2) With the coming of Christ we are no longer under the Law. (3) Christians are to "cast out" the old covenant and those who promote its being kept.

Romans

In the book of Romans Paul teaches that Christians are not under old covenant law. He does this, however, in a very tactful way and in so doing we learn additional insights which we would otherwise miss. As we observed in Chapter 13, the church at Rome was a mixed church containing Christians from both Jewish and Gentile backgrounds. Throughout this book Paul addresses one group and then the other. In Romans 1:16 Paul says,

> For I am not ashamed of the gospel, for it is the power of God for salvation to every one who believes, to the *Jew* first and also to the *Greek*.

Paul shows in the remaining verses of Chapter 1 that the *Gentiles* are under condemnation because they did not honor God even though they knew about Him from natural revelation.

In Chapter 2 Paul addresses his *Jewish* readers. He concludes that the Jews are under condemnation because even though they had the law they did not keep it.

In Chapter 3 Paul shows that *all* have sinned. Then he says,

> But now apart from the Law the righteousness of God has been manifested, being witnessed by the Law and the Prophets; even the righteousness of God through faith in Jesus Christ for all those who believe; for there is no distinction; for all have sinned and [continue to] fall short of the glory of God being justified as a gift by His grace through the redemption which is in Christ Jesus (Rom. 3:21–24).

At this point Paul's Jewish readers are about to quit reading and rebel at his teaching. They see that he is putting the believing Gentiles who are not involved with the law on the same level as the Jews who have the law. Therefore he quickly adds,

> Do we then nullify the Law through faith? May it never be! On the contrary, *we establish the Law* (Rom. 3:31).

Now Paul must show *from the law* how the Gentiles can be saved *without the law*. In other words, Paul is "establishing the law" not as now binding, but as a witness to the new covenant gospel that he is preaching. Notice carefully his reasoning.

A Better Law

> What then shall we say that Abraham, our forefather according to the flesh, has found? For if Abraham was justified by works, he has something to boast about; but not before God. For what does the Scripture say? "And Abraham believed God, and it was reckoned to him as righteousness." Now to the one who works, his wage is not reckoned as a favor but as what is due. But to the one who does not work, but believes in Him who justifies the ungodly, his faith is reckoned as righteousness... How then was it reckoned? While he was circumcised, or uncircumcised? Not while circumcised, but while uncircumcised; and he received the sign of circumcision, a seal of the righteousness of the faith which he had while uncircumcised, that he might be the father of all who believe without being circumcised, that the righteousness might be reckoned to them...For this reason it is by faith, that it might be in accordance with grace, in order that the promise may be certain to *all* the descendants, *not only* to those who are of the Law, *but also* to those who are of the faith of Abraham, who is the father of us *all* (Rom. 4:1–5, 10, 11, 16).

In these verses Paul shows how the promise of righteousness by faith was made to Abraham *before* he was circumcised. Then he shows that *both* the Jews and the Gentiles are included in this promise. The Jews are descendants of Abraham and experienced living *under the law,* yet that experience did *not* bring them into the righteousness which is by faith. The Gentiles, on the other hand, did *not* experience living under the law and came directly into the righteousness which is by faith when they believed in Christ. In other words, Paul says the believing Gentiles experienced the righteousness which is by faith, completely *bypassing Sinai and all old covenant law.* This is illustrated on the next page.

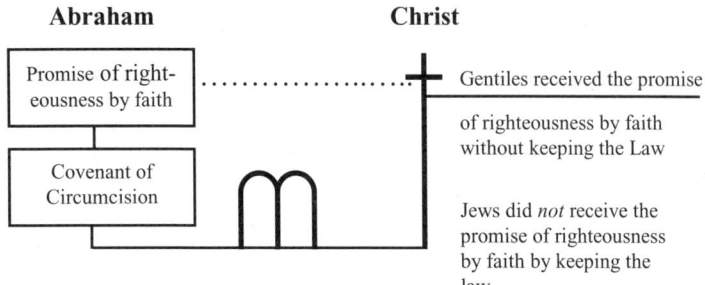

In Chapter 5 Paul explains the meaning and results of righteousness by faith and then says, The law came in that the transgression might increase; but where sin increased, grace abounded all the more (Rom. 5:20).

In Chapter 6 Paul shows that the believing Christian is free from the controlling power of sin.

> Even so consider yourselves to be dead to sin, but alive to God in Christ Jesus...But now *having been freed from sin* and enslaved to God, you derive your benefit, resulting in sanctification, and the outcome, eternal life (Rom. 6:11, 22).

In Chapter 7 Paul shows that *Jewish Christians* (as well as Gentile Christians) are *free from the law.*

> Or do you not know, brethren (for I am speaking to those who know the law), that the law has jurisdiction over a person as long as he lives? For the married woman is bound by law to her husband while he is living; but if her husband dies, she is released from the law concerning the husband. So then if, while her husband is living, she is joined to another man, she shall be called an adulteress; but if her husband dies, she is free from the law, so that she is not an adulteress, though she is joined to another man. Therefore, my brethren, you also were made to die to the Law through the body of Christ, that you might be joined to another, to Him who was raised from the dead, that we might bear fruit for God. For while we were in the flesh, the sinful passions, which were aroused by the Law, were at work in the members of our body to bear fruit for death. But now we have been released from the Law, having died to that by which we were bound, so that we **_serve_** in newness of the Spirit and not in oldness of the letter (Rom. 7:1–6).

A Better Law

It is important to note that Paul is *not* speaking about the *condemnation* of the law, from which the Christian is also free,[1] but rather he is speaking about Christian **service**. In other words Paul is telling the Jewish Christians in Rome that the law no longer serves as a guideline for Christian living. Notice also how Christians serve in the *newness of the Spirit,* a clear reference to the new covenant, in contrast to *the oldness of the letter,* a clear reference to the Sinaitic Covenant.

Illustration of Romans 7:1–6

The old covenant relationship: bound by the law.

So then, if while her husband is living she is joined to another man, she shall be called an adulteress; but if her husband dies, she is free from the law, so that she is not an adulteress though she is joined to another man (Rom. 7:3)

---

[1] Rom. 8:1

The work of Christ in freeing us from the law:

He made Him who knew no sin to be sin on our behalf, so that we might become the righteousness of God in Him (2 Cor. 5:21). Therefore, my brethren, you also were made to die to the Law through the body of Christ, so that you might be joined to another, to Him who was raised from the dead, in order that we might bear fruit for God (Rom. 7:4).

The new covenant relationship:

But now we have been released from the Law, having died to that by which we were bound, so that we serve in newness of the Spirit and not in oldness of the letter (Rom. 7:6). For Christ is the end of the law for righteousness to everyone who believes (Rom. 10:4).

A Better Law

A Christian who is joined to Christ *and* the law:

```
S    A
P    D
I    U
R    L
I    T
T    E
U    R
A    Y
L
```

This sounded like heresy to the Jewish Christians in Paul's day and it also sounds like heresy to some Christians today. Nevertheless we must take Paul at his word and let him explain what he means. To answer the questions which would immediately come to his readers' minds Paul quickly adds,

> What shall we say then? Is the Law sin? May it never be! On the contrary, I would not have come to know sin except through the Law; for I would not have known about coveting if the Law had not said, "You shall not covet." But sin, taking opportunity through the commandment, produced in me coveting of every kind; for apart from the Law sin is dead (Rom. 7:7, 8).

In Romans 7:9–25 Paul illustrates what life is like when one serves God *from the perspective of the Sinaitic Covenant*. I encourage you to read these verses. In summary Paul shows that one may try as hard as possible to live in conformity to the law but it is impossible to meet the full demands of the law. There is a continuous struggle between indwelling sin and the requirements of the law.

Again, it is important that we not forget the major thesis of this chapter: *Christians are released from the law as a guide for Christian service.* We know that Paul uses "law" to refer to the old covenant law, including the Ten Commandments, as he specifically mentions "You shall not covet."

In Romans 8, by contrast, Paul illustrates what life is like when one serves God *from the perspective of the new covenant.*

> There is therefore now no condemnation for those who are in Christ Jesus. For the law of the Spirit of life in Christ Jesus [new covenant] *has set you free from the law of sin and death* [old covenant]. For what the Law [old covenant] could not do, weak as it was through the flesh, God did: [new covenant] sending His own Son in the likeness of sinful flesh and as an offering for sin, *He condemned sin in the flesh,* in order that the requirement of the Law might be fulfilled in us, who do not walk according to the flesh, but according to the Spirit (Rom. 8:1–5).

Here Paul shows that under the dynamics of the new covenant the believer actually attains "the requirement of the law." Some have argued that this statement of Paul puts Christians back under the law and therefore as Christians we should use the law as a guide for Christian service. However, this cannot be the right interpretation for it is in direct contradiction to his clear statement.

> But now we have been released from the Law, having died to that by which we were bound, so that we serve in the newness of the Spirit and not in the oldness of the letter (Rom. 7:6).

Paul's argument in Romans 8 is that "the requirement of the law" can be fulfilled *only* within the arrangements of the new covenant. He is building on what he established before. Namely, that Christ is our righteousness. He is not seeking to place Christians back under the old covenant law. Rather, he is showing that under the new covenant, where the Christian *has been* justified by faith (Rom. 5:1) he can now "walk according to the Spirit" who testifies of Christ and empowers the believer. Thus, "what the Law could not do, God did…" (Rom. 8:3).

In the new covenant the Spirit of God indwells the believer (Rom. 8:8–11). In the new covenant God's requirements are given in basic principles, "This is My commandment, that you love one another, just as I have loved you" (Jn. 15:12). Paul adds, "Love therefore is the fulfillment of the law" (Rom. 13:10). In contrast to the shadowy nature of the old covenant, the new comes in the radiance of God's glory (Heb. 1:2). In the new covenant sins are really forgiven, "Having been freed from sin" (Rom. 6:22). "There is therefore now no condemnation for those who are in Christ Jesus" (Rom. 8:1).

It is only under this arrangement that true fellowship between man and God can develop. Paul can say that the "requirement of the law" is fulfilled in those who walk according to the Spirit (Rom. 8:4). Therefore the Christian living under the new covenant may experience a fellowship with God which was not possible under the old covenant.

> For all who are being led by the Spirit of God these are the sons of God. For you have *not* received a spirit of slavery leading to fear again, but you have received a spirit of adoption as sons by which we cry out, "Abba! [Daddy] Father!" The Spirit Himself bears witness with our spirit that we are children of God, and if children, heirs also, heirs of God and fellow heirs with Christ…(Rom. 8:14–17).
>
> For I am convinced that neither death, nor life, nor angels, nor principalities, nor things present, nor things to come, nor powers, nor height, nor depth, nor any other created thing, shall be able to separate us from the love of God, which is in Christ Jesus our Lord (Rom. 8:38, 39).

In the next few chapters Paul deals with the failure of Israel and then in Chapter 10 he says,

> For Christ is the end of the law for righteousness to everyone who believes (Rom. 10:4).

With the explanation Paul has now given, he can repeat what he said in Chapter 3 without losing his Jewish readers. Thus he says,

For there is no distinction between Jew and Greek; for the same Lord is Lord of all, abounding in riches for all who call upon Him (Rom. 10:12).

In summary Paul shows in his letter to the Romans that the Gentiles can come within the promised blessing of righteousness by faith given to Abraham by completely bypassing the Sinaitic Covenant and all of its laws. He does this without nullifying the law (Rom. 3:31). Rather, he uses the law to prove this (Rom 4:1–16 cf. Gen. 15). Then he teaches that even Jewish Christians have been released from the law as a guide for Christian service, because the law no longer applies to one who has died with Christ (Rom. 7:4–6). He shows the law is holy, and the commandment is holy and righteous and good (Rom. 7:12). It served it's intended purpose to show the Jews who said, "All that the Lord has said, we will do", that it was an impossibility to keep the law and that they needed to move from the old covenant understanding into the everlasting covenant of faith in God. Paul now concludes that

> Christ is the end of the law for righteousness to *everyone* who believes (Rom. 10:4).

He can say this without hesitation or misunderstanding since "there is no distinction between Jew and Greek" (Rom. 10:12).

Ephesians

When writing to the church in Ephesus, which was probably composed mostly of converted Gentiles, Paul again shows that the Christian is not under old covenant law. We should note that the context deals with the covenants and the relationship between the Jews, Gentiles and Christ. Therefore, this, too, has the very highest teaching authority. He starts by reminding the Gentiles of their lost condition before they believed in Christ.

A Better Law

> Remember that you were at that time separate from Christ, excluded from the commonwealth of Israel, and strangers to the covenants of promise, having no hope and without God in the world. But now in Christ Jesus you who formerly were far off have been brought near by the blood of Christ. For He Himself is our peace, who made both groups into one, and broke down the barrier of the dividing wall, *by abolishing in His flesh the enmity, which is the Law of commandments contained in ordinances,* that in Himself He might make the two into one new man, thus establishing peace, and might reconcile them both in one body to God through the cross, by it having put to death the enmity (Eph. 2:12–16).

Here Paul says Christ abolished the enmity that existed between Jews and Gentiles. He defines this "enmity" as "the law of commandments contained in ordinances." The Greek simply says, "the law of commandments in decrees." The main points of separation between Jew and Gentile were circumcision, laws regarding clean and unclean and the Sabbath.[2]

Philippians

The church in Philippi was a favorite with Paul. These Christians had accepted the Gospel and demonstrated their love by supporting Paul's ministry on more than one occasion. Yet even this church was bothered by those who wanted to enforce old covenant laws upon Christians. Paul's counsel to them is full of insight.

> Beware of the dogs, beware of the evil workers, beware of the false circumcision; for we are the true circumcision, who worship in the Spirit of God and glory in Christ Jesus and put no confidence in the flesh, although I myself might have confidence even in the flesh. If anyone else has a mind to put confidence in the flesh, I far more; circumcised the eighth day, of the nation of Israel, of the tribe of Benjamin, a Hebrew of Hebrews, as to the Law, a Pharisee; as to zeal, a persecutor of the church, as to the righteousness which is in the Law, found blameless. But

---

[2] See Ex. 12:48; Ex. 31:12–17; Isa. 56:3–6.

whatever things were gain to me, those things I have counted as loss for the sake of Christ. More than that, I count all things to be loss in view of the surpassing value of knowing Christ Jesus my Lord, for whom I have suffered the loss of all things, and count them but rubbish in order that I may gain Christ, and may be found in Him, not having a righteousness of my own derived from the Law, but that which is through faith in Christ, the righteousness which comes from God on the basis of faith (Phil. 3:2–9).

In this one sweeping, majestic statement Paul clearly shows the weakness of old covenant law and the surpassing value of the new covenant. In doing so He shows the very essence of what the covenant was intended to do: provide relationship between man and God. He speaks of the surpassing value of "knowing Christ Jesus my Lord." He rejoices knowing that he has "gained Christ" and is now "found in Him." He exalts in "the righteousness which comes from God on the basis of faith." He clearly points out that this righteousness is *not "derived from the law."*

Colossians

In the chapter "Sabbath in the Epistles", we studied Colossians in relationship to the Sabbath. A quick review shows that this letter agrees with the other epistles in its treatment of law.

> Having canceled out the certificate of debt consisting of decrees against us and which was hostile to us; and He has taken it out of the way, having nailed it to the cross (Col. 2:14).

Some teach that what Paul calls the "certificate of debt" does not refer here to the law itself, but to a list of specific violations of the law. Therefore, what was nailed to the cross were the violations (sins) without any reference to the law itself. While it may be true that Paul was using this custom as an illustration, it does not follow that he was not at the same time including the law in what was nailed to the cross. That the law was hostile to those under its dominion is evident. It was a "yoke" that neither the Jews of Christ's day nor their forefathers could bear.[3] The law itself was intended to be a witness against the Israelites.[4]

In summarizing this section, Scripture clearly states in a number of places through contextual teaching that the old covenant law, including the Ten Commandments and the regulations for divine worship, is obsolete, ready to disappear, and should be cast out. It clearly shows that the Gentiles do not come under Sinaitic law and that even Jewish Christians have been released from the law as a guide for Christian living. However, as soon as we speak about casting out the old covenant, the words of which include the Ten Commandments, many questions come to mind. Are we saying that the moral laws of the Ten Commandments are no longer binding? Under the new covenant is it permissible to kill, steal and commit adultery? These questions deserve thorough answers.

The Ten Commandments

For many the Ten Commandments are seen to be the very high point of God's revelation of truth. How then can the new covenant speak of not being under this law written with the very finger of God?

It is my prayer that the following may bring harmony to the clear statements of Scripture which declare that the Ten Commandments are no longer binding upon Christians while maintaining the moral principles upon which they are based.

We have already shown that one cannot divide the old covenant into the two subdivisions of moral and ceremonial. It is not biblical and requires an artificial forcing of the context to do so. I believe the following subdivisions make more sense and harmonize with Scripture.

---

[3] Acts 15:10.
[4] Deut. 30:15–19; 31:26

Old covenant

Moral laws: These laws would include *all* the moral laws within the Ten Commandments and *many other* moral laws in the "book of the law." Moral is here defined as that which in itself has *intrinsic value* in man's relationship with man, or man's relationship with God.

Gospel shadows: These laws include the ritual laws and ceremonies which in some way pointed forward to and were fulfilled by Christ. In this group would be the Sabbath, the seven seasonal feasts, sabbatical years, the morning and evening sacrifice, the various sacrifices for sin, the tabernacle, the candlestick, the showbread, the laver, etc.

Covenant signs: circumcision and Sabbath. The Sabbath was both a ritual law and a covenant sign. That is why it is included within the Ten Commandments. It is of interest to note that even the Jews understood the Sabbath as a ritual law.[5]

Civil laws: These laws include the many instructions given to Israel living under a theocracy and include interpretations and applications of these laws to the specific time and culture. In this group would be those laws which dealt with slavery, divorce, retaliation, etc.

New covenant

Moral principles: All the moral laws of the old covenant would be included here but *not* in old covenant form. Instead of many detailed laws the new covenant gives a few basic principles falling under the one chief moral commandment of "you shall love one another as I have loved you." Therefore Paul could say,

---

[5] "...the Sabbath's importance is suggested by its being the only ritual law in the Ten Commandments." Rabbi Joseph Telushkin, *Biblical Literacy,* p. 429.

A Better Law

> For he who loves his neighbor has fulfilled the law. For this, "You shall not commit adultery, You shall not murder, You shall not steal, You shall not covet." and if there is any other commandment, it is summed up in the saying, "You shall love your neighbor as yourself." Love does no wrong to a neighbor; love therefore is the fulfillment of the law (Rom. 13:8–10).

Gospel: Christ's life, death and resurrection and how we participate in that finished work by faith in Christ.

Covenant signs: Baptism (and the sealing of the Holy Spirit) and the Lord's Supper.

Civil duties: These principles would include how the Christian is to relate to society and the governing authorities and would include interpretations and applications of new covenant principles to the specific time and culture.

The following diagrams show how the laws of the old and new covenants relate to eternal, moral principles.

Gospel Shadows Sacrifices Rituals	**Covenant Signs** Circumcision Sabbath	**O L D**
Civil Laws Interpretations Applications	**Moral Laws** **Moral Principles**	**Civil Duties** Interpretations Applications
N E W	**Covenant Signs** Baptism Lord's Supper	**Gospel of Christ**

The following illustration may help clarify this concept. The ancestors of the founders of the United States lived under English rule. There were "moral" laws in England which dealt with killing, stealing, and many other such crimes. England was ruled by a king with a House of Lords and a House of Commons. The document of renown was the Magna Carta. Their flag was the Union Jack. The founders of our country patterned many of their laws after the laws in England. There were, however, important differences not only in the laws, but also in the administration of the laws. The United States does not have a king, a House of Lords, or a House of Commons. Rather our government has an elected president to administer the laws made by the Senate and House of Representatives. Our document of renown is the Constitution; our flag is the Stars and Stripes. As a U.S. citizen I am *not* under English rule. Their laws do *not* apply to me in *any* way. However, that does not give me the right to kill, steal and commit other crimes. Why? Because under U.S. law these things are *also* forbidden. Such is the relationship between the old and new covenants.

<u>Both the old and new covenants embrace the moral principles given by God</u>. They differ, however, in the *administration* of those principles, and they have different "flags"— *covenant signs*.

Thus, while the new covenant clearly embraces *all* the moral laws of the old covenant, it presents these laws differently (general principles rather than specific details), it has a different emphasis (grace [done] rather than law [do]), it has a broader scope (all nations rather than just Israel) and it has a different flag (Lord's Supper rather than Sabbath).

Does this mean that the Old Testament is no longer of value to Christian Bible study? Never! The Old Testament is a gold mine of truth. But woe to the person who tries to apply old covenant law according to old covenant guidelines! What we must do, however, is interpret *all* old covenant statements in light of the new covenant.

Many have stumbled in their interpretation of Scripture in trying to make the covenant signs intrinsically moral. They are not moral in themselves and have religious value *only* as they are celebrated in connection with the covenant of which they are signs. There is no religious value in being submerged in water *unless* it is done as Christian baptism. There is no religious value in eating bread or drinking wine (or grape juice) *unless* it is done in remembrance of Christ's death. There was no religious significance to circumcision *unless* it was done as a sign of the covenant community of the "sons of Israel." Likewise there is no religious significance in resting on the Sabbath *unless* it is done as a sign of the covenant between God and the sons of Israel.

It is vitally important to realize that when we speak of the old covenant, including the Ten Commandments, being superseded by the new covenant, we are speaking of the old covenant in totality, yet at the same time we are *not* doing away with *any* of the *moral principles* contained within the old covenant. We must also understand that for society to function without anarchy it must continue to have *specific moral laws* to restrain the evil of the unregenerate heart. Today modern society is reaping the results of the violation of God's moral law. God's eternal moral principles are not optional for a successful society.

Modern secular humanists who disregard God's moral principles will reap the inevitable results. We are seeing within the United States and throughout the world a growing anarchy and human degeneration as a direct result of disobedience to God's moral laws.

However, the history of the Jews living under the old covenant gives ample illustration of the limitations of *specific laws* to govern *righteous living*. The Jews were continually faced with the interpretation of numerous laws for specific life situations. The new covenant, on the other hand, offers a much better guide for righteous living in that it operates from basic principles and the Christian has the indwelling Holy Spirit to interpret these principles to specific life situations and to give the power for living the Christ-like life.

Sabbath Command not in the "Better Law"

The chart below shows that all the moral principles found in the Ten Commandment law of the old covenant, have been repeated in the new covenant with the exception of the Sabbath command. This fact adds strength to our conclusion that the Sabbath is a ritual law associated only with the old covenant and is not an eternal moral principle.

Decalogue	**O.C. command**	**N.C. Parallel**
No other gods	Ex. 20:3	1 Cor. 8:6
	Deut. 5:7	Eph. 4:6
No idols	Ex. 20:4–6	1 John 5:21
	Deut. 5:8–10	Rom. 1:23, Eph. 5:5
Not take God's	Ex. 20:7	1 Tim. 6:1
name in vain	Deut. 5:11	Mt. 6:9
Keep the Sabbath	Ex. 20:8–11	None
	Deut. 5:12–15	None
Honor parents	Ex. 20:12	Eph. 6:2, 3
	Deut. 5:16	Mk. 10:19
Not murder	Ex. 20:13	Rom. 13:9
	Deut. 5:17	1 Jn. 3:15
No adultery	Ex. 20:14	Rom. 13:9
	Deut. 5:18	Gal. 5:19–21, Mt. 5:27, 28
Not steal	Ex. 20:15	Rom. 13:9
	Deut. 5:19	Eph. 4:28

No false testimony	Ex. 20:16	Rom. 13:9
	Deut. 5:20	Mk. 10:19
Not covet	Ex. 20:17	Rom. 13:9
	Deut. 5:21	Heb. 13:5; Mk. 7:22

The Jerusalem Council

The Jerusalem Council, as recorded in Acts 15, was called for the express purpose of determining how a Christian was to relate to old covenant law. After much debate the council's written conclusion was,

> For it seemed good to the Holy Spirit and to us to lay upon you [Gentile Christians] no greater burden than these essentials: That you abstain from things sacrificed to idols and from blood and from things strangled and from fornication; if you keep yourselves free from such things, you do well. Farewell (Acts 15:28, 29).

In the light of our previous study, this short summary is full of insight. Some have argued that this statement implies the Ten Commandments are still binding, or they would have given instruction regarding killing, stealing, etc., which obviously a Christian should not do. However, upon closer investigation, just the opposite is the case. Rather than take for granted that the Ten Commandments are still binding—which flies in the very face of the clear, contextual statements we studied above and the whole conclusion of the Jerusalem Council—we must take for granted that these new covenant Christians were under the new covenant principle of "Love one another as I have loved you." And because of this one far-reaching, basic moral principle, there was no need to spell out the details "You shall not kill," "You shall not steal," etc.

As we look at what *was* requested of the Gentile Christians one thing becomes immediately apparent: The required items were an addition to the basic new covenant principle of love, or were an interpretation of that principle. There were three requests the church council made of the Gentile converts. First, they were asked to abstain from eating food which had been sacrificed to idols. First Corinthians 8 is devoted to this issue. In summary they were asked to abstain so they would not be a stumbling block to those weak in faith.

Second, these new Christians were asked to abstain from blood and from things strangled. This request was probably made because these practices were most offensive to the Jews and would therefore hinder Christian witness.

The third request of the Jerusalem Council was that Gentiles abstain from fornication. Why this request? Because there was danger then, as there is danger today, that someone might interpret "love one another" in a selfish, lustful way and the Gentiles were known to come from a very immoral society.[6] Also, as F.F. Bruce suggests, it served to keep Gentile Christians within the scope of proper marriage bounds.[7]

Some have argued that if the Sabbath were not binding in the New Testament church there would have been as heated a discussion regarding it as there was over circumcision. But this argument is flawed because it leaves out one important fact. In Judaism, Sabbath observance was required *only* if one was a member of the covenant community of which circumcision was the entrance sign.[8]

---

[6] Lenski, *Commentary on the New Testament, 1-2 Corinthians,* (Hendrickson Publishers, 1937, 1963), p. 12.

[7] See Deut. 18 and F.F. Bruce, *Paul: Apostle of the Heart Set Free,* (Eerdmans Publishing Co., Grand Rapids MI, 1977), p. 185.

[8] "The biblical evidence is that the Sabbath was inaugurated for the people of Israel to be celebrated as a weekly sign of the covenant. The Sabbath is not viewed as a universal ordinance for all mankind but as a

A Better Law

Let me illustrate this same principle in the new covenant. What Christian would seek to enforce the celebration of the Lord's Supper upon someone who had not accepted Christ and had not been baptized? Rather, the Lord's Supper in most churches is given *only* to those who have been baptized into Christ. The issue in the New Testament church was not circumcision, per se; rather it was whether Christians should observe the old covenant regulations. The reason circumcision held such a prominent place in the discussions of the early church is that it was the entrance sign for the old covenant community and thus stood for *all* old covenant practices. Here is the important point: If circumcision was not required for Gentile Christians, then neither would Sabbath observance be required, for the Sabbath was reserved only for members of the old covenant community. There is no hint in Scripture that the Sabbath was ever given to any nation or people other than the children of Israel.

> The sons of Israel shall observe the sabbath, to celebrate the sabbath throughout their generations as a perpetual covenant. It is a sign between Me and the sons of Israel forever (Ex. 31:16, 17).

Not only was circumcision not required in the New Testament church, it was forbidden for religious purposes.

> It was for freedom that Christ set us free; therefore keep standing firm and do not be subject again to a yoke of slavery. Behold I, Paul, say to you that if you receive circumcision, Christ will be of no benefit to you. And I testify again to every man who receives circumcision, that he is under obligation to

---

specific institution for Israel. As a sign of the covenant it was to last as long as that covenant." Harold H.P. Dressler, "The Sabbath in the Old Testament" in *From Sabbath to Lord's Day,* p.34. "Judaism as a whole considered the Sabbath to be binding on Israel alone." Max M.B. Turner, "The Sabbath, Sunday, and the Law in Luke/Acts" in *From Sabbath to Lord's Day,* p.128.

keep the whole Law. You have been severed from Christ, you who are seeking to be justified by law; you have fallen from grace (Gal. 5:1–4).

If Paul took a strong stand against those who were circumcised for *religious reasons* would he not do the same thing to those who wanted to keep Sabbath, the other sign of the old covenant? I believe he did in Colossians 2:16, 17 and Galatians 4:10, 11, as was pointed out in Chapter 14 of this study.

The Jerusalem Council settled the issue to which this book is devoted. It did so, however, not by dealing with the Sabbath directly, but by way of eliminating the entrance sign into the old covenant: circumcision.

Chapter Summary

1. Christians are not under the authority of the old covenant.
   a. Hebrews 8 and 9 specifically mention the "tables of the covenant" and "regulations for divine worship" and say this covenant is old and ready to disappear.
   b. Galatians 3 states that the law was in effect *until* Christ came.
   c. Galatians 3 states that Christians are no longer under Sinaitic law.
   d. Galatians 4 states that Christians are to cast out the bondwoman (a term Paul uses for the old covenant) and those who try to enforce old covenant laws upon Christians.
   e. Romans 4 states that the Gentiles can partake of the promise of righteousness by faith given to Abraham, completely bypassing all old covenant law.

A Better Law

    f. Romans 7 states that even Jewish Christians are released from the law as a guide to Christian service.
    g. Romans 8 states that only the Christian who "walks by the Spirit" can enter into full fellowship with God.
    h. Romans 10 states that Christ is the end of the law for righteousness to everyone who believes.
    i. Ephesians 2 states that Christ abolished the enmity which "is the law of commandments contained in ordinances."
    j. Philippians 3 states that righteousness comes from God on the basis of faith, not in obedience to law.
    k. Colossians 2 states that the certificate of debt which was hostile to us (the old covenant) was nailed to the cross.
2. The old covenant laws can best be divided into four sections:
    a. Moral laws
    b. Gospel shadows, including the Sabbath
    c. Covenant signs: circumcision and Sabbath
    d. Civil laws
3. The new covenant laws can best be divided into four sections:
    a. Moral principles
    b. Gospel
    c. Covenant signs: baptism (and sealing of the Holy Spirit) and the Lord's Supper
    d. Civil duties
4. The moral principles of the new covenant contain *all* the moral principles upon which the old covenant moral laws were based.
5. God's moral principles are not an option. They are eternal and apply to all mankind.

6. Covenant signs have value *only* when they are celebrated in relationship to the covenant of which they are a sign. They are not moral in themselves.
7. The moral principles behind the Ten Commandments are all repeated in the New Testament. The command to keep the Sabbath holy is not repeated in the New Testament indicating that the Sabbath is a ritual law associated with the old covenant and not an eternal moral principle.
8. The Jerusalem Council settled the question regarding the Christians' duty to observe the old covenant. Its decision was that Gentiles did not have to observe the old covenant. The point of discussion was circumcision as it was the entrance sign to the old covenant and stood for all old covenant practices.
   a. The Jerusalem Council took for granted that the Christians would be under the law of Christ, and the command to "love one another as Christ loved us" would cover the moral principles.
   b. The Jerusalem Council instructed the Gentile believers to:
      1) Abstain from eating food offered to idols—to keep them from being a stumbling block to the weak.
      2) Abstain from blood and things strangled—most offensive to their Jewish brothers.
      3) Abstain from immorality—a needed clarification of the commandment to love one another.
9. Paul states that if a Christian receives circumcision for *religious reasons* he will fall from grace. The required observance of old covenant signs places one in the position of having to obey the *whole* old covenant.

CHAPTER EIGHTEEN

JESUS, THE LAW'S FULFILLMENT

Matthew 5:17–19

Matthew 5:17–19 has been a very important text to Sabbath keepers and others who want to support the continuing nature of the Ten Commandments. These verses deserve our careful study.

> Think not that I have come to abolish the Law or the Prophets; I did not come to abolish, but to fulfill. For truly I say to you, until heaven and earth pass away, not the smallest letter or stroke shall pass away from the Law, until all is accomplished. Whoever then annuls one of the least of these commandments, and so teaches others, shall be called least in the kingdom of heaven; but whoever keeps and teaches them, he shall be called great in the kingdom of heaven (Mt. 5:17–19).

The meaning of this text hinges on the meaning of two key words: Law and fulfill. Does "Law" refer to the Ten Commandments? Or, does "Law" refer to the whole old covenant? Does "fulfill" mean "do, and keep on doing" or does it mean "do," in the sense that when it is once done, it is accomplished and no longer needs to be done again? Two widely differing interpretations have been given to these verses.

The first goes something like this: "By this statement, Jesus unmistakably teaches that the Ten Commandments are to continue and will not come to an end. This means that Christians must live in harmony with the Ten Commandment law, which includes Sabbath observance, for not even the smallest letter or stroke is to be removed from this law. Those who teach that the law is abolished are clearly going against the will of Christ."

The second interpretation says that "Jesus clearly teaches that the whole law (including all that is written in the Torah) is to remain in force 'until all is fulfilled.' By His life, death, and resurrection Jesus fulfilled all the old covenant law (and prophecies) so this law is no longer binding on Christians."

To interpret these verses correctly we must first define the meaning of the two key words, "law" and "fulfill." This is best done by comparing all the other passages in the book of Matthew which use these two words and finding the meaning Matthew gives to them in other settings. Then with this information we can interpret these verses accordingly.

The "law" in Matthew

The following quotations contain all the usages of the word "law" in the book of Matthew.

> Therefore, however you want people to treat you, so treat them, for this is the *Law* and the Prophets (Mt. 7:12).

As used in this verse "Law" refers to the whole Torah (books of Moses) for it is associated with prophets. Thus, we have represented here two of the three divisions of the Old Testament Scriptures which were divided into Law, Prophets, and Psalms. Without doubt the Ten Commandments are included in this law, but we cannot limit "law" as used here to the Ten Commandments.

> For all the prophets and the *Law* prophesied until John (Mt. 11:13).

In this verse the "Law" refers to the whole Torah for again it is linked with prophets.

Jesus, the Law's Fulfillment

> Or have you not read in the *Law,* that on the Sabbath the priests in the temple break the Sabbath, and are innocent (Mt. 12:5).

The portion of the "Law" referred to here is not the Ten Commandments but Lev. 24:5–9, which gives the duties of the priests.

> "Teacher, which is the great commandment in the *Law?"* And He said to him, "You shall love the Lord your God with all your heart, and with all your soul, and with all your mind." This is the great and foremost commandment. And a second is like it, "You shall love your neighbor as yourself" (Mt. 22:36–39).

The first quotation is taken from Deuteronomy 6:5 and the second is from Leviticus 19:18. No portion of the Ten Commandments is quoted.

> On these two commandments depend the *whole Law* and the Prophets (Mt. 22:40).

Again the "whole Law and the Prophets" makes it mandatory that we define "Law" as the Torah, and not limit it to the Ten Commandments.

> Woe to you, scribes and Pharisees, hypocrites! For you tithe mint and dill and cummin, and have neglected the weightier provision of the *law*: justice and mercy and faithfulness; but these are the things you should have done without neglecting the others (Mt. 23:23).

Again, "law" as used here is more than the Ten Commandments.

These are all the passages in the book of Matthew which use "Law," other than the use of this term in Matthew 5:17–19. Therefore, unless there are strong contextual reasons for interpreting "law" as the Ten Commandments in Matthew 5:17–19, we must understand "law" as referring to the Torah, the books of Moses, because in *every other* use of the word "law" in the book of Matthew it *never once* refers to the Ten Commandments alone, but *always* to the whole law, or to portions of the law *other than* the Ten Commandments.

When we look at the context of Matthew 5:17–19 we immediately recognize Jesus uses "Law" with the "Prophets." "Think not that I have come to abolish the Law or the Prophets..." Even the context here leans heavily in favor of understanding "Law" to be the Torah. We must, therefore, conclude that the "Law" Jesus has reference to is the *entire* old covenant law, which included the Ten Commandments.

"Fulfill" in the book of Matthew

Below are listed all the passages where Matthew uses the word "fulfill." In each passage seek to determine what Matthew means when he uses this word. Does he use "fulfill" to apply to an event which was done once and needs never to be done again, or does he use "fulfill" in the idea of "do and keep on doing"?

> Now all this took place that what was spoken by the Lord through the prophet might be *fulfilled,* saying, "Behold, the virgin shall be with child, and shall bear a Son and they shall call His name Immanuel," which translated means, "God with us" (Mt. 1:22, 23).

Here "fulfilled" is used in connection with the virgin birth of Jesus, an event which was done only once. There is no other fulfillment by Christians intended.

> And [Joseph with Jesus] was there until the death of Herod; that what was spoken by the Lord through the prophet might be *fulfilled,* saying, "Out of Egypt did I call My Son" (Mt. 2:15).

Jesus was called out of Egypt only once. The believer in Christ has nothing to do with this fulfillment.

> Then that which was spoken through Jeremiah the prophet was *fulfilled* saying, "A voice was heard in Ramah, weeping and great mourning, Rachel weeping for her children" (Mt. 2:17).

This prophecy was "fulfilled" once by the events connected with the birth of Jesus. There is no ongoing fulfillment in view here.

Jesus, the Law's Fulfillment

> And [Joseph with Jesus] came and resided in a city called Nazareth; that what was spoken through the prophets might be *fulfilled*, "He shall be called a Nazarene" (Mt. 2:23).

There was no ongoing fulfillment of this prophecy. It was done once and is not to be repeated by Christians.

> But Jesus answering said to him, "Permit it at this time; for in this way it is fitting for us to *fulfill* all righteousness." Then he permitted Him (Mt. 3:15).

The context is the baptism of Jesus by John. In this passage fulfill can be understood as "do". Also, the fact that Jesus says "us" indicates that it is something a Christian is expected to do. Note, however, that the context has nothing to do with the Ten Commandments.

> This was to *fulfill* what was spoken through Isaiah the prophet, saying, "The land of Zebulun and the land of Naphtali, by the way of the sea, beyond the Jordan, Galilee of the Gentiles—The people who were sitting in darkness saw a great light, and to those who were sitting in the land and shadow of death, upon them a light dawned" (Mt. 4:14–16).

Jesus, by coming to the area named in this prophecy, fulfilled this Old Testament prophecy. There is nothing for obedient Christians to do here.

> Again, you have heard that the ancients were told, "You shall not make false vows, but shall *fulfill* your vows to the Lord" (Mt. 5:33).

In context, Jesus quotes from the old covenant and then says, "But I say unto you..." showing his authority *over* old covenant law. Then in the next verses he *contrasts* His teaching to that of the law.

> In order that what was spoken through Isaiah the prophet might be *fulfilled*, saying, "He Himself took our infirmities, and carried away our diseases" (Mt. 8:17).

There is no further fulfillment by Christians in this verse as Christ is the only sin-bearer and He did this only once.

In order that what was spoken through Isaiah the prophet, might be *fulfilled* saying, Behold, My Servant whom I have chosen; My Beloved in whom My soul is well pleased; I will put My Spirit upon Him and He shall proclaim justice to the Gentiles. He will not quarrel, nor cry out; nor will anyone hear His voice in the streets. A battered reed He will not break off, and a smoldering wick He will not put out, until He leads justice to victory. And in His name the Gentiles will hope (Mt. 12:17–21).

Christ fulfilled this prophecy once.

And in this case the prophecy of Isaiah is being *fulfilled,* which says, "You will keep on seeing, but will not perceive; for the heart of this people has become dull" (Mt. 13:14, 15).

The people of Jesus' day fulfilled this prophecy by their rejection of Jesus.

Now this took place that what was spoken through the prophet might be *fulfilled,* saying, "Say to the daughter of Zion, Behold your King is coming to you, gentle, and mounted upon a donkey, even upon a colt, the foal of a beast of burden" (Mt. 21:4, 5).

Christ and Christ alone fulfilled this prophecy once.

Or do you think that I cannot appeal to My Father, and He will at once put at My disposal more than twelve legions of angels? How then shall the Scriptures be *fulfilled,* that it must happen this way? (Mt. 26:53, 54).

Christ fulfilled this prophecy once.

"But all this has taken place that the Scriptures of the prophets may be fulfilled," Then all the disciples left Him and fled (Mt. 26:56).

The disciples fulfilled this prophecy once. There is no ongoing fulfillment.

Then that which was spoken through Jeremiah the prophet was *fulfilled,* saying, "And they took the thirty pieces of silver, the price of the one whose price had been set by the sons of Israel; and they gave them for the Potter's Field, as the Lord directed me" (Mt. 27:9, 10).

Jesus, the Law's Fulfillment

This prophecy was fulfilled when Judas betrayed Christ for thirty pieces of silver.

In the book of Matthew every time—with two possible exceptions—when the word "fulfill" is used, it is employed in connection with the life of Christ, or the events connected with it. In these possible exceptions[1] the Ten Commandments are not in view. In all the other instances it was one event which "fulfilled" the prophecy with no ongoing fulfillment intended for Christians.

For these reasons we should interpret the word "fulfill" in Matthew 5:17–19 as referring to something that Jesus would do in connection with His work as the Messiah unless there are strong contextual reasons to do otherwise.

With this background, let us return to Matthew 5:17–19.

> Think not that I have come to abolish the Law or the Prophets; I did not come to abolish, but to *fulfill*. For truly I say to you, until heaven and earth pass away, not the smallest letter or stroke shall pass away from the Law, until all is accomplished. Whoever then annuls one of the least of these commandments, and so teaches others, shall be called least in the kingdom of heaven; but whoever keeps and teaches them, he shall be called great in the kingdom of heaven.

In John we read,

> After this, Jesus, knowing that *all things had already been accomplished,* in order that Scripture might be *fulfilled,* said, "I am thirsty" (Jn. 19:28–30).

This verse is extremely important to a correct understanding of Matthew 5:17–19. Here we find that Jesus had already accomplished all but one of the prophecies regarding the life and death of the Messiah. One thing, however, still remained to be fulfilled, so Jesus said, "I thirst."

When we let Scripture be our interpreter, the meaning of this passage becomes evident. Notice how it fits perfectly into the context. In the book of Matthew we find this

---

[1] Mt. 3:13; Mt. 5:33.

passage coming soon after Jesus gives His "blessings" on the mount. It comes *just before* the six times He says, "You have heard...but I say unto you." In the context it is evident that Jesus is taking authority to Himself greater than that of old covenant law. It would be very easy for His listeners to conclude that He was completely doing away with the binding nature of the old covenant. This He will do, but not before He *completely fulfills* the prophecies, types and shadows which pointed forward to His work as the Messiah and Savior of the world which are recorded in the law. Therefore, the law must continue *until* He has *accomplished* everything. This happened, according to John, at the death of Jesus. This harmonizes perfectly with the teaching of Paul in Romans and Galatians.

This interpretation is the only one supported by the contextual setting. If one were to conclude that Jesus was teaching the continuing nature of the law in this passage, the Christian would immediately be faced with a dilemma. For this Scripture expressly states that *not one thing, not even the smallest punctuation mark, is to be removed from the law.* Thus, if the Christian is going to use this text to prove the perpetuity of the old covenant law, he must also use it to prove the binding nature of *all* old covenant law. In writing to the Galatians Paul warned his readers that they could *not* take only part of the law and leave the rest.

> I testify again to every man who received circumcision, that he *is under obligation to keep the whole law* (Gal. 5:3).

We are left with only two choices: Jesus fulfilled the law for us and thus freed us from the dominion of the old covenant, or we must keep *every bit* of the old covenant. <u>There are no other choices</u>.

How Jesus fulfilled the law

All would agree that Jesus fulfilled the prophecies, but how, some ask, did He fulfill the law? First we have His clear statement.

Jesus, the Law's Fulfillment

> You search the Scriptures, because you think that in them you have eternal life; and it is these that bear witness of Me; and you are unwilling to come to Me that you might have life (Jn. 5:38, 39).
>
> For if you believed Moses [books of the law], you would believe Me; for he wrote of Me (Jn. 5:46).

The context of this last quotation from John is in connection with a Sabbath healing. This suggests that the Sabbath was one of the ways the law spoke of Christ.

On the day of His resurrection Jesus joined two disciples as they walked to Emmaus. Luke gives a summary of the discussion.

> And beginning with Moses and with all the prophets, He explained to them the things concerning Himself in all the Scriptures (Lk. 24:27).

Following is a partial list of things in the law which pointed forward to Christ and were fulfilled by Him.

Burnt offering	Continual forgiveness (1 Jn. 2:1, 2)
Blood of sacrifice	Blood of Christ (Heb. 10:19)
Most Holy Place	Presence of God (Heb. 10:19–23)
Tabernacle	Incarnation (Jn. 1:1–3, 14)
Shekinah	Glory of God's Son (Jn. 1:14)
Uplifted serpent	The cross of Christ (Jn. 3:14)
Laver	Regeneration (Heb. 10:22; Tit. 3:5)
Showbread	The bread of life (Jn. 6:48)
Candlestick	The light of world (Jn. 8:12)
Veil of tabernacle	The flesh of Christ (Heb. 10:20)
Regular priest	Christ's intercession (Heb. 7:23, 25)
High priest	Redemption (Heb. 9:11, 12)
Circumcision	Removal of the "flesh" (Col. 2:11f.)
Passover	Lamb of God (Jn. 1:36)
Day of Atonement	Expiation for sin (Heb. 10:14)
Sabbath	The rest of grace (Heb. 4:8–11)
Sabbatical years	God's provision (Mt. 6:31–34)
Jubilee	Liberation (Lk. 4:18, 19)

The same theme of fulfillment/transformation, shadow/reality is seen throughout the epistles

2 Corinthians 3

Ministry of death	Ministry of righteousness

Galatians 3

The law was our tutor	To lead us to Christ
No longer under the tutor	You are sons of God

Colossians 2

A mere shadow	In Him you are complete
of what was to come	The substance is Christ

Hebrews 1:1–3

God spoke (partially)	God has spoken (finally)
Long ago	In these last days
To the fathers	In His Son
In many portions	Who is the radiance of His glory
In many ways	The exact representation of His nature

Hebrews 8

Obsolete covenant	New and better covenant

> If you believed Moses, you would believe Me; for he wrote of Me (Jn. 5:46).

Jesus, the fulfillment of the Law's moral principles

At this point some may ask, "Has Jesus also fulfilled the *moral* principles of the law?" The answer is a resounding *YES!* That is the good news of the Gospel!

> So then as through one transgression there resulted condemnation to all men; even so through one act of righteousness [the life and death of Jesus] there resulted justification of life to all men. For as through the one man's disobedience the many were made sinners, even so through the obedience of the One the many will be made righteous (Rom. 5:18, 19).

The heart of the new covenant gospel is that we are accepted, not on the basis of our own moral law keeping, but upon the perfect righteousness of Christ which far surpasses the righteousness of the law. It is this fact, and this fact *alone,* that gives us the assurance of salvation. It is this "one act of righteousness"—by "the obedience of the One"—that is the only foundation stone of Christian assurance.

In Him you have been made complete (Col. 2:10). [Therefore]…we have confidence to enter the [most] holy place by the blood of Jesus (Heb. 10:19). For by *one offering* He has perfected for all time those who are being sanctified (Heb. 10:14).

Does this mean that the Christian does not have to live a moral life? Never! In Greek "being sanctified" is in the present continuous tense indicating that God has us all in the process of "being made holy." The Christian's moral life is not the *basis* of his acceptance with God, rather it is the *result* of it. As paradoxical as the following statement sounds, it is nevertheless true. Whenever the new covenant gospel is presented in its *clarity* there is danger of *misunderstanding.* It was true in Paul's day; it is true in ours. I am reminded of the time some years ago when one of our sons and I climbed Mt. Shasta. We spent a sleepless, bitterly cold night near the top of this 14,000-foot windy, snow-covered mountain. The next morning we started our descent. I'll never forget the mixed feeling of exhilaration and fear I had as we inched our way along the steep, slippery spine of a ridge. One step too far to the left and we would slide hundreds, if not thousands, of feet down an icy precipice of the mountain. One step too far to the right and we would fall over a steep cliff. A mistake on either side would prove fatal. So it is with the gospel. Jesus said

> For the gate is small and the way is narrow that leads to life... (Mt. 7:14).

Were it not for the Spirit's continuous ministry in each life, no one could ever make it. When we understand the heights and depths of grace we must be careful that the freedom of the gospel does not give license, on one hand, to live in sin. On the other hand, we must never let our holy living enter into the basis of our acceptance with God.

For example, in the book of Romans, Paul lays a solid foundation of justification by faith in Chapters 3–5.

> For we maintain that a man is justified by faith apart from works of the Law (Rom. 3:28).

He speaks of Christ's "one act of righteousness," and "the obedience of the One." As Paul climbs the towering mountain of grace he senses the danger of taking just one step off the path of truth. "What shall we say then? Are we to continue in sin that grace might increase?" (Rom. 6:1). Notice carefully the reasoning of his argument.

> May it never be! How shall we who died to sin still live in it? Or do you not know that all of us who have been baptized into Christ Jesus have been baptized into His death? Therefore we have been buried with Him through baptism into death, in order that as Christ was raised from the dead through the glory of the Father, so we too might walk in newness of life...even so consider yourselves to be dead to sin, but alive to God in Christ Jesus (Rom. 6:2–4, 11).

Because of what Christ has *already* done for us we can now "consider" ourselves to be dead to sin and free to live for God. In Romans 13 Paul gives admonition regarding Christian living. Quoting from a portion of the Ten Commandments, he says,

> Owe nothing to anyone except to love one another; for *he who loves his neighbor has fulfilled the law.* For this, "You shall not commit adultery, You shall not murder, You shall not steal, You

Jesus, the Law's Fulfillment

shall not covet," and if there is any other commandment, it is summed up in one saying, "You shall love your neighbor as yourself." Love does no wrong to a neighbor; *love therefore is the fulfillment of the law* (Rom. 13:8–10).

In these verses Paul clearly shows that the law of love encompasses *all* the moral principles of the Ten Commandments.

In the book of Galatians Paul gives the same advice.

> For you were called to freedom, brethren; only do not turn your freedom into an opportunity for the flesh, but through love serve one another. *For the whole Law is fulfilled in one word, in the statement, "You shall love your neighbor as yourself"* (Gal. 5:13, 14).

By His life, death and resurrection, and the events connected with them, Jesus fulfilled the law and the prophecies pointing forward to the Messiah.

> Now He said to them, "These are My words which I spoke to you while I was still with you, that all things which are written about Me in the Law of Moses and the Prophets and the Psalms must be fulfilled" (Lk. 24:44).
>
> And when they had carried out all that was written concerning Him, they took Him down from the cross and laid Him in a tomb (Acts 13:29).
>
> For as many as may be the promises of God, in Him they are yes; wherefore also by Him is our Amen to the glory of God through us (2 Cor. 1:20).

Chapter Summary

1. In Matthew 5:17–19 Jesus clearly teaches that the whole law (including all that is written in the Torah) was to remain in force until all was fulfilled. By His life, death, and resurrection Jesus fulfilled all the old covenant law (and prophecies) so this law is no longer binding on Christians.
    a. Every time the word "law" is used in the book of Matthew it is *always* used for the whole old covenant or for some portion of the old covenant *other than* the Ten Commandments.

      b. Every time the word "fulfill" is used in the book of Matthew it is always used in connection with the events surrounding the life of Christ. It is *never* used in the context of an ongoing practice in the life of a Christian.
      c. The interpretation above harmonizes with the context of Matthew and the other gospel writers.
      d. If Matthew 5:17–19 is interpreted to prove the perpetuity of the old covenant law, then one must keep the whole old covenant law, for not even a punctuation mark is to be removed.
2. The New Testament clearly shows how the ceremonies and practices of the old covenant pointed forward to some aspect of the life, death or resurrection of Christ.
3. By His perfect life, sacrificial death and resurrection Jesus fulfilled God's moral requirements for us.
4. The freedom of the gospel does not give Christians the liberty to sin.
5. The holy living of the Christian is never the basis of his acceptance with God, but the result of it.
6. All the moral principles upon which the Ten Commandments are founded and other old covenant moral laws can be summed up in the one principle of love.
7. The morality taught in the new covenant supersedes the morality taught in the old covenant.

CHAPTER NINETEEN

THE REST THAT REMAINS

Hebrews 3 and 4

We now come to the good news of this study on the Sabbath: the "rest" that remains for the believer. There is real gold, so to speak, in these two chapters of Hebrews. These are not easy chapters to read or understand. Therefore to extract the precious "gold" will require concentrated effort on our part. Hebrews was written to Jewish Christians who had undergone some persecution and who would be faced with more in the future. It was intended to show the superiority of Christianity over Judaism. Or, to put it in other words, these chapters show how much better the new covenant is than the old. Notice how this theme of "betterness" is central to this book.

- Jesus is a better revelation of truth (Heb. 1:1–3)
- Jesus is better than the angels (Heb. 1:3–14)
- Jesus is better than Moses (Heb. 3:1–6)
- Jesus is better than Aaron (Heb. 5)
- Jesus is a better high priest (Heb. 6, 7)
- The new covenant has a better law (Heb. 7:12)
- The new covenant is a better covenant (Heb. 8:6)
- The new covenant has better promises (Heb. 8:6)
- The new covenant has a greater temple (Heb. 9:11)
- The new covenant has better sacrifices (Heb. 9:23)

- The new covenant has a better possession (Heb. 10:34)
- The new covenant has a better country (Heb. 11:16)
- The new covenant has a better resurrection (Heb. 11:35)
- The new covenant has something better (Heb. 11:40)
- The new covenant has better blood (Heb. 12:24)
- The new covenant has better atonement (Heb. 10:1–5)

In this list from Hebrews we have left out the last part of Chapter 3 and all of Chapter 4. Here our author argues that the new covenant has *a better Sabbath*. We will study one or two verses at a time, extract the facts from these verses and summarize what is taught. We will consider the concept of rest within the context of the whole book of Hebrews. Then we will simply review the summaries, and the meaning will become clear.

In the third and fourth chapters of Hebrews the writer shows how Jesus is greater than Moses. He demonstrates this by showing that Moses, as a servant, did not give his household (Israel) "God's rest." Then he proves that Christ, as a faithful Son over His household (the church), does give "God's rest." It is important to note that the author of Hebrews is drawing upon Psalm 95 for his support. Follow closely as he works out this truth.

> Now Moses was faithful in all His house [Israel] as a servant (Heb. 3:5).
>
> Christ was faithful as a Son over His house [the church] whose house we are, if we hold fast our confidence and the boast of our hope firm until the end (Heb. 3:6).

Israel, the household of Moses, lost faith because the people hardened their hearts (Heb. 3:8). Here we know that our author is referring to the experience recorded in Exodus 17:7 where Israel put the Lord to the test. We know this because the author of Hebrews quotes Psalm 95, which in turn mentions "Meribath and Massah" by name. Because of the unbelief demonstrated at Meribath and Massah, Israel was left to wander in the wilderness for forty years (Heb. 3:9). "As I swore in My wrath, they shall not enter My rest" (Heb. 3:11). Then our author brings a timely warning to his readers,

> But take care, brethren, lest there should be in any one of you an evil, unbelieving heart, in falling away from the living God. But encourage one another *day after day,* as long as it is still called *"Today,"* lest any one of you be hardened by the deceitfulness of sin. For we have become partakers of Christ, if we hold fast the beginning of our assurance firm until the end (Heb. 3:12–14). *Today* if you hear His voice, do not harden your hearts (Heb. 3:15). And to whom did He swear that they should not enter *His rest,* but to those who were disobedient? And so we see that they were not able to enter because of unbelief (Heb. 3:18, 19).

So far we can extract five important facts from these words. (1) As Israel lost faith on the very borders of the promised land, so the Church needs to be certain that it not lose faith. (2) Israel (those who tested God as recorded in Ex. 17:7) did not enter *God's rest.* (3) They did not enter God's rest because of unbelief. (4) Emphasis is placed on "today" as the day of decision. (5) "Today" is an extended period of time: "as long as it is called today."

> Therefore, let us fear lest, while *a promise remains of entering His rest,* any one of you should seem to have come short of it (Heb. 4:1).

The author clearly states that there *remains a promise of entering God's rest.* Notice carefully in the next few verses *how* one enters God's rest!

> For indeed we have had *good news* preached to us, just as they also; but the word they heard did not profit them, because it was not united by faith in those who heard. For *we who have believed enter that rest;* just as He has said, "As I swore in My wrath, they shall not enter My rest," although His works were *finished* from the foundation of the world (Heb. 4:2, 3).

Here we find three more facts which need to be underlined in our thinking. (1) The rest of God has to do with the *"good news."* (2) We enter the rest of God by *believing.* (3) This "rest" is in some way related to the *finished* work of creation.

> For He has thus said somewhere concerning the *seventh day,* "And God rested on the seventh day from all His works"; and again in this passage, "They shall not enter My rest" (Heb. 4:4, 5).

Here, as if to add emphasis, our author repeats two important points: (1) The "rest" is related to the seventh-day creation rest. (2) This "rest" Israel did *not* experience.

> Since therefore it remains for some to enter it, and those who formerly had good news preached to them failed to enter because of disobedience, He again fixes a day, *"Today,"* saying through David after so long a time just as has been said before. *"Today"* if you hear His voice, do not harden your hearts" (Heb. 4:7).

Here the author of Hebrews shows that Israel, *in the time of David,* had not yet entered God's rest. Then he quotes Psalm 95:7, stressing the idea that *"Today"* we are not to harden our hearts. He drives this point home.

> For if Joshua had given them rest, He would not have spoken of *another day* after that (Heb. 4:8).

While it is obvious that if Israel had not yet entered God's rest by the time of David, certainly they could not have entered it in the days of Joshua, as Joshua lived long before David. Nevertheless it is of interest to note what is said about Joshua and rest. Our author states forthrightly that Joshua did *not* give Israel "rest." But did he? Notice carefully these verses taken from the book of Joshua.

> And the Lord gave them *rest* on every side, according to all that He had sworn to their fathers, and no one of all their enemies stood before them; for the Lord gave all their enemies into their hand. Not one of the good promises which the Lord had made to the house of Israel failed; all came to pass (Josh. 21:43–45).

The Rest that Remains

Here, on one hand, the writer of Hebrews states forthrightly that Joshua did *not* give Israel rest and Israel had not yet even entered God's rest in the time of David, yet on the other hand, Joshua states that the Lord *did* give Israel rest. We will see that this is not a contradiction because they are speaking of *two different types of rest.*

First, our author states that the Israelites *who rebelled* and lost faith did not enter God's rest (Heb. 3:11). But these were the very people to whom God gave the *seventh-day Sabbath.* These people were present at the giving of the Ten Commandments at Sinai. These were the very people who participated in the wilderness tabernacle services. Without question we know that *they* were given the *seventh-day Sabbath rest of Sinai.* But notice that Hebrews states these Sabbath-keeping Israelites did *not* enter "God's rest." Here we see that our author is definitely referring to a type of "rest" *other than the seventh-day Sabbath rest of Sinai.*

Second, the author says that *Joshua* did *not* give the people "rest." Here he is referring to a different group of people—not the ones who rebelled at Massah and Meribath, because they died in the wilderness. The people Joshua brought into the land of Canaan were *the children of those who died in the wilderness.*

> For the sons of Israel walked forty years in the wilderness, until all the nation, that is, the men of war who came out of Egypt, perished because they did not listen to the voice of the Lord, to whom the Lord had *sworn* that He would not let them see the *land* which the Lord had sworn to their fathers to give us, a *land* flowing with milk and honey. And their children whom He raised up in their place…(Josh. 5:6, 7).

In this quotation from Joshua we see that the oath of God regarding the Israelites who did not listen to the voice of God had to do with their entering the *promised land.* And Joshua, in the quotation listed above, states that God did give them (the children of those who rebelled) "rest on every side" and "all the promises of God came to pass." In other words, the "rest" which Joshua gave Israel was *rest from their enemies.*

Therefore, the "rest of God" mentioned in Hebrews *cannot be rest from enemies.* This is why David, many years later, could say, "Today, if you would hear His voice, Do not harden your hearts" (Ps. 95:7).

Summarizing the above evidence leads to three more facts. (1) Israel, *at the time of Joshua,* did not enter "God's rest." (2) The "rest" the author is encouraging his readers to enter into is *not* the "rest" from their enemies. (3) Israel had not yet entered into God's rest in the time of David.

Now that we have seen what the author of Hebrews is *not* referring to when he speaks of "God's rest," we now turn our attention to what he *does* mean by "God's rest."

> There remains therefore a Sabbath rest for the people of God. For the one who has entered His rest has himself also rested from his works, as God did from His. Let us therefore be diligent to enter *that rest,* lest anyone fall through following the same example of disobedience (Heb. 4:9–11).

Here we have several more facts. (1) This rest is called a "Sabbath rest." The Greek word used here for "Sabbath rest" is *sabbatismos.* This is the *only* place in Scripture where this word is used and it is the first known use of this word anywhere. Therefore, I believe the writer of Hebrews coined this word because he wanted to convey a unique meaning. (2) We are told this promise of "Sabbath rest" *remains* for the people of God. (3) The one who has entered this rest *has also rested* (ceased) from his works. (4) "Has rested" in Greek is in the aorist tense, which means that this action happened *in an instant* and took place at some point of time *in the past.* (5) This "rest" from "works" is to be of the same nature as God's seventh-day creation rest when he ceased from the work of creation. (6) We are to be diligent to enter "that rest." Now let us simply line up all these scriptural facts and see what conclusions we find.

1. The church is encouraged not to lose faith.

2. The Israelites who were alive in the experience recorded in Exodus 17:7 did not enter into the "rest of God" but they did *receive and keep the seventh-day Sabbath of Sinai.*
3. Israel did not enter into "rest" because of unbelief.
4. The author places much stress on "today" as the day of decision.
5. "Today" is an ongoing period of time: "as long as it is called today."
6. The "rest of God" is associated with the *"good news."*
7. We enter the "rest of God" *by believing.*
8. This "rest of God" is associated with God's *finished,* seventh-day creation rest when God ceased his work of creation.
9. Israel, at the time of Joshua, did not enter "God's rest" but they did enter the promised land and experience "rest" from their enemies and had the seventh-day Sabbath rest of Sinai.
10. Israel, at the time of David, had not yet entered "God's rest."
11. This "rest of God" is called a "Sabbath rest"—a unique rendering of the word.
12. The promise of entering "God's rest" *remains.*
13. Those who enter "God's rest" *have rested (ceased) from their works* as God did from His.
14. Those who have rested from their work did so in *a point of time in the past.*

Conclusions:

"God's Rest" is not the Seventh day Sabbath

This "rest" cannot be the seventh-day Sabbath of the Fourth Commandment for five reasons:

First, the Israelites who disbelieved, as mentioned in Exodus 17:7, were the same people to whom God gave the Sabbath as recorded in Exodus 16 (the giving of the manna). They were the same people to whom God gave the Ten Commandments at Sinai (Ex. 20). They were the same people who kept the seventh-day Sabbath, and the other sabbaths included in the "appointed times of the Lord" (Lev. 23). The author of Hebrews states three times that these people *did not enter the rest of God* to which he is referring (Heb. 3:11, 18, 19).

Second, the next generation of Israelites who were not included in the oath of God which stated "They shall not enter My rest" (Heb. 3:11) according to the author of Hebrews, also did not enter into the rest of God to which he was referring. Nor had Israel entered God's rest in the time of David (Heb. 4:7, 8), but *all* of these groups had the Sabbath of the Fourth Commandment.

Third, the concept of "believing" is *never* associated with keeping the seventh-day Sabbath in the old covenant. Rather, the way an Israelite entered into the Sabbath rest of the Fourth Commandment was by complete physical rest, not doing any work, not carrying a load, not building a fire, not going out of one's place, not buying or selling, and not cooking. However, the writer of Hebrews states "For we who have *believed* enter that rest" (Heb. 4:3).

Fourth, those who rested from their works on the seventh-day Sabbath were required to repeat their Sabbath rest every seven days. The writer of Hebrews, however, by using the Greek *aorist* tense in connection with "has rested," shows that the believer who rests from his works did so *at one point of time in the past.*

Fifth, the author of Hebrews states that the promise of entering God's rest is good "today" and shows that "today" is an extended period of time: "as long as it is called today." This "today" is *not* every seventh day.

"God's Rest" is the "rest of grace"

The "rest of God," referred to in Hebrews 3 and 4, *must* refer to the "rest of grace" which is characterized by a renewed relationship between man and God because of the following ten important reasons.

First, this rest of God is associated with the "good news"—the gospel of Christ. (Heb. 4:2, 6).

Second, one enters this "rest" *by believing* (Heb. 4:3).

Third, the one who "has himself also rested from his works" did that resting at *a point in past time.* This must refer to the point of salvation when a person believes in Christ and quits trying to be acceptable to God on the basis of his own "works" and "rests" in God's grace!

Fourth, this "rest" is associated, *not with the rest of Sinai, but with the seventh-day rest of creation.* The creation rest of God was a *cessation* of activity. This is the true "Sabbath rest" which the blind beggar experienced in John 9. He had been called, healed, washed, forgiven and found by the Creator and was worshipping in His very presence while the Pharisees who were keeping the Sabbath rest of the Fourth Commandment rejected the Messiah.

Fifth, the writer of Hebrews characterizes this rest as a "Sabbath rest" by using a word which is unique to Scripture. I believe he did this to give it special meaning just as we do when we put quotation marks around a word as I have done with the term "God's rest." As pointed out above, the author is showing how much better the new covenant is than the old. I believe the truth he is trying to convey is that the "Sabbath" (*sabbatismos,* Gr.) of the new covenant is better than the Sabbath (*sabbaton,* Gr.) of the old covenant.

Sixth, the writer of Hebrews is showing that this "Sabbath" rest of the new covenant is even better than the "rest" God gave Israel when they conquered Canaan and it is also better than the rest Israel experienced under their hero, King David.

Seventh, Hebrews was written for the purpose of encouraging Hebrew Christians to remain faithful and *not* fall back under old covenant law and worship. Near the end of this book it is written:

> For you have *not come to a mountain* that may be touched and to a blazing fire, and to darkness and gloom and whirlwind, and to the blast of a trumpet and the sound of words which sound was such that those who heard begged that no further word should be spoken to them. [This is a graphic description of the giving of the Ten Commandments. See Ex. 19:16–25; 20:18.] But you have come to Mount Zion and to the city of the living God, the heavenly Jerusalem, and to myriads of angels, to the general *assembly and church* of the firstborn who are enrolled in heaven, and to God the judge of all, and to the spirits of righteous men made perfect, and to Jesus the mediator of a *new covenant* (Heb. 12:18–24).

Eighth, in the old covenant the "rest" was experienced once each seventh day. The writer of Hebrews stresses the word "today" on several occasions. In the new covenant, one can enter into God's rest "today." He does not have to wait until the end of the week. In Hebrews 13 we have a beautiful definition of new covenant worship:

> Through Him [Jesus] then let us *continually* offer up a sacrifice of praise to God, that is, the fruit of lips that give thanks to His name. And do not neglect doing good and sharing; for with such sacrifices God is pleased (Heb. 13: 15, 16).

The new covenant believer is to rejoice in God's rest *continually.*

Ninth, both the promise of rest and the rest itself *remain.* This rest does not end. Just as the phrase, "and there was evening and there was morning, a seventh day," was omitted in the record of that Eden rest, the new covenant rest *remains* for the people of God. I praise God for the better "Sabbath rest"—the rest of God's gracious, intimate fellowship which remains for the one who has believed and has ceased trying to be righteous by his own works!

Tenth, we see the larger picture of "God's rest" in the context of the whole book of Hebrews when we consider the author's stress on the *finished* work of God at creation (Heb. 4:3) and Christ's *finished* work of redemption.

Considering the context of this whole book, one must conclude that the Christian is *not* to look to Sinai for law or leadership. Jesus is better than Moses. The Christian is *not* to look to Sinai for priesthood. The priesthood of Jesus is far superior to that of Aaron. The believer is *not* to look to Sinai for forgiveness of sin. Jesus forgives our sin, which the blood of animals could not do. And the Christian is *not* to look to Sinai for God's rest. Jesus brings a better "Sabbath rest"—the rest of His grace, which has its foundation in the *finished* atonement of Christ and resembles the rest of God when He *finished* creation.

Matthew 11:28–30

> Come unto Me, all you who are weary and heavy laden, and I will give you rest. Take my yoke upon you, and learn from Me, for I am gentle and humble in heart; and you shall find rest for your souls. For My yoke is easy, and My load is light.

These words are found *just before* the incident of Jesus walking through the grainfields on the Sabbath. They are, by context and theme, closely associated with the topic of Sabbath. Jesus and His disciples are living in the reality of Jubilee. Like Adam and Eve in Eden, they are gathering their food direct from nature.

Jesus is inviting the weary and heavy laden to come to Him for true rest. Jesus is the center of rest for Christians. It is only "in Him" that we can be free from the burden of sin and the weary impossibility of trying by our own works to be acceptable to God. The rest that Jesus offers is not the rest of the Fourth Commandment of Sinai, rather it is rest for the soul. It is restored fellowship with the Creator of the universe! His invitation is not limited to the people who were to keep the Sinai Sabbath—the sons of Israel—but to *"all* you who are weary and heavy laden." The new covenant gospel trumpet sounds to *all* nations: "Whoever believes in Him" will not perish (Jn. 3:16). Whoever comes will not be disappointed. All who receive Him receive the right to sonship in the restored family of God (Jn. 1:12).

What is the "yoke" Jesus asks us to take? First, we note it is *His yoke*. It is *not* the yoke of Moses, but the yoke of Jesus. Second, we see that Scripture often uses the word "yoke" for the old covenant law. In the Jerusalem Council there were those gathered who wanted to require Gentile Christians to keep the "Law of Moses" (Acts 15:5). Peter, in responding to these legalistic believers said,

> Now therefore, why do you put God to the test by placing upon the neck of the disciples a yoke which neither our fathers nor we have been able to bear? (Acts 15:10).

Here, without question, "yoke" refers to the old covenant. Further, this yoke is implied to be a heavy yoke, which neither the Jews of New Testament times nor their ancestors were able to bear.

In Galatians 4, Paul gives the allegory of the two women which ends with "cast out the bondwoman." As we studied before, this can, in context, mean nothing else than cast out the old covenant and those who try to get Christians to keep it. In Galatians 5:1 we read,

> It was for freedom that Christ set us free; therefore keep standing firm and do not be subject again to a *yoke of slavery*.

With this usage of yoke in mind, let us return to Christ's words: "Take my yoke upon you." Here He is saying, "Take my law of love upon you." Note how the context supports this interpretation, "and learn from Me." Jesus, as we saw before, is the new covenant. He is the way, the truth and the life. In the new covenant we are not pointed back to Sinai, but, like Mary, we are to sit at His feet and learn from Him. As the experience on the mount of transfiguration teaches, we are to see no one but Jesus only. While Sinai was associated with violent shaking, darkness, gloom, and fear, the new covenant, Jesus Himself, is "gentle and humble in heart." While old covenant Israel experienced only the rest of the fourth commandment—physical rest—those who come to Jesus find true rest of soul. While the old covenant, according to Peter, was so heavy that no one in the Jewish nation, fathers or sons, was able to bear it, the new covenant law of Jesus is "easy." His commandment is light.

So in the context of the Jews desperately trying to keep the letter of the Sinaitic Sabbath laws, condemning the very people who were following the One who was restoring Eden's rest, we find Jesus offering the true "Sabbath rest."

We now are able to summarize the various facets of biblical "rest". First, there is the rest of Eden's seventh day; a day when all was in perfect harmony when man and His God held face to face communion.

Second, there is the Sabbath rest of the Fourth Commandment. Israel was commanded to rest and behave very much like Adam and Eve did living in Eden's garden. It served to help Israel to remember from where they had fallen and also pointed them forward through the other sabbatical rests to the coming Jubilee which was fulfilled in Christ.

Third, God, through the leadership of Joshua, for a short time gave the people of Israel rest from their enemies.

Fourth, Christ gives the believer *true rest of soul*. The believer is now justified, at peace with God, filled with the Holy Spirit and is a new creation. This is the better "Sabbath rest" for the Christian. The writer of Hebrews shows that this "rest of God" is of the same nature as the rest of Eden's seventh day.

Fifth, in the age to come, we will be delivered from the presence of sin and then we will *fully* enjoy the perfect Eden rest again.

Jesus is the true rest—the *rest* which *remains* for the one who *believes!* Will you enter His rest? You can do it *today!*

Christ is the end of the law for righteousness

CHAPTER TWENTY

RIGHTEOUSNESS BEYOND THE LAW

Paradigm shift needed

Now it is time to shift paradigms and we start with a few statements to take our thinking outside the box. Moral *laws* do not make something right or wrong. Rather, laws are made to cause people to behave in such a way that they line up with moral *principles* which were there before the laws were written. Moral principles are broad and eternal. Laws are usually written with some specific situation(s) in mind to guide or enforce conduct to those who are immature in their thinking and/or behavior. Usually there is one of two underlying reasons behind any law. Either the law is made to protect the immature from him/herself or to protect society from the actions of the immature. *The degree of immaturity is directly proportional to the number and specificity of laws that are required.*

One of the programmed responses I often hear in discussions about the new covenant Christian not being under the law is, "Well, then, you are saying it is OK to kill, steal and commit adultery, etc." No. Not at all!

If you, the reader, have been brought up on law, let me ask you a question. If you believed that the law—yes all the Ten Commandments—had REALLY come to an end, would you start doing the things prohibited in the Ten

Commandments? I hope not. Anybody who did would be a very immature Christian.

Some have defined righteousness as obedience to the law. This may be true for old covenant righteousness, but it falls *far below* that presented in the new covenant. Note how the following New Testament references *contrast* law and righteousness.

But now *apart from the Law the* righteousness of God has been manifested, being witnessed by the Law and the Prophets (Rom. 3:21).

For the promise to Abraham or to his descendants that he would be heir of the world was *not through the Law*, but through the righteousness of faith. For if those who are of the Law are heirs, faith is made void and the promise is nullified (Rom. 4:13-14).

What shall we say then? That Gentiles, who did not pursue righteousness, attained righteousness, even the righteousness which is by faith; but Israel, pursuing a *law of righteousness, did not arrive at that law* (Rom. 9:30, 31).

For not knowing about God's righteousness and seeking to establish their own, they did not subject themselves to the righteousness of God. *For Christ is the end of the law for righteousness* to everyone who believes (Rom. 10:3, 4).

I do not nullify the grace of God, for *if righteousness comes through the Law,* then Christ died needlessly (Gal. 2:21).

You have been severed from Christ, *you who are seeking to be justified by law;* you have fallen from grace (Gal. 5:4).

...and may be found in Him, *not having a righteousness of my own derived from the Law,* but that which is through faith in Christ, the righteousness which *comes* from God on the basis of faith (Phil. 3:9).

The above verses indicate that the righteousness of God which comes on the basis of faith *is not even associated with the law*. Rather, it is a much higher righteousness beyond the righteousness of the law.

Personal Illustrations

When I was a seminary student at Andrews University I worked nights at the YMCA in Benton Harbor, Michigan. About midnight, one cold winter night, I was crossing the street with the manager of the YMCA. We came to an intersection where the facing light was red. There were no cars in sight in any direction. However, I, a good law keeper, stood there waiting for the light to turn green. Suddenly, I realized my friend was walking into the red light. He said to me, "You are still under law. I am under grace." While his statement may not fully apply, nevertheless it was instructive. The law of red and green lights was designed to prevent accidents and help drivers "take turns". However in our case there was no chance to get hit by a passing car as none was in sight. It was therefore appropriate to violate *the letter of the law* as long as it did not violate *the principle of safety*—as long as no legalistic cops were watching!

The other day I was at the busy post office getting the mail for Life Assurance Ministries. A mother was there with two small girls. As they approached the parking lot she said, "Now you must take mommy's hand as there are many cars here." This was a *very good law* for two little girls; however, don't put your 16 year old boy under the same *law!* Rather as soon as he is old enough, teach the *principle* of "safety first"! That principle will serve him well the rest of his life no matter what the circumstances.

I believe this is the way we should consider many of the old covenant laws. They were holy, just and good for the conditions and immature people[1] to whom they were given. Remember the old covenant law was given to the Israelites who had been slaves for generations. There are many good moral laws and good moral principles behind many of these laws. Now, however, life in the Spirit moves us to live *beyond* the letter of the law to follow the *principles* taught by Christ which modify and expand the letter of the law to general principles which are on a higher moral plain than old covenant law. Under the new covenant these principles

---

[1] Read the Old Testament history of the exodus, book of Judges, etc. for many examples of immature people.

are written on our heart by the Holy Spirit. We are no longer children; we are sons and daughters of God.

Biblical Teaching

> But before faith came, we were kept in custody under the law, being shut up to the faith which was later to be revealed. Therefore the Law has become our tutor *to lead us* to Christ, so that we may be justified by faith. But now that faith has come, we are no longer under a tutor. For you are all sons of God through faith in Christ Jesus (Gal. 3:23–26).
>
> But when the fullness of the time came, God sent forth His Son, born of a woman, born under the Law, so that He might redeem those who were under the Law, that we might receive the adoption as sons (Gal. 4:4, 5).
>
> But now that you have come to know God, or rather to be known by God, how is it that you turn back again to the weak and worthless elemental things, to which you desire to be enslaved all over again? You observe days and months and seasons and years. I fear for you, that perhaps I have labored over you in vain (Gal. 4:9–11).

In essence what Paul is saying here is that the Judaizers were seeking to enforce grade-school rules on mature Christians. Paul gave them the mature gospel of faith in the finished work of Christ. They had the witness of the Holy Spirit who was doing miracles among them yet now they were trying to go backward in their maturity and wanted to be under grade-school rules again. How foolish!

Moral vs. Ritual

New covenant Christians must be diligent here. It is human nature to give moral significance to established ritual customs. I was taught that communion bread *must* be made out of whole-wheat flour and olive oil, and of these two ingredients, the whole-wheat flour was the most important. I was almost scandalized when I visited a church that used white flour! It was instructive to me that a detailed recipe was given in the old covenant law for the bread of the presence and how it should be laid out.[2] In the new covenant, however, no such details are given. New covenant righteousness deals with heart issues not rituals. Some argue over which way to baptize: forward, backward, three times, in the name of Jesus only or in the name of the Father, Son and Holy Spirit. We could even extend the controversy over baptism to sprinkling or immersion.[3] Again, the most important thing is our commitment to Christ, inviting Him to be Lord and Master of our lives! Anytime rituals become the important thing, the moral and ethical nature of new covenant righteousness is compromised.

Righteousness Beyond the Law Found Only In Christ

New covenant Christians have a much higher model to pattern after than the old covenant law. There is nothing in the new covenant or "living under grace" that opens any door to willfully living in sin. Rather, new covenant morality is *far above and beyond* that of old covenant law. When we say this there are two considerations that must be emphasized lest we misunderstand the good news of the gospel. The first is *motive*. When living under the law there is a motive to try to perfectly keep the law *so that we can be fully accepted*. This, as many of us can testify, is continually frustrating *if we take the law seriously.* However the new covenant motive is different. Our sanctified living is not done from the motive of trying to be good enough to be accepted. Rather, it springs from the *fact* of acceptance! We were accepted by God while we were

---

[2] Lev. 24:5–8.
[3] As a pastor I have always baptized by immersion as I think this is the biblical model and more fully follows the symbol of the reality. We must, however, keep ritual in its place and not allow it to take precedence over the ethical and moral commitment of the person being baptized.

still helpless, ungodly sinners and enemies of God.[4] *We strive to live like sons and daughters of God because that is who we now are!* Our goal is to live like the kind of persons we *now* are in Christ!

The second consideration we must understand is that perfect new covenant righteousness is found *only* in Christ! We look to Him and Him *alone* as our Representative and Substitute! If we are Christ's then we, with the Apostle Paul may say,

> More than that, I count all things to be loss in view of the surpassing value of knowing Christ Jesus my Lord, for whom I have suffered the loss of all things, and count them but rubbish so that I may gain Christ, and may be found in Him, not having a righteousness of my own derived from *the* Law, but that which is through faith in Christ, the righteousness which *comes* from God on the basis of faith (Phil. 3:8–9).

In the Law of Christ we have moral and ethical principles above and beyond that of old covenant law.[5] We have been declared righteous on the basis of our faith in Christ which has nothing to do with the law.[6] We are accepted in Him. Now we have life in the Spirit that empowers us to follow after the example of Christ. We can by faith claim Christ's righteousness which far surpasses the righteousness of the law.

Chapter Summary

1. Laws do not make something right or wrong; rather laws only reflect the eternal moral principles behind the laws.

---

[4] Rom. 5:6–10.
[5] "The New Testament forbids not only evils condemned in the Decalog, but also scores of others not mentioned in that code, such as drunkenness. Love of pleasure, pride, anger, impatience, selfishness, boasting, filthy talk, evil thoughts, foolishness, uncleanness, strife, hatred, envyings, revelings, etc." H. M. Riggle, *The Sabbath and the Lord's Day,* (Faith Publishing House, Guthrie, OK, 1922). p. 86.
[6] Gal. 5:4.

Righteousness Beyond the Law

2. Laws are usually made to restrict or define the behavior of the immature.
3. Laws are made to keep the immature from hurting themselves or to keep them from hurting society at large.
4. New covenant righteousness is not derived by perfect obedience to the law; rather it comes *apart from the law* and is received only through faith in Christ.
5. New covenant righteousness is found only in Christ.
6. The laws of the old covenant were holy, just and good for the people to whom they were given.
7. New covenant morality does not open any door to sin. Rather, it raises the moral bar to new moral heights—the very righteousness of God.
8. The full acceptance by God and the imputed righteousness of Christ provide a much better motivation for righteous living than trying to perfectly keep the letter of the law.

But now we have been released from the Law…so that we serve in newness of the Spirit and not in oldness of the letter

CHAPTER
TWENTY ONE

LIFE IN THE SPIRIT

Law and the Spirit

> But now we have been released from the Law, having died to that by which we were bound, so that we serve in newness of the Spirit and not in oldness of the letter (Rom 7:6).

At this juncture we need to understand the central role the Holy Spirit plays in the new covenant. Without this insight we will be left with nagging questions. Without His indwelling, we will be left longing for Sinai! When Jesus entered His ministry as the Covenant Messenger He was baptized in water by John, and

> ...while He was praying, heaven was opened, and the Holy Spirit descended upon Him in bodily form like a dove (Lk. 3:21, 22).

From that point on we see Jesus being led by the Spirit and demonstrating all the gifts of the Spirit!

> Jesus full of the Holy Spirit...was led about by the Spirit (Lk. 4:1). And Jesus returned to Galilee in the power of the Spirit (Lk. 4:14). The Spirit of the Lord is upon Me (Lk. 4:18).

After the outpouring of the Spirit on the day of Pentecost we see the central role the Holy Spirit played in the church, God's new covenant people. In Peter's sermon he quotes Joel and says,

> It shall be in the last days, God says, that *I will pour forth of My spirit upon all mankind;* and your sons and your daughters shall prophecy, and your young men shall see visions, and your old men shall dream dreams; even upon My bondslaves, both men and women, I will in those days pour forth of My Spirit and they shall prophesy (Acts 2:17, 18).

Peter proclaimed to the people,

> Repent and let each one of you be baptized in the name of Jesus Christ for the forgiveness of your sins; and *you shall receive the gift of the Holy Spirit.* For the promise is for you and your children, and for all those who are far off, as many as the Lord our God shall call to Himself (Acts 2:38, 39).

The history of the new covenant church is a history of the working of the Holy Spirit. "Filled with the Holy Spirit," they began "to speak the word of God with boldness" (Acts 4:31). The deacons were "full of the Holy Spirit" and they did "great wonders and signs among the people" (Acts 6:3, 8). "The Spirit said to Philip, 'Go up and join this chariot'" (Acts 8:29). "The Spirit of the Lord snatched Philip away" (Acts 8:39). Ananias laid His hand upon Saul and he was filled with the Holy Spirit (Acts 9:17). The disciples were comforted by the Spirit (Acts 9:31). By the Spirit they foretold coming events (Acts 11:28). The Spirit spoke to the church (Acts 13:4). Paul was "sent out by the Holy Spirit" (Acts 13:4). They were filled with the joy of the Holy Spirit (Acts 13:52). By the power of the Holy Spirit the sick were healed, the dead were raised, demons were cast out and the power of the enemy was broken. Here we see the fulfillment of the promise of Jesus.

> ...He Himself will baptize you in the Holy Spirit and fire (Lk. 3:16).
>
> I will ask the Father, and He will give you another Helper, that He may be with you forever; that is the Spirit of truth, whom the world cannot receive, because it does not see Him or know Him, but you know Him because He abides with you and will be in you (Jn. 14:16, 17).

> But the Helper, the Holy Spirit, whom the Father will send in My name, He will teach you all things, and bring to your remembrance all that I said to you (Jn. 14:26).
>
> When the Helper comes, whom I will send to you from the Father, that is the Spirit of truth who proceeds from the Father, He will testify about Me (Jn. 15:26).
>
> But when He, the Spirit of truth, comes, He will guide you into all the truth; for He will not speak on His own initiative, but whatever He hears, He will speak; and He will disclose to you what is to come (Jn. 16:13).

An accurate knowledge of the role of the Holy Spirit is fundamental for a correct understanding of the new covenant and it is also necessary for a right interpretation of the Sabbath. *The role the law filled in the old covenant is filled by the Holy Spirit in the new.* Scripture compares and contrasts the law with the Spirit in many ways. A subtle example of this is seen in the events surrounding the giving of both covenants. After the law was given, the children of Israel immediately went into disobedience and fell under condemnation. They made a golden calf, worshipped it, sacrificed to it, and said, "This is your God, O Israel, who brought you up from the land of Egypt" (Ex. 32:8). Because of this sin "about three thousand men of the people fell that day" (Ex. 32:28). These *three thousand* were killed by their brothers at the command of God.

At the giving of the Spirit in the new covenant, on the other hand, we find a different and better outcome! "There were added that day about *three thousand* souls" (Acts 2:41). I believe these numbers are recorded to point out the contrasting nature of the two covenants and show the relationship between the law and the Spirit.

Notice thoughtfully how the Holy Spirit takes the place of the law in Paul's comparisons and contrasts between the old and new covenants in 2 Cor. 3:3–18.

The old covenant:	**The new covenant:**
Written with ink	Written with the Spirit
On tablets of stone	On tablets of the heart

Not of the letter	But of the Spirit
The letter kills	The Spirit gives life
Ministry of death	Ministry of the Spirit
Ministry of condemnation	Ministry of righteousness
Came with glory	Abounds in glory
Glory has faded away	Glory remains

Unless the new covenant Christian understands the role of the Holy Spirit and experiences His presence, he will long for Sinai. It is only the indwelling and empowering of the Holy Spirit that can write the principles of the new covenant law of love on our hearts so that we have an ever-present Person who will teach us all things (Jn. 14:26), guide us into all truth (Jn. 16:13), and testify to us of Christ (Jn. 15:26). The old covenant law was external—written on stone. The new covenant law is internal—written on our hearts. The new covenant Lawgiver is present in our hearts by the Holy Spirit.

> If anyone loves Me he will keep my word; and My Father will love Him, and *We will come to him, and make Our abode with him* (Jn. 14:23).

The Spirit, the Word and Prayer

Today the church has, to a large degree, bought into the western world view, which eliminates the supernatural. That is *not* the view of Scripture. The book of Acts, as well as the whole of Scripture, is filled with the supernatural working of the Holy Spirit. It is my belief that the New Testament Christian who rejects the present-day "gifting" of the Holy Spirit is not experiencing the fullness of new covenant life: a personal relationship with the indwelling Christ

> ...who is able to do exceeding abundantly beyond all that we ask or think, *according to the power that works within us* (Eph. 3:20).

Life in the Spirit

The Bible makes it clear that the Holy Spirit's preferred way of working is though the word of God, the Bible. We believe that the Bible is the Spirit inspired word (*logos*) of God and as we *prayerfully* read and study it, The Holy Spirit speaks to us the living word (*rhema*) of God.

> And take the helmet of salvation, and the sword of the Spirit, which is the word of God (Eph. 6:17).

Those who seek to live by the "promptings of the Holy Spirit" without a corresponding study of the word of God and regular prayer place themselves in a position where they may think they are receiving specific direction from the Holy Spirit when, in reality, they are hearing from their own subconscious mind or wishful thinking. Sometimes we hear people saying, "God told me this" or "God told me that" and following these comments are statements that are incongruent with the written word.

While the work of the Holy Spirit cannot be boxed in or perfectly described, it is important that the Christian not try to live by the written word without the Holy Spirit as a guide to interpret it, nor to live by the Holy Spirit without allowing the Holy Spirit to speak through the written word.

How, then do we live?

In the book of Galatians we have the clearest teaching about the reign of law. It came in with Moses and ceased with Christ.[1] Paul, under the direct guidance of the Holy Spirit, foresaw the questions some of the immature Christians in Galatia who had been sidetracked by a law-focus "gospel" would ask. Therefore, we have his clear answer to the implied question: "Paul, if we are not under the law anymore, then how do we live?" His answer is clear, powerful, and relevant to those of us who come from a law-centered religion. Read this section through in context and then we will clarify what is taught.

---

[1] Gal. 3:15–29.

> But I say, walk by the Spirit, and you will not carry out the desire of the flesh. For the flesh sets its desire against the Spirit, and the Spirit against the flesh; for these are in opposition to one another, so that you may not do the things that you please. But if you are led by the Spirit, you are not under the Law. Now the deeds of the flesh are evident, which are: immorality, impurity, sensuality, idolatry, sorcery, enmities, strife, jealousy, outbursts of anger, disputes, dissensions, factions, envying, drunkenness, carousing, and things like these, of which I forewarn you, just as I have forewarned you, that those who practice such things will not inherit the kingdom of God. But the fruit of the Spirit is love, joy, peace, patience, kindness, goodness, faithfulness, gentleness, self-control; against such things there is no law. Now those who belong to Christ Jesus have crucified the flesh with its passions and desires. If we live by the Spirit, let us also walk by the Spirit. Let us not become boastful, challenging one another, envying one another (Gal. 5:16–26).

The above section is so important that I want to comment on each key element:

Paul's statement, "if you are led by the Spirit, you are not under the Law" agrees perfectly with out findings thus far. To be led by the Spirit is to follow just where the Spirit leads. The Christian no longer needs an external set of rules *if* he is in step with the Holy Spirit and feeding on the Word of God coupled with a consistent prayer life.[2]

The struggle is not between the Christian and the law, as portrayed in Romans 7:7–24 where Paul depicts what life is like for the Christian *who lives according to the old covenant*. Rather, the war the Christian must fight is between the Spirit and the flesh. The outcome is determined by who is master of our lives: the Spirit or the flesh.

Paul does not define evil as transgression of the law because Christians are free from the law. Rather he defines

---

[2] To whet your appetite for a consistent devotional life of prayer, Bible study and listening to God I highly recommend Tom Elliff, *A Passion for Prayer*, (Crossway Books, Wheaton, IL, 1998), and Bill Hybles, *To Busy Not to Pray*, (InterVarsity Press, Downers Grove, IL, 1988).

evil as the deeds of the flesh. These deeds are the natural outgrowth if we follow the promptings of our fallen nature.

These "deeds of the flesh" Paul says "are evident". The mature Spirit-filled Christian[3] does not need to be told these are wrong. The Holy Spirit working in the conscience of the believer grounded in Scripture is a sufficient guide.

The deeds of the flesh

Now let us consider Paul's list of the deeds of the flesh which can be subdivided into five categories:[4]

Sexual sins:

"Sexual immorality" would include adultery, sex outside of marriage or we might say the "natural sexual sins".

"Impurity" would include the unnatural sexual sins such as homosexuality, lesbianism, incest and bestiality.

"Sensuality" has the overtones of portraying, even in public, an attitude of indifference or inappropriateness to the sexual sins and desires.

Loyalty sins:

"Idolatry" is allowing oneself to become infatuated and enamored with anything or anybody apart from Almighty God. This sin is rampant in the western world and in the church.

"Sorcery" has two basic connotations. The root word implies a use of drugs. Later the meaning of this word came to be used for any activity involved with the powers of evil including secret meetings with evil spirits. Today it would include a vast number of activities associated with the occult. Practicing sorcery is seeking power or guidance from some source—often evil—other than God. This would

---

[3] i.e. Genuine Christian who allows the Holy Spirit to reign in his life.
[4] Some of the insights presented here were gathered from Clinton Chisholm's excellent tape set, "The Christian and the Mosaic Law" available from Life Assurance Ministries.

include Ouija boards, horoscopes, fortune tellers, books on extra-sensory perceptions, etc. All power is not of God!

Social or relationship Sins:
"Enmities" are hostile negative feelings.

"Strife" refers to people taking sides, fighting wars of words, forming cliques and doing unloving acts.

"Jealousy" is seen when we envy others and often secretly hate them because they are perceived as being better than we are.

"Outbursts of anger" are hurtful words hastily spoken when strife and enmities are present.

"Disputes" refer to arguments as to who is right and who is wrong.

"Dissensions" reflect division, disloyalty and negative attitudes.

"Factions" are an outgrowth of the above works of the flesh when people align in groups and the groups then champion their own agenda without concern of others.

"Envying" is inordinate desire to possess what someone else has such as wealth, popularity, prestige, position and power, etc.

Self-control sins:
"Drunkenness" is abusing any substance to such a degree that it affects one's thinking and/or hurts one's self or others.

"Carousing" refers to activities such as wild parties which are often associated with people who are out of control and where unnecessary temptation and evil are present.

"And things like these." Here Paul implies that this list could be greatly enlarged. However, he has been specific enough so that his readers will understand what he is speaking about.

We must also note Paul's clear warning against those who make it a practice to give in to the deeds of the flesh.

He did not say that they will go to heaven but just not get the same rewards as those who do not do such deeds of the flesh. Rather, he said, "as I have forewarned you, that those who practice such things will not inherit the kingdom of God." In other words, those who make it a practice to follow the deeds of the flesh are not genuine Christians. They are not controlled by the Holy Spirit. They have another lord and master. Within the new covenant there is no open door to "living in sin" and having the assurance of salvation. True, we all fall short, but our loyalty to God is seen as we keep in step with the Holy Spirit residing in our lives and not following the flesh.

The fruit of the Spirit

Having outlined the deeds of the flesh, Paul now turns to the fruit of the Spirit that will be manifest in the genuine Christian's life.

> But the fruit of the Spirit is love, joy, peace, patience, kindness, goodness, faithfulness, gentleness, self-control; against such things there is no law (Gal. 5:22, 23).

Here is another insight worth underlining. The new covenant law can be summed up in one basic overarching principle.

> This is My commandment, that you love one another, just as I have loved you (Jn. 15:12).

In Galatians we find that the fruit (singular) of the Spirit is manifest first in love. We love because He first loved us. Here is the guideline for new covenant living! While the "gifts" of the Spirit are given severally as the Spirit wills, all are to participate in the fruit of the Spirit. *These virtues are a greater evidence of the Spirit's control than any of the more spectacular gifts as mentioned in Corinthians 12–14.* Let's examine the wonderful thing called the fruit of the Spirit. We will note that all the aspects of the fruit of the Spirit are supernatural and are outside the realm of personal achievement without the power of the indwelling Holy Spirit.

"Love" is agape love—a selfless love that loves not for its own sake but for the sake of the other person who needs our love. It is a sacrificial love, an unconditional love and a never ending love. It is a wholesome attitude toward others that results in positive actions and is supremely modeled by Christ.

> But God demonstrates His own love toward us, in that while we were yet sinners, Christ died for us (Rom. 5:8).
> Walk in love, just as Christ also loved you and gave Himself up for us... (Eph. 5:2)

This love is not a natural love that can be worked up; it is truly a "fruit of the Spirit".

> ...the love of God has been poured out within our hearts through the Holy Spirit who was given to us (Rom. 5:5).

"Joy" is an inner attitude of cheerfulness that is not dependant upon circumstances. It is a supernatural joy often expressed in the very face of persecution and difficulty.

> But the Jews incited the devout women of prominence and the leading men of the city, and instigated a persecution against Paul and Barnabas, and drove them out of their district. But they shook off the dust of their feet in protest against them and went to Iconium. And the disciples were continually filled with joy and with the Holy Spirit (Acts 13:50–52).
> But even if I am being poured out as a drink offering upon the sacrifice and service of your faith, I rejoice and share my joy with you all (Phil. 2:17).

"Peace" is an inner contentment and serenity of mind. It is what I call "living the eternal kind of life." It is knowing that we are saved and that no matter what happens to us, we will be with Christ. It is experiencing eternal life NOW. Peace is the assurance that everything is right between us and God. It is a supernatural gift of the gospel. It is peace *with* God.

Life in the Spirit

> Therefore, having been justified by faith, we have peace with God through our Lord Jesus Christ (Rom. 5:1).

It is also the peace *of* God.

> And the peace of God, which surpasses all comprehension, will guard your hearts and your minds in Christ Jesus (Phil. 4:7).

"Patience" is the endurance that waits hopefully for God's timing. It is a divine quality that allows us to endure other people and their offensive actions without these circumstances triggering the deeds of the flesh and causing us to retaliate. It is seeing those who cause us frustration or real hurt as needing our offer of forgiveness and our prayer of encouragement.

> The Lord is not slow about His promise, as some count slowness, but is patient toward you, not wishing for any to perish but for all to come to repentance (2 Pet. 3:9).
>
> The Lord's bond-servant must not be quarrelsome, but be kind to all, able to teach, patient when wronged (2 Tim. 2:24).

Patience is tested not just when we have to wait for something, patience is also demonstrated when we have been wronged and do not react to the one who wronged us.

"Kindness" is not only an attitude that wishes others well, but a divine quality that moves us to positive actions which are appreciated by others.

> Or do you think lightly of the riches of His kindness and tolerance and patience, not knowing that the kindness of God leads you to repentance? (Rom. 2:4).

It will be the supernatural quality of kindness expressed to others that will point them to our kind God.

"Goodness" is a divine quality that motivates us to be good people. Good people avoid hurting others and seek the good of all.

> The good man brings out of his good treasure what is good; and the evil man brings out of his evil treasure what is evil (Mt. 12:35).

In the quotation of Jesus above, it is clear that the heart must be renewed by the Holy Spirit. It is the "new man" that must be present on the inside before we can bring something good from the heart. In its unregenerate condition the heart is desperately wicked and unclean.

"Gentleness" is a divine quality that is careful not to cause hurt or harm. It is a quality that is needed when we seek to restore others.

> Brethren, even if anyone is caught in any trespass, you who are spiritual, restore such a one in a spirit of gentleness; each one looking to yourself, so that you too will not be tempted (Gal. 6:1).

Gentleness has a long reach—even if *anyone* is caught in *any* trespass he/she is to be treated with a sprit of gentleness!

"Self-control" is an all encompassing virtue given by the Spirit. A self-controlled person is not one to have outbursts of anger or disputes. Self-control allows one to be truly free—free to choose how he/she will respond to varying and adverse circumstances rather than be controlled by unbridled passions and lusts. A self-controlled person is a mature person, one who needs few, if any, external laws to govern behavior.

Paul concludes this section by saying,

> ...against such things there is no law. Now those who belong to Christ Jesus have crucified the flesh with its passions and desires. If we live by the Spirit, let us also walk by the Spirit. Gal. 5:23–25.

It becomes patently clear that one who walks by the Spirit does not need the old covenant law to govern external behavior for he has the internal guide and power of the Holy Spirit. Life in the Spirit is mature life—a life lived by a few overarching principles taught by Christ and interpreted and applied by the grace and power of the Holy Spirit. Thoughtfully look over the list of the deeds of the flesh and the fruit of the Spirit. They *cannot* coexist! Both are expressions of the inner man, or heart. Either one is motivated by the flesh or by the Spirit. Yes, indeed, life in the Spirit produces righteousness far beyond the law! Now it becomes clear how and why the Spirit replaces the function of old covenant law in the life of the believer!

Chapter Summary

1. The Holy Spirit plays an indispensable role in the life of a Christian teaching him "all things", "testifying about Christ", "guiding into all truth." And "disclosing what is to come."
2. In the new covenant the Holy Spirit plays much the same role as did the law in the old covenant.
3. The Holy Spirit actually indwells the believer and there is the secret of life in the Spirit.
4. If a Christian is led by the Spirit he/she is not under the dominion of old covenant law.
5. Paul defines evil, not as transgression of the law, but as the deeds of the flesh.
6. The deeds of the flesh are "evident" to a Spirit led Christian.
7. The fruit of the Spirit is a supernatural manifestation of the qualities of love.
8. The Holy Spirit indwelling the believer is a better guide to righteous living than old covenant law.
9. The Holy Spirit works in conjunction with the word of God, the Bible.
10. The Holy Spirit not only guides the believer but supplies the power to live the Christian life.

On the first day of the week, when we were gathered together to break bread

CHAPTER TWENTY TWO

THE FIRST DAY OF THE WEEK

A study on the topic of the Sabbath would not be complete without an examination of the New Testament "first day" and "Lord's day" references. Most Christian groups worship on Sunday but their reasons for doing so vary widely. Some believe the sacredness of the old covenant seventh-day Sabbath was transferred over to Sunday in the new covenant and they keep Sunday holy (some call it Sabbath) by not working on this day. Others worship on Sunday "in honor of the Lord's resurrection," and make no attempt to "keep" the day. They feel perfectly free to return home from church and go to work, or to engage in other activities which would be forbidden by old covenant Sabbath law. I hope the findings of this chapter, when integrated with the other material in this book, will give the worshipping Christian greater insight regarding the day of worship.

We will examine every first-day text in the New Testament to discover what is taught or not taught regarding the first day of the week.

Resurrection Day, First-day References

> Now late on the Sabbath, as it began to dawn toward the first day of the week, Mary Magdalene and the other Mary came to look at the grave (Mt. 28:1).

> And when the Sabbath was over, Mary Magdalene, and Mary the mother of James, and Salome, bought spices, that they might come and anoint Him. And very early on the first day of the week, they came to the tomb when the sun had risen (Mk. 16:1, 2).
> Now the women who had come with Him out of Galilee followed after, and saw the tomb and how His body was laid. And they returned and prepared spices and perfumes. And on the Sabbath they rested according to the commandment. But on the first day of the week, at early dawn, they came to the tomb, bringing the spices which they had prepared. And they found the stone rolled away from the tomb (Lk. 23:55–24:2).

From these three passages several facts emerge. (1) Jesus was resurrected on the first day of the week. (2) The women who followed Jesus felt it more important to keep the Sabbath "according to the commandment" than to anoint the body of Jesus. (3) There was no mix-up in days at the time of the death, burial and resurrection of Jesus.

First-day Appearances of the Resurrected Lord

Scripture records seven appearances of the resurrected Lord. Five of these occurred on the first day of the week. In the other two accounts, by the sea of Tiberius (Jn. 21) and the ascension (Acts 1:6–10), there is no record of what day it was. Jesus appeared on the first day of the week to:

Mary, the morning of the resurrection
(Mt. 28:8–10; Mk. 16:9; Jn. 20:11–18)

> Mary Magdalene and the other Mary…departed from the tomb with fear and great joy and ran to report it to His disciples and behold, Jesus met them and greeted them. And they came up and took hold of His feet and worshipped Him. Then Jesus said to them, "Do not be afraid; go and take word to My brethren to leave for Galilee, and there they will see Me" (Mt. 28:8–10).

The two disciples on their way to Emmaus
(Lk. 24:13–33; Mk. 16:12, 13)

The First Day of the Week

In this account Cleopas and an unnamed disciple were traveling from Jerusalem to Emmaus.

> Jesus himself approached, and began traveling with them... And He said to them, "O foolish men and slow of heart to believe in all that the prophets have spoken!"...And beginning with Moses and with all the prophets, He explained to them the things concerning Himself in all the Scriptures...And it came about that when He had reclined at table with them, He took the bread and blessed it, and breaking it, He began giving it to them. And their eyes were opened and they recognized Him; and He vanished from their sight...(Lk. 24:15–31).

Simon (Lk. 24:34)

> The Lord has really risen, and has appeared to Simon.

The disciples on the evening of resurrection Sunday
(Mk. 16:14–18; Lk. 24:36–44; Jn. 20:19–23)

> When therefore it was evening, on that day, the first day of the week, and when the doors were shut where the disciples were for fear of the Jews, Jesus came and stood in their midst, and said to them, "Peace be with you." And when He had said this, He showed them both His hands and His side. The disciples therefore rejoiced when they saw the Lord. Jesus therefore said to them again, "Peace be with you, as the Father has sent Me, I also send you." And when He had said this, He breathed on them, and said to them, "Receive the Holy Spirit. If you forgive the sins of any, their sins have been forgiven them; if you retain the sins of any, they have been retained" (Jn. 20:19–23).

To the eleven "eight days later" (Jn. 20:26–29)

> And after eight days [a week later—see margin] again His disciples were inside, and Thomas with them. Jesus came, the doors having been shut, and stood in their midst, and said, "Peace be with you." Then He said to Thomas, "Reach here your finger, and see My hands; and reach here your hand, and put it into My side; and be not unbelieving, but believing." Thomas answered and said to Him, "My Lord and my God!"

Jesus said to him, "Because you have seen Me, have you believed? Blessed are they who did not see, and yet believed."

Summary of first-day appearances

Several things should be mentioned from these records of first-day appearances. First, there are no planned "first day of the week" meetings, as if Christ had told His disciples before His death to meet on the first day of the week. Rather, the disciples were taken by surprise. They were apparently afraid for their own lives and were hiding behind locked doors "for fear of the Jews."

Second, while the events which happened on this day seem not to have been planned by the disciples, that in no way diminishes the importance of what did transpire in the sovereign will of God.

We should also remember that the gospel accounts as well as Acts were written many years after the events described therein. The fact that the first day of the week is mentioned so often reflects the beginning of special significance accorded that day in New Testament times.

1. On Sunday morning Mary "worshipped Him."
2. On Sunday evening Jesus took bread, blessed it, broke it and began to give it to the disciples in Emmaus. It is of importance to note that these two disciples recognized Jesus in the breaking of the bread. Only a few days earlier He had broken bread, given it to His disciples and said, "Do this in remembrance of Me" (Lk. 22:19). When they did recognize Jesus, He suddenly vanished from their sight.
3. Sunday night Jesus said, "Peace be with you," two times.
4. Sunday evening Jesus commissioned His disciples by saying, "As the Father has sent Me, I also send you."
5. On the evening of the first day of the week Jesus breathed on His disciples and said, "Receive the Holy Spirit."

The First Day of the Week

6. Sunday evening Jesus gave His disciples the authority to proclaim forgiveness to those who believe in Him.

    The meeting on the Sunday evening a week after the resurrection is of interest on two accounts. First, why were the disciples meeting on Sunday evening? This question, for our purposes, has only two possible answers. If the disciples were purposely meeting on the first day of the week it would show that some significance was given to this day. On the other hand, they may have been meeting together on many evenings or even living together and it just happened to be on this evening that Jesus appeared to them. If the former is correct then it appears that the *disciples* were giving some significance to the first day of the week. However, if the latter is the case, then *Jesus* is the one who chooses to reveal Himself on the first day of the week.

7. In either case, some significance must be given to the fact that Jesus appeared to the disciples "eight days later"—a commonly accepted term for "next week."[1]

8. It was on this occasion that Thomas said, "My Lord and my God!"

9. When a day is mentioned in connection with the appearances of the risen Lord it is *always* the first day of the week.

Pentecost

While there is no mention of the first day of the week in the record of the day of Pentecost as recorded in Acts 2, the fact that Pentecost fell that year on the first day of the week is well attested.[2] John 19:31 states that the day Jesus was in

---

[1] See Leon Morris, *The Gospel According to John, The New International Commentary of the New Testament,* p. 852, (Wm. B. Eerdmans Publishing Co. Grand Rapids, MI, 1971)

[2] F. F. Bruce, *The Book of the Acts, The New International Commentary on the New Testament,* (Wm. B. Eerdmans Publishing Co. 1983), p. 53.

the grave was a "high day." This term was used when the annual sabbath of the Passover and the weekly Sabbath came together. If we accept this, then fifty days later would bring us to the first day of the week. Again, very significant events happened on this day, but the fact that the first day of the week is *not* mentioned in connection with these events may mean little significance should be given to the fact that Pentecost fell on Sunday. In other words, the *event* of the outpouring of the Holy Spirit is more important than the *day* upon which it was given. We would expect this under the new covenant, where reality takes precedence over form.

Acts 20:6–12

> And we sailed from Philippi after the days of Unleavened Bread, and came to them at Troas within five days; and there we stayed seven days. And on the first day of the week, when we were gathered together to break bread, Paul began talking to them, intending to depart the next day, and he prolonged his message until midnight. And there were many lamps in the upper room where we were gathered together. And there was a certain young man named Eutychus sitting on the windowsill, sinking into a deep sleep; and as Paul kept on talking, he was overcome by sleep and fell down from the third floor, and was picked up dead. But Paul went down and fell upon him and after embracing him, he said, "Do not be troubled, for his life is in him." And when he had gone back up, and had broken the bread and eaten, he talked with them a long while, until daybreak, and so departed. And they took away the boy alive, and were greatly comforted.

This is a very complex section, as we will soon see. If Luke is using Jewish time this evening meeting was on Saturday night. In Jewish reckoning the new day always started at sundown. However, this was a Gentile Christian church which probably used Roman time. Nevertheless, Luke says this meeting took place on the first day of the

The First Day of the Week

week. The fact that there were "many lamps in the upper room" where they were gathered (Acts 20:8) is evidence that this evening meeting was not a holdover meeting from a Sabbath morning service as some have argued. The many lamps show that the people came prepared for the evening service. The weight of evidence is that this was a Sunday evening meeting, probably the regular meeting time for the Christians in Troas.[3]

Luke states they "were gathered together to break bread," indicating this was the purpose of their meeting together. Some have argued this was a specially called meeting as Paul was "intending to depart the next day." Paul could have left Troas earlier and gone by ship but he chose to wait and then walk some thirty miles to Assos. Why did he wait? The most probable reason was that Paul wanted to address the Christian believers in Troas before he left and he waited until their *regular* meeting time to do so.

The term "break bread" should not be confused with the Jewish expression "to eat bread." The latter is a common Jewish term for a regular meal. To "break bread," however, is commonly associated with the Lord's Supper.[4]

> And having taken some *bread,* when He had given thanks, He *broke it,* and gave it to them, saying, "This is My body which is given for you; do this in remembrance of Me" (Lk. 22:19).
>
> And it came about that when He had reclined at table with them, He took *bread* and blessed it, and *breaking it,* He began giving it to them. And their eyes were opened and they recognized Him; and He vanished from their sight (Lk. 24:30, 31).
>
> And they began to relate their experiences on the road and how He was recognized by them in the *breaking of the bread* (Lk. 24:35).
>
> And day by day continuing with one mind in the temple, and *breaking bread* from house to house, they were taking their meals together with gladness and sincerity of heart (Acts 2:46).

---

[3] Max M. B. Turner, "The Sabbath, Sunday, and the Law in Luke/Acts", in *From Sabbath to Lord's day,* p. 130.

[4] *Ibid.,* p. 130.

There are several other things we should note regarding the last verse (Acts 2:46) above. First, it is clear that the early Christians continued to worship in the temple. We should also recognize that the Jews would not have allowed the Christians to practice the Lord's Supper in the Jewish temple or synagogue. This necessitated their meeting "from house to house" in order to practice the Lord's Supper. Second, the fact that this breaking of bread was said to be a daily occurrence does not mean *every home* was visited on a daily basis. Third, the Lord's Supper was often taken at a fellowship meal. The fact that Luke records they were "breaking bread from house to house" *and* "taking their meals together," would make him redundant if he were not speaking of *two different things*: communion and a fellowship meal. Therefore, the evidence is weighted heavily in favor of interpreting "breaking bread" in Acts 2:46 to be the Lord's Supper.

In 1 Corinthians 11:23, 24 we find,

> For I received from the Lord that which I also delivered to you, that the Lord Jesus in the night in which He was betrayed took *bread;* and when He had given thanks, He *broke* it, and said, "This is My body, which is for you; do this in remembrance of Me."

In the early church "to gather together" and "to break bread" appear to be a standard formula for Christian meetings where the Lord's Supper was practiced.[5]

The weight of evidence seems to support F. F. Bruce's conclusion regarding Acts 20:7.

> The statement that at Troas the travelers and their fellow Christians dwelling in that port met together for the breaking of the bread "upon the first day of the week" is the earliest

---

[5] *Ibid.,* p. 132.

The First Day of the Week

unambiguous evidence we have for the Christian practice of gathering together on that day.[6]

To summarize: (1) This meeting was "on the first day of the week." (2) It was probably Sunday evening. (3) Luke says they were "gathered together to break bread," indicating the purpose of the meeting. (4) "Breaking bread" was probably the Lord's Supper. (5) This was a Christian church meeting. (6) It is the earliest strong evidence of Christians meeting on the first day of the week.

1 Corinthians 16:1, 2

> Now concerning the collection for the saints, as I directed the churches of Galatia, so do you also. On the first day of every week let each one of you put aside and save, as he may prosper, that no collection be made when I come.

This is an important verse because the instruction given this church is the same instruction Paul had given to a number of other Christian churches. This instruction includes specific mention of the first day of the week. From my research I have been unable to find any *good* reason for Paul to specifically mention the first day of the week, *unless* this day held a degree of importance to the New Testament Christians.

The Greek construction "put aside and save" literally means, "put by himself." However, it is not proof that it could not have been at a church meeting, although nothing is said about a church meeting or putting this money into the collection plate. Perhaps Paul was telling the believers to save *some* of their offering money at home *before* they went to church each Sunday. This would keep them from putting all their offering money into the local church expense. Therefore, when Paul came he would simply call

---

[6] O. Cullmann, *Early Christian Worship,* as quoted by F. F. Bruce, *The New International Commentary of the New Testament, The Book of Acts,* pp. 407, 408.

for the money which the believers would by then have already saved up for the saints in Jerusalem. This hypothesis provides a possible reason for the facts in this verse.

In summary we have the following: (1) Paul saw some significance to the first day of the week. (2) Paul instructed all the churches of Galatia to follow the instruction given here. (3) The Greek construction suggests that the money may have been put aside privately.

Revelation 1:10

> I was in the Spirit on the Lord's day, and I heard behind me a loud voice like the sound of a trumpet...

At first this verse seems to say very little regarding the Sabbath or the first day of the week. This verse is found in a section of Scripture which is dealing with other subject matter. But what does it say? Really all it says is that John received a vision "on the Lord's day." What did He mean? One can hardly use this text to form a theology of Sabbath or Sunday, rather this is a verse which must fit into that theology *and* it must *also* fit the history of the early church. This verse, for all practical purposes, will be interpreted on the basis of other study and other conclusions.

The Reformation/Continuation, Saturday sabbatarian school of thought reasons like this. Here it says the Lord has a day. Matthew 12:8 (Mk. 2:27) says that "the Son of Man is Lord of the Sabbath." Therefore, John must have been "in the Spirit" on the seventh-day Sabbath.[7] In fact SDA's *Clear Word* (Bible)[8] renders Revelation 1:10 as follows:

---

[7] See Desmond Ford, *The Forgotten Day*, (Desmond Ford Publications, Newcastle, CA, 1981), p. 224.
[8] Jack Blanco, *The Clear Word Bible*, (Review and Herald Publishing Association, Hagerstown, MD. 1994). This work has been revised since this date and is now simply called *The Clear Word*.

> One Sabbath morning when I had gone to the rocky island shore to meditate and worship...

Those who place significance on the first day of the week use the same reasoning, but instead of Sabbath being the Lord's day, they see the first day of the week, the day of the resurrection, as the Lord's day. While they do not have any specific Scripture which calls the first day of the week "the Lord's day," they point to the frequent mention of the first day of the week in connection with the risen Lord, and to extra-biblical use of the "Lord's day" in connection with the first day of the week.[9]

Which is correct? First we must note that the phrase "The Son of Man is Lord of the Sabbath" (Mt. 12:8) does not mean that the Sabbath is the Lord's day. Rather, as we saw in Chapter 7, the context shows that Jesus was *not* submitting Himself to old covenant Sabbath law but He was exercising His authority *over* Sabbath law. He made this statement in the context of excusing His disciples' questionable Sabbath activities.

Second, we know from the historical record that the term "Lord's day" was a common title for the first day of the week.

> Pliny wrote to Trajan concerning the Christians: "They were wont to meet together, on *a stated day* before it was light, and sang among themselves alternately a hymn to Christ as God."—*Home's Introduction* (vol. 1, chap. 3, sec. 2, p. 84). Early in the morning the Christians assembled "before it was light." These meetings were on a "certain stated day." On what day were the early morning meetings held? Eusebius the historian answers: "By this is prophetically signified the service which is performed very early and every morning *of the resurrection day throughout* the whole world."—*Sabbath Manual* (p. 125). The day on which Christ rose was the "stated day" on which the Christians met for worship. Pliny was governor of Bithynia, Asia Minor, A. D. 106–108. This was the very place where the

---

[9] See R. J. Bauckham, "The Lord's Day", in *From Sabbath to Lord's Day,* pp. 224–250 for a thorough study of this verse.

apostles labored, and the time only eleven years after John died.[10]

In the Epistle to Barnabus, written between 70–132 AD We read,

> "...your new moons and Sabbaths I cannot stand." Therefore he has abolished these things, in order that the new law of our Lord Jesus Christ, which is free from the yoke of compulsion, might have its offering, one not made by man.[11]
> ....this is why we spend the eighth day in celebration, the day on which Jesus both arose from the dead, after appearing again, ascended into heaven.[12]

Ignatius of Antioch, 107–110 AD, wrote,

> ... for if we continue to live in accordance with Judaism, we admit that we have not received grace...If, then, those who had lived in antiquated practices come to newness of hope, no longer keeping the Sabbath but living in accordance with the *Lord's day,* on which our life also arose through him..."[13]

This statement was made only a few years after Revelation was written.

Justin Martyr, ~150 AD wrote,

> But Sunday is the day on which we hold our common assembly, because it is the first day of the week and Jesus our saviour on the same day rose from the dead.[14]

Those wishing to do more research into the Sabbath/Sunday practices of the early church in general and the use of "Lord's Day" specifically are encouraged

---

[10] H.M. Riggle, (Faith Publishing House, Guthrie, OK, 1922) p. 121.
[11] *Epistle of Barnabas,* in *The Apostolic Fathers,* Translated by J.B. Lightfoot and J. R. Harmer, (Baker book House, Grand Rapids, MI, 1989), p. 163.
[12] *Ibid.,* p. 183.
[13] Ignatius of Antioch, *Epistle to the Magnesians,* in *The Apostolic Fathers,* Translated by J.B. Lightfoot and J. R. Harmer, (Baker book House, Grand Rapids, MI, 1989), p. 95.
[14] First apology of Justin, Chp. 68. See also H.M. Riggle, *The Sabbath and the Lord's Day,* p. 123.

The First Day of the Week

to read, R. J. Bauckham's extensive research as published in *From Sabbath to Lord's day*. Here is his conclusion:

> It seems clear that by the end of the second century this [the Lord's day] (with its Latin equivalent dies dominica) was the ordinary designation of the weekly day of worship throughout the greater part of the Christian world.[15]
>
> From the latter second century onwards it is clear that Sunday was the regular day of Christian worship everywhere, and there is no record of any controversy over whether worship should take place on Sunday...It therefore becomes extremely likely that "Lord's day"[16] in Revelation 1:10 also means Sunday....to claim that Revelation 1:10 refers to Easter (or to the Sabbath) is mere speculation with no evidence whatever to support it. The wholly consistent usage of second-century writers indicates Sunday.[17]

The weight of evidence is in favor of accepting "The Lord's day" in Revelation 1:10 as a reference to Sunday.

The Lord's Day Is a Voluntary Celebration of the Resurrection of Christ

It seems evident that the early Christians did not worship on the first day of the week because the Sabbath had been changed to Sunday. Rather, they chose that day because of the many important events that happened on the first day of the week, the greatest of which was the resurrection of Christ. First-day worship is a *voluntary* celebration of Christ's gift of new life to the Christian. Just as a wedding anniversary or a birthday celebration is not a thing to be legislated, so first-day worship is a joyous occasion for us to reflect back to the greatest event in world history: the resurrection of Christ from the dead! This was

---

[15] *Ibid.*, p. 230.
[16] "Lord's Day" in the quote is given in Greek letters.
[17] R. J. Bauckham, "The Lord's Day", in *From Sabbath to Lord's Day*, p. 231.

the theme of the new covenant proclamation.[18] This event is the basis of all the new covenant blessings and promises. Therefore it is most appropriate to make the first day of the week a special day for gathering together with other Christians to celebrate the Christ event.

That the early church voluntarily started this practice is not wrong or unusual. Throughout biblical history God's people have voluntarily celebrated important events to help them remember the mighty works of God. Following are just two examples, many could be given.

After Esther succeeded in delivering the Jews from the wicked Haman who wanted to exterminate them, then,

> Mordecai recorded these events, and he sent letters to all the Jews who were in all the provinces of King Ahasuerus, both near and far, obliging them to celebrate the fourteenth day of the month Adar, and the fifteenth day of the same month, annually, because on those days the Jews rid themselves of their enemies, and it was a month which was turned for them from sorrow into gladness and from mourning into a holiday; that they should make them days of feasting and rejoicing and sending portions of food to one another and gifts to the poor (Esth. 9:20–22).

In John 10:22 and following, we find that Jesus went to the temple during the feast of Hanukkah, sometimes called the Festival of Lights, which was a voluntary celebration of the cleansing of the sanctuary by Judas Maccabaeus after its profanation by Antiochus Epiphanes.[19]

Therefore, we should not be surprised that the people of God would celebrate the greatest event in world history by *voluntarily* meeting together on the first day of the week to celebrate the Lord's Supper, read the gospel and encourage one another in Christ! *It is the most appropriate thing to do!*

---

[18] The resurrection is mentioned over 75 times in the New Testament outside of the Gospels.
[19] 1 Maccabees 4:36–61.

The first day of the week and sun worship

Some sabbatarians accuse those who worship on the first day of the week of sun worship because in Roman times this day was called "Sunday". There is no evidence that I have seen that indicates that any body of main-stream Christians ever worshiped on the first day of the week *to worship the sun*. When Christians met at sunrise, it was not to worship the sun, but to celebrate the resurrection event which took place early Sunday morning. The fact that the first day of the week is called Sunday is no more significant to Christians than the seventh day of the week is called Saturday. As sabbatarians do not worship Saturn, neither do those who worship on Sunday worship the sun.[20]

Chapter Summary

1. Jesus rose from the dead on the first day of the week.
2. There was no mix-up in days at the death, burial and resurrection of Jesus.
3. The women who were associated with Jesus felt it more important to keep the Sabbath "according to the commandment" than to anoint Jesus' body.
4. Mary worshipped Jesus on resurrection Sunday.
5. Jesus took bread, blessed it, broke it, and gave it to two of His disciples on the first day of the week.
6. Jesus spoke peace to His disciples on the first day of the week.
7. Jesus commissioned His disciples on the first day of the week. "As the Father has sent Me, I also send you."
8. On the first day of the week Jesus breathed on His disciples and said, "Receive you the Holy Spirit."
9. On the first day of the week Jesus gave His disciples the authority to proclaim forgiveness.

---

[20] See Riggle, *The Sabbath and the Lord's Day* for extensive documentation on this topic.

10. Of the seven recorded post-resurrection appearances of Jesus, five of them were on the first day of the week.
11. Every time a day is mentioned in connection with the appearance of the risen Lord, it is always the first day of the week.
12. Pentecost, and the outpouring of the Holy Spirit, took place on the first day of the week, but that fact is not mentioned in Scripture.
13. The Christians in Troas "gathered together to break bread" on the first day of the week. This was probably a Sunday evening meeting where the Lord's Supper was celebrated.
14. Paul told all the churches in the region of Galatia and Corinth to "put aside and save" money for the Jerusalem saints on "the first day of every week."
15. John, when writing the book of Revelation, speaks of the "Lord's day." There is good evidence to believe this has reference to the first day of the week.
16. Every time the first day of the week is mentioned in the New Testament it is in connection with believing Christians.
17. Every time the first day of the week is mentioned in the New Testament it is in a positive setting.
18. There is no specific command to keep *any* day holy in the New Testament.
19. There is no specific command to worship on the first day of the week in the New Testament.
20. Worship on the first day of the week is a voluntary celebration of the Christ event.
21. There are many biblical examples of God's people celebrating the mighty acts of God.
22. Worship on the first day of the week is not sun worship.

CHAPTER
TWENTY THREE

SABBATH FULFILLMENT IN CHRIST

We have studied each Sabbath passage in its own contextual setting. It is now time to review the key findings and to reach a conclusion on this topic.

Review of the key facts of our study

- The Genesis account says nothing about man resting or keeping a Sabbath.
- There is no mention of Sabbath keeping before the time of Moses.
- The Ten Commandments are the very words of the Sinaitic Covenant.
- The Book of the Covenant was an expansion and application of the Ten Commandments to the life of Israel.
- The Sabbath is the sign of the Sinaitic Covenant.
- One purpose of the Sabbath was a reminder of God's rest at the end of creation's sixth day.
- One purpose of the Sabbath was a reminder of redemption from Egyptian bondage.
- The Sabbath was given only to the nation of Israel.
- The stipulations of the Sinaitic Covenant were not given to Abraham.
- The Sabbath is mentioned with moral laws of the Sinaitic Covenant two times.

- The Sabbath is mentioned with ritual laws of the Sinaitic Covenant at least a dozen times and is part of the sabbatical system pointing forward to the Jubilee.
- The Sabbath was to be kept by the whole Israelite family, their slaves, their animals and their land.
- The laws for Sabbath observance were stringent and clearly spelled out.
- Violators of the Sabbath were to be put to death and were cut off from the covenant community.
- The Sabbath is inseparably linked with every aspect of the Sinaitic Covenant.
- Jesus is the new covenant center.
- The New Testament defines the old, or first, covenant as including *both* the Ten Commandments and the other laws of the Torah.
- The new covenant is a more complete and a better revelation of truth than was the old.
- We must allow the new covenant to interpret, transform and apply all old covenant law(s) in a Christ-centered way.
- Jesus always let moral and ethical considerations determine His actions even if his actions violated old covenant ritual law.
- Jesus expanded old covenant moral laws given to Israel into eternal moral principles for all nations.
- By His actions it is clear that Jesus understood the Sabbath laws to be ritual laws.
- Jesus purposely went out of His way to create controversy regarding Sabbath law. In doing so, He was trying to help the people become Christ centered rather than old-covenant-law centered.
- The apostle John states that Jesus was continually breaking or destroying the Sabbath.
- Nowhere in the book of Acts is there record of Christian assemblies being held on the Sabbath. All

Sabbath Fulfillment in Christ

Sabbath meetings in the book of Acts are in Jewish gatherings.
- The old covenant law was given 430 years after Abraham and was to rule until Christ.
- The old covenant law was given to lead Israel to Christ but when Christ came they were no longer under old covenant law.
- Christians are free from the law and serve in the newness of the Spirit and not in the oldness of the letter.
- Christians who try to be "married" to both the law and Christ are committing spiritual adultery.
- Colossians 2:16 is a clear reference to the Seventh-day Sabbath and links it with the other old covenant ritual laws which were a mere shadow of Christ.
- Galatians 4:10 is probably a reference to the holy days of the old covenant and when observed by Christians as a necessary duty pervert the gospel of faith in Christ alone.
- Romans 14:5 probably refers to the Seventh-day Sabbath. Controversy over opinions regarding holy days is not to be a cause for disunity in the church.
- The epistles never give instruction regarding Sabbath keeping.
- The epistles never give a command to keep the Sabbath.
- The epistles never mention Sabbath breaking in any lists of sins.
- The Sabbath is not the seal of God for new covenant believers.
- New covenant believers are sealed with the Holy Spirit at the moment they believe in Christ as their Lord and Savior.
- New covenant righteousness is beyond and above that of old covenant, law-based righteousness.

- In the new covenant the Holy Spirit fills the role that the law served in the old covenant and is the guide to righteous living.

Conclusion:

The epistles, in contextual teaching, state that the Sinaitic Covenant is not binding in any way upon the Christian. This covenant, which was good for its time, has been superseded by the new, better covenant. The new covenant law of love interpreted by the New Testament writings and applied under the guidance of the Holy Spirit *far surpasses* the laws given to Israel. Scripture makes it clear, however, that the *moral principles* upon which many of the Sinaitic Covenant laws were based are included in the *moral principles* of the new covenant. However, in the new covenant there is a different administration of the moral principles, and the new covenant has different signs.

Under the new covenant the emphasis is no longer on sign and symbol, rather it is on reality and relationship. There are no long lists of minutely detailed laws, rather the new covenant is characterized by general principles which have application to *all nations and cultures,* not just the sons of Israel in the promised land. The epistles teach that Christians can add nothing to the righteousness provided for them in Christ. Those who seek to add their own works of obedience to the perfect, finished work of Christ by keeping any of the ritual observances of the old covenant are in serious danger of falling from grace.[1] The new covenant writings show one cannot pick and choose among the old covenant laws. If one is seeking to be under Sinaitic

---

[1] "You observe days and months and seasons and years. I fear for you, that perhaps I have labored over you in vain" (Gal. 4:10, 11).

Sabbath Fulfillment in Christ

law, he must be under the *whole* law.[2] However, to do this is to fall from grace.[3]

There is no biblical evidence which proves the Sabbath of the seventh day was transferred to the first day of the week. While there are many important events which transpired on the first day of the week, there is no biblical command to keep it holy. Nevertheless, it appears that the first day of the week did have significance for New Testament believers and the Christians of the Early Church because of the important events which happened on that day. It is necessary that Christians have a time to worship. It is necessary that time be given to pursue the things of God. In harmony with established biblical custom, many Christians in the early Church voluntarily made the first day of the week a special time to celebrate the resurrection, observe the Lord's Supper and meet for Christian fellowship and teaching. The first day of the week, however, should never be seen in the same light as the Sabbath of the old covenant. Rather, the emphasis is on *what* happened rather than on *when* it happened. New covenant worship is a voluntary celebration rather than a legislated duty.

Nearly every ceremony in the old covenant in some way pointed forward to the work of Christ. The writer of Hebrews unequivocally shows that the rest which remains *for the Christian* is not the seventh-day Sabbath of Sinai, nor is it the "rest" which Israel experienced under the leadership of Joshua or David. Rather, the rest of the new covenant is the "rest" of a restored relationship between man and God similar to the rest of creation's seventh day which one *enters by believing*.

---

[2] "And I testify again to every man who receives circumcision, that he is under obligation to keep the whole Law" (Gal. 5:3).

[3] "You have been severed from Christ, you who are seeking to be justified by law; you have fallen from grace" (Gal. 5:4).

All the Sinaitic Sabbaths—seventh-day Sabbaths, seasonal sabbaths, sabbatical years and Jubilee—seem to have been like small oases in the desert where the sons of Israel pretended they were back in the Garden of Eden. These sabbaths not only pointed *back* to that seventh-day rest of creation, but they pointed *forward* to the restored relationship which was to take place within the new covenant: the fellowship of the Holy Spirit indwelling the heart of the believer who is saved by grace. These sabbaths served a very important function in giving roots, purpose, direction and hope to the people of Israel. But like the dozens of other pointers, which were also shadows of good things to come, their value ended in the presence of the Creator. Jesus drew all these old covenant signs and shadows of hope to Himself.

The Pharisees demonstrated the heartbreaking paradox of old covenant Sabbath law. The laws that were designed to point forward to the open fellowship between man and God were the very laws which blinded their eyes to the present reality of the Creator standing in their midst. Jesus said,

> You search the Scriptures, because you think that in them you have eternal life; and it is these that bear witness of Me; and you are unwilling to come to Me, that you may have life (Jn. 5:38, 39).

The actions of the Pharisees can be likened to a person driving from the East Coast of the U.S. to visit California's Yosemite Valley. For thousands of miles the traveler has been following a road map to Yosemite. During this time he becomes so intent on watching the map—lest he make a wrong turn—that when he reaches Yosemite he fails to see the beauty of the country. With one eye on the road and the other eye on the map he drives through Yosemite Valley without ever seeing El Capitan, Half Dome or Yosemite Falls. Finding a parking place, with his eyes still glued to his packet of instructions, he reads about the beautiful park but never leaves the seat of his car to personally walk the trails and never lifts his eyes to the majesty above.

The map and trail guide of the Sabbath served important functions. But upon arrival at the destination it is time to put the map down and look up. So it is with the Sabbath. Rather than seek to keep a *day* holy let us put the day down and step into the arms of our holy *Creator*. Let us enter "today" into fellowship, into a "rest" which *remains* for those who have believed. The Redeemer has come to bring true deliverance from the bondage of guilt and sin.

Jesus was continually seeking those who would come to *Him*. "Come unto *Me* all you who are weary and heavy laden" (Mt. 11:28). "Follow *Me*" was his often-repeated phrase to those who were seeking to obey God.

> Now on the last day, the great day of the feast, Jesus stood and cried out, saying, "If any man is thirsty, let him come to *Me* and drink" (Jn. 7:37, 38).

New covenant worship is not concerned with times and places. The woman of Samaria said to Jesus,

> "Our fathers worshiped in this mountain; and you people say that in Jerusalem is the place where men ought to worship." Jesus said to her, "Woman, believe Me, an hour is coming when neither in this mountain, nor in Jerusalem, shall you worship the Father…an hour is coming and *now is,* when the true worshipers shall worship the Father in *spirit* and *truth;* for such the Father seeks to be His worshipers. God is spirit; and those who worship Him must worship in spirit and truth" (Jn. 4:20–24).

To understand that God is actually seeking people like you and me to worship Him fills us with a sense of both humility and tremendous self-worth!

> He jealously desires the spirit which He has made to dwell in us (Jas. 4:5).

The "sabbatismos" (Gr.) rest of the new covenant is better than the "sabbaton" (Gr.) rest of the old covenant, for it deals with the *reality* to which the old covenant Sabbath only prefigured. It moves from *observance* to *experience*.

Do This in Remembrance of Me

Jesus developed a close relationship with His disciples during His three-and-a-half-year ministry. They had come to believe in Him as the Messiah. They had learned to trust His wisdom and power in times of sickness and emergency, as well as in everyday life. They had walked with Him, talked with Him, and listened to His teaching.

Just before His death, and the resulting physical separation from His disciples, Jesus chose a ceremony (ritual) by which His disciples could express their continued faith in Him. In the days and years to come this ceremony would also demonstrate the continued presence of Jesus, even though He would be invisible to the gathered assembly.

To express His deep feeling of love to His disciples, Jesus chose a simple meal of bread and wine. Through the ensuing years this has become variously known as the Lord's Supper, Holy Eucharist, or the communion service. During the Last Supper with His disciples Jesus inaugurated this service using these words, "Do this in remembrance of Me."

> And having taken some bread, when He had given thanks, He broke it, and gave it to them, saying, "This is My body which is given for you; *do this in remembrance of Me.*" And in the same way He took the cup after they had eaten, saying, "This cup which is poured out for you is *the new covenant* in my blood" (Lk. 22:19, 20).

By partaking in the Lord's Supper, we demonstrate our continued belief and trust in Jesus Christ as our Covenant Keeper.

Bread and the presence of the Lord

From its very beginning the Lord's Supper has been associated with the *presence of the risen Lord.* On Resurrection Sunday two grieving, confused disciples were on their way to Emmaus. As they sorrowfully made their way along the trail they were joined by a fellow traveler. When they arrived at their destination they invited the traveler to eat with them and stay overnight. The traveler accepted their invitation. During the evening meal this traveler picked up the bread and began to break it and suddenly they realized this traveler was none other than the risen Lord. It was *during the breaking of the bread* that they recognized the presence of the risen Lord, the very symbol He had given to His disciples when He said, "Do this in remembrance of Me"!

> And it came about that when He had reclined at table with them, He took the bread and blessed it, and breaking it, He began giving it to them. And their eyes were opened and they recognized Him; and He vanished from their sight (Lk. 24:30, 31).

Later, to emphasize the connection between the breaking of the bread and the presence of the risen Lord, Luke records,

> And they began to relate their experiences on the road and how He was recognized by them *in the breaking of the bread.* And while they were telling these things, He Himself stood in their midst (Lk. 24:35, 36).

Today, during the celebration of the Lord's Supper, the same presence of the living Lord is realized in the heart of the believer as he partakes of the *bread* and the *wine*. The bread is a symbol of Christ's body which He gave for us.

> And while they were eating, Jesus took some bread, and after a blessing, He broke it and gave it to the disciples, and said, "Take, eat; this is My body" (Mt. 26:26).

In the eastern world bread is considered the staff of life. Jesus took this well-known necessity of life and made it a symbol of His body, given for the life of the world. In the symbol of the bread we are also to remember the experience of the manna in the wilderness. Jesus said,

> I am the bread of life. Your fathers ate the manna in the wilderness, and they died. This is the bread which comes down out of heaven, so that one may eat of it and not die. I am the living bread that came down out of heaven; if any one eats of

this bread, he shall live forever; and the bread also which I shall give for the life of the world is My flesh (Jn. 6:48–51).

Wine, on the other hand, is symbolized in Scripture in two ways. It is both a symbol of joy and a symbol of God's wrath. The wine of the Lord's Supper should be seen in both ways.

Wine as joy

In the book of Psalms we read of the Lord's blessings and care over all His works in these words.

> He causes the grass to grow for the cattle, and vegetation for the labor of man, so that he may bring forth food from the earth, and wine which makes man's heart glad, so that he may make his face glisten with oil, and food which sustains man's heart (Ps. 104:14, 15).

According to the Gospel of John, Jesus' public ministry started at a wedding feast in Cana of Galilee. The joy of the celebration was interrupted when the wine ran out. Jesus met this need by miraculously providing some one hundred and twenty gallons of the finest wine (Jn. 2:6–11).

Wine as wrath

> And Babylon the great was remembered before God, to give her *the cup of the wine of His fierce wrath* (Rev. 16:19).
>
> If any one worships the beast and his image, and receives a mark on his forehead or upon his hand, he also will drink of the wine of the wrath of God, which is mixed in full strength in the cup of His anger (Rev. 14:10).

Doubtless the association between wine and the wrath of God sprang from the custom of treading the winepress during the grape crush. People coming from the winepress looked like they had come from a bloody battle.

One truth Jesus communicates in giving us the cup—a symbol of God's wrath—is that if we partake of the cup *now* we will escape the *coming wrath* which will be poured out on those who reject God's invitation of mercy. It is a symbolic way of teaching,

He who hears My word, and believes Him who sent Me, has eternal life, and *does not come into judgment,* but has passed out of death into life (Jn. 5:24).

We are reminded how the blood sprinkled on the doorposts the night of the Passover protected those "under the blood" from the destroying angel. In the same way the blood of Christ, symbolized by the communion wine, will protect us from the coming wrath pictured by the Revelator in these words:

> And the angel swung his sickle to the earth, and gathered the clusters from the vine of the earth, and threw them into the great *wine press of the wrath of God.* And the wine press was trodden *outside the city,* and blood came out from the wine press, up to the horses' bridles, for a distance of two hundred miles (Rev. 14:19, 20).

At the Last Supper Jesus

> ...took a cup and gave thanks, and gave it to them, saying, "Drink from it, all of you; for this is *My blood of the covenant,* which is to be shed on behalf of many for forgiveness of sins" (Mt. 26:27, 28).

When Jesus speaks of "My blood of the covenant" it is rich with meaning. At Sinai Moses

> ...took the Book of the Covenant and read it in the hearing of the people; and they said, "All that the Lord has spoken we will do, and we will be obedient!" So Moses took the blood and sprinkled it on the people, and said, "Behold, the blood of the covenant, which the Lord has made with you in accordance with all these words" (Ex. 24:7, 8).

When Jesus speaks of "My blood of the covenant" He understands the violent and sacrificial death He is about to undergo as He inaugurates with His people the new covenant. As the Passover Lamb, His blood will soon be "poured out."[4]

---

[4] See D. A. Carson, "Commentary on Matthew", *The Expositor's Bible Commentary,* Vol. 8, pp. 536, 537.

In the Garden of Gethsemane Jesus began to feel the weight of sin being placed upon Him.

> "My soul is deeply grieved, to the point of death..." And He went a little beyond them, and fell on His face and prayed, saying, "My Father, if it is possible, let this cup pass from Me; yet not as I will, but as Thou wilt" (Mt. 26:38, 39).

Therefore, Jesus also, that He might sanctify the people through His own blood, suffered *outside the gate* (Heb. 13:12).

As mentioned before, the Gospel of John is full of details which provide insight into the deeper message of this Gospel. John records the public ministry of Jesus starting with a joyous wedding celebration where He provided the "best" wine. It is no accident that John records the end of Jesus' ministry with His drinking "sour wine" given to Him on the branch of hyssop—the same instrument used to apply the blood of the Passover lamb to the lintel and doorposts.

> After this, Jesus, knowing that all things had already been accomplished, in order that the Scripture might be fulfilled, said, "I am thirsty." A jar full of *sour wine* was standing there; so they put a sponge full of the *sour wine* upon a branch of hyssop, and brought it up to His mouth. When Jesus therefore had received the *sour wine,* He said, "It is finished!" And He bowed His head and gave up His spirit (Jn. 19:28–30).

It was the sin of Adam and Eve which brought to an end that perfect "rest" of creation and led them into the bondage of sin. It was because of this sin that God "drove the man out" and placed the cherubim with the flaming sword to guard the gate of the Garden of Eden (Gen. 3:24). It was because of Adam's sin that the ground was cursed and brought forth thorns and thistles (Gen. 3:17–19) and Adam was forced to eat bread by the sweat of his brow (Gen. 3:19).

At the entrance of sin God began the "work" of redemption. This work came to an end when Jesus, wearing the crown of thorns "suffered outside the gate" in Adam's place. This work of redemption was complete when Jesus said, "It is finished," and died for the sins of the world. Contrary to what Seventh-day Adventists teach,[5] the book of Hebrews pictures Christ, not standing, pleading his blood, as did the high priest in the old covenant Day of Atonement, but *seated, resting, having completed the atonement.* For the Christian, celebrating the Lord's Supper is a time of deep and meaningful reflection. We learn to value ourselves by the price paid for our redemption. While the signs of the covenant are *not moral in themselves* they are nonetheless invaluable *to the covenant community.* Celebrating the Lord's Supper serves as a renewing of the covenant. We express our belief and trust in the risen Lord,

---

[5] In contrast to the book of Hebrews where Christ is pictured as having *completed* His atonement for sin and "sat down" at the right hand of God, Seventh-day Adventists see Jesus as *now standing and pleading His blood before the Father.* They also *do not see a completed atonement* as noted in the following quotations by Ellen White, whose "writings are a continuing and authoritative source of truth..." (See SDA Fundamental Beliefs No. 17 "The Gift of Prophecy". Printed in SDA Year books and listed on the SDA official web site at: http://www.adventist.org/beliefs/index.html.

"Therefore the announcement that the temple of God was opened in heaven and the ark of His testament was seen points to the *opening* of the most holy place of the heavenly sanctuary *in 1844* as Christ entered there to perform the *closing work of the atonement.* Those who by faith followed their great High Priest as He *entered* upon His ministry in the most holy place, beheld the ark of His testament. As they had studied the subject of the sanctuary they had come to understand the Savior's change of ministration, and they saw that He was *now officiating before the ark of God, pleading His blood in behalf of sinners."* E. G. White, *The Great Controversy,* p. 433.

"Then again was held up before me those who were not willing to dispose of this world's goods to save perishing souls by sending them the truth while Jesus *stands* before the Father *pleading His blood..."* E. G. White, *Early Writings,* p. 50 (See also E. G. White, *Spirit of Prophecy,* Vol. 4, p. 273; *Signs of the Times,* 1850-64-01; 1890-06-02; *Review and Herald,* 1870-04-19; 1911-06-29)

who fulfilled the covenant requirements *for us*. And we rehearse His covenant promises *to us*. More than that, during the communion service we experience the presence of the risen Lord.

Jesus took some bread, and after a blessing, He broke it and gave it to the disciples, and said, "Take, eat; this is My body." And He took a cup and gave thanks, and gave it to them, saying, "Drink from it, all of you; for this is My blood *of the covenant, which is to be shed on behalf of many for forgiveness of sins* (Mt. 26:26–28).

For those living in the new covenant the verdict is clear. It is no longer "remember the Sabbath *day* to keep it holy," but

DO THIS IN

REMEMBRANCE

OF ME.

The Lord's Supper causes us to look forward to the time when our Lord will drink it new with us in the Father's kingdom (Mt. 26:29).

Evaluation

As we mentioned in Chapter 1, Sabbath understanding can be categorized in three main areas, recognizing that there are varying interpretations within each group: Sunday keeping, which we called transfer/modification, Saturday keeping which we named reformation/continuation, and fulfillment/transformation or just "Sabbath in Christ".

Which one of these understandings best fits the biblical evidence?

Transfer/modification

This is perhaps one of the most popular understandings. It teaches that the seventh-day Sabbath of the Old Testament was *transferred* to Sunday in the New Testament and the rules for Sabbath keeping have been *modified*. Even though many Christian interpreters have supported this motif, or some variation of it, it is my judgment that this interpretation has little *biblical* support. First, there is no command *in Scripture* which would warrant the transfer of the Sabbath, and all that it stood for, to Sunday. Second, there are few, if any, biblical guidelines for a modification of Sabbath observance. One must, however, recognize that within *church history* this view is well supported.

Reformation/continuation

This has been a minority view well documented in Christian history. This view holds that the seventh-day Sabbath of the Fourth Commandment is as valid today as it was at Sinai. Supporters of this view believe the Sabbath is one of the most important moral laws, if not the most important commandment in the law.[6] Those who hold this view believe that the Sabbath encounters of Jesus were designed to bring *reform* to the Sabbath and free it from the extra-biblical rules which Jewish tradition had placed upon it. This view holds that the seventh-day Sabbath is to continue into the new covenant and even into the age to come. It has some biblical evidence to support it, but it has *several major weaknesses*. First, it ignores the evidence that

---

[6] "The four on the first table shone brighter than the other six. *But the fourth, the Sabbath commandment, shone above them all; for the Sabbath was set apart to be kept in honor of God's holy name. The holy Sabbath looked glorious—a halo of glory was all around it.*" Ellen. G. White, *Early Writings,* p. 33.

Christ treated the Sabbath like the other ritual laws of the old covenant.

Second, it portrays Paul as a Sabbath keeper and ignores that all of his Sabbath meetings were in Jewish settings.

Third, it cannot explain why Paul never gave any instruction regarding Sabbath observance or listed Sabbath breaking in any of his lists of sins.

Fourth, it does not take seriously the differences between the old and new covenants.

Fifth, it ignores the many clear biblical statements which show that the reign of law started with Moses and ended with Christ.

Sixth, it ignores the many clear biblical statements which teach that Christians are no longer under the law.

Seventh, because it ignores the differences between the covenants, it is faced with the dilemma of Sabbath observance. While it wants to hold many of the Old Testament statements regarding Sabbath as normative for the Christian, it is at a loss to show why *all* the old covenant statements regarding Sabbath observance—and all the other convocations of the old covenant as well—are not also valid today.

Eighth, history has shown that often those holding this motif struggle with legalism.[7]

Fulfillment/transformation—or Sabbath in Christ

This view holds that the Sabbath of the old covenant was *fulfilled* by Jesus. It sees the old covenant Sabbath pointing backward to the *rest of God* lost in Eden when man sinned, and pointing forward to the *rest of Christ*

---

[7] Author's note: Legalism has been a constant battle in many Sabbath keeping churches. This was and is true in the Seventh-day Adventist Church in which I grew up. I have found it true in other Sabbath keeping churches, such as The Church of God, Seventh-day, the Worldwide Church of God, until the recent major change in its theology and also in some Sunday sabbatarian churches.

which started when, after completing the atonement, He *sat down* at the Father's right hand. As the rest of the old covenant is transformed into the rest of the new covenant, so the vehicles of symbolism have also been *transformed* into other vehicles. While aspects of this view have been supported within the Christian church throughout its history, it seems to have been most clearly articulated in recent times.[8]

It is my judgment that this motif is the *only* view which harmonizes with *all* of Scripture. There were four main streams of symbolism that were carried by the Sabbath: creation rest, redemption from bondage, the sign of the covenant, and the day for worship. Notice how the new covenant takes these ideas and *transforms* them.

True rest

The Sabbath of the Fourth Commandment as recorded in Exodus 20:11 was a symbol of the rest of creation's seventh day. The new covenant shows that Jesus *fulfilled* this concept of rest. He is now the one that *provides true rest*. When we believe we enter into *His rest*—the rest of the completed atonement. Hebrews 3 and 4 show that in the new covenant God's rest *cannot* be the seventh-day Sabbath and *must* be the rest of grace.

Real redemption

The Sabbath of the Fourth Commandment as recorded in Deuteronomy 5:15 was a symbol of redemption from Egyptian bondage. The new covenant shows that Jesus provides the true redemption from the bondage of sin.

Covenant sign

The Sabbath of the Fourth Commandment was the "remembrance sign" of the Sinaitic Covenant. In the new cove-

---

[8] For a scholarly and well-footnoted study of this topic see *From Sabbath to Lord's Day,* edited by D. A. Carson.

nant it is clear that for the Christian the "remembrance sign" is the Lord's Supper.

Center of worship

The Sabbath of the Fourth Commandment was a day of worship. However, it is important to note that the concept of the Sabbath *as day of worship* is *not* in the old covenant Sabbath statements themselves. Rather, the Sabbath was portrayed as a day of *physical* rest. It was not until *after* the Babylonian captivity when the synagogue was instituted that the Sabbath became a regular day for worship and religious teaching.[9] While there are hints of special Sabbath activities, such as special sacrifices, etc., the concept is in germ form. In like manner the new covenant lacks specific commands for worship on the first day of the week. There are many *indicators* that the first day of the week held special significance, but the regular practice of Christian worship on Sunday came as a voluntary celebration of the resurrection of Christ.

The following diagram illustrates the fulfillment/transfer motif:

O.C. Sabbath concepts   vs   **N.C. Transformation**

Creation rest

Physical rest (Ex. 20)   →   Rest of grace (Heb. 4)

Redemption

Redemption from Egypt   →   Redemption from Sin
(Deut. 5:15)   (1 Cor. 1:30[10])

---

[9] See C. Rowland, "A Summary of the Sabbath Observance in Judaism at the Beginning of the Christian Era", in *From Sabbath to Lord's Day*, pp. 50, 51.

[10] "But by His doing you are in Christ Jesus, who became to us wisdom from God, and righteousness and sanctification, and redemption" (1 Cor. 1:30).

Sabbath Fulfillment in Christ

Covenant sign

Sabbath (Ex. 31) → Lord's Supper (Lk. 21)

Day of worship

Seventh day (History) → First day (History)[11]

Therefore we see that the fulfillment/transformation motif takes seriously *all* the scriptural evidence regarding the Sabbath and its meaning and shows how this meaning was fulfilled and/or transformed by Christ.

Yes, our Sabbath is in Christ!

- Christ is our true Rest.[12]
- Christ is our real Redemption.[13]
- Christ is our Covenant Keeper. [14,15]

---

[11] Author's note: The first day of the week in the new covenant should not be considered in the same way as was the seventh day of the week in the old covenant. There is nothing wrong with a new covenant church or Christian worshiping on the seventh day as long as it is not done for old covenant reasons.

[12] "Come to Me, all who are weary and heavy-laden, and I will give you rest. Take My yoke upon you and learn from Me, for I am gentle and humble in heart, and YOU WILL FIND REST FOR YOUR SOULS." (Mt.11:28, 29)

[13] "But by His doing you are in Christ Jesus, who became to us wisdom from God, and righteousness and sanctification, and redemption" (1 Cor. 1:30).

[14] "Behold, My Servant, whom I uphold; My chosen one in whom My soul delights. I have put *My Spirit* upon him; He will bring *justice* to the *nations*...I am the Lord, I have called you [the Messiah] in righteousness, I will also hold you by the hand and watch over you, and *I will appoint you as a covenant to the people,* as a light to the *nations.* To open blind eyes, *to bring out* prisoners from the dungeon, and those who dwell in darkness from the prison...Behold, the *former things* have come to pass, now I declare *new things.* Sing to the Lord a *new song"* (Isa. 42:1, 6, 7, 9, 10).

- Christ is the Seal of God[16].
- Christ is our focus of worship.

And every created thing which is in heaven and on the earth and under the earth and on the sea, and all things in them, I heard saying, "To Him who sits on the throne, and to the Lamb, be blessing and honor and glory and dominion forever and ever." And the four living creatures kept saying, "Amen." And the elders fell down and worshiped (Rev. 5:13, 14).

Yes, Christ is our Sabbath rest!

---

[15] "Therefore when Jesus had received the sour wine, He said, 'It is finished!' And He bowed His head and gave up His spirit" (Jn. 19:30).

[16] "Do not work for the food which perishes, but for the food which endures to eternal life, which the Son of Man will give to you, for on Him the Father, God, has set His seal" (Jn. 6:27).

CHAPTER TWENTY FOUR

SABBATH ARGUMENTS

Notwithstanding the biblical evidence we have already discovered, it is necessary for us to carefully look at several arguments from the sabbatarian point of view and honestly evaluate them.

The Sabbath and the Fall of Jerusalem

Sabbatarians often use Matthew 24:20 to support the ongoing validity of the seventh-day Sabbath of Sinai. Speaking of the coming destruction of Jerusalem Jesus said,

> But pray that your flight may not be in the winter, or on a Sabbath.

We should note that the context of the teaching is *not* dealing with the Sabbath, rather Jesus is answering the question the disciples asked in Matthew 24:3:

> Tell us, when will these things [destruction of the temple] be and what will be the sign of Your coming and of the end of the age?

The destruction of Jerusalem to be like the abomination of desolation

By the wording of this passage it is clear that Jesus is making a connection between the destruction of Jerusalem and events surrounding the abomination of desolation, an idol of the Olympian Zeus erected over the altar of burnt offerings by Antiochus Epiphanes IV in 167 B.C. Antiochus defiled the Jerusalem sanctuary, sacrificed pigs on its altars, burned all the books of the law he could find and killed many loyal Jews. These events are recorded in 1 Maccabees. Protestants generally have not included this book in the biblical canon, however most believe this to be an accurate, historical record of the events described therein and it is found in many Bibles. The first nine chapters of this book are well worth reading. I have listed below a verse or two from the context of Matthew 24:20 with a corresponding section from 1 & 2 Maccabees.[1] At times I have quoted from the historian Josephus, who lived in the first century A.D. Notice the close parallel in wording, ideas, and content.

"Abomination of desolation" in Holy Place

> Therefore when you see the abomination of desolation which was spoken of through Daniel the prophet, standing in the Holy Place (let the reader understand) (Mt. 24:15).
>
> The King (Antiochus) erected the abomination of desolation above the altar (1 Mac. 1:57).

The Jewish historian, Josephus, in commenting on this incident says:

> For so it was, that the temple was made desolate by Antiochus, and so continued for three years...And this desolation came to pass according to the prophecy of Daniel, which was given four hundred and eighty years before; for he declared that the Macedonians would dissolve that worship [for some] time.[2]

Leave possessions and flee to the mountains

> Then let those who are in Judea flee to the mountains; let him who is on the housetop not go down to get the things out

---

[1] 2 Maccabees may not be as historically accurate as 1 Maccabees.
[2] Flavious Josephus, *Antiquities of the Jews,* (Kregel Publications, Grand Rapids, MI, 1960), Book XII, Chapter VII, Paragraph 6.

Sabbath Arguments

that are in his house; and let him who is in the field not turn back to get his cloak (Mt. 24:16–18).

Then Mattathias went through the town, shouting at the top of his voice, "Let everyone who has a fervour for the Law and takes his stand on the covenant come out and follow me." Then he fled with his sons into the hills, leaving all their possessions behind in the town (1 Mac. 2:27, 28).

Woe to women and babies

But woe to those who are with child and to those who nurse babes in those days (Mt. 24:19).

Her babies have been slaughtered in her streets, her young men by the enemy's sword...Mattathias and his sons tore their garments, put on sackcloth, and observed deep mourning (1 Mac. 2:9,14).

Pray that it not be in winter or on the Sabbath

But pray that your flight may not be in the winter, or on a Sabbath (Mt. 24:20).

...And many...went down to the desert and stayed there, taking with them their sons, their wives and their cattle...A strong detachment went after them preparing to attack them on the sabbath day..."Enough of this! Come out and do as the king [Antiochus] orders and you shall be spared." But they answered, "We refuse to come out, and we are not going to obey the king's orders and so profane the sabbath day." The others at once went into action, but they offered no opposition; not a stone was thrown, there was no barricading of the hiding places. They only said, "Let us all die innocent; let heaven and earth bear witness that you are massacring us with no pretense of justice." The attack was pressed home on the sabbath itself, and they were slaughtered, with their wives and children and cattle, to the number of one thousand persons. When the news reached Mattathias and his friends, they mourned bitterly for the victims, and said to one another, "If we all do as our brothers have done, and refuse to fight the pagans for our lives and institutions, they will only destroy us the sooner from the earth." So then and there they came to this decision, "If anyone attacks us on the sabbath day, whoever he may be, we will resist him; we must not all be killed, as our brothers were in the hiding places" (1 Mac. 1:57; 2:29, 32–41).

The "abomination of desolation" was set up in winter, on December 8, 176 B.C.[3]

A great tribulation

> For then there will be *a great tribulation,* such as has not occurred since the beginning of the world until now, nor ever shall (Mt. 24:21).

First Maccabees 1–7 records the terrible three-and-a-half-year war between Antiochus and the loyal Jews. This was a determined attack on the worship of YHWH with the intent of completely wiping out the covenant people and all traces of their worship.

> Then the king [Antiochus] issued a proclamation to his whole kingdom that all were to become a single people, each renouncing his particular customs...The king also sent instructions by messenger to Jerusalem and the towns of Judah directing them to adopt customs foreign to the country, banning holocausts [burnt offerings], sacrifices and libations from the sanctuary, *profaning sabbaths* and feasts, defiling the sanctuary and the sacred ministries, building altars, precincts and shrines for idols, sacrificing pigs and unclean beasts, leaving their sons uncircumcised, and prostituting themselves to all kinds of impurity and abomination, so they should forget the Law and revoke all observance of it. Anyone not obeying the king's command was to be put to death (1 Mac. 1:41–53).
>
> Any books of the Law that came to light were torn up and burned. Whenever anyone was discovered possessing a copy of the covenant or practicing the Law, the king's decree sentenced him to death...Women who had their children circumcised were put to death according to the edict with their babies hung round their necks, and the members of their household and those who had performed the circumcision were executed with them (1 Mac. 1:59–64).

---

[3] See footnote in the Jerusalem Bible at 1 Mac. 1:57. "December 8th, 167."

Sabbath keepers at the destruction of Jerusalem

Jesus foresaw there would be many people still observing the Sabbath when Jerusalem would be destroyed. Obviously there would be many Jews who were not Christians keeping the Sabbath. On the other hand, as we have pointed out in Chapter 11, there were also many Jewish Christians who were still observing the Sabbath. We know this from the record in the book of Acts.

> But certain ones of the sect of the Pharisees *who had believed,* stood up, saying, "It is necessary to circumcise them, and to direct them *to observe the Law of Moses"* (Acts 15:5).
>
> You see, brother, how many thousands there are among the Jews of those *who have believed, and they are all zealous for the Law;* and they have been told about you, that you are teaching all the Jews who are among the Gentiles to forsake Moses, telling them not to circumcise their children nor to walk according to the customs (Acts 21:20).

There were many thousands of Christians who continued to follow "Moses," practice circumcision, and live according to "the customs" which certainly included Sabbath observance.

Matthew written to Jewish Christians

It is interesting to note that Matthew is the only Gospel writer to include "Pray that your flight may not be in the winter, or on a Sabbath." Mark simply states, "Pray that it may not happen in the winter (Mk. 13:18). He includes no mention of Sabbath. Luke's account of Jesus' Olivet address does not mention either the Sabbath or winter. Most scholars believe Matthew was written specifically to the Jewish-Christian community.

> The Gospel of St. Matthew was intended for Jewish Christians.[4]
>
> This Gospel [Matthew] has a strong Judaic background.[5]

---

[4] Alfred Wikenhauser, *New Testament Introduction,* (Herder and Herder, New York, NY), p. 195.
[5] Everett F. Harrison, *Introduction to the New Testament,* p. 161.

The gospels of Mark and Luke, however, are intended for Gentile audiences.[6]

Conclusions

What, then, does Matthew 24:20 teach regarding the Sabbath? "But pray that your flight may not be in the winter, or on a Sabbath." Considering the evidence above leads us to the following conclusions:

First, Jesus may have mentioned the Sabbath in connection with the other specifics, such as babies, winter, and fleeing, and tribulation, to help the reader realize the close connection between the coming destruction of Jerusalem and the "abomination of desolation" which had taken place under the persecution of Antiochus.[7] Note that Matthew says, "Let the reader understand," indicating that special insight would be needed. By the wording of this passage, any Jew, or Christian familiar with Jewish history, would have immediately understood the connection between Jesus' statement and the persecution of Antiochus. Jesus made this association to indicate the extent of the terrible conditions which were coming with the destruction of Jerusalem.

Second, Jesus asked his followers to pray that the flight from the destruction of Jerusalem would not happen on the Sabbath because He knew there would still be many thousands of people (Jews and Jewish Christians) still keeping the Sabbath in Jerusalem and He knew that fleeing on the Sabbath would create extra hardship. They would have to choose between breaking Sabbath law or being massacred as did the Jews in the time of Antiochus.

Third, the fact that Matthew is the only Gospel writer to include the mention of Sabbath in Christ's Olivet discourse,

---

[6] Wikenhauser, *New Testament Introduction,* pp. 169, 219.
[7] Many believe that the prophecy of Daniel and the events of Antiochus and the Jews may have more than one application or fulfillment.

coupled with the fact that his Gospel was specifically written for Jewish Christians, indicates that this admonition was not needed by Gentile Christians. Acts 15 and 21 indicate that thousands of Jewish Christians were still zealous for the law and still observed the customs of Moses, which would include Sabbath keeping. This would also explain why other Gospel writers who wrote for Gentile audiences did *not* include Christ's mention of Sabbath. The Gentile Christians would not have needed this counsel for three reasons: (1) They would not be in Jerusalem. (2) They would not be concerned about Sabbath observance. (3) They might not know the history of Antiochus.

Evaluation

All of the above conclusions fit perfectly with the other biblical evidence we have discovered. Therefore we may conclude that Matthew 24:20 indicates many would still be keeping the Sabbath at the time of the destruction of Jerusalem but it *cannot* be used as evidence that *all* Christians were observing, or should be required to observe, the Sabbath.

The Sabbath of the Lord

Some use the following reasoning to support the continued observance of the seventh-day Sabbath. "The Bible clearly states that the seventh day is 'the Sabbath of the Lord.' If it is His day, then it should be observed by all His people. We, as Christians, are His people; therefore, we ought to observe His day."

The biblical support for this argument is as follows:

> Remember the sabbath day, to keep it holy. Six days you shall labor and do all your work, but the seventh day is the sabbath *of the Lord your God* (Ex. 20:8–10).

This argument is based upon two assumptions: (1) The Sabbath belongs to the Lord. (2) If something is stated as belonging to the Lord, then it becomes obligatory.

It is certainly a scriptural fact that the seventh-day Sabbath is said to be "the sabbath of the Lord your God." However, if we are going to argue that the seventh-day Sabbath is binding *because* it belongs to the Lord, then to be consistent, we must also argue for the other old covenant convocations which come with the same credentials. Note the following:

> The *Lord's* appointed times which you shall proclaim as holy convocations—My appointed times are these...These are the appointed *times of the Lord* (Lev. 23:2, 4, 37).

Then follows a listing of the "Lord's appointed times," which not only include the seventh-day Sabbath, but also the seven annual sabbaths, or feasts.

> [It] is the LORD*'s Passover* (Lev. 23:5).
> He shall bring the tenth of an ephah of fine flour for a sin offering...and offer it up in smoke on the altar, with the *offerings of the* LORD by fire (Lev. 5:11, 12).
> ...present it as an offering to the LORD before the *tabernacle of the* LORD (Lev. 17:4).
> A sacrifice of peace offerings...the holy thing of the LORD (Lev. 19:5–8).
> Take the *grain offering* that is left over from the LORD*'s offerings* by fire...(Lev. 10:12).
> A *first-born* belongs to the LORD...*it is the* LORD*'s* (Lev. 27:26).
> The Levitical priests...shall eat the LORD*'s offerings* (Deut. 18:1).

Evaluation

If we are going to observe the seventh-day Sabbath because it is "the sabbath *of the* LORD*,"* then to be consistent we must also be willing to observe the seven annual sabbaths, the grain offerings, the burnt offerings, the tabernacle services, the peace offerings, and the offering of the firstborn, *all of which are said to be "of the* LORD*."*

Therefore the above reasoning does not support continued Sabbath observance.

The Sabbath in the New Earth

> "For just as the new heavens and the new earth which I make will endure before Me," declares the Lord, "so your offspring and your name will endure. And it shall be from new moon to new moon and from sabbath to sabbath, all mankind will come to bow down before Me," says the Lord (Isa. 66:23).

It has often been argued that if the Sabbath will be kept in the new earth, then that is evidence it should be kept here and now. Is this good reasoning? This quotation from Isaiah and the argument derived from it deserves our careful consideration.

Let us look closely at the argument. It is based upon two assumptions: (1) that in the new earth all mankind will keep the Sabbath; (2) that because all mankind will keep the Sabbath in the new earth, they should keep it now.

The perspective of old covenant prophecy is limited

The first assumption appears to be valid if we take Isaiah 66:23 at face value. But before we do so, however, we should consider an important characteristic of Old Testament prophecy. The old covenant prophets, when describing the age to come, described it through *old covenant eyes*. In other words, *old covenant eschatology is set forth in old covenant terminology*. Here are just a few samplings to illustrate.

In Isaiah 66:20, 21, which is the immediate context of Isaiah 66:23, we read,

> "Then they shall bring all your brethren [Israelites assumed] from all the nations [Israel was in captivity at this point] as a grain offering to the Lord, on horses, in chariots, in litters, on mules, and on camels, to My holy mountain Jerusalem," says the Lord, "just as the *sons of Israel* bring their grain offerings in a clean vessel to the house of the Lord. I will also take some of

them [the returning Israelites] as *priests* and for *Levites,"* says the Lord (Isa. 66:20, 21).

Will the Levitical priesthood be restored in the new earth? The purpose of the Levitical priesthood was to perform the many ceremonies which *pointed forward* to Christ. In the presence of God, there would surely be no need for the restoration of this old covenant priestly function. In Isaiah 65:17–25 we have a prophetic description of the "new heavens and a new earth." In these verses we note the mention of "Jerusalem," "My holy mountain," "My people" and "My chosen ones." This is not to say the new earth will not have a "Jerusalem" or the people there will not be the Lord's "chosen ones," but what must be seen is that the prophet sees this new earth through "old covenant eyes."

Should new earth observances be practiced now?

First, if it is to be argued that the Sabbath should be kept today because in an Old Testament prophetic description of the new earth the inhabitants are said to bow down before the Lord from Sabbath to Sabbath, then it must also be argued that new moon celebrations should be observed today for they too are said to be observed in the new earth. It is not a valid method of interpretation to use only half of the data in a text while ignoring the other half. It was pointed out in the chapter "Shadows of Hope" that the seventh-day Sabbath is often mentioned with the new moon celebrations in old covenant services. The fact that the Sabbath and the new moon celebrations are mentioned together in Isaiah only reinforces the fact that old covenant prophets described the age to come using old covenant terminology.

Second, if the activities described in these verses are to be observed now, then we could argue that the Levitical priesthood should also be observed now. But there is abundant biblical evidence showing the Levitical priesthood should *not* be restored now. One of the themes of the book of Hebrews is that the ministry of Christ far supersedes the Levitical priesthood (Heb. 5–7) which came to a functional end with the death of Christ.

Third, even if a certain practice may be observed in the new earth it does not, in and of itself, mean that it should be practiced now. Isaiah pictures the new earth with the wolf and the lamb grazing together. He describes the lion eating straw like an ox (Isa. 65:25). However, it is *not* a currently recommended practice to pasture wolves and sheep together! Nor would we advise zookeepers to feed their lions straw! The Old Testament prophet pictured the world to come with a little boy leading a leopard (Isa. 11:6) and a nursing child playing by the hole of a cobra (Isa. 11:8), but these are *not* safe practices now. In the same way it is not good interpretation to find a practice which *may* be observed in the "new earth" and urge its practice today.

Conclusion

Those who make an argument for the present observance of the Sabbath from Isaiah 66:23 are left on the horns of a dilemma. Either they must see this verse as "colored" by the limited perspective of the old covenant prophet, or they must also be willing to argue for the observance of new moon celebrations and the restoration of the Levitical priesthood, which according to Paul would mean placing oneself back under the old covenant and falling from grace. For these reasons we must conclude that Isaiah 66:23 is not a valid support for present-day Sabbath observance.

Sabbath at Creation

There is a relationship between the rest of Eden's seventh day and the Sabbath of Sinai in the biblical data we have studied. There are some sabbatarians, however, who want to push this relationship to make them fundamentally *equal,* seeking support for the continued observance of the seventh-day Sabbath. They do this by arguing that the Sabbath *of the Fourth Commandment* was actually instituted by God *at creation*. Then they argue that all the involved relationships between the seventh-day Sabbath and the old covenant are meaningless because Sabbath observance for man had its origin at creation. Their reasoning is based upon a comparison of Exodus 20:11 with Genesis 2:3.

> For in six days the LORD made the heavens and the earth, the sea and all that is in them, and rested on the seventh day; therefore the LORD blessed the sabbath day and made it holy (Ex. 20:11).
>
> Then God blessed the seventh day and sanctified it, because in it He rested from all His work which God had created and made (Gen. 2:3).

By comparing these two references, it seems to indicate the "Sabbath day" (of the Sinaitic Covenant) started in Eden. However, when one carefully reads the Sabbath commandment, it is clear that it refers to the family, the servants, the cattle and even the sojourner. This clearly cannot be from Eden. Remember, there is no record of any man or woman keeping the Sabbath until the time of Moses.

Scripture is very clear that the covenant made with Israel at Sinai, the words of which were the Ten Commandments, was *not made with the fathers* (See Chapter 4). There is a great amount of detail regarding the life of Abraham, even more regarding Jacob and his sons, but *never once* is the Sabbath even alluded to. To this evidence we must add the clear statement of Paul that the Law was given 430 years *after* Abraham. (See Chapters 13).

There are a number of anachronisms in the writings of Moses[8] and it was written from *his perspective in time*. Some have argued that the blessing and sanctifying of the seventh day in Genesis 2 is also an anachronism. If one accepts this reasoning, then the record of God's blessing the seventh day as *recorded* by Moses in Genesis 2 *actually*

---

[8] See Gen. 2:5, 10–14, 23, 24; Ex. 16:34 cf. 31:18

took place at Sinai. However, my study leads me to conclude that the seventh day was sanctified *for God's rest* on creation's seventh day. True, Adam and Eve participated in that perfect fellowship but it was not the same as the Sinaitic Sabbath.

Third, the evidence of the New Testament is weighted heavily against *required* Sabbath observance. (See Chapter 13.) Hebrews 3 and 4 make it clear that the "Sabbath rest" for the Christian *cannot* be the seventh-day Sabbath of Sinai. (See Chapter 19.)

For these reasons one cannot argue for the present day observance of the seventh-day Sabbath from Genesis 2.

Jesus and Sabbath Reform

Some have argued that Jesus' Sabbath miracles and encounters on the Sabbath must be seen as Sabbath reform. Then they argue that He would not have reformed the Sabbath if it were soon to pass away.[9] Jesus did, however, bring reform to other aspects of the old covenant, which soon *did* pass away. At both the beginning and end of Jesus' ministry He sought to bring reform to the temple services (Jn. 2:13-22; Mt. 21:12-17). Yet at His death the "veil of the temple was torn in two from top to bottom" (Mt. 27:51), indicating that *from God's perspective* the temple services were over. As Jesus approached Jerusalem a few days before His death he said,

> O Jerusalem, Jerusalem, who kills the prophets and stones those who are sent to her! How often I wanted to gather your children together, the way a hen gathers her chicks under her wings, and

---

[9] "He [Jesus] even risked His mission and life in performing seven (recorded) miracles on the holy day to demonstrate that true Sabbathkeeping brought blessing not injury. Never did He defend any institution soon to pass away." Desmond Ford, *The Forgotten Day*, p. 209.

you were unwilling. Behold, *your house is being left to you desolate* (Mt. 23:37, 38).

Jesus sought to bring reform regarding the way people were offering sacrifice in connection with interpersonal relationships.

> If therefore you are presenting your offering at the altar, and there remember that your brother has something against you, leave your offering there before the altar, and go your way, first be reconciled to your brother, and then come and present your offering (Mt. 5:23, 24).

We should also question the very hypothesis upon which this argument is based. In the Sabbath activity and teaching of Jesus, the emphasis was not in bringing reform to the Sabbath as much as it was in showing that His *work* of Jubilee ministry was not to be restricted by old covenant (or rabbinical) Sabbath law. The main emphasis of Jesus with regard to the Sabbath was in *fulfilling* the Sabbath by showing that He, Himself, was the *true rest,* the *real redemption,* the *covenant keeper* and the focus of *genuine worship.*

In our study we have seen that the Sabbath is a ritual law and Jesus often did not follow the ritual laws as prescribed by the old covenant. We also discovered that John, His closest disciple, clearly says that Jesus "was breaking" or "was destroying" the Sabbath. This is not Sabbath reform but Sabbath fulfillment: moving people away from the ritual Sabbath rest to the real Sabbath Rest: Jesus Christ our Lord.

God does not change

Some have argued that because God does not change He certainly would not change the Sabbath law which He wrote with His own finger in stone.

> Jesus Christ is the same yesterday and today and forever (Heb. 13:8).

> For I, the Lord, do not change; therefore you, O sons of Jacob, are not consumed (Mal. 3:6).

However, the context of all statements must be considered. There are many Bible references which speak of God changing His mind.

> Now therefore amend your ways and your deeds and obey the voice of the Lord your God; and *the Lord will change His mind* about the misfortune which He has pronounced against you (Jer. 26:13).
> ...He instructed them that they should take nothing for their journey, except a mere staff—no bread, no bag, no money in their belt (Mk. 6:8).
> And He said to them, "When I sent you out without money belt and bag and sandals, you did not lack anything, did you?" They said, "No, nothing." And He said to them, "But now, whoever has a money belt is to take it along, likewise also a bag, and whoever has no sword is to sell his coat and buy one...(Lk. 22:35, 36).
> For when the priesthood is changed, of necessity there takes place a *change of law* also (Heb. 7:12).

We have already listed the references from Romans and Galatians which clearly state that the law was to reign "until Christ."

We conclude, therefore, that just because there are places in Scripture that state God does not change, does not mean that He never changes instructions, laws or commands. Rather, it means that His unchangeableness relates to His character and attributes.

Questions about Law

Romans 2:13

I have received dozens of calls from people using Romans 2:13 to prove that one is justified by keeping the Ten Commandments and cannot be justified without keeping them.

> For it is not the hearers of the Law who are just before God, but the doers of the Law will be justified.

At face value one could use this text in this way. However, one must consider the context. In this section Paul is showing that all are sinners and in need of salvation. He starts in Romans 1 showing that the Gentiles are worthy of death because they knew about God from nature but did not honor Him. In Chapter 2, Paul shows that both the moral person and the Jew are worthy of death. This becomes clear in Chapter 3 where Paul clearly states that all have sinned and there are none who are righteous. In other words, while the law promises justification to those who are "doers of the Law", in practice the law only condemns.

Later in Romans, Paul makes it clear that

> by the works of the Law no flesh will be justified in His sight; for through the Law comes the knowledge of sin (Rom. 3:23).

We must also recognize that the law here probably stands for the whole law or Torah.

Romans 7:12

> So then, the Law is holy, and the commandment is holy and righteous and good (Rom. 7:12).

Nowhere is context more important than in the book of Romans. Paul follows a very tight outline and Romans 7 is not designed to put Christians back under the law, rather, the key theme of Romans 7 is verse 6.

> But now we have been released from the Law, having died to that by which we were bound, so that we serve in newness of the Spirit and not in oldness of the letter (Rom. 7:6).

Paul's argument in verse 12 is simply that the law was good for its purpose: to show Israel her sin. Later, after he fully develops his argument he will conclude:

> For Christ is the end of the law for righteousness to everyone who believes (Rom. 10:4).

James 2:8–12

> If, however, you are fulfilling the royal law according to the Scripture, "You shall love your neighbor as yourself," you are doing well. But if you show partiality, you are committing sin and are convicted by the law as transgressors. For whoever keeps the whole law and yet stumbles in one point, he has become guilty of all. For He who said, "Do not commit adultery," also said, "Do not commit murder." Now if you do not commit adultery, but do commit murder, you have become a transgressor of the law. So speak and so act as those who are to be judged by the law of liberty. For judgment will be merciless to one who has shown no mercy; mercy triumphs over judgment (Jas. 2:8-13).

The argument goes something like this. "James says that if you break one commandment you break them all. That the Ten Commandments are in view here is clear for he quotes from them in verse 11. He clearly states that we are to be judged by this law in verse 12. Therefore, if one breaks the Fourth Commandment he is guilty of breaking all Ten and will be judged accordingly."

Two things must be said. First, we know that James presided over the important church counsel recorded in Acts 15 where it was decided that Gentile believers did not come under the laws of Sinai. However, it appears that James was still sympathetic with Jewish Christians, perhaps even some Judaizers, who continued to promote the laws of Sinai.

> For prior to the coming of certain men from James, he [Barnabas] used to eat with the Gentiles; but when they came, he began to withdraw and hold himself aloof, fearing the party of the circumcision (Gal. 2:12).

Here we see that James, or at least his followers, may not yet have fully accepted the freedom of the gospel, at least for the Jewish Christians.

Second, I believe that careful study of this passage will show that James has two laws in view. The first is the "law of liberty" or Christ's law and the second is by way of illustration, the Ten Commandments. Also the context is not the Sabbath but showing partiality in favoring the rich over the poor. James speaks of showing mercy and mercy is not even mentioned in the Ten Commandments. As Greek Scholar, R.C.H., Lenksy states,

> James tells his readers ever to speak and ever to act (present, durative imperative) as people who are about to be judged by God, not by means of the law, i.e. the Ten Commandments, two of which have just been quoted, not by the summation of the second table (v. 8,11), but by "liberty's law" (both anarthrous nouns are qualitative). The readers will then escape the condemnation of the law. "Liberty's law" will be their merciful salvation.[10]

Liberty's law is the law of Christ. It is loving one another as He loved us. It is living under the grace of God and allowing that grace to flow out of our lives to those around us. This text has no bearing on the Sabbath.

Chapter Summary

1. Matthew 24:20
    a. Jesus foresaw a close association between the abomination of desolation by Antiochus Epiphanes and the destruction of Jerusalem by the Romans. This is seen in close parallel between Matthew 24:15–21 and 1 Maccabees 1–7 and may account for His mention of the Sabbath in these verses.
    b. Jesus foresaw that many people, Jews and Jewish Christians, would be observing the seventh-day Sabbath at the time of the destruction of Jerusalem.
    c. The Gospel of Matthew is specifically written to people of Jewish background. While all the Synoptic Gospels record Christ's Olivet discourse,

---

[10] R.C.H. Lenski, *Commentary on the New Testament*, "Hebrews James", p. 573.

Sabbath Arguments

Matthew is the *only one* to record the mention of the Sabbath. The reason the other Gospel writers did not include mention of the Sabbath probably is that the Gentile Christians to whom they were writing were not observing the Sabbath, therefore they did not need that instruction.

d. Matthew 24:20 cannot be used to prove continued Sabbath observance for all Christians.

2. The reasoning which says that because the Sabbath is said to be "of the Lord" and therefore should be kept by the "Lord's people" is invalid.
   a. Many old covenant practices are said to be "of the Lord."
   b. To argue for one would be to argue for all.
3. Isaiah 66:23 cannot be used in support of present-day Sabbath observance.
   a. Old Testament prophets picture the age to come in old covenant terminology.
   b. New earth practices cannot be used as guides for present-day behavior.
   c. If one is going to observe the Sabbath today because it *may* be observed in the new earth, then to be consistent, one must also observe the new moon celebrations, for they are mentioned in the same verse, and one must also argue for the reinstitution of the Levitical priesthood now.
4. The Sabbath of the Fourth Commandment was not given at the time of creation.
   a. The laws for Sabbath keeping would have been without meaning to Adam and Eve.
   b. While there is considerable detail regarding the life of Abraham, Isaac, Jacob and his sons, never is the Sabbath mentioned or even alluded to.
   c. The covenant God made with Israel at Sinai was not made with the "fathers" of Israel (Abraham, Isaac and Jacob). The fact that the Sabbath was the

seal of that covenant gives evidence that the fathers did not have the Sabbath.
   d. There are a number of anachronisms in the writings of Moses. The Genesis record states the seventh day was blessed but makes no mention of man resting.
   e. The Biblical evidence indicates the Sinaitic Sabbath was patterned after the rest of Eden's seventh day but they are not equal.
   f. If one wants to read into the Genesis account some command for man to rest, it must be considered an anachronism.
5. While Jesus, in a sense, did bring Sabbath reform, He also reformed other old covenant practices which were soon to pass away. His main emphasis in relationship to the Sabbath was in showing that His work of redemption did not come under old covenant or rabbinical law, as He fulfilled the Sabbath by providing the true rest of which the Sabbath was a type.
6. The fact that John clearly states that Jesus "was breaking" the Sabbath[11] indicates that Jesus understood the Sabbath to be a ritual that pointed forward to Him.
7. Romans 2:13 is in Paul's outline under the heading "why all are sinners." He speaks of the doers of the law being justified but goes on to show that no one has kept the law and therefore one must be justified by faith apart from works of the Law (Romans 3:28).
8. Romans 7:12 studied in its context does not teach that Christians are to be put back under the law.
9. James 2:8–13 speaks of two laws: the Law of Liberty (Christ's law of love) and the Ten Commandments. We are to be judged by the law of liberty. This verse says nothing about the Sabbath.

---

[11] John 5:18.

CHAPTER TWENTY FIVE

THE SABBATH
AND SEVENTH-DAY ADVENTISTS

I feel it is vitally important in connection with this study on the Sabbath to clarify and evaluate several Seventh-day Adventist (SDA) teachings and practices relative to this topic.[1]

In some sections of the Adventist church there is now (2003) considerable openness to understand the Sabbath in a Christ centered way as long as one does not teach against SDA's historic understanding of the Sabbath or other church doctrines. Many SDA pastors no longer believe in a number of the "unique teachings" of historic Adventism. However, most hold their views in private and share them only with trusted associates. This chapter deals with the historic Adventist understanding of the Sabbath. Adventist evangelists, however, usually still rely on the historic Adventist teachings to persuade their attendees to join the Seventh-day Adventist Church and continue to be very successful, especially in third world countries.

---

[1] The author was a fourth-generation Seventh-day Adventist, grew up in an Adventist home, received all of his schooling from first grade through graduate school in SDA educational institutions, taught Bible in a SDA educational institution, and served as a Seventh-day Adventist pastor for thirteen years. He still has communication with a number of SDA pastors.

The Sabbath and the True Church

Many people who leave the Seventh-day Adventist church have unanswered questions regarding which church is the "true" or "remnant" church and what part, if any, the Sabbath has in connection with the "true church."

Seventh-day Adventists are taught to believe that the SDA church is God's last-day, true church, or "the remnant church."[2] The support for this belief is derived mainly from two passages in the book of Revelation.

> And the dragon was enraged with the woman, and went off to make war with the *rest* of her offspring, who keep the *commandments of God* and hold to the *testimony of Jesus* (Rev. 12:17).

> And I fell at his feet to worship him...And he said to me, "Do not do that; I am a fellow-servant of yours and your brethren who hold the testimony of Jesus; worship God...For *the testimony of Jesus is the spirit of prophecy"* (Rev. 19:10).

Seventh-day Adventists believe these verses teach that the SDA church is the only, true, remnant church. Their reasoning goes like this: The "woman" represents the church. The "rest" ("remnant" KJV) of her offspring must be the portion of the church living in the *last days* (our time). Revelation 12:17 lists two identifying marks of this last church: (1) It will "keep the commandments of God" and (2) "hold to the testimony of Jesus." But what is "the testimony of Jesus"? By comparing Revelation 19:10 they find that the "testimony of Jesus is the spirit of prophecy." They interpret "commandments of God" to mean the Ten Commandments of Sinai, including the Fourth Commandment, which leads them to conclude the end-time church will be a seventh-day, Sabbath-keeping church. They interpret "spirit of prophecy" to mean a last-day prophet giving a prophetic message. They believe this last-day prophet is

---

[2] See Fundamental Beliefs of Seventh-day Adventists, No. 12, "The Remnant and Its Mission," and No. 17, "The Gift of Prophecy."

Ellen G. White, whose writings they refer to as "The Spirit of Prophecy" or "The Testimonies." The SDA church accepts her writings as "a continuing and authoritative *source* of truth."[3] Seventh-day Adventists believe and teach that the SDA church is the *only, true, last-day church* because it is the *only* seventh-day, Sabbath-keeping church which has a modern-day prophet (even though Ellen White died in 1916).

Is this a correct interpretation? It is based upon three fundamental assumptions: (1) "Commandments of God" *must* refer to the Ten Commandments of Sinai and specifically include the Sabbath commandment, (2) the "testimony of Jesus" is an undefined term except for its use in Revelation 19:10, and (3) the "spirit of prophecy" must refer to a modern-day prophet. Let us study these three terms of Scripture, evaluate the underlying assumptions in the above reasoning and draw some conclusions.

Commandments of God

The word "commandments," as used in the New Testament, may refer to one or more of the Ten Commandments. However, this term does not *always* refer to the Ten Commandments, and when it does, only *once* is it used in connection with the Sabbath commandment. That one time is:

> And they returned and prepared spices and perfumes. And on the Sabbath they rested according to *the commandment* (Lk. 23:56).

---

[3] "One of the gifts of the Holy Spirit is prophecy. This gift is *an identifying mark* of *the remnant church* and was manifested in the ministry of Ellen G. White. As the Lord's messenger, her writings are a *continuing and authoritative source of truth* which provide for the church comfort, guidance, instruction, and correction. They also make clear that the Bible is the standard by which all teaching and experience must be tested. (Joel 2:28,29; Acts 2:14–21; Heb. 1:1–3; Rev. 12:17; 19:10.)" Doctrinal point No. 19 taken from *Fundamental beliefs of Seventh-day Adventists.* (Emphasis supplied.)

Other uses of the term commandment or commandments of God include the following:

> Circumcision is nothing, and uncircumcision is nothing, but what matters is the keeping of the commandments of God. Let each man remain in the condition in which he was called (1 Cor. 7:19, 20).

There is no evidence that *entolon theou* ("the commandments of God") was a technical term which would have been understood as referring exclusively (or even primarily) to the Decalogue.[4]

We must remember that we are seeking to define "commandments" as used by *John,* the author of Revelation.[5] While Luke used the Greek word commandment *(entole)* to refer to the Sabbath commandment, John *always,* uses the word "Law" *(nomos)* when referring to old covenant law.[6]

---

[4] D. R. De Lacy, "The Sabbath/Sunday Question and the Law in the Pauline Corpus", in *From Sabbath to Lord's Day,* p. 176.

[5] This assumes that John the Evangelist is the same person as John the Revelator, which some question.

[6] The following is a complete list of the usages of the word "Law" in the writings of John: "For the Law [*nomos*] was given through Moses; grace and truth were realized through Jesus Christ" (Jn. 1:17). "Philip found Nathanael and said to him, 'We have found Him of whom Moses in the Law [*nomos*] and also the Prophets wrote, Jesus of Nazareth, the son of Joseph.'" (Jn. 1:45). "Did not Moses give you the Law [*nomos*], and yet none of you carries out the Law [*nomos*]? Why do you seek to kill Me?" (Jn. 7:19). "If a man receives circumcision on the Sabbath that the Law [*nomos*] of Moses may not be broken, are you angry with Me because I made an entire man well on the Sabbath?" (Jn. 7:23). "But this multitude which does not know the Law [*nomos*] is accursed" (Jn. 7:49). "Our Law [*nomos*] does not judge a man, unless it first hears from him and knows what he is doing, does it?" (Jn. 7:51). "Now in the Law [*nomos*] Moses commanded us to stone such women; what then do You say?" (Jn. 8:5). "Even in your law [*nomos*] it has been written, that the testimony of two men is true" (Jn. 8:17). "Jesus answered them, 'Has it not been written in your Law [*nomos*], "I SAID, YOU ARE GODS"?'" (Jn. 10:34). "The multitude therefore answered Him, 'We have heard out of the Law [*nomos*] that the Christ is to remain forever; and how can You say, "The Son of Man must be lifted up"? Who is this Son of Man?'" (Jn. 12:34). "But they have done this in order that the

When John uses the word "commandment" *(entole)* it *never* refers to the old covenant law and usually refers to the new covenant law of love.⁷ I encourage the reader to refer to

---

word may be fulfilled that is written in their Law [*nomos*], 'THEY HATED ME WITHOUT A CAUSE.'" (Jn. 15:25). "Pilate therefore said to them, 'Take Him yourselves, and judge Him according to your law [*nomos*].' The Jews said to him, 'We are not permitted to put anyone to death'" (Jn. 18:31). "The Jews answered him, 'We have a law [nomos], and by that law [*nomos*] He ought to die because He made Himself out to be the Son of God'" (Jn. 19:7). The word "Law" (*nomos*) is not used in Revelation.

⁷ The following is a complete listing of the word "commandment" in the writings of John: "No one has taken it away from Me, but I lay it down on My own initiative. I have authority to lay it down, and I have authority to take it up again. This commandment [*entole*] I received from My Father" (Jn. 10:18). "For I did not speak on My own initiative, but the Father Himself who sent Me has given Me commandment [*entole*], what to say, and what to speak. And I know that His commandment [*entole*] is eternal life; therefore the things I speak, I speak just as the Father has told Me" (Jn. 12:49, 50). "A new commandment [*entole*] I give to you, that you love one another, even as I have loved you, that you also love one another" (Jn. 13:34). "If you love Me, you will keep My commandments [*entole*]" (Jn. 14:15). "He who has My commandments [*entole*] and keeps them, he it is who loves Me; and he who loves Me shall be loved by My Father, and I will love him, and will disclose Myself to him" (Jn. 14:21). "But that the world may know that I love the Father, and as the Father gave Me commandment [*entole*], even so I do. Arise, let us go from here" (Jn. 14:31). "If you keep My commandments [*entole*], you will abide in My love; just as I have kept My Father's commandments [*entole*], and abide in His love" (Jn. 15:10). "This is My commandment [*entole*], that you love one another, just as I have loved you" (Jn. 15:12). "And by this we know that we have come to know Him, if we keep His commandments [*entole*]. The one who says, 'I have come to know Him,' and does not keep His commandments [*entole*], is a liar, and the truth is not in him" (1 Jn. 2:3, 4). "Beloved, I am not writing a new commandment [*entole*] to you, but an old commandment [*entole*] which you have had from the beginning; the old commandment [*entole*] is the word which you have heard. On the other hand, I am writing a new commandment [*entole*] to you, which is true in Him and in you, because the darkness is passing away, and the true light is already shining" (1 Jn. 2:7, 8). "And whatever we ask we receive from Him,

footnotes 6 and 7 where *all* the passages in John's writings which contain the words "law" and "commandment" have been listed. It will become immediately evident that when used in John, "commandment" *(entole)* does not refer to the Ten Commandments, or other portions of the old covenant.

Here are a few of the places where the Greek word *(entole)*, used for "commandments" in Revelation 12:17 and Revelation 14:12, is used by John in his other writings.

> If you love Me, you will keep My commandments (Jn. 14:15). He who has My commandments, and keeps them, he it is who loves Me…(Jn. 14:21). If you keep My commandments, you will abide in My love; just as I have kept My Father's commandments, and abide in His love…This is My commandment, that you love one another, just as I have loved you…This I command you, that you love one another (Jn. 15:10, 12, 17).
>
> And this is His commandment, that we believe in the name of His son Jesus Christ, and love one another, just as He commanded us. And the one who keeps His commandments abides in Him, and He in him. And we know by this that He abides in us, by the Spirit which He has given us (1 Jn. 3:23, 24).

---

because we keep His commandments [*entole*] and do the things that are pleasing in His sight. And this is His commandment [*entole*], that we believe in the name of His Son Jesus Christ, and love one another, just as He commanded [*entole*] us. And the one who keeps His commandments [*entole*] abides in Him, and He in him. And we know by this that He abides in us, by the Spirit whom He has given us" (1 Jn. 3:22–24). "And this commandment [*entole*] we have from Him, that the one who loves God should love his brother also" (1 Jn. 4:21). "By this we know that we love the children of God, when we love God and observe His commandments [*entole*]. For this is the love of God, that we keep His commandments [*entole*]; and His commandments [*entole*] are not burdensome" (1 Jn. 5:2, 3). "I was very glad to find some of your children walking in truth, just as we have received commandment [*entole*] to do from the Father. And now I ask you, lady, not as writing to you a new commandment [*entole*], but the one which we have had from the beginning, that we love one another" (2 Jn. 1:4, 5). "And this is love, that we walk according to His commandments [*entole*]. This is the commandment [*entole*], just as you have heard from the beginning, that you should walk in it" (2 Jn. 1:6). The word "commandment" (*entole*) is used only two times in Revelation: Rev. 12:17 and 14:12.

And this commandment we have from Him, that the one who loves God should love his brother also (1 Jn. 4:21).

By this we know that we love the children of God, when we love God and observe His commandments. For this is the love of God, that we keep His commandments; and His commandments are not burdensome (1 Jn. 5:2, 3).

We conclude that the term, "commandments of God" as used by John in Revelation 12:17 and 14:10 does *not* refer to the Ten Commandments. If he were referring to the Ten Commandments He would have used the Greek word *(nomos)* "Law"

The testimony of Jesus

The word, "testimony" comes from a root word which in its various forms in Greek means testifying, testimony, witness and martyr. The underlying meaning is the proclamation of truth regardless of consequences. The "of Jesus" part of this phrase can be understood in two ways. It can mean the testimony *from* Jesus, or it can mean the testimony *concerning* Jesus. The first meaning stresses the fact that this testimony has Jesus as its *source*. The second meaning stresses the idea that this testimony has Jesus as the *subject matter*. Either interpretation is valid as far as the Greek syntax is concerned.

In other words, the phrase "testimony of Jesus" means proclaiming the truth of (either from or about) Jesus. When we stop to think about it, this is not a bad definition of the gospel. It is a proclamation of the truth both from and about Jesus. From a linguistic definition we would say the "testimony of Jesus" is a term which stands for the gospel as it is fearlessly proclaimed.

Let us now look at *all* the passages in the book of Revelation which use the terms "testimony of Jesus" or just "testimony" and seek to discover the meaning of this term.

> The Revelation of Jesus Christ, which God gave Him to show to His bond-servants, the things which must shortly take place; and He sent and communicated it by His angel to His bond-servant John; who bore witness to the word of God and to

the *testimony of Jesus* Christ, even to all that he saw (Rev. 1:1, 2).

I, John, your brother and fellow partaker in the tribulation and kingdom and perseverance which are in Jesus, was on the island called Patmos, because of the word of God and the *testimony of Jesus* (Rev. 1:9).

And when He broke the fifth seal, I saw underneath the altar the souls of those who had been slain because of the word of God, and because of the *testimony* which they had maintained (Rev. 6:9).

And I saw thrones, and they sat upon them, and judgment was given to them. And I saw the souls of those who had been beheaded because of the *testimony of Jesus* and because of the *word of God,* and those who had not worshipped the beast or his image, and had not received the mark upon their forehead and upon their hand; and they came to life and reigned with Christ for a thousand years (Rev. 20:4).

In these verses the "testimony of Jesus" or just "the testimony" is used as a term for the gospel. John bears witness to the gospel, the truth about (or from) Jesus (Rev. 1:1, 2). The souls under the altar had been slain *because* they maintained the truth about (or from) Jesus.

With this background let us now return to the two texts in question and see if our definition of "testimony of Jesus" fits within their context.

And the dragon was enraged with the woman, and went off to make war with the rest of her offspring, who keep the commandments of God and hold to the testimony of Jesus (Rev. 12:17).

Who are these people with whom the dragon is angry? They are the people who keep the *new covenant* commandments of God and hold to the truth about (or from) Jesus! Notice the close parallel verse in Revelation 14:12.

Here is the perseverance of the saints who keep the commandments of God and their faith in Jesus.

These two verses seem to say the same thing. In one the saints are described as those who keep the commandments of God and hold to the testimony of Jesus. In the other they keep the commandments of God and their faith in Jesus. Therefore, the term "testimony of Jesus" and keeping their "faith in Jesus" are parallel in meaning.

It is quite evident that the term "testimony of Jesus" has reference to the gospel. It is the truth about (or from) Jesus. If this is true, then what does the Revelator mean when he says "the testimony of Jesus is the spirit of prophecy"?

> And I [John] fell at his feet to worship him [the angel] and he said to me, "Do not do that; I am a fellow-servant of yours and your brethren who hold the testimony of Jesus; worship God. For *the testimony of Jesus is the spirit of prophecy"* (Rev. 19:10).

Here the angel says he also holds the "testimony of Jesus." In other words, the angel also believes the truth about (or from) Jesus. Focusing on the last phrase, we read, "the testimony of Jesus is the spirit of prophecy." To paraphrase, "The truth about Jesus is the spirit of prophecy." Notice how this verse is variously translated or paraphrased.

> Those who bear testimony to Jesus are inspired like the prophets (*The New English Bible*).
>
> For the truth revealed by Jesus is the inspiration of all prophecy (*Weymouth*).
>
> For the testimony of Jesus is what inspires prophecy (*Goodspeed*).
>
> It is the truth concerning Jesus which inspires all prophecy (*Knox*).
>
> The purpose of all prophecy and of all I have shown you is to tell about Jesus (*Living Bible*).

These translators have captured the essence of what John is seeking to communicate. All prophecy, when rightly interpreted, in some way points to the truth concerning Jesus.

> You search the *Scriptures,* because you think that in them you have eternal life; and *it is these that bear witness of Me* (Jn. 5:39).
>
> "O foolish men and slow of heart to believe *in all that the prophets have spoken!* Was it not necessary for the Christ to

suffer these things and to enter into His glory?" And beginning with Moses and with all the prophets, He explained to them the things *concerning Himself* in all the Scriptures (Lk. 24:25–27).

There is one instance in Revelation where the ark of the covenant (or testimony) is mentioned.

And the temple of God which is in heaven was opened; and the ark of His covenant appeared in His temple, and there were flashes of lightning and sounds and peals of thunder and an earthquake and a great hailstorm Rev. 11:19.

However, the context of this is totally different from that of Revelation 19:10. It must also be pointed out that Revelation is a book that is saturated with Old Testament imagery. This imagery, however, does not have a one to one correspondence. Rather, it is presented as symbolic of ideas that must be transformed into new covenant truth.

Good theology does not have its foundation in apocalyptic prophecy. The book of Revelation has been interpreted in many, many ways throughout the history of the Christian church and even today most honest scholars will tell you that much of it is still remains somewhat of a mystery.

Our conclusion is that Revelation 19:10 and 12:17 have *nothing whatever* to do with the writings of Ellen White, even if these writings are known by Seventh-day Adventists as "the Spirit of Prophecy" or "Testimonies to the Church." John was imprisoned on the isle of Patmos *not* because he had the writings of Ellen White or because he was a prophet, but because he held to the truth concerning Jesus. The church derives its "trueness" as it submits to the head of the church, Jesus Christ.

By using this text as "proof" that the SDA church is the "remnant church of Bible prophecy", the Adventist church has, in essence, substituted the writings of Ellen G. White in the place of the gospel of Christ!

We conclude that the reasoning used by Seventh-day Adventists to prove they are the true, remnant church of the last days is *faulty on every count*. Not only is this claim of

Adventism faulty on every count, *it is heretical at its very core*. It has removed the gospel of Christ and in its place substituted the writings of their dead "prophet", Ellen White.

Are you looking for "the true church"? You will find no *one* human organization which is *the* true church. Rather look for a *local gathering* of Christian believers who confess and worship Jesus Christ as their Lord and Savior, who make Him the center of their theology, who demonstrate the fruits of the Spirit in their lives, who proclaim the simple gospel of God's grace, who practice water baptism and celebrate the Lord's Supper, who study and obey God's word, and who express their forgiven condition by loving one another—even immature sinners who need God. There you will find God's true church regardless of its name.

The Sabbath and SDA Evangelism

The Sabbath doctrine has proven to be a manipulative tool in Seventh-day Adventist evangelism. The evangelistic method often used is to "show" from portions of Scripture (often out of context) the binding nature of the seventh-day Sabbath, demonstrate that the SDA church keeps the Sabbath and explain to the people that if they want to be saved and not receive the "mark of the beast" then they should join the SDA church, which is God's *only* true, remnant church. Seventh-day Adventists teach the seventh-day Sabbath is the "seal of God" and Sunday worship will become the "mark of the beast."[8] This manipulative method has brought hundreds of thousands if not millions

---

[8] "The Sabbath will be the great test of loyalty; for it is the point of truth especially controverted…The Fourth Commandment…contains the seal of God, affixed to His law as evidence of its authenticity and binding force. While one class, by accepting the sign of submission to earthly powers [in context, Sunday worship], receive the mark of the beast, the other, choosing the token of allegiance to divine authority, receive the seal of God." E. G. White, *The Great Controversy,* p. 605.

of "converts" into the SDA church. It continues to be used in their "traditional evangelism."[9] This method creates several serious problems. (1) It is unbiblical. Nowhere in the New Testament is this type of evangelism *taught* or *practiced*. Rather, New Testament evangelism is *always* a proclamation of *the good news of the gospel of Jesus Christ!* (2) The SDA "traditional evangelistic method," as mentioned above, undermines the gospel. It takes the gospel out of the center and makes Sabbath observance "the testing truth."[10] (3) It damages church unity. It is contrary to Christ's prayer "that they may all be one" (Jn. 17:20, 21). (4) It creates unneeded social concerns and economic problems for new converts. Often people are

---

[9] "By keeping the seventh day holy, God's people show their loyalty to their Creator and Recreator. God designed the seventh-day Sabbath to be His sign or seal to distinguish those who worship Him from those who do not...Those who keep the Sabbath receive God's seal and demonstrate their loyalty to Him. In contrast, those who reject God's control and choose to follow the beast power receive its mark. (See Revelation 13:16, 17.) The contrast is clear." R. Russell Holt, *Signs of the Times* (the missionary journal of SDAs), February and March 1990. See also Marvin More, *The Antichrist and the New World Order* (Pacific Press Publishing Association, Boise, ID, 1993) The book, *The Ultimate Rip-off,* by Bill Stringfellow, (Concerned Publications, Bemidji, MN, 1987) gives a popular—if not sensational—presentation of the "traditional Adventist" evangelistic agenda.

As the author was revising this chapter, Seventh-day Adventists left the book, *National Sunday Law,* by A. Jan Marcussen, at his home and in the homes in the author's neighborhood. This must be a common practice as the flyleaf of the book states "7 million in print." This book contains sensational material designed to call attention to the Sabbath and the mark of the beast.

[10] "Before Jesus comes, the entire world will stand divided over the great issue of loyalty to God and His commandments—especially the Fourth Commandment...Loyalty to God and His commandments will be the test." R. Russell Holt, *Signs of the Times,* February and March 1990. "The Sabbath will be the great test of loyalty, for it is the point of truth especially controverted." E. G. White, *The Great Controversy,* p. 605.

counseled to quit jobs, disobey marriage partners or parents in order to "keep the Sabbath" from sundown Friday until sundown Saturday. Thus, like the Jews of New Testament times, the observance of Sabbath law takes precedence over relationships. The paradox is that the Sabbath laws were to point forward to a restored relationship. In the new covenant, relationship takes precedence over ceremony.

Following is a letter I received two days before I revised this chapter in 1995. It illustrates how Seventh-day Adventists use the Sabbath as a manipulative tool in their evangelism.

> Dear sir,
> I have purchased your book *Sabbath in Crisis,* and have found it to be enlightening and biblically correct.
> Let me tell you something about myself. I am a twenty-eight-year-old black female. I am a born-again Christian for eight years now and an active church member. I am a member of the ____ church.
> The reason for my writing to you is I have a male friend whom I love very much. We have known each other for about three years. He is an Adventist. At first there was not much of a problem. We are both Christians, serving the same God.
> Two months ago, the Seventh-day Adventist Conference of ____ started tent meetings. The preacher is an Adventist minister from ____.
> I have heard him preach. He has been preaching that if a person does not keep the Sabbath they are in unbelief and are lost. He says persons who go to church on Sundays have the mark of the beast. He says God (1) cannot change, (2) cannot lie, (3) cannot hear a law breaker's prayer, among other things. He also teaches that in 1st, 2nd, and 3rd John, it says that if we do not keep the commandments we are lost, among other things.
> My friend of three years, whom I pray with, who visits my church, and I his, is now faced with two problems. He is being taught that I am not a Christian.
> The preacher is very persuasive and the Adventists do not question anything he says. My friend who was already baptized went and was baptized again. Over four hundred persons are baptized every Saturday for the past two weeks.

> Now Adventists are coming up to persons who are not Adventists and telling these persons they have the mark of the beast.
> My friend does not want to lose my friendship, or I his, but this thing has become a mountain.
> I think I read that you were once an Adventist; why did you leave? Could you write back to me and just give me an idea of what you think of what I have written you about…[11]

What this young woman writes is typical of Adventist "traditional evangelism" and how they use the Sabbath as a manipulative tool.

That Adventists are still using this manipulative method is evident from an email I received May 14, 2002.

> I am currently attending a seminar sponsored by the Seventh-day Adventist Church in which Verne Snow is presenting the Prophecies for the End Times. Two of my friends went forward last night, and I am being pressured to join the local Adventist Church. I am Faith Wesleyan, and what the Adventists say about the Sabbath being changed to Sunday by the Catholic Church, and the fact that we are worshipping on Sundays, and thus not keeping the Sabbath, is weighing on my heart. I am saved by the grace of our Lord. However, if I am breaking the True Sabbath, [and] have I fallen from Grace, becomes the question. They say if I recognize that Saturday is the Lord's Holy Day, but worship on Sunday, I am not keeping the 4th Commandment. This makes sense, but I do not agree with "voting" anyone into a church. That is Christ's decision alone. I really have no desire to change churches, but if Saturday is the true Sabbath, I want the Church I attend to worship on Saturday, in keeping the Sabbath Holy. [Do you have] any advice for me?

One can see SDA's manipulative method still being used here. A born-again Christian is told that she will fall from grace if she does not keep the seventh-day Sabbath! Paul, on the other hand, said that those who were trying to keep the law were the ones who were likely to fall from grace![12]

---

[11] Used by permission of the author who requested anonymity.
[12] Gal. 5:4.

It is clear that SDAs still believe that if a person "understands" the Sabbath and Adventist doctrine, and then leaves, they will be lost. Following is a quote from the current (2003) President of the General Conference of Seventh-day Adventists, Jan Paulsen.

> ...We believe that being Seventh-day Adventists has a direct bearing on our salvation; that while a believer can be saved as a Catholic, I would risk my whole spiritual life and salvation were I to leave what I am now and join any other community.[13]

The Sabbath and the "Seal of God"

For Seventh-day Adventists the Sabbath holds considerable significance, more than most other Christians realize. It is seen as the "testing truth" for the last days. They believe that sometime "soon" true Christians will be separated from false "Christians" and the point of separation will be loyalty to God *as manifested by the observance of the seventh-day Sabbath*. Those who reject the "truth" of the seventh-day Sabbath message will at that time receive the mark of the beast, which they believe to be enforced Sunday worship. Thus, according to their eschatology, *all* Christendom will fall into one of these two camps: true seventh-day Sabbath keepers who have the "seal of God" and those who worship on Sunday who will receive the "mark of the beast."[14]

---

[13] Jan Paulson, "The Theological Landscape" No. 4, "The Idea of Remnant" printed in the *Adventist Review,* (Review and Herald Publishing Association, Hagerstown, MD, 2002).

[14] "The sign, or seal, of God is revealed in the observance of the seventh-day Sabbath, the Lord's memorial of creation. 'The Lord spake unto Moses, saying, Speak thou also unto the children of Israel, saying, Verily My Sabbaths ye shall keep: for it is a sign between Me and you throughout your generations; that ye may know that I am the Lord that doth sanctify you.' Exodus 31:12,13. Here the Sabbath is clearly designated as a sign between God and His people. The mark of the beast is the opposite—the observance of the first day of the week. This mark distinguishes those who acknowledge the supremacy of the papal

This is not some sideline theology within the SDA church; it is the very *heart of traditional Adventism.* It is called "The Third Angel's Message" (From Rev. 14:6–12). It is the basis of their official logo, which may be seen on many SDA churches and in many of their periodicals. It is this "message" which gives purpose to their existence. It is this "truth" which mandates their continuing presence in the world.

Because of this understanding many who leave the Seventh-day Adventist church live under fear and guilt.[15] They fear they may be deceived and may end up receiving the mark of the beast rather than the seal of God. They suffer guilt since they no longer worship with the "true, remnant church." Many who leave the SDA church feel isolated. They are not comfortable to worship in any local Christian church which worships on Sunday for fear they may receive the mark of the beast. For this reason many flounder in their spiritual life clinging desperately to friends on the fringes of the Adventist church, or to some other sabbatarian group.

The chapter, *Christ: The Testing Truth,* provides a solid, scriptural foundation for those who are uncertain about their acceptance with God. However, let us now consider the SDA doctrine regarding the Sabbath and the Seal of God.

---

authority from those who acknowledge the authority of God." E. G. White, *Testimonies for the Church,* Vol. 8, p. 117.

[15] "It is Satan's plan to weaken the faith of God's people [SDA members] in the *Testimonies* [Writings of Ellen G. White]. Next follows skepticism in regard to the vital points of our faith, the pillars of our position, then doubt as to the Holy Scriptures, and then the downward march to perdition. When the *Testimonies,* which were once believed, are doubted and given up, Satan knows the deceived one will not stop at this; and he redoubles his efforts till he launches them into open rebellion, which becomes incurable and ends up in destruction." E. G. White, *Testimonies for the Church,* Vol. 6, p. 335. (see also footnote No. 18, 19).

The following quotation is taken from the SDA "Summary of Doctrinal Beliefs" as found on the back of their Certificate of Baptism.

> The seventh day of the week is the eternal sign of Christ's power as Creator and Redeemer, and is therefore the Lord's day, or the Christian Sabbath, constituting the *seal of the living God.* It should be observed from sunset Friday to sunset Saturday.

The traditional support for the seventh-day Sabbath as the seal of God comes from the common understanding of what a seal is: it is a mark which shows authenticity by (1) giving the *name* of the one in authority, (2) the *title* of the one in authority, and (3) the *dominion* of the one in authority. Seventh-day Adventists show that the Sabbath of the Fourth Commandment has all of this information: "The Lord" (name), "The Lord your God" (title), "Who made the heavens and the earth, and sea and all that is in them" (dominion).

This may be good human reasoning, but the New Testament *never* speaks of the Sabbath as the seal of God. Because the Sabbath commandment was placed in the very center of the Ten Commandments, it served as the dynastic seal of the Sinaitic Covenant. On several occasions *within the old covenant* we find the Sabbath called a *sign*. In context it is *always* the sign between God and the sons of Israel.

> But speak to the *sons of Israel,* saying "You shall surely observe My *sabbaths;* for this is a *sign between Me and you throughout your generations"* (Ex. 31:13).
> It [the Sabbath] is a sign between Me and the sons of Israel forever (Ex. 31:17).
> And also I gave them My *sabbaths* to be a *sign between Me and them* that they might know that I am the LORD who sanctifies them (Ez. 20:12).
> I am the LORD your God; walk in My statutes, and keep My ordinances, and observe them. And sanctify My *sabbaths;* and they shall be a *sign between Me and you,* that you may know that I am the LORD your God (Ez. 20:20).

Never is the Sabbath called a seal or a sign within the new covenant. During the ministry of Jesus He was the seal.

> Do not work for the food which perishes, but for the food which endures to eternal life, which the Son of Man will give to you, for on Him the Father, God, has set His seal (Jn. 6:27).

Now that Jesus has ascended to the Father, Christ's representative, the Holy Spirit, is the seal which the Christian receives when he believes.

> Now He who establishes us with you in Christ and anointed us in God, who also *sealed* us and gave us *the Spirit* in our hearts as a pledge (2 Cor. 1:21, 22).
>
> In Him, you also, after listening to the message of truth, the gospel of your salvation—having also believed, you were *sealed in Him with the Holy Spirit of promise,* who is given as a pledge of our inheritance, with a view to the redemption of God's own possession, to the praise of His glory (Eph. 1:13, 14).
>
> And do not grieve the *Holy Spirit* of God, by whom you were *sealed* for the day of redemption (Eph. 4:30).
>
> The Spirit Himself testifies with our spirit that *we are children of God* (Rom. 8:16).

According to the New Testament, the sealing takes place when a person places his faith in Christ alone for salvation and he is regenerated by the sovereign work of the Holy Spirit. It is simultaneous to our entering into the true rest of God.

According to Scripture the seventh-day Sabbath is *not* the seal of God. According to the New Testament the seventh-day Sabbath is *not* the sign which is to be remembered by Christians; rather Christians are to celebrate the Lord's Supper (the new covenant sign) in remembrance of Christ. Christians are sealed with the Holy Spirit.

The Dilemma of Sabbath Observance

If the Sabbath is going to be the final test as Adventists teach, then it must be observed by certain behavior. Who is going to decide what behavior will pass the test? I sent out

The Sabbath and Seventh-day Adventists

over a dozen draft manuscripts of this book to Seventh-day Adventist pastors and theologians for their evaluation. I was amazed at their comments regarding Sabbath keeping.

One retired SDA theologian said "God leaves the details of Sabbath observance up to the individual." If that is true, then how can this be a life and death test? What will the man who was stoned for picking up sticks on the Sabbath say to this?

Another well known Adventist theologian expressed to me that the Sabbath law in the Ten Commandments was the only moral Sabbath law and the other Sabbath laws in Scripture were all ceremonial. If this is true, then why do Seventh-day Adventists keep the Sabbath from sundown to sundown and publish the exact time of sunset each week in their papers?

Yet another retired Adventist professor said, "Keeping the Sabbath is not a work of the law—it is resting in God's grace." If this is true, then why do Adventists make such an important issue in their Evangelistic meetings over Rev. 12:17 and "keeping the commandments" which they interpret to be the Ten Commandment law?

Endless discussions will never do away with biblical statements. There is no biblical evidence which suggests that some of the Old Testament Sabbath commands are still to be followed while others are not. There is little logic in the way Seventh-day Adventists observe certain of the old covenant Sabbath commands while neglecting others.[16] The chief support for their form of Sabbath observance is dependence upon the writings of Ellen White. However, who is willing to keep the Sabbath according to her rules?[17] Few can measure up to all of her Sabbath laws,

---

[16] Seventh-day Adventists in general follow many of the old covenant laws regarding Sabbath observance, yet the author has never known any Adventist to follow the clear biblical law, "You shall not kindle a fire in any of your dwellings on the sabbath day" (Ex. 35:3).

[17] "On Friday let the preparation for the Sabbath be completed. See that all the clothing is in readiness and that all the cooking is done. Let the

and if one does not he is under condemnation.[18,19] Yet if one does keep all the Sabbath rules laid down by Ellen White he must again face Scripture for she, herself, says,

---

boots be blacked and the baths taken. It is possible to do this. If you make it a rule you can do it. The Sabbath is not to be given to the repairing of garments, to the cooking of food, to pleasure seeking or to any other worldly employment. Before the setting of the sun let all secular work be laid aside and all secular papers be put out of sight." Ellen G. White, *Testimonies for the Church,* Vol. 8, p. 355. "Let not the precious hours of the Sabbath be wasted in bed. On Sabbath morning the family should be astir early." Ibid., p. 357. "If we desire the blessing promised to the obedient, we must observe the Sabbath more strictly. I fear that we often travel on this day when it might be avoided. In harmony with the light which the Lord has given in regard to the observance of the Sabbath, we should be more careful about traveling on the boats or cars on this day...When starting on a journey we should make every possible effort to plan so as to avoid the company of those who would draw our attention to worldly things...We should not talk about matters of business or engage in any common, worldly conversation. At all times and in all places God requires us to prove our loyalty to Him by honoring the Sabbath." Ibid., p. 360. "God requires that His holy day be as sacredly observed now as in the time of Israel. The command given to the Hebrews should be regarded by all Christians as an injunction from Jehovah to them." E. G. White, *Patriarchs and Prophets,* p. 296.

[18] "Those who would in any way lessen the force of the sharp reproofs which God has given me to speak, must meet their work at the judgment." E. G. White, *Testimonies for the Church,* Vol. 5, p. 19. "If you feel just as safe in following your own impulses as in following the light given by God's delegated servant [E. G. White], the peril is your own; you will be condemned because you rejected the light which heaven had sent to you." *Ibid.,* p. 674.

"It is Satan's plan to weaken the faith of God's people in the *Testimonies." Ibid.,* p. 672.

"God has given sufficient evidence so that all who desire to do so may satisfy themselves as to the character of the *Testimonies;* and, having acknowledged them to be from God, it is their duty to accept reproof, even though they do not themselves see the sinfulness of their course...Those who despise the warning will be left in blindness to become self-deceived." *Ibid.,* p. 682.

[19] Author's note: The quotations from Ellen G. White in Note 18 express the cultic control of fear and guilt. This is *not* God's method.

The Sabbath and Seventh-day Adventists

God will have a people upon the earth to maintain the Bible, and the *Bible only,* as the standard of *all* doctrines and the basis of *all* reforms.[20]

The biblical laws for Sabbath observance include *all* the following: not going out of one's place, not baking or boiling, not doing *any* work, not building a fire, not buying or selling, not carrying a load or burden, not doing your own pleasure. The commands for Sabbath observance were to keep it holy, to have a day of *complete* rest, observe, do, or celebrate, and delight oneself in the Lord.[21] Sabbaths were to be carefully observed from sundown Friday to sundown Sabbath.[22] Penalties for the violation of the Sabbath law included being put to death and cut off from the covenant people.[23] Again I ask, how is one to observe the Sabbath?

I have many friends who remain in the Seventh-day Adventist church who call themselves "liberated Sabbath-keepers." They continue to worship on the Sabbath in that

---

He invites us to come and reason together (Isa. 1:18). It is the *love of Christ* which controls us (2 Cor. 5:14). God invites us to study *for ourselves* and compare what others say with the truth of Scripture (Acts 17:11). We should never allow the keeping of our souls to be given to another human being. In essence, Ellen White is saying that if a person once believed in her writings, and then rejected them, he/she is lost. It should be known that she also condemned those who rejected the *false* message of William Miller's 1843 prediction of the second coming of Christ. (See E. G. White, *Spiritual Gifts,* Vol. 1, p. 140.) She condemned those who said the door of mercy was still *open* after 1844. (See E. G. White, *Day Star* 1846 as printed in *1844 and the Rise of Sabbatarian Adventism,* p. 146, and the "Camdon Vision" as printed in Ford, *Daniel 8:14, The Day of Atonement and the Investigative Judgment,* p. 356 ff.) All of these *false* condemnations came as a result of her "visions" where God showed her the "truth" which in retrospect is blatant error.

[20] E. G. White, *The Great Controversy,* p. 595.
[21] Review "Prohibition" and "Admonitions" in the chapter, "Shadows of Christ".
[22] See Lev. 23:32.
[23] See Ex. 31:15; 35:2, 3.

they go to church on Saturday. However, they have been "liberated" from what they call the "legalistic aspects" of the Sabbath. They feel free to go out to eat in a restaurant after church where they have to buy their meal, they have no problem with stopping at the supermarket to get needed (not necessarily emergency) items, watching TV, playing on the computer, or even working on Sabbath afternoon.

This "liberated Sabbath keeping" is not Sabbath keeping at all. One cannot claim the (supposed) biblical benefits of Sabbath observance while ignoring the biblical rules for Sabbath observance. If these "liberated Sabbath keepers" still think the Seventh-day Sabbath applies today, then they ought to fear, for in reality their "liberated Sabbath keeping" is really nothing but self-deceptive Sabbath breaking.

To My Seventh-day Adventist Friends

Many years ago when I conducted a seven-month study of the Sabbath I felt no compulsion to persuade any of you to change your beliefs concerning the Sabbath. Nor did I feel that way when I started to write *Sabbath in Crisis*. However, now that many intervening years have transpired and I have restudied this subject in greater depth, especially in the light of the covenants, and have, in the intervening years, received hundreds—probably many thousands—of phone calls, letters and emails from both current and former Sabbath keepers, I now feel I must share with you my deep concern as I write *Sabbath in Christ*. Prayerfully consider the following.

Seventh-day Adventists believe they will be judged in relation to the Ten Commandment law of Sinai.[24] They believe the Sabbath is the seal of God, the seal of the covenant under which they live, and use the reference in Exodus

---

[24] "The great principles of God's law are embodied in the Ten Commandments...These precepts are the basis of God's covenant with His people and the standard in God's judgment..." No. 18, *Fundamental Beliefs of Seventh-day Adventists*.

31:12–17 to support this view.[25] They believe the Sabbath is the "testing truth" for the last days.[26] Remember however what Scripture *clearly* teaches. The Ten Commandments are the *words* of the Sinaitic Covenant.[27] The seventh-day Sabbath is the *sign* of the Sinaitic Covenant.[28] The Sinaitic Covenant was made *only* with the "sons of Israel."[29] The Sabbath is at the *very heart* of the Sinaitic Covenant and is *inseparably connected* with *every* aspect of it.[30] The New Testament calls the Sinaitic Covenant the "first" or "old" covenant.[31] The New Testament says this "first" or "old" covenant is obsolete, is ready to disappear and should be "thrown out."[32] Paul said those who want to be under this covenant must keep *all* the stipulations of this covenant or they are *cursed*.[33] Paul says those who keep this covenant for religious reasons have *fallen from grace*.[34] If you are seeking to be under this law, remember

> There is no partiality with God...all who have sinned under the Law will be judged by the Law; for not the hearers of the Law are just before God, but the doers of the Law will be justified (Rom. 2:11–13).

---

[25] E. G. White, *Testimonies for the Church,* Vol. 8, p. 117.
[26] "The Lord has said that the Sabbath was a sign between him and his people forever. The time is coming when *all* those who worship God *will be distinguished by this sign.* They will be known as the servants of God, *by this mark* of their allegiance to Heaven. But all man made tests will divert the mind from the great and important doctrines that constitute the present truth." Ellen G. White, *Review and Herald,* 1888-05-29. See also the *Youth's Instructor,* 1898-10-20.
[27] See Ex. 31:18; 34:28; Deut. 9:9, 11, 15; 1 Ki. 8:9, 12.
[28] See Ex. 31:12–17.
[29] See Ex. 20:1, 2; 31:13, 16, 17; Deut. 5:1–3.
[30] See Lev. 23 and review "Sabbath Relationships" in the chapter, "The Shadows of Christ".
[31] See Heb. 9:1–4; 2 Cor. 3:2–7; Gal. 4:21–31.
[32] See Heb. 9:1–4; 2 Cor. 3:2–7; Gal. 4:21–31 and review the chapter, "A Better Law".
[33] See Gal 3:13; 5:1–4.
[34] See Gal. 5:4.

Paul says that *required* Sabbath observance *undermines the gospel.* It has been my experience, personally, and in working with hundreds of others, that this is usually true. When the Galatians started observing days, months, seasons, and years, Paul was fearful that he had labored over them in vain.[35]

As pointed out above it is the Holy Spirit, *not* the Sabbath, that is the new covenant seal of God. It is the Lord's supper, not the Sabbath, that is the repeatable sign new covenant Christians are to remember.

I know some of you have some understanding of the gospel. I know many of you are trusting Christ for your salvation. I know many of you are honestly seeking to follow God. Make sure your understanding of the Sabbath and the covenants is *biblical.*

I also know that there are *many* SDA pastors, college and university professors and some administrators and evangelists both currently employed and retired who have communicated with me that they do not hold many of SDA's unique teachings, including the Sabbath being the seal of God or the testing truth for the last days, Sunday as the Mark of the Beast, SDA 1844 sanctuary theology, the writings of Ellen White "as a continuing and authoritative source of truth" or the Adventist church being "the remnant church of Bible prophecy." These people need our prayers. On the one hand they want to be loyal to their church, on the other they are seeking to help the church drop its cultic historic teachings and move the denomination to a Christ-centered, *sola scriptura,* organization that focuses on the pure, simple gospel of Jesus Christ. It is my prayer that this book may in some small way help in this transition and that you, the reader, will find your *Sabbath in Christ* who is *the True Rest, the Real Redemption, the Covenant Keeper* and the *only One worthy of genuine worship*—on any and every day of the week.

---

[35] See Col. 2:16, 17; Gal. 3:10, 11, 21.

Come to Me, all you who are weary and heavy laden, and I will give you rest. Take My yoke upon you, and learn from Me, for I am gentle and humble in heart; and you shall find rest for your souls. For My yoke is easy, and My load is light (Mt. 11:28–30).

But an hour is coming, and now is, when the true worshipers will worship the Father in spirit and truth; for such people the Father seeks to be His worshipers. "God is spirit, and those who worship Him must worship in spirit and truth" (Jn. 4:23, 24).

Through Him then, let us *continually* offer up a sacrifice of praise to God, that is, the fruit of lips that give thanks to His name. And do not neglect doing good and sharing, for with such sacrifices God is pleased (Heb. 13:15, 16).

Not forsaking our own assembling together

CHAPTER TWENTY SIX

ASSEMBLING AND RESTING

> Since therefore, brethren, we have confidence to enter the [most] holy place by the blood of Jesus, by a new and living way which He inaugurated for us through the veil, that is, His flesh, and since we have a great priest over the house of God, let us draw near with a sincere heart in full assurance of faith, having our hearts sprinkled clean from an evil conscience and our body washed with pure water. Let us hold fast the confession of our hope without wavering, for He who promised is faithful; *not forsaking our own assembling together,* as is the habit of some, but encouraging one another; and all the more, as you see the day drawing near (Heb. 10:19–25).

It is important for us to hear what these verses teach. Those of us who have come from a strict Sabbath-keeping background can appreciate one thing about the Sabbath. It made us take time to focus our attention on God. While the new covenant is not concerned with specific times and places, it does, nonetheless, stress the importance of meeting together on a regular basis and taking time to be with the Lord.

It is very easy for those who once kept the Sabbath but now no longer do so, to work seven days a week and to crowd out time for God. I believe this problem stems from the "pendulum effect." When the legal restrictions were taken away, it was easy to let the pendulum swing too far into personal freedom. It is for this reason that I have included this short chapter which deals with Christian assembly and physical rest.

Christian Assembly/Church Attendance

The passage quoted above gives several admonitions and I believe also tells us how to keep these admonitions. The following may help.

- Let us draw near…in full assurance
- Let us hold fast the confession of our hope
- Let us consider how to stimulate one another to love and good deeds

(by)

- not forsaking our own assembling together

Fellowship needed for faith

All Christians should understand why regular Christian meetings and regular time devoted to God are so necessary. In the new covenant we are saved, not by works, but *by faith*.

> And without faith it is impossible to please Him, for he who comes to God must believe that He is, and that He is a rewarder of those who seek Him (Heb. 11:6).
>
> So faith comes from hearing and hearing by the word of Christ (Rom. 10:17).

The early church had a living faith in their Lord. We have this short, but important, description of its activities.

> So then, those who had received his word were baptized; and there were added that day about three thousand souls. And they were *continually* devoting themselves to the apostles' teaching, and to fellowship, to the breaking of bread and prayer (Acts 2:41, 42).

Christ is present in Christian fellowship

Jesus said that where two or three are gathered together He would be in their midst (Mt. 18:20). And the appearances of the risen Lord, most of which were on the first day of the week, are designed to teach us the *reality* of His promise. When Christians come together for the celebration of the Lord's Supper His presence is manifest, especially in the breaking of the bread.

Today we live in a secular culture and are constantly bombarded with information which is targeted to undermine our faith. In order to combat this we must be careful to regularly feed upon the word of God. It is *only* when we meet together with *other Christians* that we are able to follow the admonition of Hebrews 10. It is imperative that Christians meet together on a *regular* basis to experience the presence of the risen Lord.

Fellowship needed for personal growth

In the new covenant, the Holy Spirit fills the place which the law held in the old.[1] It is the Holy Spirit that guides the believer in how to implement the new covenant law of love. Therefore we find Paul's beautiful exposition on love recorded in 1 Corinthians 13 sandwiched between 1 Corinthians 12 and 1 Corinthians 14, two chapters dealing with the gifts of the Holy Spirit. In these chapters Paul shows how *all* Christians have some gift of the Spirit. In order for these gifts to operate, the church must *come together* in order to become the "body of Christ." It is only within the fellowship of believers that the Holy Spirit can lead us to become all that He wants us to be. Each Christian is likened to an organ of the body with every Christian ministering to and receiving ministry from every other "organ" of Christ's "body." In His final talk with the disciples before His death, Jesus said, "This is my commandment, that you love one another, just as I have

---

[1] Review Chapter 21.

loved you" (Jn. 15:12). Just as the "book of the law" interpreted and applied the "tablets of the law" in the old covenant so the epistles interpret and apply the law of love in the new covenant. One-another ministry is an example of this interpretation and application. One-another ministry is not an option if we are to experience authentic Christianity. Following is a partial list of "one-another" passages in the New Testament which serve to guide us in one-another ministry:

- Greet one another. Rom. 16:16
- Accept one another. Rom. 15:7
- Be kind to one another. Eph. 4:32
- Care for one another. 1 Cor. 12:25
- Be at peace with one another. Mk. 9:50
- Be members of one another. Eph. 4:25
- Be devoted to one another. Rom. 12:10
- Give preference to one another. Rom. 12:10
- Be of the same mind toward one another. Rom. 12:16
- Admonish one another. Rom. 15:14
- Wait for one another. 1 Cor. 11:33
- Bear one another's burdens. Gal. 6:2
- Show forbearance to one another. Eph. 4:2
- Be subject to one another. Eph. 5:21
- Bear with one another. Col. 3:13
- Teach one another. Col. 3:16
- Comfort one another. 1 Thess. 4:18
- Stimulate one another to love and good deeds. Heb. 10:24
- Confess your sins to one another. Jas. 5:16
- Pray for one another. Jas. 5:16
- Forgive one another. Col. 3:13
- Be hospitable to one another. 1 Pet. 4:9
- Build up one another. 1 Thess. 5:11
- Encourage one another. 1 Thess. 5:11
- Serve one another. Gal. 5:13

While Christians should meet together in weekly worship celebration, "one another" ministry often works best in small home groups where authentic, dynamic Christianity really lives.

Pastoral teaching needed for spiritual growth

Every Christian does not have the skill, time or training to be a thorough Bible student. It is the duty of the pastor to "equip the saints for the work of service, to the building up of the body of Christ" (Eph. 4:12). Thus it is important for the Christian to receive weekly teaching from one who does have the time and training to dig out the precious ore of Bible truth and refine it so that it is relevant for today. This does not mean the Christian is to blindly follow what the pastor says. Nor does it mean that the Christian layperson cannot be individually guided in his Bible study by the Holy Spirit. Rather, the Christian is to examine the Scriptures to see if the pastor's teaching is true. (See Acts 17:11.) But a Christian who does not regularly attend Bible study and church *is* going to be stunted in his personal growth. Our Lord wants us all to experience authentic, dynamic Christianity; therefore, He gives us pastoral leaders.

Fellowship needed for evangelism

The church is commissioned to take the gospel to all the world (Mt. 28:18–20). The fellowship of believers plays an important part in this expansion of the church. It was the church that sent out Paul and Barnabas on their missionary trips (Acts 13:1–3). The Philippian church on several occasions sent money to Paul so he could spend more time in preaching the gospel (Phil. 4:15, 16).

The New Testament knows nothing about Christians who are outside of fellowship. Even when they were in jail, the New Testament Christians wrote letters to encourage others to hold fast their faith in Christ (2 Tim. 4). Those who were not in jail visited and encouraged those who were

(Phil. 2:25). The underlying dynamic of new covenant life is *relationship*. And regular fellowship is a prerequisite for this relationship.

Thus, with the fellowship present in New Testament times even Paul's imprisonment was an asset to the spreading of the gospel.

> Now I want you to know, brethren, that my circumstances have turned out for the greater progress of the gospel, so that my imprisonment in the cause of Christ has become well known throughout the whole praetorian guard and to everyone else, and that *most of the brethren,* trusting in the Lord because of my imprisonment, *have far more courage to speak the word of God without fear* (Phil. 1:12, 13).

Fellowship needed for worship

It is true that the Christian can worship God by himself.

> Through Him then let us *continually* offer up a sacrifice of praise to God, that is, the fruit of lips that give thanks to His name. And do not neglect doing good and sharing; for with such sacrifices God is pleased (Heb. 13:15, 16).

It is equally true that the Christian can experience complete, corporate worship only in fellowship with other Christians. In Acts 4:24–30 we have the account of the congregation lifting up "their voice to God with one accord." After this time of rehearsing God's power and His work they prayed that they might

> ...speak Thy word with all confidence...the place where they had gathered together was shaken, and they were all filled with the Holy Spirit, and began to speak the word of God with boldness.

Thus, it is imperative that Christians have a regular time for worship. It is imperative that they assemble together in order to strengthen their faith, to meet in Christ's presence, for personal Christian growth, for the extension of the kingdom, and for corporate worship.

> Since therefore, brethren, we have confidence to enter the [most] holy place by the blood of Jesus, by a new and living

way which He inaugurated for us through the veil, that is, His flesh, and since we have a great priest over the house of God, let us draw near with a sincere heart in full assurance of faith, having our hearts sprinkled clean from an evil conscience and our body washed with pure water. Let us hold fast the confession of our hope without wavering, for He who promised is faithful; *not forsaking our own assembling together,* as is the habit of some, but encouraging one another; and all the more, as you see the day drawing near (Heb. 10:19–25).

Physical Rest

There is little *direct* teaching in the New Testament regarding physical rest. However, from what is recorded and from basic principles which are clearly stated the Christian is not left without guidance.

Jesus and physical rest

It appears that for Jesus the Sabbath was not His main time for physical rest and relaxation. Often His Sabbaths were filled with teaching in the synagogue followed by some type of ministry.

> …He entered the synagogue on the Sabbath, and stood up to read (Lk. 4:16).
>
> And He came down to Capernaum, a city of Galilee. And He was teaching them on Sabbath days (Lk. 4:31).
>
> And it came about on another Sabbath, that He entered the synagogue and was teaching (Lk. 6:6).

Most pastors will tell you that their hardest day is the day of worship. Preaching, teaching and personal ministry can be exhausting. For Jesus, however, His "work" often did not end when the synagogue service was over. On one occasion, after the conclusion of the synagogue service, Jesus went to the home of Peter and healed Peter's mother-in-law (Lk. 4:38, 39). After sundown, Jesus ministered to the crowd which had gathered (Lk. 4:40, 41). On another occasion He was invited to the home of a Pharisee for Sabbath dinner and ended up healing a man with dropsy and having a confrontation with the Pharisees (Lk. 14:1–6).

It is clear, however, that Jesus did take time for rest and relaxation. After a full Sabbath of ministry we find Jesus seeking to get away from the multitudes.

> And when day came, He departed and went to a lonely place (Lk. 4:42).
>
> And in the early morning, while it was still dark, He arose and went out and departed to a lonely place, and was praying there (Mk. 1:35).

It appears from the gospel record that Jesus had a *regular habit* of slipping away to some place of solitude for rest, private prayer and meditation.

> But He Himself would often slip away to the wilderness and pray (Lk. 5:16).
>
> And it was at this time He went off to the mountain to pray (Lk. 6:12).

Jesus taught His disciples by example and personal association. Thus, after Jesus and His disciples had been involved in intense times of ministry, He would say to them,

> "Come away by yourselves to a lonely place and rest a while." (For there were many people coming and going, and they did not even have time to eat.) And they went away in the boat to a lonely place by themselves (Mk. 6:30–32).

After Jesus heard about the death of John the Baptist,

> He withdrew from there in a boat, to a lonely place by Himself (Mt. 14:13).

Not only do we have the example of Jesus to guide us, but we also have fundamental principles. The New Testament teaches that our bodies are temples of God.

> Or do you not know that your body is a temple of the Holy Spirit who is in you, whom you have from God, and that you are not your own? For you have been bought with a price: therefore, glorify God in your body (1 Cor. 6:19, 20).

In context, Paul is not dealing with physical rest, rather he is addressing the problem of immorality. However, one characteristic of the new covenant is that instead of there being many specific laws to follow, we have a few basic principles *which can be applied to differing situations* as the need demands. Such is the case here. Because our bodies are temples of God, then it becomes a part of Christian discipline to care for our bodies so that we can be in the best of health and thus give to God the most effective service. Regular times of physical rest are required for sound mental, physical and spiritual health. Not only will the Christian schedule for worship and physical rest, but will also eat, drink, sleep, and exercise for optimal physical, mental and spiritual health.

> I urge you therefore, brethren, by the mercies of God, to present your bodies a living and holy sacrifice, acceptable to God, which is your spiritual service of worship (Rom. 12:1).

Conclusion

I believe that the day of worship is often an excellent day to devote to the things of God by setting aside one's regular work. However, the Christian must remember he is not under the old covenant Sabbath laws. Rather, he should be guided by the general principles of the new covenant, including the principles of health, which may be applied differently for different situations, to bring glory to God. While the New Testament gives several admonitions regarding the worship service itself, it has no specific behavior requirements regarding what one should, or should not do, before, or after, the worship service. It does, however, give general principles to guide us. Therefore, the Christian living under the new covenant may experience total rest. True believers will experience the "rest of grace" and find true rest for their souls. They will bring glory to God in all that they do, including getting the physical rest appropriate for their needs.

Chapter Summary

1. It is vitally important for Christians to assemble together on a regular basis.
   a. Fellowship is necessary for faith.
   b. Christ is present in Christian fellowship.
   c. Fellowship is needed for "one-another" ministry where authentic Christian living takes place.
   d. Pastoral teaching is needed for spiritual growth.
   e. Fellowship is needed for the implementation and support of evangelism.
   f. Fellowship is needed for complete, corporate worship.
2. The New Testament has little *direct* teaching regarding physical rest.
3. From the example of Jesus we learn the following:
   a. Jesus often taught during the synagogue services on Sabbath.
   b. After the synagogue service was over, Jesus often continued His ministry.
   c. It was the regular habit of Jesus to go out to a lonely place for rest, prayer and meditation. Often these occasions came after a busy day of ministry.
   d. Jesus taught His disciples to take time from their successful ministry and encouraged them to go out to a place of solitude.
4. From basic principles in the new covenant we learn that our bodies are the temple of the Holy Spirit and should be cared for by keeping them in good health.
   a. The Christian should sleep, eat, drink and exercise for optimal physical, mental and spiritual health.
   b. These principles may be applied differently under different situations with the intended result of glorifying God.
5. While the New Testament gives several admonitions regarding the worship service itself, it has no specific

behavior requirements regarding what one should, or should not do, before, or after, the worship service.

The free gift of God is eternal life in Christ Jesus our Lord

CHAPTER Twenty Seven

THE TESTING TRUTH

The purpose of this chapter is twofold. First, I want to bring hope and a biblical understanding of "the testing truth" to the many thousands who have left the fellowship of the Adventist church over the past years and are experiencing a certain amount of uncertainty regarding their assurance of salvation. Second, perhaps this material will be of help to others who minister to those who come from legalistic, Sabbath keeping backgrounds.

In Colossians 2 and Galatians 3–5, Paul listed the old covenant observance of the Sabbath as one of the things which could undermine a Christian's standing in Christ. It has been my experience that sabbatarians[1] often do not have a clear understanding of the gospel. For this reason, it is vital to our study to outline the way of salvation as set forth in the new covenant. This will serve two purposes. First, it will help those who read this book, who may come from backgrounds where the gospel was not clearly understood, to find a solid base for their acceptance with God. Second, it will show how the continued *required* observance of the Sinaitic Sabbath undermines that assurance. With this short introduction, let us examine what the New Testament teaches regarding the way of salvation and what it defines as the testing truth.

---

[1] Either Sabbath or Sunday sabbatarians.

Salvation in the New Covenant

Eternal life is a free gift

The wages of sin is death, but the *free gift* of God is eternal life (Rom. 6:23).

Not by works of righteousness which we have done, but according to *His mercy* He saved us (Tit. 3:5).

Being justified as a *gift by His grace* through the redemption which is *in Christ Jesus* (Rom. 3:24).

The good news of the new-covenant gospel is that the "work" of salvation has *already been completed.* Jesus is *seated* at the right hand of God. Never let anyone take away the glad tidings of the new covenant gospel. Salvation is a free gift based upon the work of Jesus Christ alone!

God has given us heaven's best

I am come that they might have life and that they might have it more abundantly (Jn. 10:10).

Blessed be the God and Father of our Lord Jesus Christ, who has blessed us with every spiritual blessing in the heavenly places in Christ, just as He chose us in Him before the foundation of the world, that we should be holy and blameless before Him. In love He predestined us to adoption as sons through Jesus Christ to Himself, according to the kind intention of His will (Eph. 1:3–5).

Now to Him who is able to do exceeding abundantly beyond all that we ask or think, according to the power that works within us… (Eph. 3:20).

In ourselves we are all sinful and lost

It is a good thing that salvation is free, for God's word clearly teaches that we all sin in the following ways. First, *by our own actions we have all sinned.*

For all have sinned and fall short of the glory of God (Rom. 3:23).

An understanding of the Greek verbs used in this verse adds additional insight. "Have sinned" refers to past actions of sin. However, "fall short" relates to a *present ongoing activity.* A literal rendering of the last part of this verse would read, "and *continue* to fall short of the glory of God." This verse means that those who are seeking to be justified by their own right behavior will not make it. For we all have sinned *in the past* and we all *continue* to fall short of God's requirement in the present.

A second way we all sin is by the *sin of thought.*

> Everyone who is *angry*...shall be guilty (Mt. 5:22).
> Everyone who looks on a woman to *lust* for her has already committed adultery with her in his heart (Mt. 5:28).

Here we see again how Jesus raised the moral level of new covenant righteousness far above that of the old covenant law. Who of us can claim to never sin by our thoughts?

A third way we all sin is by the *sin of neglect.* Jesus said,

> To the extent that you did *not* do it to one of the least of these, you did it *not* unto me (Mt. 25:45).

How many times have we neglected to do good to someone who was in need and by that neglect have actually sinned against Christ?

A fourth way we all sin is through the sin of *lack of faith.*

> Whatever is *not of faith* is sin (Rom. 14:23).

Then if these four ways were not enough to condemn us all, there is yet a fifth which we cannot escape. Our fallen, human nature is sinful at the core.

> We too...were *by nature* children of wrath (Eph. 2:3).

We are called to repentance and confession

When we see our own sinfulness and utter helplessness in contrast to the holiness, purity and righteousness of God which is far above that represented by the law, we are led to repentance. Repentance is a godly sorrow for our sin and a turning away from it. Jesus said,

> I have not come to call the righteous but sinners to repentance (Lk 5:32).

On the day of Pentecost when Peter outlined the magnitude of Israel's sin in putting Christ to death, the response of the people was, "What shall we do?" Peter's answer was,

> Repent therefore and return, that your sins may be wiped away, in order that times of refreshing may come from the presence of the Lord (Acts 3:19).

As repentant sinners we understand our lost condition and our need for God's saving grace. We recognize that if we are depending upon our *own* good behavior for our right standing with God not one of us has the slightest chance! Understanding our completely helpless condition we are now *willing* to accept God's solution to the sin problem.

Confession is the completion of repentance. We move from being willing to turn from sin, to actual confession or acknowledgment of sin. We agree with God's verdict that we are sinners. The confession of sin is linked with God's promise of forgiveness.

> If we confess our sins, He is faithful and righteous to forgive us our sins and to cleanse us from all unrighteousness (1 Jn. 1:9).

Evangelists who have insisted on specific confession of sin have had the best long-term results.

> It was found by actual research that over eighty-five in every hundred persons professing conversion to Christ in Finney's meetings remained true to God, whereas seventy percent of those professing conversion in the meetings of even so great an evangelist as Moody afterwards became backsliders. Finney seems to have had the power of impressing the consciences of

men with the necessity of holy living in such a manner as to procure the most lasting results.[2]

Those who have read the writings of Charles Finney cannot but be impressed by his insistence upon total and specific repentance and confession of every known sin.[3]

Repentance and confession of sin are sometimes glossed over in modern Christendom. They are, however, important steps in allowing God's grace to rule in the life.

While repentance is necessary in coming to Christ, it should never be thought of as a human work. It, too, is a gift of God.

> God exalted him [Christ] to his own right hand as Prince and Savior that he might *give* repentance and forgiveness of sins to Israel (Acts 5:31).

Love finds a way

God is love (1 Jn. 4:8).

> For God so loved the world, that He gave His only begotten Son, that whoever believes in Him should not perish, but have eternal life (Jn. 3:16).

God knew there was no way we could be good enough to make it to heaven so He graciously provided a way of salvation which would meet our needs.

Jesus Christ is the only way

> Jesus said to him, "I am the way, and the truth, and the life; no one comes to the Father, but through Me" (Jn. 14:6).

Jesus calls Himself the "good shepherd" and says,

> I am the door; if anyone enters through Me, he shall be *saved,* and shall go in and out, and find pasture (Jn. 10:9,11).

---

[2] James Gilchrist Lawson, *Deeper Experiences of Famous Christians*, (Glad Tidings Publishing Company, 1911), p. 243.
[3] See Charles Finney, *Lectures on Revivals of Religion,* (Fleming H. Revell Co., New York, NY, 1868), pp. 35–47.

> And there is salvation in no one else; for there is no other name under heaven that has been given among men, by which we must be *saved* (Acts 4:12).

It is important to remember that in the New Testament the covenant partners are God the Father and His Son Jesus Christ. Jesus is God's elect One. He is a "covenant to the people." The old covenant was made between God and the "the sons of Israel." The old covenant was faulty because the "sons of Israel" could not keep their promises.

> For finding fault with them...Says the Lord...I will effect a new covenant (Heb. 8:8).

The new covenant is far better for us than was the old covenant in that we are not the ones who must keep the covenant contract. The loving behavior and righteous living of *Jesus* satisfied the new covenant.

> We shall be saved by *His life* (Rom. 5:10).
>
> So then as through one transgression [Adam's] there resulted condemnation to all men; even so through *one act of righteousness* [Jesus'] there resulted justification of life to *all* men (Rom. 5:18).

While the new covenant is better *for us,* it was costly *for Jesus.* Under the old covenant the sons of Israel were the ones who had to demonstrate covenant loyalty by their obedience to the commandments. Under the new Christ had to perfectly obey His Father's will. Under the old covenant the sons of Israel received the curses of the broken covenant. In the new covenant we find that,

> Christ redeemed us from the curse of the Law, having become a curse for us (Gal. 3:13).

Under the old covenant atonement for sin was typified by the death of animals. However, under the new covenant Christ gave His life to reconcile us to Himself.

> He made Him who knew no sin to be sin on our behalf, that we might become the righteousness of God in Him (2 Cor. 5:21).

For I delivered to you as of first importance what I also received, that Christ died for our sins (1 Cor. 15:3).

The new covenant and us

Salvation is a free gift. We are all sinners on at least five counts. God understands our predicament and out of His gracious love made a new and better covenant. In the new covenant it is Christ's behavior, not ours, which matters. Now we must ask how this affects us. How do we participate in the blessings of the new covenant? The following is vital to our understanding of personal salvation and our understanding of the Sabbath. Here is the important question: How do I as a sinner become incorporated into the blessings of the new covenant if Jesus is the obedient covenant partner?

First, let us see how we do *not* enter into the new covenant blessings.

> He saved us, *not on the basis of deeds which we have done in righteousness,* but according to His mercy, by the washing of regeneration and renewing of the Holy Spirit (Tit. 3:5).
>
> For we maintain that a man is justified by faith *apart from works of the Law* (Rom. 3:28).
>
> You have been severed from Christ, you who are seeking to be justified by law; you have fallen from grace (Gal. 5:4).

These are forceful verses of Scripture for those who seek to make Sabbath keeping a testing truth which will determine a person's eternal destiny!

If our good behavior will not entitle us to the blessings of the new covenant, what will?

> They said therefore to Him, "What shall we do that we may work the works of God?" Jesus answered and said to them, "This is the work of God, that you *believe* in Him whom He has sent" (Jn. 6:29).
>
> ...that is the *word of faith* which we are preaching, that *if you confess* with your mouth Jesus as Lord, and believe in your heart that God raised Him from the dead, you shall be saved; for with the heart man *believes,* resulting in righteousness, and with the mouth he confesses, resulting in salvation. For the Scripture

says, "Whoever *believes* in Him will not be disappointed" (Rom. 10:8–11).
Truly, truly, I say to you, he who *believes* has eternal life (Jn. 6:47).

Scripture is not muddy or unclear regarding the way of salvation in the new covenant. It was the work of Jesus to provide the righteousness we needed. He did that. It was the work of Jesus to receive the curse of sin. He did that. It is our work to *believe* in Him, and in so doing we enter *by faith* into the blessings of the new covenant—without works. Under the new covenant salvation is by grace through faith in Christ plus nothing!—and even saving faith is a gift of God![4]

But what do we mean by "faith" and "belief"? The story is told of a tight-rope walker who a number of years ago stretched a cable across Niagara Falls. The newspapers carried the story that he was going to walk across this dangerous place on a given day. That day hundreds gathered to watch this man perform his risky skill. Shortly before he was to go out on the cable this tight-rope walker made his way into the crowd. He would approach people and ask them if they believed he could make it across without falling to his death. Most said he could. He came up to a young man and said, "Do you believe I can safely walk across this cable above the falls?"

"Yes," answered the young man. "You are a tight-rope walker and have the necessary skills to do it."

"Do you *really believe* I can do it?" asked the tight-rope walker.

"Yes, I really believe you can do it," answered the young man.

"Good," said the tight-rope walker. "You are just the person I am looking for. I want to push this wheelbarrow across the falls and I want you to sit in it!"

---

[4] Eph. 2:8,9.

Did the young man get in? No, for his "belief" was only an *intellectual concept;* it was not *trust.* He was not willing to trust his life to his belief. When Scripture speaks of faith or belief (they are the same word in Greek) it means *both* belief and trust. In other words, the condition for salvation in the new covenant is simply to *believe* in who Jesus is—the divine Son of God who perfectly obeyed His Father's will, died for our sins, and was raised from the dead for our justification—and *trust* our eternal salvation to what *He did.* We must, so to speak, climb into the wheelbarrow and let Christ push us across. We must recognize there is no way we can ever be good enough. We must trust our very life to His work. Too many of us, however, want to get out and help Christ push the wheelbarrow!

Christ is our true redemption so we can live a life of full assurance

> But as many as received Him to them He gave the right to become children of God, even to those who believe in His name (Jn. 1:12).
> If we confess our sins, He is faithful and righteous to *forgive* us our sins and to *cleanse* us from all unrighteousness (1 Jn. 1:9).
> Christ redeemed us from the curse of the Law, having become a curse for us—for it is written, "Cursed is everyone who hangs on a tree"— in order that in Christ Jesus the blessing of Abraham might come to the Gentiles, so that we would receive the promise of the Spirit through faith (Gal. 3:13, 14).
> Therefore, having been justified by *faith,* we *have peace* with God through our Lord Jesus Christ (Rom. 5:1).
> For if while we were enemies, we were reconciled to God through the death of His Son, much more, *having now been reconciled,* we shall be saved by *His life* (Rom. 5:10).

In the new covenant we can come with confidence into the very presence of God because of the blood of Jesus.

> Since therefore, brethren, we have confidence to enter the [most] holy place by the blood of Jesus…(Heb. 10:19).

God wants us to experience true "rest"

The writer of Hebrews says, "There remains therefore a Sabbath rest for the people of God." He admonishes us to "be diligent to enter that rest." And he says "we who have *believed* enter that rest" (Heb. 4:3, 9, 11). Christians who believe enter the "rest" of fellowship with God, the "rest" of Eden's seventh day when all was very good. We *now* have eternal life (Jn. 6:47)! We now *know* we have eternal life (1 Jn. 5:13). We *now* have peace with God (Rom. 5:1). We *now* have been reconciled to God (Rom. 5:10). Our old self (man) *was crucified* with Christ (Rom. 6:6.). We are *now* to consider ourselves to be *dead* to sin (Rom. 6:11). We are *now* freed from sin (Rom. 6:18, 22; 1 Jn. 3:8, 9). We are *now* dead to the law (Rom. 7:4). We *now* have been released from the law! (Rom. 7:6). We *now* serve in the newness of the Spirit and not in the oldness of the letter! (Rom. 7:6). There is *now* no condemnation to those who are in Christ Jesus! (Rom. 8:1). We have *now* received the spirit of adoption! (Rom. 8:15). We *now* overwhelmingly conquer through Him who loved us! (Rom. 8:37). We are *now* sealed with the Holy Spirit of promise! (Eph. 1:13). We are *now* saved through faith! (Eph. 2:8). We are *now* the dwelling of the Holy Spirit (Eph. 2:22). We are *now* chosen in Christ (Eph. 1:4). We *now have* redemption through his blood (Eph. 1:7). God is *now* at work in us to will and to do *His* good pleasure (Phil. 2:13). We are *now* qualified to share in the inheritance of the saints in light (Col. 1:12). We have *now* been transferred to the kingdom of His beloved Son (Col. 1:13).We *now* have each received a spiritual gift (Rom. 12; 1 Cor. 12; Eph. 4). The Spirit *now* helps our weaknesses (Rom. 8:26). We have *now* been predestined to be like Christ (Rom. 8:29). And this is just the beginning! Do you see why the gospel is "good news"? One cannot work righteousness from the outside in—that

The Testing Truth

was the old covenant way[5] and it *never* worked. Rather, in the new covenant God creates or regenerates our spirits. We are born of God. (Jn. 3:3–5) We have the divine DNA, God's life living in us and that life is perfect.[6]

> If anyone loves Me he will keep My word; and My Father will love him, and *We will come to him, and make Our abode with him* (Jn. 14:23).
>
> What we have seen and heard we proclaim to you also, that you also may have fellowship with us; and indeed *our fellowship is with the Father, and with His Son Jesus Christ*. And these things we write, so that our joy may be made complete (1 Jn. 1:4).

This intimate fellowship with the Lord is the "rest" which "remains." This is the "rest" which can be entered "today." This is the true "rest" Jesus had in mind when He said,

> Come unto Me, all you who are weary and heavy laden, and I will give you rest. Take My yoke upon you, and learn from Me, for I am gentle and humble in heart; and you shall find rest for your souls. For My yoke is easy and My load is light (Mt. 11:28–30).

According to the New Testament the testing truth is faith in Jesus. It is *not* the seventh-day Sabbath. Don't let anyone take away from you the simple gospel of faith in Christ!

> If you confess with your mouth Jesus as Lord, and believe in your heart that God raised Him from the dead, you will be saved; for with the heart a person believes, resulting in righteousness, and with the mouth he confesses, resulting in salvation (Rom. 10:9, 10).

"If you abide in My word, then you are truly disciples of Mine; and you shall know the truth and the truth shall set you *FREE*" (Jn. 8:31, 32).

---

[5] "It will be righteousness for us if we are careful to observe all this commandment before the LORD our God, just as He commanded us" (Deut. 6:25).

[6] 1 Cor. 6:19; Rom. 8:9–12, 1 Cor. 2:12; 1 Cor. 3:16.

BIBLIOGRAPHY

I have not listed the publisher for the Ellen G. White books as this information has little practical use. Her books are sold at Adventist Book Centers throughout the U.S. People wishing to purchase her books may call any Seventh-day Adventist church for referral to the nearest Adventist Book Center. For a complete listing of her works, contact the Ellen G. White Estate, Inc. General Conference of Seventh-day Adventists, 12501 Old Columbia Pike, Silver Spring, MD, 20904-6600.

Anderson, Dirk, *White Out—An Investigation of Ellen G. White,* (Life Assurance Ministries Publications, Glendale, AZ, 1999)

Andrews, J. N. *History of the Sabbath and the First Day of the Week,* (Review and Herald Publishing Co., Battle Creek, MI, 1873)

Bacchiocchi, Samuele, *The Sabbath in the New Testament,* (Biblical Perspectives, Berrien Springs, MI, 1990)

_____, *The Sabbath Under Crossfire,* (Biblical Perspectives, Berrien Springs, MI, 1998)

Blanco, Jack, *The Clear Word Bible,* (Review and Herald Publishing Association, Hagerstown, MD, 1994).

Bible Readings for the Home Circle, (Review and Herald Publishing Co., Battle Creek, MI, 1888)

Bird, Herbert S., *Theology of Seventh-day Adventism,* Wm. B. Eerdmans Publishing Co., Grand Rapids, MI, 1961)

Brinsmead, Robert D. *Judged by the Gospel,* (Verdict Publications, Fallbrook, CA, 1980)

_____, *Verdict,* "The Covenants", (Verdict Publications, Fallbrook, CA, 1980)

Bruce, F.F., *Paul: Apostle of the Heart Set Free,* (Wm. B. Eerdmans Publishing Co., Grand Rapids, MI, 1977)

_____, *The Book of the Acts, The New International Commentary on the New Testament,* (Wm. B. Eerdmans Publishing Co., Grand Rapids, MI, 1983)

Carson, D. A., *Commentary on John,* (Wm. B. Eerdmans Publishing Co., Grand Rapids, MI, 1991)

_____, Editor, *From Sabbath to Lord's Day,* (Zondervan, Grand Rapids, MI, 1982)

_____, *Gospel of Matthew, The Expositor's Bible Commentary,* Vol. 8 (Zondervan, Grand Rapids, MI, 1984)

_____, *Showing the Spirit,* (Baker Book House, Grand Rapids, MI, 1987)

Chisholm, Clinton, "The Christian and the Mosaic Law", cassette tape set (available from Life Assurance Ministries Publications, Glendale, AZ)

Elliff, Tom, *A Passion for Prayer,* (Crossway Books, Wheaton, IL, 1998)

Finney, Charles, *Lectures on Revivals of Religion,* (Fleming H. Revell Co., New York, NY, 1868)

Finley, Mark, *The Almost Forgotten Day,* (The Concerned Group, Inc. Siloam Springs, AR, 1988)

Ford, Desmond, *Daniel 8:14, The Day of Atonement and the Investigative Judgment* (Euangelion Press, Casselberry, FL, 1980), Available from Life Assurance Ministries Publications, Glendale, AZ.

_____, *The Forgotten Day,* (Desmond Ford Publications, Newcastle, CA, 1981)

Fredericks, Richard, "Sabbath in Christ", a cassette tape series, (Damascus Road Community Church, Damascus, MD, 1998)

"Fundamental Beliefs of Seventh-day Adventists." These were revised in 1980 and remain current in 2003. See http://www.adventist.org/beliefs/index.html for the complete listing of all twenty seven. These are also printed in Ratzlaff, *The Cultic Doctrine of Seventh-day Adventists.*

Gladson, Jerry, *A Theologians Journey from Seventh-day Adventism to Mainstream Christianity,* Life Assurance Ministries Publications, Glendale, AZ, 2000)

Harrison, Everett H. *Introduction to the New Testament,* (Wm. B. Eerdmans, Grand Rapids, MI, 1971)

Hendriksen, William, *New Testament Commentary, The Gospel of Matthew,* (Baker Book House, Grand Rapids, MI, 1973)

Holt, R. Russell, *Signs of the Times,* Pacific Press Publishing Association, Nampa, ID, February and March, 1990. (The missionary journal of SDAs)

Hybles, Bill, *Too Busy Not to Pray,* (InterVarsity Press, Downers Grove, IL, 1988)

Ignatious of Antioch, *Epistle to the Magnesians,* in *The Apostolic Fathers,* Translated by J. B. Lightfoot and J. R. Harmer, (Baker book House, Grand Rapids, MI, 1989)

Josephus, Flavius, *Antiquities of the Jews,* (Kregel Publications, Grand Rapids, MI, 1960)

Kittel, Gerhard, Editor, *Theological Dictionary of the New Testament,* Vol. I, (Wm. B. Eerdmans Publishing Co., Grand Rapids, MI, 1963)

_____, *Theological Dictionary of the New Testament,* Vol. IV, (Wm. B. Eerdmans Publishing Co., Grand Rapids, MI, 1967)

Kline, Meredith G., *Treaty of the Great King,* (Wm. B. Eerdmans Publishing Co., Grand Rapids, MI, 1963)

Knight, George, *1844 and the Rise of Sabbatarian Adventism,* (Review and Herald Publishing Association, Hagerstown, MD, 1994)

LaRondell, Hans K., *Light for the Last Days,* (Pacific Press Publishing Association, Nampa, ID, 1999)

Lawson, James Gilchrist, *Deeper Experiences of Famous Christians,* (Whitaker House, Pittsburgh, PA, 1998. Originally Published by Glad Tidings, 1911)

Lenski, R.C.H., *Commentary on the New Testament, Matthew,* (Hendrickson Publishers, Inc., Grand Rapids, MI, 1998)

Lightfoot, J.B. and J. R. Harmer, *The Apostolic Fathers,* (Baker Book House, Grand Rapids, MI, 1989)

Marcussen, A. Jan, *National Sunday Law* (Now available on the Internet at http://home.netvigator.com/~jskfung/co/books/ sunlaw.pdf)

Martin, J. Mark, *Seventh-day Adventism and the Writings of Ellen G. White,* (Calvary Community Church, Phoenix, AZ, 1997)

Martin, Walter, *The Kingdom of the Cults,* (Bethany House, Bloomington, MN, 1997)

Ministerial Association of the General Conference of Seventh-day Adventists, *Seventh-day Adventists Believe...,* (Review and Herald Publishing Association, Hagerstown, MD, 1988)

Moore, Marvin, *The Antichrist and the New World Order,* (Pacific Press Publishing Association, Boise, ID, 1993)

_____, *The Crisis of the End Times,* (Pacific Press Publishing Association, Boise, ID, 1992)

Morris, Leon, *The New International Commentary of the New Testament, The Gospel According to John,* (Wm. B. Eerdmans Publishing Co. Grand Rapids, MI, 1971)

Nichol, Francis D., *Answers to Objections,* (Review and Herald Publishing Association, Washington, D.C., 1952)

Paulson, Jan, "The Theological Landscape" "No. 4, The Idea of 'Remnant'" *Adventist Review,* (Review and Herald Publishing Association, Hagerstown, MD, 2002), Find this on the Internet at: http://www.adventistreview.org/2002-1524/story3.html

Paxton, Geoffrey, J., *The Shaking of Adventism,* (Baker Book House, Grand Rapids, MI, 1978)

Peck, Clayton, "An Appeal From The Heart," (Cassette tape set on the topic of the Sabbath, Grace Place, Berthoud, CO, 2001)

Pestes, Sam, *The Stone Cutter's Bride,* or *Abraham, Messenger to the Twenty First Century,* [Alternate title] (Published by Sam Pestes, Kelowna, BC, Canada, 2002). Tapes and CDs of this study are available from Life Assurance Ministries Publications, Glendale, AZ.

Peterson, Eugene H., *The Message,* (Navpress, Colorado Springs, CO, 1994)

Ratzlaff, Dale, *The Cultic Doctrine of Seventh-day Adventists,* (Life Assurance Ministries Publications, Glendale, AZ, 1996)

_____, *The Truth About Seventh-day Adventist "Truth",* (Life Assurance Ministries Publications, Glendale, AZ, 2000)

Rea, Walter T., *The White Lie,* M & R Publications, Turlock, CA, 1982)

Reiner, Edwin, *The Covenants,* (Southern Publishing Association, Nashville, TN, 1967)

Riggle, H. M., *The Sabbath and the Lord's Day,* (Faith Publishing House, Guthrie, OK, 1922). This book has been reprinted and is now available from Life Assurance Ministries Publications, Glendale, AZ.

Smith, Uriah, *Daniel and the Revelation,* (Southern Publishing Association, Nashville, TN, 1944)

Streifling, Verle, *Proclamation,* (Life Assurance Ministries, Inc. Glendale, AZ, 2001)

Stringfellow, Bill, *The Ultimate Rip-off,* (Concerned Publications, Bemidji, MN, 1987)

Telushkin, Rabbi Joseph, *Biblical Literacy,* (William Morrow and Co., Inc., New York, NY, 1948)

The Jerusalem Bible, (Doubleday & Co., Inc, Garden City, NJ, 1966)

Vandeman, George E., *When God Made Rest,* (Pacific Press Publishing Association, Boise, ID, 1987)

Watson, Alan, *Jesus and the Law,* (University of Georgia Press, Athens, GA, 1996),

Wikenhauser, Alfred, *New Testament Introduction,* (Herder and Herder, New York, NY, 1958)

Wheeler, Gerald and Bill Cleveland, Editors, *My Covenant Getting Ready to Meet Jesus,* (Review and Herald Publishing Association, Hagerstown, MD, 1998).

White, Ellen G., *Early Writings,* 1882

_____, *Patriarchs and Prophets,* 1890

_____, *Review and Herald,* 1870-04-19; 1911-06-29

_____, *Signs of the Times,* 1850-64-01; 1890-06-02

_____, *Spirit of Prophecy,* Vol. 4, 1870–1884

_____, *Spiritual Gifts,* Vols. 1, 2, 3, 4, 1858, 1860, 1864, 1864

_____, *Testimonies to the Church,* Vols. 5, 6, 8, 1889, 1900, 1904

_____, *The Great Controversy,* 1888, 1911

_____, *Youth's Instructor,* 1898-10-20.

White, Ellen G. Web sites:

http://www.whiteestate.org (This is the official web site of the SDA White Estate.)

http://www.ellenwhite.org (This site shows the self contradictions in the writings of Ellen White, the contradictions between her writings and Scripture, her copious plagiarism, false prophecies, historical errors and unscientific statements.)

Scriptural Index

Reference	Page	Reference	Page
Gen. 1:5	21	Ex. 2:24	83,231
Gen. 1:8	21	Ex. 3:8	83,231
Gen. 1:13–31	22	Ex. 3:15	53
Gen. 2	362,363	Ex. 4:5	53
Gen. 2:1	24	Ex. 4:24,25	61
Gen. 2:1–3	21	Ex. 4:24–26	224
Gen. 2:2,3	25,362	Ex. 12:14	68
Gen. 2:5	362	Ex. 12:15	62
Gen. 2:6	75	Ex. 12:17	68
Gen. 2:10–14	362	Ex. 12:43,44,48	55
Gen. 2:15	25	Ex. 12:48	82,251
Gen. 2:16,17	77	Ex. 15:1,2	33,45
Gen. 2:23,24	362	Ex. 16	285
Gen. 3:16–18	26	Ex. 16:4,5	84
Gen. 3:17–19	38,75,342	Ex. 16:21	35,47
Gen. 3:21	26	Ex. 16:23	72
Gen. 3:24	342	Ex. 16:23–26	138
Gen. 12:2,3	30	Ex. 16:23,30	84
Gen. 12:3	97,234	Ex. 16:27,28	85
Gen. 12:13	36	Ex. 16:29	71,138,165
Gen. 13:15	82	Ex. 16:34	362
Gen. 13:17	36	Ex. 17:7	281,285
Gen. 15	250	Ex. 19:4,5	52
Gen. 15:1	30	Ex. 19:7,8	52,58
Gen. 15:4–6	31,57	Ex. 19:8	235
Gen. 15:6	234	Ex. 19:16–25	288
Gen. 15:17,18	31	Ex. 19:18	32
Gen. 17:1–8	29,33	Ex. 19:24	235
Gen. 17:9–11	33	Ex. 20	51,285,348
Gen. 17:9–14	54,82,224	Ex. 20:1,2	56,393
Gen. 17:13	55,58	Ex. 20:2	44
Gen. 17:14	62	Ex. 20:3	258
Gen. 17:15–18	34,36	Ex. 20:4–6	258
Gen. 18:12	34	Ex. 20:4–11	258
Gen. 21:12	123	Ex. 20:7	258
Gen. 22	35	Ex. 20:8	13,73
Gen. 22:15–18	36,37,235	Ex. 20:8–10	357
Gen. 26:4,5	36,37	Ex. 20:8–11	80,83
Gen. 27,28	123	Ex. 20:10	56,71,83,138,165
Gen. 30:22	231	Ex. 20:11	74,77,347,362
Gen. 32:24–30	235	Ex. 20:12	54,258
Ex. 2:23,24,3:8	31,43,83	Ex. 20:13–15	258

Ex. 20:16,17	259	Ex. 32:28	303
Ex. 20:18	32,288	Ex. 34:1	60
Ex. 20:18,19	77	Ex. 34:7	49
Ex. 20:19	230	Ex. 34:14	48
Ex. 20:22	234	Ex. 34:21	72,138
Ex. 21:1–23,33	48	Ex. 34:24	50
Ex. 21:15	49	Ex. 34:28	46,94,234,393
Ex. 21:17	49	Ex. 35:1,3	72
Ex. 21:18	49	Ex. 35:2	74,154,391
Ex. 21:20	48,49	Ex. 35:3	49,211,389
Ex. 21:28,29	49	Ex. 38:21	81
Ex. 22:1	49	Ex. 40:20	47,94
Ex. 22:2–4	49	Lev. 3:17	59
Ex. 22:5	49	Lev. 5:4	50
Ex. 22:8	49	Lev. 5:11,12	358
Ex. 22:20	48	Lev. 6:3–8	50
Ex. 23:1	50	Lev. 7:20	62
Ex. 23:12	83,84	Lev. 7:21	62
Ex. 23:31	82	Lev. 7:25	62
Ex. 24:1–7	64	Lev. 7:27	62
Ex. 24:3	52,58,235	Lev. 10:9	59
Ex. 24:3–8	235	Lev. 10:12	358
Ex. 24:7	51,52,58,94	Lev. 11	107,205
Ex. 24:7,8	341	Lev. 12:1–3	54
Ex. 25:16	81	Lev. 12:3	82
Ex. 27:21	58	Lev. 13:45,46	104
Ex. 29:9	58	Lev. 15:19–25	105
Ex. 30:8	59	Lev. 16:29,31	69
Ex. 30:11–15	107,108	Lev. 17:1–4	62
Ex. 30:33	62	Lev. 17:4	358
Ex. 30:38	62	Lev. 18:5	58
Ex. 31	349	Lev. 18:6–18,29	62
Ex. 31:12,13	14,385	Lev. 18:16–30	49
Ex. 31:12–18	50,54,251,393	Lev. 18:19,20	62
Ex. 31:13	49,57,85,234,387	Lev. 18:22,29	62
Ex. 31:12–18	49,54,80,82,224 251,392,393	Lev. 18:23,29	62
		Lev. 19:1–8	62
Ex. 31:14	62,96	Lev. 19:3	49
Ex. 31:14,15	74,154	Lev. 19:4	49
Ex. 31:15	73,138,165,391	Lev. 19:5–8	358
Ex. 31:15,17	84	Lev. 19:18	267
Ex. 31:16	68,73,234	Lev. 20:3	62
Ex. 31:16,17	50,57,85,261	Lev. 20:6	62
Ex. 31:17	23,81,82,157,387	Lev. 20:10	49
Ex. 31:18	34,46,94,362,393	Lev. 20:11	49
Ex. 32:8	303	Lev. 20:12	49
Ex. 32:15	60	Lev. 20:24	48

Scriptural Index

Reference	Pages
Lev. 22:32	49
Lev. 23	67,73,81,195,232,238,286,393
Lev. 23:1,2	68
Lev. 23:1–3	81
Lev. 23:2,4,37	358
Lev. 23:3	68,73
Lev. 23:5	68,358
Lev. 23:6–8	68
Lev. 23:7	73
Lev. 23:10–14	68
Lev. 23:13	63
Lev. 23:14,21,41	59
Lev. 23:15–21	69
Lev. 23:19	63,233
Lev. 23:21,24,27,35	73
Lev. 23:23–25	69
Lev. 23:27–32	69
Lev. 23:29	62
Lev. 23:32	49,73,391
Lev. 23:33–44	69
Lev. 24:2	63
Lev. 24:5,6	231,232
Lev. 24:5–9	63,140,267,297
Lev. 24:10–13	49
Lev. 24:16	49
Lev. 25:1–4	82
Lev. 25:1–7	81
Lev. 25:2–7	70
Lev. 25:4	83,84
Lev. 25:8–12,20,21	70
Lev. 25:8–17	81,125
Lev. 25:10	125
Lev. 25:11	84
Lev. 25:12	77
Lev. 25:34	59
Lev. 26:1	49
Lev. 26:14,15	61
Lev. 26:34,35	82
Lev. 27:26	358
Lev. 28:18,25	73
Num. 1:50,53	80
Num. 9:13	62
Num. 15:27,30	61
Num. 15:32–36	154
Num. 15:35,36	62
Num. 15:38	120
Num. 16:44–48	64
Num. 18:19	59
Num. 19:11–13	106
Num. 21:4–9	64
Num. 28:9,10	140
Num. 28:11	69
Num. 29:1,7,12	73
Num. 30:1–15	114
Deut. 1:6,7	82
Deut. 1:8	53
Deut. 3	82
Deut. 4:13	46,234
Deut. 4:40	82
Deut. 5	51
Deut. 5:1,2	234
Deut. 5:1–3	57,393
Deut. 5:1–21	53
Deut. 5:3	53,239
Deut. 5:7	258
Deut. 5:8–11	258
Deut. 5:12,15	83
Deut. 5:12–19	258
Deut. 5:15	77,130,347,348
Deut. 5:20,21	259
Deut. 6:5	267
Deut. 6:10	53
Deut. 6:13	115
Deut. 6:20,21	44
Deut. 6:24,25	58,234,419
Deut. 7:17–19	44
Deut. 7:25	50
Deut. 9:5	53
Deut. 9:9	46,393
Deut. 9:11	46,234,393
Deut. 9:15	47,234,393
Deut. 10:2	47
Deut. 10:5,8	47
Deut. 10:12	48
Deut. 10:18,19	91
Deut. 10:20	115
Deut. 14	107
Deut. 15:12–15	44
Deut. 18:1	358
Deut. 19:18–21	50
Deut. 21:18–21	49
Deut. 22:12	96
Deut. 23:19,20	116

Deut. 23:21–23	114	Isa. 56:3–6	56,251
Deut. 25:5–10	96	Isa. 58:13,14	73
Deut. 28:15–20	230	Isa. 58:14	73
Deut. 29:1	48	Isa. 59:2	24
Deut. 29:1,9	51	Isa. 61:1	122
Deut. 29:17–21	49	Isa. 61:1,2	125
Deut. 30:15–19	253	Isa. 62:1	32
Deut. 30:20	53	Isa. 65:17–25	360,361
Deut. 31:26	50,94,190,253	Isa. 66:20,21	359,360
Deut. 32:21	49	Isa. 66:23	80,193,359,361
Josh. 5:6,7	283	Jer. 11:10,11	43
Josh. 21:43–45	282	Jer. 17:27	72,152,154
Jug. 11:29–31,39	115	Jer. 26:13	365
1 Sam. 21:1–6	139	Jer. 31:31	59
2 Sam. 11,12	140	Jer. 31:32	239
1 Ki. 8:8,9,21	94,393	Ez. 20:12	387
1 Ki. 8:9,21	47	Ez. 20:20	387
1 Ki. 11:11	43	Ez. 45:17	79,194
2 Ki. 4:23	80,192	Ez. 46:1,3–7	192
1 Chron. 16:15–17	54	Ez. 46:1–7	80
1 Chron. 23:31	79,193	Dan. 7:13	143
2 Chron. 2:4	69,79,81,193	Dan. 8:27	98
2 Chron. 8:12,13	79,193	Dan. 9:11,12	60
2 Chron. 13:5	123	Dan 12:9	98
2 Chron. 31:3	79,193	Hos. 2:11	80,193
Neh. 1:15	72	Hos. 6:6	141
Neh. 10:31	72	Joel 2:28,29	373
Neh. 10:33	80,193	Amo. 8:5	72,193
Esth. 9:20–22	328	Mich. 5:2	124
Ps. 95	280	Mal. 3:6	365
Ps. 95:1–5	45	1 Mac. 1–7	354
Ps. 95:7	282,284	1 Mac. 1:41–53	354
Ps. 104:14,15	340	1 Mac. 1:57	352,353,354
Ps. 105	54	1 Mac. 1:59–64	354
Ps. 106:1,2,8,9	45	1 Mac. 2:9,14	353
Ps. 121:4	23	1 Mac. 2:27,28	353
Isa. 1:13,14	80,193	1 Mac. 2:29,32–41	353
Isa. 1:18	390	1 Mac. 4:36–61	328
Isa. 11:6	361	2 Mac.	352
Isa. 11:8	361	Mt. 1:22,23	268
Isa. 42	125	Mt. 2:15	219,268
Isa. 42:1,6,7,9,10	123,349	Mt. 2:17	268
Isa. 42:6	124,217,235	Mt. 2:23	269
Isa. 42:7	123	Mt. 3:13	271
Isa. 42:10	130	Mt. 3:14,15	224
Isa. 49:8	218	Mt. 3:15	269
Isa. 56:1–8	82	Mt. 4:14–16	269

Scriptural Index

Reference	Page
Mt. 5:	113
Mt. 5:1–12	219
Mt. 5:17–19	265,267,268,271
Mt. 5:21,22	113,220
Mt. 5:27,28	114,220,258
Mt. 5:22	411
Mt. 5:23,24	120,364
Mt. 5:28	411
Mt. 5:31,32	220
Mt. 5:33	269,271
Mt. 5:33,34	220
Mt. 5:33–37	114
Mt. 5:38–42	220
Mt. 5:43–47	220
Mt. 5:43–48	115
Mt. 6:31–34	273
Mt. 7:12	266
Mt. 7:14	276
Mt. 8:17	269
Mt. 9:20	120
Mt. 11:12,13	110,119
Mt. 11:13	266
Mt. 11:28	337,349
Mt. 11:28–30	138,143,144,289
	395,419
Mt. 12:1,2	127,143,144,191
Mt. 12:5	140,267
Mt. 12:6	141
Mt. 12:7	141
Mt. 12:8	324,325
Mt. 12:1–8	137
Mt. 12:5–7	138
Mt. 12:11,12	148
Mt. 12:9–14	147
Mt. 12:17–21	270
Mt. 12:35	311
Mt. 12:41,42	141
Mt. 13:14,15	270
Mt. 13:53–58	122
Mt. 14:13	404
Mt. 17:24–27	108
Mt. 18:20	232,399
Mt. 21:4,5	270
Mt. 21:12–17	363
Mt. 22:36–39	267
Mt. 22:40	267
Mt. 23:23	267
Mt. 23:37,38	364
Mt. 24:3	351
Mt. 24:15	352
Mt. 24:16–18	353
Mt. 24:19	353
Mt. 24:20	351,352,353,356,357
Mt. 24:21	354
Mt. 25:45	411
Mt. 26:26	339
Mt. 26:26–28	226,344
Mt. 26:27,28	341
Mt. 26:29	344
Mt. 26:38,39	342
Mt. 26:53,54	270
Mt. 26:56	270
Mt. 26:61	141
Mt. 27:9,10	270
Mt. 27:51	363
Mt. 28:1	315
Mt. 28:8–10	316
Mt. 28:18–20	117,401
Mt. 29:19	234
Mt. 28:19,20	225
Mk. 1:21–28	134
Mk. 1:21–34	133
Mk. 1:25	104
Mk. 1:29–31	134
Mk. 1:32–34	135
Mk. 1:35	404
Mk. 1:39	136
Mk. 1:40–45	104
Mk. 2:5	126
Mk. 2:23–28	137,138
Mk. 2:25,26	139
Mk. 2:27	324
Mk. 2:27,28	142
Mk. 3:1–6	147
Mk. 3:5	148
Mk. 5:21–43	105
Mk. 6:1–6	122
Mk. 6:8	365
Mk. 6:30–32	404
Mk. 7:3	214
Mk. 7:14–19	205
Mk. 7:14–23	106,107
Mk. 9:3–8	221
Mk. 9:50	400

Mk. 10:19	258	Lk. 15	171
Mk. 11:15–18	120	Lk. 16:16	110,119
Mk. 13:18	355	Lk. 21	349
Mk. 15.37,38	218	Lk. 22:11	120
Mk. 16:1,2	316	Lk. 22:19	318,321
Mk. 16:9	316	Lk. 22:19,20	226,338
Mk. 16:12,13	316	Lk. 22:35,36	365
Mk. 16:14–18	317	Lk. 23:55–24:2	316
Lk. 2:10,11	126	Lk. 23:56	373
Lk. 2:21	17,120	Lk. 24:13–33	316
Lk. 2:41,42	120	Lk. 24:15–31	317
Lk. 3:16	302	Lk. 24:25–27	380
Lk. 3:21,22	301	Lk. 24:27	273
Lk. 4:1	122,301	Lk. 24:30,31	321339
Lk. 4:1,14	124	Lk. 24:34	317
Lk. 4:14	126,301	Lk. 24:35	321
Lk. 4:16	126,128,403	Lk. 24:35,36	339
Lk. 4:16–21	122	Lk. 24:36–44	317
Lk. 4:16–30	122,124,128	Lk. 24:44	277
Lk. 4:18	125,301	Lk. 24:46,47	127
Lk. 4:18,19	273	Lk. 24:47	124
Lk. 4:31	128,136,403	Jn. 1:1–3,14	155,273
Lk. 4:31–36	124,127	Jn. 1:12	289,417
Lk. 4:31–44	133	Jn. 1:14	141
Lk. 4:36	124	Jn. 1:17	374
Lk. 4:38,39	124,127,403	Jn. 1:36	273
Lk. 4:39	135	Jn. 1:41	124
Lk. 4:40	124,127,403	Jn. 1:45	374
Lk. 4:41	127,403	Jn. 2:6–11	340
Lk. 4:42	404	Jn. 2:13	120
Lk. 4:43	124	Jn. 2:13–22	363
Lk. 4:43,44	127,136	Jn. 2:19	153
Lk. 5:16	404	Jn. 3:3–5	419
Lk. 5:20	127	Jn. 3:14	273
Lk. 5:32	412	Jn. 3:16	219,289,413
Lk. 6:1–5	137	Jn. 3:17	219
Lk. 6:6	403	Jn. 4:8	214
Lk. 6:6–11	147	Jn. 4:20	232
Lk. 6:9	191	Jn. 4:20–24	337
Lk. 6:12	404	Jn. 4:23,24	395
Lk. 7:21	127	Jn. 4:24	232
Lk. 7:22	124	Jn. 4:34	165,218
Lk. 10:16	200	Jn. 5:1	120
Lk. 13:10–17	126,127,129,131	Jn. 5:1–9	151
Lk. 13:11	130	Jn. 5:1–18	150
Lk. 13:13	130	Jn. 5:9–18	153
Lk. 14:1–6	149,404	Jn. 5:19	156

Scriptural Index

Jn. 5:21–39	156,158	Jn. 9:29,30	169
Jn. 5:24	341	Jn. 9:31–33	170
Jn. 5:27	219	Jn. 9:32–34	170
Jn. 5:30	218	Jn. 9:35–38	171
Jn. 5:37	165	Jn. 9:39–41	173
Jn. 5:38,39	273,336	Jn. 10:7	219
Jn. 5:39	111,379	Jn. 10:9,11	413
Jn. 5:45–47	156	Jn. 10:10	410
Jn. 5:46	273,274	Jn. 10:11,14	218
Jn. 6:4	151	Jn. 10:18	375
Jn. 6:27	218,350,388	Jn. 10:22	120,328
Jn. 6:27–29	27	Jn. 10:34	374
Jn. 6:29	415	Jn. 11:11	106
Jn. 6:47	416,418	Jn. 11:25	219
Jn. 6:48	219,273	Jn. 12:34	374
Jn. 6:48–51	340	Jn. 12:46–50	222
Jn. 7:2,10	120	Jn. 12:49,50	375
Jn. 7:14–24	150	Jn. 13:34,35	222,375
Jn. 7:19	374	Jn. 14:6	218,413
Jn. 7:21–24	157	Jn. 14:9	98
Jn. 7:23	374	Jn. 14:15	91,223,375,376
Jn. 7:25–27	170	Jn. 14:16,17	302
Jn. 7:37,38	219,337	Jn. 14:21	223,375,376
Jn. 7:49	374	Jn. 14:23	304,419
Jn. 7:51	374	Jn. 14:26	303,304
Jn. 8:5,17	374	Jn. 14:31	375
Jn. 8:12	219,273	Jn. 15:10	218,375
Jn. 8:24	221	Jn. 15:10,12,17	223,376
Jn. 8:28	109	Jn. 15:12	249,309,375,400
Jn. 8:31	222	Jn. 15:14	223
Jn. 8:31,32	419	Jn. 15:17	223
Jn. 8:51	222	Jn. 15:25	375
Jn. 8:56	29,35,36	Jn. 15:26	303,304
Jn. 8:58	155,219	Jn. 16:13	303,304
Jn. 9	163	Jn. 17:20,21	382
Jn. 9:1,2	173	Jn. 18:31	375
Jn. 9:1–5	163	Jn. 19:7	375
Jn. 9:3	163	Jn. 19:28	218
Jn. 9:6,7	165	Jn. 19:28–30	271,342
Jn. 9:7	165	Jn. 19:30	218,349
Jn. 9:8–12	166	Jn. 19:31	319
Jn. 9:13–16	167	Jn. 19:42	151
Jn. 9:17	171	Jn. 20:11–18	316
Jn. 9:17–23	167	Jn. 20:19–23	317
Jn. 9:22	171	Jn. 20:26–29	317
Jn. 9:24–27	169	Jn. 20:30,31	121
Jn. 9:28	169	Jn. 20:31	151,165

Jn. 21	316	Acts 18:4	180,214
Jn. 21:25	121	Acts 18:6–8	180
Acts 1:6–10	316	Acts 18:18	208
Acts 1:12	182	Acts 18:28	214
Acts 2	119	Acts 19:8,9	181
Acts 2:14–21	373	Acts 20:6–12	320
Acts 2:17,18	302	Acts 20:7	322
Acts 2:38,39	302	Acts 20:8	320
Acts 2:41	303	Acts 20:16	208
Acts 2:41,42	398	Acts 21	357
Acts 2:46	321,322	Acts 21:20	355
Acts 3:19	412	Acts 21:20,21,25	203
Acts 4:12	414	Acts 21:23–26	208
Acts 4:24–30	402	Acts 26:2	214
Acts 4:31	302	Rom. 1:16	242
Acts 5:31	413	Rom. 1:23	258
Acts 6:3,8	302	Rom. 2:4	311
Acts 8:29	302	Rom. 2:11–13	393
Acts 8:39	302	Rom. 2:13	365
Acts 9:17	302	Rom. 3–5	267
Acts 9:31	302	Rom. 3:21	294
Acts 10, 11	107	Rom. 3:21–24	242
Acts 10:20	214	Rom. 3:23	366,410
Acts 11:28	302	Rom. 3:24	410
Acts 13:1–3	401	Rom. 3:28	234,276,415
Acts 13:4	302	Rom. 3:31	242,250
Acts 13:13–52	177	Rom. 4	262
Acts 13:14–16	177	Rom. 4:1–16	250
Acts 13:27	177	Rom. 4:1–5,10,11,16	38,243
Acts 13:29	277	Rom. 4:9–11	235
Acts 13:42–50	177,178	Rom. 4:9–25	29
Acts 13:43	214	Rom. 4:13	37
Acts 13:50–52	310	Rom. 4:13,14	294
Acts 13:52	302	Rom. 4:16	38
Acts 15	259,357,367	Rom. 5:1	310,417,418
Acts 15:5	189,203,290,355	Rom. 5:5	310
Acts 15:10	253,290	Rom. 5:6–10	298
Acts 15:20	182	Rom. 5:8	310
Acts 15:21	182	Rom. 5:10	414,417,418
Acts 15:28,29	203,259	Rom. 5:18	414
Acts 16:3	208,214	Rom. 5:18,19	275
Acts 16:11–40	178	Rom. 5:20	244
Acts 16:12–15	179	Rom. 6:1	276
Acts 17:1–9	179	Rom. 6:2–4,11	276
Acts 17:11	19,391,401	Rom. 6:3	225
Acts 17:13	214	Rom. 6:6	418
Acts 18:1–11	180	Rom. 6:9–12,18	92

Scriptural Index

Reference	Page
Rom. 6:11	418
Rom. 6:11,22	244
Rom. 6:18,22	418
Rom. 6:22	249
Rom. 6:23	410
Rom. 7	262
Rom. 7:1–6	244,245
Rom. 7:4	188,418
Rom. 7:4–6	250
Rom. 7:6	234,248,301,366,418
Rom. 7:7,8	247
Rom. 7:7–24	306
Rom. 7:9–25	247
Rom. 7:12	250,366
Rom. 8	248,263
Rom. 8:1	190,245,249,418
Rom. 8:1–5	248
Rom. 8:3	248
Rom. 8:4	249
Rom. 8:8–11	249
Rom. 8:9–12	419
Rom. 8:14–17	249
Rom. 8:15	418
Rom. 8:16	388
Rom. 8:26	418
Rom. 8:29	418
Rom. 8:37	418
Rom. 8:38,39	249
Rom. 9:6–8	234
Rom. 9:30,31	294
Rom. 10	263
Rom. 10:3,4	294
Rom. 10:4	250,366
Rom. 10:4,5	234,249
Rom. 10:8–11	416
Rom. 10:12	250
Rom. 10:17	398
Rom. 12	418
Rom. 12:1	233,405
Rom. 12:10	400
Rom. 12:16	400
Rom. 13:8–10	255,277
Rom. 13:9	258,259
Rom. 13:10	249
Rom. 14	204
Rom. 14:5,6	201,333
Rom. 14:14	107
Rom. 14:14,20	205
Rom. 14:20	205
Rom. 14:23	411
Rom. 15:7	400
Rom. 15:14	400
Rom. 15:18,19	
Rom. 16:5	182
Rom. 16:16	400
1 Cor. 1:30	348,349
1 Cor. 2:12	419
1 Cor. 3:16	419
1 Cor. 6:15,19,20	90
1 Cor. 6:19,20	404,419
1 Cor. 7:19,20	374
1 Cor. 8:6	258
1 Cor. 9:16	91
1 Cor. 9:20–21	204,209
1 Cor. 9:19–23	207
1 Cor. 11:6	224
1 Cor. 11:23,24	322
1 Cor. 11:24,25	232
1 Cor. 11:26	232
1 Cor. 11:33	400
1 Cor. 12	418
1 Cor. 12,13,14	309,399
1 Cor. 12:13	226
1 Cor. 12:25	400
1 Cor. 15:3	415
1 Cor. 16:1,2	323
1 Cor. 16:19	182
2 Cor. 1:20	277
2 Cor. 1:21,22	388
2 Cor. 3	274
2 Cor. 3:2–7	95,393
2 Cor. 3:3	229
2 Cor. 3:3–18	303
2 Cor. 3:6–11	99
2 Cor. 3:7–11	93
2 Cor. 3:13–18	100
2 Cor. 3:14–18	164
2 Cor. 3:15,16	172
2 Cor. 5:14	91,390
2 Cor. 5:17	173
2 Cor. 5:21	26,109,231,414
Gal. 1:6–9	206
Gal. 2:12	367
Gal. 2:13	214

Gal. 2:21	294	Eph. 1:7	418
Gal. 3	111,274	Eph. 1:13,14	388,418
Gal. 3:1	200	Eph. 2:	263
Gal. 3–5	409	Eph. 2:3	411
Gal. 3:10,11,21	394	Eph. 2:6	
Gal. 3:12	58,234	Eph. 2:8	418
Gal. 3:13	393,414	Eph. 2:8,9	234,416
Gal. 3:13,14	417	Eph. 2:12–16	251
Gal. 3:14–18	29,38	Eph. 2:22	418
Gal. 3:15–29	305	Eph. 3:12	
Gal. 3:17	234,239	Eph. 3:20	304,410
Gal. 3:19	239	Eph. 4	418
Gal. 3:22	240	Eph. 4:2	400
Gal. 3:23–26	296	Eph. 4:6	258
Gal. 3:25	234	Eph. 4:12	401
Gal. 3:24,25	199	Eph. 4:25	400
Gal. 3:26–29	234	Eph. 4:28	258
Gal. 3:27	26,226	Eph. 4:30	388
Gal. 4	262,290	Eph. 4:32	400
Gal. 4:4	17,120	Eph. 5:2	310
Gal. 4:4,5	296	Eph. 5:5	258
Gal. 4:1–5	187	Eph. 5:21	400
Gal. 4:9–11	198,199,296	Eph. 6:2,3	258
Gal. 4:10	201,333	Eph. 6:17	305
Gal. 4:10,11	262,334	Phil. 1:12,13	402
Gal. 4:21	199,203,239	Phil. 2:1–4	90
Gal. 4:21–31	234,235,240,393	Phil. 2:5–8	91
Gal. 4:24	95	Phil. 2:13	418
Gal. 4:30,31	241	Phil. 2:17	310
Gal. 5:1	290	Phil. 2:25	402
Gal. 5:1–4	261,393	Phil. 3	263
Gal. 5:1–6	194	Phil. 3:2–9	252
Gal. 5:2	17	Phil. 3:8,9	168,298
Gal. 5:2–4	207	Phil. 3:9	294
Gal. 5:3	272,335	Phil. 4:7	311
Gal. 5:4	294,298,335,384,393,415	Phil. 4:15,16	401
Gal. 5:13	401,414	Col. 1:12	418
Gal. 5:13,14	277	Col. 1:13	418
Gal. 5:16–26	306	Col. 2	263,274,409
Gal. 5:18	234	Col. 2:8	187
Gal. 5:19–21	258	Col. 2:8–23	186,190
Gal. 5:22,23	309	Col. 2:9,10	189
Gal. 5:23–25	312	Col. 2:10	275
Gal. 6:1	312	Col. 2:11,12	226,273
Gal. 6:2	400	Col. 2:11–13	189,194
Eph. 1:3–5	410	Col. 2:14	252
Eph. 1:4	418	Col. 2:14,15	190

Scriptural Index

Col. 2:16	185,190,191,192
	193,194,195,197,333
Col. 2:16,17	185,191, 262,394
Col. 2:16–18	196
Col. 2:17	197,198
Col. 2:20,21	188
Col. 3:13	400
Col. 3:16	400
Col. 4:15	182
1 Thess. 4:18	400
1 Thess. 5:11	400,401
1 Tim. 6:1	258
2 Tim. 2:24	311
2 Tim. 4	401
Tit. 3:5	273,410,415
Tit. 3:9	209
Phile. 1:2	182
Heb. 1:1,2	217
Heb. 1:1–3	93,97,99,274,279,373
Heb. 1:2	249
Heb. 1:3	99
Heb. 1:3–14	99,279
Heb. 3	279,347,363
Heb. 3,4	279,286
Heb. 3:1–3	279
Heb. 3:1–6	279
Heb. 3:5	280
Heb. 3:6	280
Heb. 3:8	280
Heb. 3:9	281
Heb. 3:11	281,283,286
Heb. 3:11,18,19	286
Heb. 3:12–14	281
Heb. 3:13	99
Heb. 3:15	281
Heb. 3:18,19	99,281
Heb. 4	280,347,348,363
Heb. 4:1	281
Heb. 4:2,3	281
Heb. 4:2,6	287
Heb. 4:3	286,287,288
Heb. 4:3,9,11	418
Heb. 4:4,5	282
Heb. 4:7	282
Heb. 4:7,8	282,286
Heb. 4:8–11	273
Heb. 4:9–11	284
Heb. 4:15	109
Heb. 5,6,7	279
Heb. 5–7	361
Heb. 5:12	188
Heb. 6,7	279
Heb. 6:9–11	99
Heb. 6:13–20	29,235
Heb. 7:12	99,279,365
Heb. 7:22	99
Heb. 7:23,25	273
Heb. 8	274
Heb. 8:6	99,218,235,279
Heb. 8:6–8	235
Heb. 8:6–10	229
Heb. 8:6–12	238
Heb. 8:8	239,414
Heb. 8:9	231
Heb. 8:10	229
Heb. 8:11	229
Heb. 8:12	230
Heb. 8:13	235,238
Heb. 9:1	238
Heb. 9:1–4	94,217,393
Heb. 9:4–10	239
Heb. 9:11	239,279
Heb. 9:11,12	273
Heb. 9:14	235
Heb. 9:23	99,279
Heb. 10	399
Heb. 10:1–4,12,14	126
Heb. 10:1–5	280
Heb. 10:9,10	239
Heb. 10:14	273
Heb. 10:14,19	275
Heb. 10:19	417
Heb. 10:19–23	273
Heb. 10:19–25	397,403
Heb. 10:20	273
Heb. 10:22	273
Heb. 10:24	400
Heb. 10:25	232
Heb. 10:34	280
Heb. 11:6	398
Heb. 11:16	99,280
Heb. 11:17–19	35
Heb. 11:32	115
Heb. 11:35	99,280

Heb. 11:40	99,280	Rev. 16:19	340
Heb. 12:18–24	288	Rev. 19:10	372,373,379,380
Heb. 12:24	99,235,280	Rev. 19:16	92
Heb. 13:5	259	Rev. 20:4	378
Heb. 13:8	364	Rev. 22:13	219
Heb. 13:12	342		
Heb. 13:15	232		
Heb. 13:15,16	92,288,395,402		
Heb. 13:20	235		
Jas. 2:8–12	367,368		
Jas. 4:5	337		
Jas. 5:16	400		
1 Pet. 4:9	400		
2 Pet. 3:9	311		
1 Jn. 1:1–3,14	273		
1 Jn. 1:4	419		
1 Jn. 1:9	412,417		
1 Jn. 2:1,2	273		
1 Jn. 2:3,4	375		
1 Jn. 2:7,8	375		
1 Jn. 3:8	153		
1 Jn. 3:8,9	418		
1 Jn. 3:14	273		
1 Jn. 3:15	259		
1 Jn. 3:23	223		
1 Jn. 3:23,24	376		
1 Jn. 4:8	413		
1 Jn. 4:21	223,376,377		
1 Jn. 5:2,3	376,377		
1 Jn. 5:13	418		
1 Jn. 5:21	258		
2 Jn. 1:4,5	376		
2 Jn. 1:6	376		
Rev. 1:1,2	378		
Rev. 1:9	378		
Rev. 1:10	324,327		
Rev. 5:12–14	93,350		
Rev. 6:9	378		
Rev. 11:19	380		
Rev. 12:17	372,373,376 377,378,380,389		
Rev. 13:16,17	382		
Rev. 14:6–12	386		
Rev. 14:9,10	15		
Rev. 14:10	340,377		
Rev. 14:12	376,378		
Rev. 14:19,20	341		

Other Books Published by Life Assurance Ministries Publications

http://www.ratzlaf.com | dale@ratzlaf.com
Information & Orders: 623-572-9549
Orders only: 800-355-7073

- *The Cultic Doctrine of Seventh-day Adventists—An Evangelical Resource, An Appeal to SDA Leadership*, by Dale Ratzlaff, 388 pages, $14.95 Ratzlaff's writing clearly possesses a spirit of meekness; it is nevertheless a *tour de force*. Patiently pursuing his subject, he lays out the evidence supporting an irresistible conclusion—Ellen White was not a true prophet or messenger from God, and the Seventh-day Adventist Church is not what it claims to be, the only true "remnant church." If Adventist leadership will heed his plea, then perhaps this church is salvageable. If not, then it is time for evangelicals everywhere to say to the Christians within Adventism, with neither malice nor exultation, but with one united and very earnest voice, "Babylon is fallen! Come out of her my people!"

- *The Truth About Seventh-day Adventist "Truth"*, by Dale Ratzlaff, 44 pages, $3.95. Seventh-day Adventist teachings are rapidly spreading around the world. For decades there has been a need for a clear and concise biblical examination of the fundamental teachings of this church. This ready reference on Adventism compares biblical Christianity with contemporary Adventism and quickly gives the reader an understanding of the major issues and answers. *The Truth About Seventh-day Adventist "Truth"* is a ministry tool that will equip many to meet the questions of those interested in Adventism as well as share the Gospel with the searching thousands within the Seventh-day Adventist church.

- ***La Verdad Sobre Las "Verdades" de Los Adventistas Del Septimo Dia*** (Spanish Translation of *The Truth About Seventh-day Adventist "Truth"*) by Dale Ratzlaff, 52 pages, $3.95.

- ***A Theologian's Journey from Seventh-day Adventism to Mainstream Christianity***, by Jerry Gladson, Ph.D., Senior Minister at First Christian Church (Disciples of Christ), Marietta, Georgia, 383 pages, $14.95. Dr. Gladson was a SDA theologian, professor and pastor serving an important role at the central core of Adventist scholarship for many years. Drawing from his meticulously kept journals, Dr. Gladson describes events at the center of the recent crisis in Adventism. He has done something few other scholars have been able to do. He has combined careful, detailed research with a gripping, narrative style of writing. The reader is forced to crawl under the skin of Dr. Gladson, see through his eyes and feel the trauma of having to choose between career and conscience. One cannot put the book down until finished. This book uncovers the hidden, toxic core of Adventism.

- ***White Washed, Uncovering the Myths of Ellen G. White***, by Sydney Cleveland, 233 pages, $12.95. *White Washed* is a comprehensive look at Ellen White's prophecies, practices and publications. Sydney Cleveland examines her claims of inspiration, her dreams and visions, the doctrines she endorsed, her personal practices that opposed her teachings and the effect of her claims on the Adventist Church. This is a well-documented overview of the little-known reality about Ellen White and her long service to the Adventist church. Sydney Cleveland was an Adventist pastor for 11 years. During an extensive study of Ellen G. White's writings, he discovered that she contradicted the Holy Bible, gave many false prophecies, and didn't even follow her own teachings.

- *White Out*, by Dr. Dirk Anderson, 160 pages, $9.95. White Out will be a challenge for Adventist leaders for it exposes, with extensive documentation, the deception regarding Ellen White that has been, and continues to be, harbored at the central core of the Adventist church. White Out covers a wide range of subject matter as it relates to Ellen White and her writings. The facts brought to light are vastly different from what is taught in "Spirit of Prophecy Classes" in Adventist education. If it were not for the fact that Ellen White claimed divine inspiration for her writings, often stating that she received her information directly through visions from God or in conversations with "her angel," one would think it unfair to treat a deceased religious leader of her reputation with such scrutiny. Yet not to do so is to continue the "white out." Many former Adventists have seen that the unique teachings of Adventism stand or fall with Ellen White because they cannot be clearly derived from Scripture without making copious and unwarranted assumptions. For this reason church administrators continue to face the dilemma of how to deal with the growing weight of evidence that proves her writings are untrustworthy. Perhaps *White Out* will be the final pound that tips the now heavily weighted scale toward administrative honesty.

- ***The Sabbath and the Lord's day,*** by H. M. Riggle, 160 pages $7.95. This book includes a discussion of Sabbath/Sunday issues in the early church and is an excellent companion to *Sabbath in Christ.*

- **Life Assurance Ministries Publications** also sells a number of other books, videos and tapes not listed here. For a current list go to our LAM Bookstore at www.ratzlaf.com/lam_book.htm.